A History of Italy

PALGRAVE ESSENTIAL HISTORIES
General Editor: Jeremy Black

This series of compact, readable and informative national histories is designed to appeal to anyone wishing to gain a broad understanding of a country's history.

Published

A History of the Low Countries   *Paul Arblaster*
A History of Italy   *Claudia Baldoli*
A History of Russia   *Roger Bartlett*
A History of Spain (2nd edn)   *Simon Barton*
A History of the British Isles (2nd edn)   *Jeremy Black*
A History of Israel   *Ahron Bregman*
A History of Ireland   *Mike Cronin*
A History of Greece   *Nicholas Doumanis*
A History of the Pacific Islands   *Steven Roger Fischer*
A History of the United States (3rd edn)   *Philip Jenkins*
A History of Denmark   *Knud J. V. Jespersen*
A History of Poland   *Anita J. Prazmowska*
A History of India   *Peter Robb*
A History of China (2nd edn)   *J. A. G. Roberts*
A History of Germany   *Peter Wende*

Series Standing Order
ISBN 1–4039–3811–3 hardback
ISBN 1–4039–3812–1 paperback

If you would like to receive future titles in this series as they are published, you can make use of the standing order facility. To place a standing order please contact your bookseller or, in case of difficulty, write to us at the address below with your name and address, the name of the series and one of the ISBNs quoted above. Please state with which title you wish to begin your standing order. (If you live outside the United Kingdom we may not have the rights for your area, in which case we will forward your order to the publisher concerned.)

Customer Services Department, Macmillan Distribution Ltd
Houndmills, Basingstoke, Hampshire RG21 6XS, England

A History of Italy

Claudia Baldoli

First published 2009 by
PALGRAVE MACMILLAN

Palgrave Macmillan in the UK is an imprint of Macmillan Publishers Limited,
registered in England, company number 785998, of Houndmills, Basingstoke,
Hampshire RG21 6XS.

Palgrave Macmillan in the US is a division of St Martin's Press LLC,
175 Fifth Avenue, New York, NY 10010.

Palgrave Macmillan is the global academic imprint of the above companies
and has companies and representatives throughout the world.

Palgrave® and Macmillan® are registered trademarks in the United States,
the United Kingdom, Europe and other countries.

ISBN 978–1–4039–8615–3   hardback
ISBN 978–1–4039–8616–0   paperback

This book is printed on paper suitable for recycling and made from fully
managed and sustained forest sources. Logging, pulping and manufacturing
processes are expected to conform to the environmental regulations of the
country of origin.

A catalogue record for this book is available from the British Library.

A catalog record for this book is available from the Library of Congress.

10 9 8 7 6 5 4 3 2 1
18 17 16 15 14 13 12 11 10 09

Printed and bound in China

Contents

CONTENTS

List of Maps, Chronologies and Boxes

MAPS

CHRONOLOGIES

BOXES

Acknowledgements

As just one of the many possible histories of Italy, this book has been influenced by readings and experiences that have accompanied me since my years at the *Liceo* in Brescia. Over the years since then, teachers, students and colleagues have inspired me with reading suggestions, discussions and exchange of ideas. The Department of History at the University of Venice has been an extraordinary place in which to study in critical and at times unconventional ways, for example during the *La Pantera* occupation of 1990, or during fieldwork at the Roma camps established as a consequence of the war in the former Yugoslavia in 1992–3. In particular I wish to thank Piero Brunello for many discussions we have had since the early 1990s, and for commenting on the modern chapters of this book. Collaboration with Mario Isnenghi has been an exciting intellectual experience, including collective work with his seminar group, which has continued to meet in the History Department in Venice down the years. In the School of Historical Studies of Newcastle University I have found an extraordinarily lively environment, both intellectually and socially. I am particularly grateful to the 'gang' (Livia, Neelam, Martin, Alejandro, Matt, James, Luc and Xavier) for the great time spent together between Newcastle and Italy while I was writing the book. As a historian of modern Italy, the most difficult task has been working on the pre-modern chapters; while any remaining mistakes are my own responsibility, these chapters have been improved greatly by comments from Trevor Dean, Chris Wickham and John Marino. Megan Trudell has been a great proofreader and adviser. My father, Mario Baldoli, provided invaluable help during the early stages of the book. Richard Overy, Tim Kirk, Camilla Russell, Marcella Sutcliffe and Matt Perry have read and commented on parts of the typescript. My family in Italy has been a constant source of ideas, affection and good times, and I wish to dedicate this book to them: Maria, Mario, Giaime and nonna Sandra.

CLAUDIA BALDOLI

ACKNOWLEDGEMENTS

The author and publishers wish to thank the following for permission to reproduce copyright material:

Harvard University Press for: Procopius of Cesarea, *Gothic Wars*, in *History of the Wars*, translation by H. B. Dewing (1960–8); *The Poetry of Giacomo da Lentino, Sicilian Poet of the Thirteenth Century*, ed. by E. F. Langley (1915); E. L. Eisenstein, *The First Professional Revolutionist: Filippo Michele Buonarroti (1761–1837)* (1959).

Laterza for: A. Barbero, *Terre d'acqua. I vercellesi all'epoca delle crociate* (2007); I. Fosi, *La giustizia del papa* (2007); M. Montanari, *Convivio: storia e cultura dei piaceri della tavola dall'antichità al Medioevo* (1989); F. Bartolini, *Rivali d'Italia: Roma e Milano dal settecento a oggi* (2006); A. Paravicini Bagliani, *La vita quotidiana alla corte dei papi nel Duecento* (1996).

Manchester University Press for T. Dean, *The Towns of Italy in the Later Middle Ages* (2000).

Shambhala for Francis of Assisi, *Canticle of the Sun*, Boston and London (2002).

Paulist Press for Jacopone da Todi, 'On the Heart's Jubilation', in *The Lauds*, translated by S. and E. Hughes (SPCK: 1982).

Cantagalli for G. Boccardi, ed., *Caterina da Siena. Una santa degli europei. Dalle lettere di Caterina: un fervido messaggio per l'Europa dello spirito, alla ricerca delle proprie radici cristiane* (2003).

Carcanet New Press for *Literature in the Vernacular* (De vulgari eloquentia), translation by S. Purcell (1981), book I.

Oxford University Press for: B. Cellini, *My Life*, translated by J. Conaway Bondanella and P. Bondanella (2002), book I, 40; C. Abba, *The Diary of One of Garibaldi's Thousand* (1962); R, Griffin, *Fascism* (1995); maps from John A. Davis, *Italy in the Nineteenth Century* (2000).

J. M. Dent (Orion Publishing) for A. Manzoni, *The Betrothed*, ed. by D. Forgacs and M. Reynolds (1997).

Il Melangolo for Stendhal, *I briganti in Italia* (2004).

Yale University Press for J. Locke, *Two Treatises of Government* and *A Letter Concerning Toleration*, ed by Ian Shapiro (2003).

Calder for Stendhal, *Rome, Naples and Florence* (1959 – repr. Oneworld Classics, 2008).

Peter Owen for E. De Amicis, *Cuore: the Heart of a Boy* (1986) p. 17; for C. Pavese, *The House on the Hill*, translated by W. J. Strachan (1965).

Dedalus for G. Verga, 'Liberty', in *Short Sicilian Novels*, translated by D. H. Lawrence (1984).

Feltrinelli for G. Salvemini, *Memorie di un fuoruscito* (1973).

Einaudi for N. Revelli, *Le due guerre: guerra fascista e guerra partigiana* (2005).

The Hogarth Press for N. Ginzburg, *Family Sayings*, translation by D. M. Low (1967).

Every effort has been made to trace all copyright holders, but if any have been inadvertently omitted the publishers would be pleased to make the necessary arrangement at the first opportunity.

Photograph by Giaime Baldoli

Introduction

The picture that precedes this introduction shows a typical Italian square with arcades. It is a neo-classical square in the medieval centre of Brescia in northern Italy built in 1823 in order to relocate the grain market. The statue that gives the square its name was erected in 1882 and dedicated to Arnaldo of Brescia, a twelfth-century monk who opposed the worldliness and opulence of the Roman Church and was burnt at the stake by order of the Pope. The statue of Arnaldo, with its severe and rather menacing aspect, points towards the city centre, and in particular in the direction of the Cathedral square, as if to indicate who was responsible for his death. The inscription at the base of the monument reads: 'Brescia remembers in liberty their Arnaldo, the precursor, the martyr of Italian free thought'. In the climate of anti-clericalism that followed Italian unification in 1870 (Rome had become the capital of Italy only twelve years earlier, terminating the temporal power of the Papacy), the unveiling of the statue was a hotly contested occasion, bringing to the city representatives of political and cultural associations from all over Italy. They not only signified the new liberal Italy, but also the ideas that had run through Italian history from the twelfth to the nineteenth centuries: ideas of the renovation of the Church, of the liberation of Rome (Arnaldo had supported one of several attempts to create a republic in the papal city), and the messianic hopes of the poor masses. Today, the square is a symbol of the city's consumerism, surrounded by bars and restaurants, and crowded until late at night with wealthy and fashionable youth. The history narrated by the square synthesizes the content of this book: an exploration of Italian history down the centuries, and in particular of the cultural, political and social aspects that shaped Italian identity long before Italy became a nation. In the square and its architecture it is indeed possible to observe the coexistence of a centuries-long religious history (of the Catholic Church, of its deep influence on Italian values and culture, its idealism and social welfare, mediation and opposition to the secular arm as much as in its complicity through censorship and intolerance, corruption and abuse of power that spawned a consequent history of anti-clericalism) alongside the birth of the Italian nation, and the transformation of Italy into a hedonistic consumer society in the second half of the twentieth century.

The book has a social and cultural focus, and is organized around the major themes that have characterized Italy's history from the Middle Ages to the present. It examines the development of ideas about Italy's frontiers and the perception of foreigners (the Alps, the Mediterranean, the concept of 'barbarian'); the cultural and social relationship between cities and countryside; social, political and religious strife, and its legacy on collective identities; localism and cosmopolitanism (framed by foreign invasions, the mass emigration after unification, and the period of the Italian Republic and of the European Community). It explores the characteristics that have shaped the country, such as literature, music, architecture, politics, art and food. Although the chapters have a strong chronological thrust, they are not based principally on a narrative of military and political events, but instead they integrate this narrative with the broader thematic elements of the story.

It is possible to describe Italy as a nation only from 1860, and while the idea of Italy, and indeed the word itself, already existed during the period from the earliest Middle Ages to the nineteenth century, until the eighteenth century it had only a weak geographical connotation. This book will therefore deal with the history of Italy as a country (*paese*), rather than as a nation (*nazione*); and will discuss the development of a modern national idea only from the eighteenth century onwards. Before that time, to be 'Italian' meant to identify with a number of collective memories, not with a 'national' memory. Florentines of the fourteenth century would have felt themselves to be very different from the inhabitants of Venice or Calabria. Yet even though they did not speak entirely the same language, they were all seen and defined abroad as 'Italians'. This book will help to explain this paradox by exploring the elements of continuity in the country's history over the past 1,500 years.

The history of Italy as a country means the intertwining (and not just the 'sum') of various local histories. The fact that Italy did not have a centralized state until unification in the nineteenth century does not mean that Italy had no state(s). Indeed, the existence of a central administration does not constitute the most important parameter in the definition of a country, and even of a nation; for example, countries with a longer unitary tradition have continued to experience the most violent centrifugal tendencies (for example, Basque separatism in Spain and the

Corsican independence movement in France); the differences in climate, food and habits can be more significant, for example between Brittany and Mediterranean France, than between northern and southern Italy, though France has been a nation for a longer time. Moreover, the state does not represent a fixed body but rather a construction, and one that continues to change.

This book considers Italy as a geographical entity, a distinct country, from the fall of the Roman Empire and throughout the invasions that followed. The legacy of the Roman Empire, and particularly the legacy of Roman law and Christianity, has continued throughout the centuries to influence Italy's culture and self-perception. The book will examine how this legacy developed and was at times revived. The country was always dismembered into a number of regional states and principalities in the centuries that followed Roman rule; however, it will be argued here that it is nevertheless still possible to trace a unitary history of the country that stretches geographically from Sicily to the Alps. As historian Ruggiero Romano suggested, the history of Italy can be regarded as an opera, where soprano and tenor, bass and baritone are not united: what matters is not each individual voice but the sound they make together in concert.

After the Roman Empire (when a unified state had been centred on, and revolved around, the capital city, Rome), the Italian peninsula and its islands were occupied by numerous invaders. In the south, the passage of Byzantines, Arabs, Normans, Angevins, and Aragonese constituted, from the early Middle Ages to the nineteenth century, a distinct political world separate from the regions north of Rome, where power was concentrated in the local communes and city-states such as Milan, Venice or Florence. However, a common cultural, religious and social identity, built from regular exchange between the regions, continued to run in the veins of the country as a kind of underground history. After 1870, the nation was born in defiance of the Papacy, which fitted well with a historiographical tradition which saw the Church as a permanent obstacle to unification, from the Lombard age onwards.

Of all the powers that sought to control Italy between the early Middle Ages and the Napoleonic period, none of them ever genuinely succeeded. Byzantines, Lombards, Swabians, Angevins from Naples, Visconti from Milan, all came close to the final goal but did not accomplish it; and when Napoleon's turn came, the Italians were already preparing for their own unification. It was impossible for any state to expand its power in Italy without coming into conflict with the Papacy;

however, this was not the only obstacle to unification, for the loyalties of Italians were also traditionally divided between two conflicting 'universal' rulers, the Pope and the emperor, between religious and secular power. City-states were also an obstacle to unification: proud of their liberty and economic success, the Italian communes only formed alliances when they were confronted by common enemies (often, in the case of central-northern city-states, the Germanic emperor). This made Italian politics a complicated and shifting system of alliances, interests, loyalties and disloyalties; and this is where the idea developed in other European countries of Italians as double-dealing and cunning, classically Machiavellian. This view of the Italian people persisted until recent times, and was revived during the wars of independence and again during the two world wars.

The responsibility of the Germanic invasions and the interference of the Papacy in the fragmentation of Italy have been matters of controversy over the centuries. Questions about the unification of Italy have been especially contentious in the modern period, focusing in particular on the two most celebrated periods in national memory: the Renaissance and the Risorgimento. This has at times produced an interpretation of the history of Italy as periods of light and darkness – of moments when an Italian 'model' triumphed and others when it declined; but the 'dark centuries' were never completely dark, and if a 'global' model collapsed, some areas of light might remain or even prosper. During the Counter-Reformation, the problem of controlling knowledge became a pressing issue, because scientific progress was, as historian Paula Findlen has observed, 'as much a religious as a philosophical question', and local Inquisitions particularly targeted heresies concerned with the interpretation of the natural world; nevertheless, Italy remained until the mid-sixteenth century the centre of the scientific world in Western Europe. The birth of melodrama and of Baroque architecture and music during the period produced cultural movements that spread out over the rest of Europe. Even when the national cultures of France, England and the Netherlands deprived Italy of its cultural primacy in the seventeenth and the eighteenth centuries, the peninsula continued to attract poets, architects and musicians from all over Europe.

The ingredients that made Italy a country between the time of the communes and the Renaissance were evident from the way in which political life was organized and conducted, and from common economic practices and institutions, as well as ways of cooking and dressing. Italians from different parts of the peninsula created these ingredients, which were each regularly described by foreigners as 'Italian'. The urban phenomenon that created the city-states and their cultural achievements was based on a flourishing economic system. In the thirteenth century, Venice, Genoa and Florence began to mint gold coins, around which all European finance revolved: foreign kings borrowed money from Italian bankers, and Italian businessmen had a prime position at trade fairs all over Europe. On the basis of this economic preponderance, Italian cities created the splendour that is still visible today in Italy's many public and private palaces, cathedrals and universities, and it was from those same cities that artists and writers of the quality of Giotto and Dante, Petrarch and Boccaccio emerged. By the fifteenth century, Italy had become what the French historian Fernand Braudel called the 'governess' of Europe. Wealthy English merchants sent their children to study or train for their profession in Italian cities; Flemish market squares only became internationally significant when Italian companies took part in their trade fairs; and Italian cookery books were translated into many different languages. This 'model' declined in the sixteenth century, when French fashion shops began to appear in Italian cities and French chefs began to influence Italian cuisine. French predominance continued for several centuries; for example, in 1766, an anonymous treatise published in Turin carried the title *The Piedmontese Cook Perfected in Paris*. However, Italy remained the favourite destination in the age of the Grand Tour between the seventeenth and the nineteenth centuries, when the European aristocracy travelled to the peninsula to complete their artistic education, studying in particular the Renaissance art and architecture.

Italian fashion flourished during the Renaissance, when dresses, like the architecture, assumed the sobriety of classic style and a perfect arrangement of colour, which is evident in the paintings of the time. From the fourteenth century onwards, fashion changed rapidly, and for the wealthy classes it was no longer enough to dress in luxury clothes, but necessary to 'appear fashionable', to follow the 'fashion of the day'. It was the sixteenth-century Dutch humanist, Desiderius Erasmus, who claimed 'all of us who are educated are Italian'; anyone who wanted to be fashionable in Europe began to dress 'Italian style'. Italian cuisine also reached a golden age during the Renaissance, but by the sixteenth century had begun to decline, becoming increasingly obsessed with mere presentation and luxury. Both in the case of food and of dress, the Italian aristocracy became more and more ostentatious between the Renaissance and the period of the Baroque. Literature also began to focus on the beauty of words, on rhetoric, rather than on content, particularly because of censorship at the time of the Counter-Reformation. The sixteenth-century French humanist, Christophe de Longueil, lamented that Italian scholars preferred eloquence to the search for truth. This was not an isolated polemic, but represented one of the ways in which Italians came to be perceived abroad: they privileged beauty over verity. Rhetoric, fashion, luxury banquets, the baroque *bella figura* or 'fine figure': by the seventeenth century, what mattered in Italy was not life but appearance.

Nationalist nineteenth-century intellectuals defined the period that followed the Renaissance, from the second half of the sixteenth century, as a dark era. Parts of Italy were either invaded or controlled by France, Spain, and later Austria. They saw the decline of the Italian 'model' in the Counter-Reformation and triumph of Catholic intolerance (with the subsequent attacks on science and philosophy); the growth of a bureaucratic aristocracy, which increased corruption and nepotism; the weakness of the armies; the fragmentation of the states; and, as was underlined by the sixteenth-century writer and political thinker Niccolò Machiavelli, the separation between princes and peoples that caused continuous civil wars. When Machiavelli and the historian Francesco Guicciardini laid down rules of political science in the early sixteenth century, Italy was already losing weight internationally; with the discovery of America, the European economy acquired new dimensions, independent of Italy.

The period between the French Revolution (and Napoleon's occupation) and the unification of Italy is defined as the Risorgimento, the rebirth of Italy that many intellectuals all over the peninsula had been anticipating for centuries; at the end of the eighteenth century, patriotic poets such as Vittorio Alfieri believed that only literature could rescue Italy from what he perceived to be its cultural and political decline. In the twentieth century, both Fascists and anti-Fascists believed they were heirs to the ideals of the Risorgimento; both Fascism and the wartime Resistance proclaimed that they could produce the rebirth of the nation. After the Second World War, an Italy covered in ruins began a period of reconstruction, and this too was perceived as the rebirth of a 'model': contemporary foreign commentators described the economic 'miracle' as a new Italian Renaissance. The 'miracles' of the 1960s and of the 1980s sought to make Italians forget about the divisions of the Fascist period and of the civil war (1943–5); but years of radical politics in the 1970s and the end of the Cold War in the early 1990s brought back divisions. Indeed, the prosperity and extension of material goods to a broader spectrum of society raised expectations and overlooked divisions that emerged and were expressed in politics, but came to the fore through economic recession and hard times.

These developments in the history of Italy can be studied through the life of its squares. The square mentioned at the start of this Introduction, which now exemplifies the consumer values of an Italian city with its rite of the evening aperitif, is only a few yards away from three other squares: Piazza Duomo contains a twelfth-century cathedral, the palace of the medieval commune and the newer eighteenth-century Baroque cathedral, and has served a mainly religious purpose down the centuries, though it often hosts music events during the summer; Piazza Vittoria is the result of an urban development in the city centre carried out during the 1930s, and represents an extreme example of Fascist architecture; Piazza Loggia is the symbol of the Renaissance city and the location of the town hall: this is the site of political demonstrations, and was where one of the neo-Fascist bomb outrages against the Left movement took place in the 1970s – a plaque there bears the names of the victims. With their mixed architecture and disparate uses, Italian squares narrate the changing political and cultural landscape that has influenced public life throughout the centuries; this book will attempt an exploration of this history.

1
....
The 'Barbarian' Middle Ages: Invasions, Culture, Religion

CHRONOLOGY

When did the Middle Ages start? The German mathematician Johann Christoph Keller, who lived at the end of the seventeenth century, suggested that they began between 313 (when Constantine's Edict legalized Christianity) and 326 (when the capital of the Roman Empire moved to Constantinople), though he also considered 395, the date of the division of the Empire by Theodosius. Others proposed different dates, such as the capture of Rome by the Visigoths (410) or the death of Justinian, the emperor of the eastern Roman Empire (565). The Belgian historian Henri Pirenne (author, among many works, of the 1937 classic *Mohammed and Charlemagne*) argued that only with the Islamic invasions around 650 was it possible to really confirm the end of the Roman tradition, and so he dated the Middle Ages from that time.

By convention, we now regard the start of the Middle Ages as 476, the year when the King of the Eruli and a general of the Roman army, Odoacer, deposed Romulus Augustolus, the last western Roman emperor. That date had no significance for the population of the time, because throughout the fifth century, the western Roman Empire was invaded repeatedly while its organization crumbled. However, in recent decades a new concept of late antiquity has been used, which comprises the third to seventh centuries, therefore eliding a specific turning point or decisive break and emphasizing a slow and imperceptible transition between ancient times and the Middle Ages. The end of the Middle Ages is often considered to coincide with the discovery of America in 1492, a date that was also meaningless to contemporary populations. It is evident that all these dates function only to produce a superficial periodization and offer little help in understanding the slow dialectic of continuity and change provoked by repeated crises and contingencies.

Despite the impossibility of defining precise temporal shifts, some factors did determine the new age and the ways in which Italy took shape as a country from the end of the Roman Empire: the diffusion of Christianity and the organization of the Church; the migration of Germanic peoples with the consequent creation of an ethnically mixed society; the end of the imperial economic system; the beginning of processes which contributed to a separation between East and West, bringing religious unity to crisis point.

During the imperial age, populations external to Roman civilization were called barbarians. There was a distinction between those who were allowed to reside within the borders of the Empire and obtained the status of *federati* (allies of Rome), and those who remained outside. The latter included numerous Germanic tribes from the west (Angles,

2

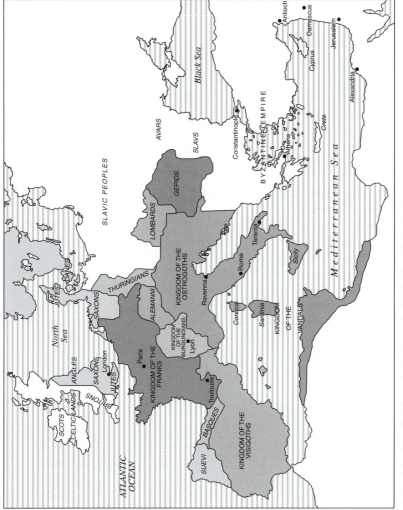

Map 1.1 The division of Europe at the beginning of the sixth century

Saxons, Suevi, Burgundians, Alemanni, Franks, Lombards) and tribes from the east (Sciri, Goths, Turcilingi). Under King Alaric, the Visigoths attacked Italy directly and sacked Rome in 410. The Vandals (with the Anglo-Saxons the only sailors among the barbarians), founded a kingdom in 429 in Roman Africa. From there, they conquered the Balearic islands, Sardinia and Corsica, and in 455 sacked Rome for fourteen terrible days: this is the origin of the expression 'vandalism', still used today. In 443, the kingdom of the Burgundians was established in Gaul, the Franks occupied the lower Rhine, and the Suevi occupied western Iberia. In 449 the Angles and the Saxons penetrated Britain and integrated with the Celts, creating seven small kingdoms.

From the time of the barbarian invasions, Italy and the Mediterranean had been major attractions for northern peoples, as Pirenne and Braudel emphasized in their seminal works about the Mediterranean during the Middle Ages. One of their concerns was to integrate history and geography as closely as possible, and they regarded the nature of the land and the climate as fundamental reasons for the invasions. According to Pirenne, the invaders' dream was 'to settle down, themselves, in those happy regions where the mildness of the climate and the fertility of the land were matched by the charms and the wealth of civilization'. Most of the chosen countries for the fifth-century invasions were in the Mediterranean; the invaders' objective was the sea, 'that sea which for so long a time the Romans had called, with as much affection as pride, *mare nostrum*'. The invaders saw Italy as the garden of the Mediterranean, an area of abundance and wealth. The Mediterranean had also been the seat of Greco-Roman hegemony and the region of classical culture – an idea later emphasized during the Renaissance, and one that encouraged continual cultural migrations, culminating in the Romantic perception of the Mediterranean shared by Protestant reformers and other northerners in the age of the Grand Tour, from the seventeenth to the nineteenth centuries.

The wars that followed the 'barbarian invasions', or, as they are also called, the 'great migrations', provoked a terrible demographic crisis. As Chris Wickham has argued, Italy was ruined not by barbarian rule but by a succession of wars during the sixth and the seventh centuries. By then, Italy was no longer at the centre of the Western Empire as a whole, and consequently lost important tax revenue. Rome in particular suffered from the loss of African tax payments. The city, which had almost a million inhabitants at the end of the fourth century, was reduced to around 30,000 by the seventh century, even though it was still the second-largest European city after Constantinople. Indeed, the crisis was not specifically Italian: in the third century, Europe had an estimated 65 million inhabitants; but by the middle of the eighth century there were fewer than 30 million.

Populations were decimated by wars and massacres, but also by famine, terrible fires and catastrophic floods. As Bryan Ward-Perkins has recently argued, archaeological evidence shows a dramatic decline in Western standards of living between the fifth and the seventh centuries. The Lombard poet and historian, Paul the Deacon, born around 720 of a Lombard family in Friuli and educated at the grammarian Flavianus's school in Pavia, wrote: 'A deep silence reigned over villages and towns. Only dogs remained barking outside the houses, and cattle wandered in the moors without cowherds.' An Italian prayer known throughout the Middle Ages probably originated from this time: *A peste a fame et bello libera nos Domine* ('From plague and hunger and war free us, O Lord').

The contemporary building of churches demonstrates that, while the Roman heritage survived, new buildings were dramatically smaller. The materials of classical architecture were re-used; capitals, funerary epigraphs and columns were embedded in the structure of new buildings. Artisan workshops were established inside decaying ancient Roman villas and fires were lit on the mosaic floors. As a consequence of the Gothic War, cities were poorer than they had been in Roman times. Archaeological evidence demonstrates that cities experienced a serious crisis, and only slowly began to recover, from the eighth century onwards. Nevertheless, and unlike other parts of the Empire, Italian cities maintained their ancient structure, and that urban continuity is still visible today.

'MAY YOU LIVE IN HARMONY': LATIN AND GOTHIC POPULATIONS IN ITALY

When the invaders settled, Italy became characterized by Roman–Barbarian kingdoms, so-called for their dual aspect: Latin-speaking and Germanic populations did not integrate, but coexisted. The double legal system, which continued until the Ostrogothic period, allowed people to be judged respectively by either Roman or Germanic law; in the same way, two different religions were observed, Christian and Arian.

Box 1.1   Arianism

Arianism is the doctrine claiming that Jesus Christ is inferior to the Father. The name came from Arius, a theologian who lived in the third/fourth centuries. He was condemned at the first Council of the Church at Nicea (325), summoned by Emperor Constantine, but, thanks to Bishop Ulfila, who translated the Bible into the Gothic language, Arianism established roots among many of the barbarian tribes.

In the state administration, Roman laws, institutions and organization persisted almost unchanged, but political power and the army were in the hands of the victors, who continued to follow their own traditions. The invaders were a small minority of the population, between 2 per cent and 20 per cent depending on the area. Government duties required a specific culture and training, and since many Germanic military chiefs were illiterate, they had to keep functionaries from the Roman administration. For this reason, many public institutions survived, particularly those related to the administration of justice and taxation.

The Germans imitated the symbols of Roman power, although no barbarian king proclaimed himself emperor until Charlemagne. The invading peoples underwent profound transformations, through a slow fusion between victors and vanquished, becoming the progenitors of the populations of modern Europe. The role that Germanic immigrants had on the creation of Italy has been a contested area for a long time. Recent historiography has moved to what Chris Wickham calls a 'Romanist direction', contesting an overemphasis on Germanic influence in the Roman provinces. The elites of the new populations, always small minorities, tended to 'make the best of what they found', even though the Roman state, its entire fiscal system and its economic networks had collapsed.

Odoacer was the first barbarian to govern Italy, from 476 to 493. He occupied Dalmatia, developed good relations with the Visigoths and the Vandals (who granted him Sicily as a tribute), and strengthened the northern borders of the empire at the eastern Alps. Although his religion was Arian he created no problems for the existing Church. However, Zeno, emperor of the Eastern Empire (which originated from the division of the Roman empire into a Western and an Eastern part after the death of Theodosius I in 395), who was either nervous of Odoacer's power or hoped to get rid of the Ostrogoths on his Balkan border, persuaded the

Ostrogoths to fight Odoacer. The Ostrogoths were led by Theodoric, who had lived in Constantinople for ten years and had been educated in the values of Roman civilization. They defeated Odoacer, and Zeno granted Theodoric the title of king of the Goths in Italy.

The Ostrogoths were a tiny minority compared with the Roman populations in Italy, but as rulers they only had to live alongside and deal with the Roman elites, not with the majority of the population. Their settlement was not homogeneous, but was concentrated mainly in the centrenorth. Under Theodoric, the Roman Church found itself inside a kingdom run by a barbarian of Arian belief, which it considered a heretical version of Christianity. The Arian Church had its own sacred sites and properties. In the urban centres where Goths and Romans cohabited there were Arian churches for the former and Roman churches (much more numerous) for the latter.

Differences between Romans and Goths were also evident in their ways of life. The Romans cut their hair and beards short and wore tunics and, among the upper classes, the toga. Goths had long hair and beards, and wore trousers. The transition from the ancient world to the Middle Ages can be interpreted as a vast process of cultural transformation that resulted from the encounter/clash between classical and barbaric civilizations. This is true also from a dietary point of view: the Greco-Roman civilization had taken shape in a Mediterranean environment, where cereal growing, and grapevine and olive tree propagation had a primary role, alongside some sheep farming, with limited use of uncultivated forests. The dietary culture was therefore based on wheat, oil and wine, supplemented with milk and cheese, though many animal bones have also been found on Roman sites. In mountainous areas, particularly from the ninth century onwards, cereals were replaced by chestnuts, which were also used to make flour. The food consumption of Celtic and Germanic populations north of the Alps was different, marked principally by the lack of olives: the economy was based mainly on forest and pasture, on the exploitation of uncultivated woods through hunting, fishing, the picking of wild fruit and pig breeding. However, cereal growing was central too, mainly used in the production of beer, which replaced wine. Once in Italy, however, Germanic peoples ate what the Italians ate.

The Roman influence became evident, particularly among Germanic elites. A famous treasure found by archaeologists in the Republic of San Marino in 1893, considered to be one of the most important finds from Italy under the Goths, includes the luxurious trousseau of an upper-class woman. The use of the bonnet and the veil, as well as the type of jewellery decoration, is typical of contemporary Mediterranean style, indicating a high degree of acculturation among Gothic communities. As an admirer of Latin civilization, Theodoric co-operated with the Romans, choosing for a number of years Senator Aurelius Cassiodorus, a prestigious intellectual from Calabria, as his adviser and secretary, and placing the philosopher Severinus Boethius, from a powerful Roman family, briefly at the head of his administration. Theodoric proclaimed the *Edict of Theodoric* which kept Romans and Ostrogoths apart, maintaining Roman law for the former and barbaric law for the latter. He restored fortifications, monuments and aqueducts that had been damaged by the invasions, and created new buildings in Verona, Pavia and Ravenna.

Theodoric regarded himself as the king of both Goths and Romans. To make clear his common kingship over the two peoples, he was buried at his request in a sarcophagus made of porphyry inside a funeral monument built for the occasion just outside Ravenna, near the lighthouse of the port. The tomb's cupola is 34 metres in circumference and made from a single block of Istrian stone. At the church of Sant'Apollinare Nuovo, a mosaic portrays Theodoric as a Byzantine emperor (though his name was later erased and replaced by that of Justinian, emperor of the Eastern Empire).

Theodoric's attempts to reconcile Latins and Goths failed, because of Justinian's intervention: the new Eastern emperor proclaimed an edict of persecution against the Arians in 524, which was extended to Italy, demonstrating that he still considered Italy to be his possession. The period of war between the Goths and the Eastern Empire from 535 to 553 was the worst time for the population of Italy since the first invasions in the fifth century. The Byzantine general, Belisarius, at the head of Justinian's army, attacked from the south, first conquering Sicily and proceeding without hindrance up to Naples. There, and later elsewhere, he finally faced stubborn resistance; the population endured a state of siege, in which they suffered violence from both sides.

Theodoric, already old and persuaded that there were conspiracies against him, condemned to death Pope John I, Symmachus, the head of the Senate, and the philosopher Severinus Boethius, who wrote from prison *On the Consolation of Philosophy*, a prose and poetry work protesting against barbarism in the name of spiritual values. Embittered by the failure of the policy of uniting Latins and Goths, Cassiodorus retreated to Vivarium, near Squillace, in Calabria, to a convent he had founded, and there wrote the *Institutions*, to promote the study and tran-

8

Box 1.2   Statements by Theodoric

Theodoric to the Goths and Latins to live in harmony
We love all of you equally, but those of you who are fond of the laws
and demonstrate a wish for peace will be most dear in our heart. We
do not like anything that is against civilisation and we loathe criminal arrogance and its perpetrators: our clemency is horrified by
violence. In litigation, the law, and not strength, shall prevail . . . Both
peoples, do listen to our wish. To you, Goths, may the Romans share
their affection just as they share their land. And you, Romans, must
love the Goths, who make the population more numerous in peace-
time and who defend the whole state during wartime. (Cassiodorus,
Variae)

Theodoric to Emperor Anastasius (Eastern Empire)
Our kingdom is an imitation of yours, it is the concrete realisation of
a good system, a special example within the wider empire; therefore,
the more we become similar to you, the easier it will be to overcome
other peoples . . . We are certain that you do not want the persistence
of discrepancies between the two states, which have always formed a
single body under the emperors of the past. On the contrary, it is
necessary that our states be united with peaceful love, and that they
help each other. May the will of the Roman Empire always be unique,
may its thought always be unique. (Cassiodorus, *Variae*)

---

scription of classical pagan and Christian masterpieces. He also inaugurated the differentiation between the arts of Trivium (grammar, rhetoric,
logic) and Quadrivium (arithmetic, geometry, music, astronomy).

At roughly the same time as Cassiodorus was writing the *Institutions,*
the first Benedictine monastery was founded in 529 at Montecassino,
near Frosinone. After three years of prayers and meditation in a cave on
the river Aniene, Benedict of Nursia (480–547) spent time in a number
of monasteries, an experience that persuaded him to forge his own path
by founding a monastery on a site where – according to Pope Gregory I
(called Gregory the Great) – there had once been a temple to Jupiter. The
surrounding land was deforested and turned into vegetable gardens;
fields and fruit trees were planted. The motto of the monastery, 'Pray
and Work', prescribed that the hours of the day should be divided
between work, study and prayer. As a result, work was revalued in a

society in which it had been thus far reserved for the inferior classes and slaves. Immersed in the silence of the abbeys, anonymous scribes illuminated manuscripts of the masterpieces of ancient authors and Church founders.

At the same time, the Church began to reform the calendar, progressively replacing pagan feasts or adapting them to its own needs. In mid-December, for example, the Romans used to celebrate the *Saturnalia*, days of noisy partying; these were considered to be too close to Christmas, so the Church moved them to February–March, the time of Carnival. Around 525, Pope John I entrusted a monk, Dionysius Exiguus, with the duty of compiling a table for the calculation of Easter. Easter falls on different days depending on the lunar cycle. Not only did Dionysius establish the time of Easter for the coming 100 years, but he also proposed establishing a dating system from the birth of Jesus, calculating it as 25 December in the Roman year 753. Until then, years were counted from the foundation of Rome, which in today's chronology would be the equivalent of 753 BC. This innovation had huge symbolic value (although it was not used very often in Italy until the tenth century) as the birth of Christ became the turning point of history, the event that divided before and after. The date was probably wrong, as today it is thought that Christ was born around 7–6 BC, but Dionysius' calendar has been adopted in the Christian world.

A PROVINCE OF THE EMPIRE

As the Western Roman Empire ceased to exist, the Eastern Empire showed great vitality and lived on for another millennium, until the Turks seized Constantinople in 1453. Its longevity was a result of minimal pressure from the barbarians at its borders, the favourable geographic position of its major cities (which were generally located on the coast), and a well-organized bureaucracy. Emperors were absolute monarchs, with both political and military powers as well as being the religious leaders of the state, God's representatives on earth. The bishops of Constantinople were dependent on them, and they could appoint bishops, summon councils, and promulgate laws on religious matters. By contrast, the bishops of Rome, who were becoming the highest religious authorities in the Western world, increasingly acquiring more autonomy from the emperors, had never ceded these prerogatives.

The difficult relationship between the Roman Church and Byzantium became particularly evident after the latter's victory over the Goths and the surrender of most of the peninsula to the Eastern Empire. The Gothic Wars, which lasted for almost twenty years (535–53), sacked and ruined the peninsula, causing the worst famine in its history. The contemporary Byzantine historian, Procopius of Caesarea, left testimony to the terrible results in his book *The Gothic Wars*:

> In the Picene no fewer than 50,000 peasants starved, and many more did so on the other side of the Ionian gulf. I can describe what they looked like and in which way they died, because I have been a spectator of those facts. Their faces became emaciated and pale. Their dry skin looked like leather and seemed to adhere to the bones while their expression became horribly absent. If some of them, tortured by hunger, saw even a herb, they avidly leapt on it and, down on their knees, sought to extract it; but they did not succeed because all their strength was exhausted, and they fell dead on the herb they were clutching in their hands; nor was there anyone to bury them, because no one was thinking about providing burial. In the meantime, hunger grew also in Rome, where almost all the inhabitants looked emaciated and their colour had little by little turned livid, making them seem like ghosts. Many, while walking and chewing nettles between their teeth, suddenly fell dead on the ground. And they even ate each other's excrement. Many, tortured by hunger, committed suicide as they could no longer find dogs or rats, or the corpses of other animals to eat.

(Procopius of Caesarea, *History of the Wars: The Gothic Wars*)

Italy was subsequently annexed to the Empire as a province, and subjected to heavy taxation. Among all Italian cities only Ravenna, the capital at the time, reaped some benefits from the Byzantine government: built by Theodoric and maintained by Justinian, it still boasts eight monuments that are considered to be world heritage sites by UNESCO because of their architectural importance and the extraordinary mosaics they contain.

The masterpiece that made Justinian famous is the *Corpus Iuris Civilis*. He decided to re-confirm Roman law throughout the Empire so that its subjects were equally protected and the emperor's laws were clear to all. From 529 to 534 several committees of jurists published the *Corpus*, a collection of legal norms divided into three sections: the *Codex Iustinianeus*, which brought together laws promulgated from the time of Emperor Hadrian (117–38); the *Pandette* or *Digest*, which collected together the judgements of Roman jurists from the classical

---

Box 1.3 Some of the great monuments of Ravenna

The Mausoleum of Galla Placidia (425–50), which portrays the Victory of Life over Death;

The *Neoniano* Baptistery (end of fourth–fifth century), octagonal with four niches, decorated with mosaics by bishop Neone;

Sant'Apollinare Nuovo (sixth century) was Theodoric's church and has the largest piece of Roman mosaic work still remaining;

The Baptistery of the Arians, an octagonal building with four small apses;

The Chapel of Sant'Andrea (sixth century) has a cruciform layout; the mosaics on the superior part represent the glorification of Christ;

The Mausoleum of Theodoric (520), a great octagonal construction, is divided into two superimposed orders: in the upper space there is a porphyry tank where the king is supposed to have been buried;

The Basilica of San Vitale (consecrated in 548) is among the most important monuments of early Christian art: a central octagonal core is surmounted by a cupola and rests on eight pillars and arches;

The Basilica of Sant'Apollinare in Classe (first half of the sixth century) is famous for its mosaics and the marble sarcophaguses of the archbishops arranged along the side aisles.

---

age; and the *New Constitutions*, which also contained Justinian's *Institutes*, a manual of law. Justinian's *Corpus* remains the basis of modern law throughout continental Europe. The stratification of Roman law provided the instruments with which to govern, to safeguard people's needs and to resolve conflicts.

After fifteen years of Byzantine dominion, the Lombards entered Italy, urged on by the Avars (a tribe probably of Turkic origin). The Lombards arrived from Pannonia (today's Hungary) led by Alboin. They enforced confiscations across the entire territory they occupied, destroyed the administrative organization of the Romans and fragmented the territory by dividing it into thirty-six duchies governed by military leaders or dukes. They settled in the Po Valley, in Tuscany and the Apennine areas of central Italy down to Benevento in the south. The Byzantines were able to keep Ravenna for two more centuries, together with the exarchate (territory around Ravenna), the pentapolis (five cities along the Adriatic coast between present Romagna and Marche – Rimini, Pesaro, Fano, Senigallia, Ancona), Venice, and much of the South.

A PROJECT FOR ITALIAN UNIFICATION? THE LOMBARDS IN THE PENINSULA

When they arrived in Italy in 568–9, the Lombard people numbered perhaps 100,000–150,000 men, women and children. They came to stay. They integrated with the Roman world, considered Italy their land and intended to occupy the whole peninsula. Most of the Po Valley was called Lombardy from the twelfth century until the early modern period. For example, in his *The Divine Comedy*, Dante called the early-fourteenth-century military leader, Cangrande della Scala from Verona, 'the great Lombard'. The Lombards were very skilled in agriculture and divided the large Roman properties into many smaller possessions. They improved agricultural techniques and became attached to their new land. The Italian landscape, after centuries of disasters wrought by invasions, plague and wars between Byzantines and Goths, was being reborn.

The Lombard kingdom was composed of an immigrant, ethnically different population that dominated and politically subordinated a Roman majority; at the same time the papacy adopted a political role in defence of the values of Roman Christianity. Much of the historiography, particularly of the nineteenth century, underlined the negative aspects of this period, comparing it with contemporary domination by the Habsburgs: the Catholic–Liberal writer Alessandro Manzoni, for example, in his tragedy *Adelchis,* depicted a society in which Romans were enslaved by Lombard occupiers, symbolizing the Italians before the Risorgimento. That 'slavery' was in fact non-existent, and the relationship between the two populations evolved and took different forms throughout the long Lombard age. Contrasting judgements of that age were given by other authors who considered Italy's history and identity in the centuries that followed. For example, in the sixteenth century, Niccolò Machiavelli saw the end of Lombard Italy as a missed opportunity for the political unification of the peninsula, as well as a typical example of the deplorable habit of inviting foreigners to settle Italy's internal political issues (referring to the Papacy's action in raising the Franks against the Lombards in the mid-eighth century). The enlightened philosophers of the eighteenth century admired the Lombard capacity to restrain the Church and its temporal interference. It remained important that 'barbarian Italy' was still an Italy inhabited mainly by Romans; the mixed character of Italian culture and institutions at that time meant that the different components did not remain separate and hostile, but influenced each other.

The Lombards chose Pavia as their capital. Regional officials employed by the duke resided in rural areas and controlled production. Once the first period of invasion and violence came to an end, daily life under the Lombards did not change very much, particularly for the peasants. New barbarian landowners replaced previous Roman landowners. Initially, Lombards and Romans remained separated socially, juridically and physically (for example, they may have lived in different areas within the same cities); however, prolonged coexistence and the Lombards' numerical inferiority favoured a slow but steady process of assimilation. In the cities, the Lombards were a small minority surrounded by a large Roman population that was organized by bishops and more used to a settled urban life. The Lombards were constantly coming into contact with Roman artisans and merchants. In these conditions, it was impossible for a militarized minority, despite its status as the ruling power, to remain separate indefinitely. Moreover, no rule forbade mixed marriages, and another determining force for unification was the Lombards' conversion to Christianity (initiated by King Agilulf, who had his son baptized, for political and diplomatic reasons), a process that was complete by the seventh century.

The Lombards at first imported an Arianism largely imbued with Germanic pagan elements, which clashed with local Christianity. This reignited religious conflict on the peninsula, a conflict that was linked directly with the political–military wars. Christians felt increasingly defenceless in the context of the declining power of the Byzantine Empire. The native Italian dominant class was destroyed in the decade 574–84, many Roman aristocrats were killed or had to serve the invaders, many cities were ruined, churches and monasteries were razed (including the community founded by Benedict at Montecassino). As recorded by Paul the Deacon, priests were massacred and bishops emigrated, leaving the churches empty. Rhetorically, he concluded that only a 'miracle' could have prevented Italic Christianity from disappearing. The new religion, on the other hand, had little chance of becoming rooted. Not only was it different from the previous religion, it was antithetical to it and had little precedent in Italy. It spread through the countryside but not in the cities, and was never adopted by cultured people. The Roman hierarchies began talking about an imminent end of the world; the future Pope Gregory the Great announced it many times, declaring that he saw signs in the Holy Scriptures. In a letter to the Milanese clergy in April 593, he wrote that sufficient evidence for such a demise could be seen by simply looking around: everything was in ruin, there were only few survivors and they lived under the shadow of the Lombard sword; the Day of Judgement was coming, and there was nothing to do but make ready for it: 'I do not know what is happening in other parts of the world, but here, in this land where we are living, the end is not only near: it has already occurred.'

The idea of the end was a powerful impulse in the discovery of a new religious path: if God's judgement was near, then all that was left was retreat, from society and from the Church, with the only objective being to please God. Many felt it was the right time to re-found the Christian experience. The common perception was that of a God who seemed to live in the cities and the villas of the powerful, taking the side of the Roman aristocrats and of emperors. While Gregory was no radical, he began describing a God who was not kind to the emperor, who condemned the rich and took the side of the poor. Moreover, this God had no interest in the origins of people, so even a barbarian could become a good Christian and be saved. Gregory's concerns were for Italy, for a southern Italy threatened by the extension of the Lombard invasion but still largely Roman, and for a northern Italy in the hands of the Lombards apart from a few Byzantine 'islands'. The south of Italy became centralized around the Roman Church; the Roman Christian religion became even more rooted in this period, to the extent that it was able to resist threats from Byzantium and Islam. In northern Italy, an explosion of monasteries replaced the traditional churches that had been destroyed by the invaders. Gregory relied largely on monasteries, as well as on the increasing belief in miracles: with the idea of the end of the world and of God's judgement, the irrational element in popular Christianity had greater appeal than anything said in priestly sermons.

Contemporary sources describe a multiplication of miracles. When floods threatened, the River Po near Piacenza obeyed the Pope and returned within its banks; in Verona, the oratory of St Zeno stopped the river Adige from flooding; at Genoa, the church of St Siro expelled from its walls the corpse of an unworthy clergyman who was to be buried there; in Brescia, the bones of the martyr St Faustinus were said to have rejected the burial of the corpse of a vicious aristocrat; at the court of Autari, a key of St Peter's killed an undignified Lombard and respected a pious one, demonstrating the power of the Roman God's justice. Gregory began to be regarded favourably even by the Lombards, though it was only about a century later that powerful Lombard kings began to support the monastic foundations, to such an extent that most of Lombard Italy, from Tuscia (an area north of Rome) to Friuli (north-east of Venice), became covered in a dense network of monasteries.

In 593, Agilulf arrived at Rome and laid siege to it, but after meeting Pope Gregory I he retreated. Such a swift change of heart generated a legendary account of the event among contemporary observers, modelled on the encounter between Pope Leo I and Attila the Hun in the previous century, which became a well-known symbol of the meeting between a Roman bishop and a barbarian, and of the beneficial effects of the Pope's protection for the Roman population. In the version made public by later sources, Gregory, unarmed, met the Lombard king on the steps of St Peter's and frightened him with the sheer strength of his faith and the power of his prayer. In fact, the Pope had probably agreed to give the king a substantial financial tribute, which the king considered more convenient than the prosecution of a military campaign that was likely to be both onerous and risky. However, in Rome the event reinforced the idea that, through the Pope, St Peter (protector of Rome, the cradle of world civilization) was the guarantor of the lives of the Romans and of the ethical and cultural values of the Roman-Christian civilization. The fusion of Lombards and Romans was also demonstrated by the presence of mixed names (traditional Roman names for the Lombards and traditional Germanic names for the Romans), and the elements of a mixed language; however, by the eighth century the Lombard language was no longer in use.

The years under King Rothari (636–52) were particularly important for territorial and political consolidation. Rothari took Liguria from the Byzantines, and his name remained famous for his codification of Lombard law, hitherto only transmitted orally. In order to avoid the proliferation of vendettas, he meticulously proscribed all types of offence. While the way in which cases were dealt with was naïve, the aim was noble: the end of personal vendetta, to be replaced by financial compensation. The Lombards' legislative initiatives demonstrate an interest in the judicial and civil culture that was at the heart of their civilization. Important additions to Rothari's edict were provided by Liutprand (king between 712 and 744), the most powerful and ambitious

Lombard king, who also contributed to Pavia's architecture, emphasizing its role as a capital city. He presented himself as a Christian king and a defender of the Pope, and crossed the River Po to occupy the region south of Ravenna, though his attempts to occupy the city itself were unsuccessful. In 728 he occupied the town of Sutri near Viterbo and donated it to Pope Gregory II; this was the first core of the Roman Church's territorial power, known as the Donation of Sutri.

The Lombards in Italy were eventually defeated by another invasion, by the Franks, who came to Italy at the Pope's request. In 751, the Lombard King Aistulf seized Ravenna, leaving the Byzantines without their capital and best-defended city. Anxious about the Lombard threat, Pope Stephen II signed an alliance with the Franks and obtained the commitment that their king Pippin the Short would intervene against the Lombards. In two expeditions, the king of the Franks liberated Ravenna and the surrounding territory and gave them to the Pope, who continued to enlarge his possessions in central Italy. The Church by then controlled a strip of land that stretched from Lazio to the Romagna coast. This was the birth of the so-called Patrimony of St Peter, the core of the state of the Church, a political entity that divided Italy in two and survived until 1870; the present Vatican State is the last residue of this.

Charlemagne, son of Pippin, continued to provide assistance to the Popes, and in 773 broke the alliance with the Lombards that he had made when he married Ermengarda, daughter of the Lombard King Desiderius. When the other king of the Franks, Carloman, died, Charles occupied his part of the kingdom (from western France to the Pyrenees), abandoned his wife Ermengarda, and, at the request of Pope Hadrian I, waged war on Desiderius. He invaded Italy, defeating and capturing Desiderius at Pavia. He quickly occupied Milan and Brescia, where it is still possible to see the Lombard monastery of S. Salvatore, and seized Pavia, which he conquered in 774 after besieging it for a year. Desiderius was imprisoned in a monastery in France. Charlemagne then occupied all the Lombard territories apart from the southern Benevento, which survived as Lombard for three more centuries. The extreme south of the peninsula and the islands remained under Byzantine control; a fragile control that was subject to Arab incursions.

The defeat of the Lombards interrupted an experiment in coexistence between the barbarian and Roman populations that had lasted for two centuries. This had huge consequences. It meant that Italy could not experience, for example, what Visigoth Spain or Frankish Gaul had done: the consolidation of a kingdom capable of providing a united

government – and identity. This fact, at the root of Italy's future complicated political situation, was caused by a number of contingent factors:
the decision of the Roman Papacy to obstruct the Lombard experiment;
the eventual retreat of Constantinople from the West; the failure of the
Lombards to conquer more than a third of Italy at any given time; and
the correspondence of Roman interests and those of the Franks.

THE MYTH OF ROME IN THE GERMANIC EMPIRE

Unlike the Goths and the Lombards, the Franks did not migrate to Italy,
but sent there only the men who were to rule it. Aristocrats, warriors and
administrators from north of the Alps slowly replaced the Lombard
rulers. As Walter Pohl has underlined, Italians did not distinguish
between their different ethnic backgrounds and called them, from the
tenth century, *theotisci* (those who speak vernacular), which was the
origin of the term used to define the Germans in Italy, *tedeschi*. The
Lombards were excluded from this designation, most of them no longer
spoke a Germanic language and they had by then mixed with the Italians
and were perceived as such. One of the most important writers of the
tenth century, Bishop Liutprand of Cremona, called the inhabitants of
Italy interchangeably either 'Lombards' or 'Itali'; and soon after 1000
the term *teutonici* was also used as the collective name for all those
coming from north of the Alps (used for the first time in the early
eleventh century by John the Deacon in *Historia Veneticorum*). The
teutonici continued to be regarded as outsiders, present in Italy only at a
political level and only because of weakness and discord among Italians.

Italy's social body was not, therefore, significantly altered by the
occupation by the Franks, and Italy continued to be inhabited by Roman
and mixed Roman–Lombard populations. This was despite the fact that
Italy's regions were controlled politically by different powers: the
Carolingians in the north, and the Byzantines in the south. Between the
two there existed a common thread, particularly at the level of cultural
exchange, which makes it impossible to consider the period as the
beginning of the divergence between the north and south of the peninsula. Moreover, the Lombard experience did not end in the south in 774,
since their kingdom survived in the Benevento area. The development
of Lombard rule in the south is exemplified by the monastery of
Benevento, which was built on the model of S. Salvatore in Brescia.
The Lombards also enlarged and strengthened the city, and began the

urban redesign of Salerno. Southern Italy returned to unified rule only with the later Norman invasion: Salerno was the last Lombard city to fall into the hands of Robert Guiscard in 1076. Lombard influence in southern Italy did not end there, however. Its legacy continued under Norman rule, as well as in many areas (for example, in the law) in northern Italy.

The Pope granted Charlemagne the title of King of the Franks and the Lombards. Through successive wars, Charlemagne extended his power from the Atlantic to the Elbe, from the Ebro river in Spain to the Danube, from the North Sea to central Italy. He became the most valuable defender of Christianity for the Church, and provided the opportunity to replace the Eastern Roman Emperor and therefore occupy the centre of European politics. On the morning of the anniversary of Christ's birth, 25 December 800, Charlemagne entered St Peter's Basilica to hear the third Christmas mass celebrated by the Pope according to ritual. After the *oratio*, in which people prayed lying down on the floor, Charlemagne got up and Pope Leo III put a crown on his head. The Romans immediately understood the meaning of this gesture and acclaimed Charles as emperor, shouting the Pope's words three times: 'To Charles, pius Augustus, to the great emperor, bearer of peace, crowned by God, life and victory!' Until then, only the Eastern Roman Emperor in Constantinople had been recognized as the universal emperor, and no French, Goth or Lombard king had ever disputed the title.

In order to give a theoretical foundation to the Pope's temporal power and a judicial foundation to the coronation of kings, the Roman Church secretly produced a document according to which the Emperor Constantine had given the Western Roman Empire to Pope Sylvester as a gift in the same year as the Edict of Milan (313) in which he had granted Christians the freedom of religion, a gift known as the donation of Constantine. The history of what is perhaps the most famous literary forgery of the Western world, written anonymously in the eighth/ninth centuries, is rooted in the conversion of the Emperor Constantine. The legend holds that, after persecuting the Christians, Constantine was punished by God and hit by leprosy. During the night, he was visited by a vision of Saints Peter and Paul, sent by Christ to cure him of his illness on condition that he re-established churches throughout the Empire, abandoned idolatry and served God's will. As Constantine woke, Pope Sylvester – having thus far eluded persecution – explained to the emperor that his visions were of the apostles, the servants of God. Constantine converted, was baptized, and halted the persecution of the

Christians in recognition of the superiority of the Roman Church. As a sign of gratitude, Constantine donated the symbols of imperial power and the material possession of the Lateran palace, the city of Rome, all the provinces and cities of Italy and the western regions to the apostles, through Sylvester and successive Popes, 'who would sit on the throne of St Peter until the end of the world'. Thus a mythical origin was invented to explain the reasons for the growth of papal power in the West. The fake document also contained an ideological core, affirming the divine origin of papal superiority in an attempt to redefine the difficult relationship between Pope and Empire. The document was created at a time when the temporal power of the Popes was increasing, and when, under Pope Gregory III (731–41), the Roman Church was looking to the Franks for possible protection from the dual menace of Lombards and Byzantines (the Franks having converted to Christianity with King Clovis at the end of the fifth century).

The document was finally unmasked in 1440 by the Italian humanist, Lorenzo Valla (which did not prevent the Popes from continuing to proclaim the donation's authority – as shown, for example, by the painting of it in the *Stanza di Costantino* in the Vatican palace under Leo X, or by its defence by Cardinal Caesar Baronius later in the sixteenth century). However, even in the Middle Ages, some intellectuals understood the harm the Constantine donation was doing the Church by prioritizing the pursuit of power over religion. In the XIX canto of his *Inferno*, Dante relegated some Popes to dwell among the simoniacs (those who bought religious titles) and lamented:

> Ah, Constantine, of how much ill was mother,
> not your conversion, but that dowry
> which the first rich Father took from you!

For centuries the German emperors supported the myth of Rome because they needed to be crowned by the Pope as a sign of legitimacy. In May 996, for the first time since Charlemagne, a 15-year old German prince, the future Emperor Otto III, entered Rome to receive the crown from Pope Gregory V. The solemn occasion was greeted by Roman crowds and German imperial aristocrats. That scene was repeated many times until 1328: German kings descended on Italy with their armies, were crowned by the Popes in the ancient Church of St Peter, built by Constantine in the Vatican on the alleged site of the apostle's martyrdom. The emperors generally remained in Rome for some time, which resulted in friction between the aristocracy and the population. Occasional revolts and urban guerrilla action took place, after which the – often defeated – emperor and his army would retreat back north of the Alps.

Despite repeatedly disappointing results, German emperors continued travelling to Rome for centuries to be awarded the prestigious title of Roman Emperor and Servant of the Roman Church – the highest political and religious consecration. Only Rome as the cornerstone of political universalism, and the Pope as the head of the Church in the West, could entitle the emperors to proclaim themselves successors to Constantine and Charlemagne – the two Christian emperors, treated by some as saints, and the memory of whom was diffused throughout the entire Christian world. Rome's prestige was felt universally; even though by around the year 1000 the city that had once had about a million inhabitants had shrunk to 30,000, it was still larger than any other city in Latin Europe of the period. However, Rome's fame was dwarfed by the splendour and power of Byzantium. By the end of the first millennium, Constantinople, first called the 'new Rome' by Constantine (who founded it on the site of the Greek town Byzantium), was one of the great metropolises of the Eastern world alongside Cairo, Damascus and Baghdad. Despite this, Rome, with its classic monuments, was able to synthesize an impressive number of memories and myths on which new ideological claims could be founded, as expressed by an anonymous seventh-century poet, quoted by the Venerable Bede:

So long as the Colosseum stands/Rome stands/When the Colosseum falls/Rome falls/When Rome falls/The world falls.

From the end of the fourth century, the Roman Church had insisted that its possession of the relics of the Saints Peter and Paul, the founders of the Church and propagators of the Gospel, gave it the unique right to lead the Christian world. No doubts could remain that Rome was the mother and Constantinople the daughter – a daughter with a great political prestige, the capital of the Empire in the East, but inferior in rank to *Roma Christiana*. If pagan Rome had dominated the world physically, Christian Rome was going to dominate its souls; the city retained both temporal and spiritual powers.

One of Rome's main legacies was the idea of empire. While the kings of France and England were creating the bases for powerful national monarchic states and the Italian city-states were increasingly affirming their autonomy, during the Middle Ages – and not only in Germany – the concept of empire remained strongly rooted, as illustrated by Charlemagne's prestige in popular imagery. It was widely believed that God wanted the empire in order to favour the diffusion of the Christian faith and justice in the world. The medieval empire was to lead people to salvation through laws in the temporal sphere, while the Roman Church was responsible for their souls. The two powers, as underlined in a letter by Pope Gelasius to the Emperor Anastasius I as early as 494, were distinct and complementary.

A NEW LANGUAGE

Latin and Greek were the two principal languages in Europe until the barbarian invasions. In the second century, the cultural prestige of Greek was matched by the use of Latin in administration, in the military and in Roman colonies throughout the Empire. Many cities were bilingual. Thanks to literary rules, the spread of schools and Rome's prestige, Latin was the same language everywhere, expressed in different accents but not distinct dialects. Local ruling classes wanted to be recognized as Roman and took their example from Rome's senatorial class; the unification of law, commercial networks, and the presence of the administration and the army, avoided the fragmentation of the language.

The barbarian groups of Germanic speakers who were allowed to settle on the border along the Rhine–Danube axis in the second century had no significant influence on the language. The populations that invaded the Empire in the fourth century spoke heterogeneous languages and their influence on Latin was only superficial. After the fall of the Empire, rules remained in the written language at school level, but schools themselves generally only survived in convents. The language began to diverge into different local forms.

Between 600 and 1000, Europe underwent a great linguistic transformation. Latin began to be modified under pressure from diverse languages. For almost two centuries from 600, a period of transition brought about a substantial break between a literary and written Latin, practised by small groups of cultured people, and the spoken language called vernacular (language of the people), used by the majority of the inhabitants of the Roman–Germanic empire. Languages live and change with the people who speak them, and so it was for the Latin of the Romans, which slowly mixed with the various local languages.

According to the Romance philologist and scholar of comparative literature, Erich Auerbach, the original language left for future generations was:

> a residue of pronunciation habits, together with morphological and syntactical patterns that the newly Romanized people made a part of the Latin they spoke. They also kept a few words of their former language, either because they were deeply rooted or because there were no equivalents in Latin. This is especially true of the names of plants, agricultural implements, clothing, food, etc, in short, all those things which are closely tied to differences in climate, rural customs and regional traditions.
>
> (Auerbach, 1961, p. 23)

Despite the collapse of the common language and local spoken languages becoming more widely used, Latin remained the language of the Church, schools, written law and administration, philosophy, theology and science throughout the early Middle Ages. During the age of Constantine, at the beginning of the fourth century, in the city of Rome alone there were twenty-eight libraries, numerous private collections, and schools with their own teachers and books. Following the sacking of Rome by Alaric in 410 and the Vandals' fourteen days of fire and pillage, the great majority of books fell into disuse, while circulation and copying stopped. Books rapidly deteriorated and were lost. Since these texts were all hand-copied, only those present in high numbers or those preferred by the Christians were rescued. The classics survived: Virgil and Cicero, for example, which – apart from their literary quality – constituted the model of Latin poetry and prose; great historical works, some technical manuals of agriculture, grammar and medicine were also saved. Between the seventh and eleventh centuries, parchment was difficult to obtain, so ancient parchment was re-used, the original scripts being washed out and written over. Manuscripts treated in this manner, known as palimpsests, can be read today, including their deleted sections, which can now be revealed by the use of X-ray equipment.

The enormous task of transcribing the texts of the classical era began in the religious houses. In order to write in good Latin, such as that of Caesar or Cicero, it was necessary to be able read their texts. In the service of God, clergymen made copies of an immense quantity of ancient literary production as well as the love poems of pagan poets, rescuing extraordinarily beautiful works in this way and transmitting past knowledge from ancient times to the present. Indeed, little has remained of the original Latin texts, and everything we read today (most of which had been copied in France) was transcribed in the Middle Ages. Monk scribes usually transcribed classic texts in the libraries of monasteries. A note in a codex from the seventh century bears witness to the terrible efforts that characterized such work:

> Dearest reader, pick up the book only after having washed your hands with care, turn the pages with gentleness, keep your finger far away from the written text so that you do not spoil it. Those who do not know how to write believe that there is no effort involved. On the contrary, how excruciating the art of writing is: it strains one's eyes, bends one's back, and all the limbs are painful. Only three fingers write, but the whole body suffers.

The books that came out of the scribes' hands looked like a series of pamphlets made of folded sheets inserted one inside another (in Latin called *codex*). The sheets were made of parchment (which was made from goatskin and replaced Egyptian papyrus). The pamphlets were then sewn together and enclosed between wooden covers bound in leather. The scribes wrote with quill pens (generally of goose feather, which was thin and hard) and the calamus (which contained ink). The *miniatores* (painters) illustrated the manuscripts, the *antiquarii* (experts in calligraphy), the *scriptores* (helpers) and *rubricatores* (painters of the initial words of paragraphs and chapters) all contributed to the final result of the manuscript.

The transition that led to the spoken Romance languages took place over a long time: the new languages were formed over five centuries across a vast territory. An oral culture developed among the populations, often popular and folkloristic, diffused by actors who recited love poems and the first heroic poems in the Germanic language in the courts. The Romance languages, which did not come from literary Latin but from the changes to which spoken Latin had been subjected, were Italian, Dalmatian, Sardinian, Ladino (spoken in the Grigioni, Tirol and Friuli), Spanish or Castilian, Portuguese, Catalan, Provençal (occitanian or *langue d'oc*), French (or *langue d'oïl*) and Rumanian. Only in the late Middle Ages did spoken (vernacular) languages become written languages, giving birth to national literatures. The appearance of texts in these languages demonstrated that there was a new consciousness of the existence of two different (now written) languages. The transition to non-Latin texts derived from the emergence of new social needs, specifically a new demand for knowledge and entertainment that could no longer be satisfied in traditional terms. This demand came from a new cultured public, defined by Auerbach as 'a high level society that expressed itself in the popular language': this was a milieu where both the producers and the consumers of literature written in the vernacular came together. The exchange between different milieux, the circulation of common values, the contact between popular themes, and the new official culture developed from the top down, through pilgrimages, feasts and mass movements promoted by the Crusades. As Mikhail Bakhtin has illustrated in his studies of the carnival-like origin of some literary genres, popular mentalities also penetrated dominant culture. The seigneurial culture was a secular culture in both its institution (the court) and its contents. From the eleventh century onwards, two cultures were established, one secular and the other religious, that at times would be in conflict and competition, at times influencing and penetrating each other. However, while in most of Europe the vernacular was the most suitable instrument to express this new culture, in Italy the common use of Latin survived until the late twelfth–early thirteenth centuries.

The following are the first documents written in Italian vernacular that have survived: the Veronese riddle; the *Placitum* of Capua; the *Postilla amiatina*; and the inscription of S. Clement. The Veronese riddle, later discovered in the chapter-house library of Verona, was written towards the end of the eighth/beginning of the ninth centuries, and is the most ancient example of Italian vernacular. It was probably produced by a copyist in the margin of a liturgical codex. It revived the genre of the enigma of the Latin early medieval tradition:

> *Se pareva boves, alba pratalia araba,*
> *albo versorio teneba, et negro semen seminaba.*
> *Gratias tibi agimus omnipotens sempiterne deus.*
> (He pushed oxen in front of him, ploughed white fields,
> carried a white plough, and sowed a black seed.
> We thank You, eternal almighty God.)

The first two lines are in vernacular, while the third is a Latin formula. The copyist must therefore have had some fun in mixing high and low styles. The solution to the riddle is the scribe, compared to a peasant who pushes the oxen (his fingers), ploughs white fields (paper), and sows a black seed (ink). The transformation of the Latin 'i' (*nigrum*) into 'e' and the disappearance of the endings are typically vernacular. From the lexical point of view, these are terms of Venetian vernacular.

The *Placitum capuano* of 960 is a sentence handed down by a judge who had to solve a border dispute between the monastery of Montecassino and a private individual. The judge reported the words of a witness in vernacular in order to be understood by all the participants in the case:

> *Sao ko kelle terre, per kelle fini que ki contene, trenta anni le possette parte Sancti Benedicti.*
>
> (I know that those lands, within the borders here indicated, were for thirty years the possession of the monastery of S. Benedict.)

The Latin endings of words and verbs were dropped, except for the Latin construction of *parte Sancti Benedicti*. The document is considered much more important than the one from Verona because it is an official document.

In the *Postilla amiatina* of 1087, the notary Rainerio, who had collected a donation for the St Salvatore abbey on Mount Amiata, added a personal comment: *ista cartula est de caput coctu ille adiuvet de ill(u) rebottu qui mal consiliu li mise in corpu* ('This paper is Capocotto's [a derogatory nickname of one of the two donors which means 'hot head', perhaps because he was drunk or in love] and may help him against the devil who put an evil suggestion into his body.'). The words have a clear Latin derivation, but are altered by the vernacular pronunciation, and the tone is playful and light-hearted. The inscription of S. Clement is from the years 1084–1100 and is situated in the underground chapel of the S. Clement Basilica in Rome. It was added to a fresco which portrays a miracle, and it is a mixture of vernacular and incorrect Latin. This inscription, a parody of paganism, was the first comic-strip of Western culture.

As the next chapter will describe, a period of high emigration during the eleventh and twelfth centuries from the centre-north to southern Italy and Sicily favoured the birth of an Italian poetic language, while the use of Greek and Arabic fell into irreversible decline. In the thirteenth century, in a period of extraordinary economic and cultural development, Tuscany became the new centre of written Italian, which then spread towards the other regions.

SELECTED FURTHER READING

C. Wickham, *Framing the Middle Ages: Europe and the Mediterranean, 400–800* (Oxford: Oxford University Press, 2005) combines history and archaeology, and is the most complete comparative history of the early medieval period. An excellent overview is M. C. La Rocca (ed.), *Italy in the Early Middle Ages, 476–1000* (Oxford: Oxford University Press, 2002). P. Horden and N. Purcell, *The Corrupting Sea. A Study of Mediterranean History* (Oxford: Blackwell, 1999) is a fascinating synthesis of pre-modern Mediterranean history. B. Kreutz, *Before the Normans: Southern Italy in the Ninth and Tenth Centuries* (Philadelphia, Pa.: University of Pennsylvania Press, 1991) provides a political and cultural history of pre-Norman southern Italy. H. Wolfram, *History of the Goths* (Berkeley, Calif.: University of California Press, 1988) is a thorough examination of the history of the Germanic invasions.

2

· · · · · · · ·

The Middle Ages of the Cities

CHRONOLOGY

YEAR 1000 AND THEREABOUTS

In the period leading up to 1000 there were fears that the millennium might herald the end of the world. Even though people did not necessarily expect the end of the world in that exact year, the eleventh century recovery appeared like the reawakening of a society which, as the historian Henri Pirenne observed, 'for a long time had seemed oppressed by a distressing nightmare'. The decades around the year 1000 were times of transition; economic and social changes intensified people's need for the kinds of reassurance typical of pre-industrial ages, and these years were characterized by mysticism, belief in miracles, heresy, and opposition to the corruption and worldliness of the clergy. As Georges Duby showed, that age of hope and fear was marked by epidemics, eclipses and famine; monks interpreted astrological signs as prefiguring the end of the world. This atmosphere of impending doom persisted for two centuries, and is the origin of many monastic orders, such as that founded by Joachim of Fiore on a mountain near Cosenza in Calabria at the end of the twelfth century. Joachim offered a bridge to make the transition less traumatic between a world in decline and a new age of hope, which was optimistically expected but still threatened by uncertainties. He did so by promoting through his writing an isolated way of life and detachment from the material world, and by founding forms of monasticism in central and southern Italy known as Florens. Like other similar experiments, this activity gave a boost to monastic architecture; the most important example of Florens architecture is the thirteenth-century Florens Abbey at S. Giovanni in Fiore. The hermitical choice was a reaction against the changes brought about by modernization and economic development, a radical opposition to the new commercial values of a society that was becoming more secular, and a revolt against a Church that was taking advantage of those changes to increase its wealth and power.

In the eleventh century, Italy maintained undisputed economic supremacy in Europe. The French medievalist Yves Renouard has described Italian businessmen at this time as 'the first capitalists of Europe'. Commercial movement from the Mediterranean came from the east through Venice and from the west through Pisa and Genoa, converging in Lombardy; as Pirenne described it, 'in this wonderful plain, cities blossomed with the same vigour as the harvests'. All the ancient cities were reborn to a new life, one much livelier than in Roman times. While in most of Europe the aristocracy despised the new wealthy social classes, in Italy aristocratic families did not hesitate to increase their fortunes by financing commercial activities; they did not share the prejudice that becoming involved in commerce entailed a loss of dignity – a prejudice that was common to most of Europe's nobility until the end of the *ancien régime*. The Church's attitude to commerce was, in theory, unfavourable, as it believed that commercial life endangered the salvation of the soul. In fact, however, the Church was so linked to the aristocracy and the economic system that it would have been impossible to sustain enmity between churchmen and merchants; and businessmen took part in religious events. During the Middle Ages, Italy was the first country to construct a society of cities, republican and commercial, city-states and merchant-cities, which united the political with the economic principles of 'civil life' and the 'practice of trading'. These aspects of Italian development were later explored by generations of political scientists, from Machiavelli to Antoine Barnave and Karl Marx.

Among the important developments during the period later known as 'the age of the communes', or 'city-states', were the reconstruction of cities as centres of social, political and economic life; the instigation of reforms in the Church following pressure from lay movements and the launch of the first crusades against Islam; the foundation of what would become the kingdom of the Two Sicilies in southern Italy, as a result of the Normans' conflict with the Byzantines and Muslims; demographic growth among both peasant and aristocratic families, as in the rest of Europe; changes in the landscape, with the extension of cultivated land resulting in the loss of areas of woodland; the beginning of a period of rebirth of commerce, thanks mainly to the importance of two European centres – Venice and southern Italy on the one hand, and the Flemish coast in the north on the other; and the beginnings of an Italian literature that spread across the peninsula from Sicily. Historians have tended to define this period as a golden age in Italian history. Despite continual wars between cities and between Popes and emperors, it was indeed an age in which some distinctive elements of the country's history began to appear: the close interdependence of cities and countryside; the involvement of the aristocracy in trade, city politics and architecture; the high levels of urban literacy; and the development of a legal culture.

MONASTIC ART AND HOLY WARS: THE ROMAN CHURCH IN THE NEW MILLENNIUM

As was seen in the previous chapter, when Charlemagne defeated Desiderius in 774 and took over Lombard territory (apart from Benevento), the regions previously under the exarch of Ravenna became Frankish territories. The Popes continued to control an area that corresponded roughly to the present region of Lazio: this remained the basis of their temporal power in the centuries that followed. However, in the ninth and tenth centuries the Empire was not strong enough to protect the Church, which was subjected to the overbearing behaviour of the Roman aristocracy. For the latter, controlling the Papacy meant access to the economic resources and government of the city. For decades until the mid-tenth century, the Roman aristocracy produced a high number of Popes; and they were often inept and vindictive individuals who brought about the considerable degeneration of the Church. For example, in 897, Pope Stephen VI removed the corpse of his predecessor, Formoso, from its coffin and brought it to trial, judging him guilty of having become Bishop of Rome when he was already a bishop somewhere else, and subsequently throwing the corpse into the River Tiber; Stephen VI was later imprisoned and strangled in his cell; Leo V was another Pope imprisoned by a rival: eventually, both he and his rival, Christopher, were murdered by the new pope, Sergius III. To conclude the series of papal crime and corruption stories, between 1044 and 1046 there were three Popes at the same time – Benedict IX, Sylvester III and Gregory VI. The high clergy was no better: it privileged political and military activities over spiritual ones, spent time banqueting or hunting, and kept concubines. Nor was the lower clergy much of an improvement; they were inadequate and ignorant to the extent that priests were not even able to read the Bible.

An effort to remedy the situation was prompted not by Rome but by the Empire. In 1046 the Emperor Henry III arrived in Rome, removed the three quarrelling Popes and appointed a new one, Clement II, the first of a series of German Popes. There was also a reaction against the Church from below, which took various forms, was generally spontaneous, and came from different sections of society. Because of its heterogeneous character, there was no common organization to lead the protests, which meant they were later absorbed and led by the Papacy itself. These movements appeared mainly in the cities, where the social body was more dynamic, ideas circulated more widely, and direct attacks on bishops were possible. Criticism of the Church by lay movements was generally more radical than that by monastic orders: the former wanted to transform ecclesiastical organization completely; but the reformist clergy often disputed the extreme views of these movements, as they represented a subversive threat to the existing order. However, there were some common issues. Among the principal targets of all reformers were the abolition of the two 'stains' that shamed the Church of the time: nicolaitism (the fact that clergymen lived with women, be they wives or mistresses); and simony (the trading of ecclesiastic careers and of sacred objects). The word 'simony' came from the legend of Simon Magus, who allegedly sought to buy from the apostle Peter the gift of making miracles. In the mid-eleventh century in Milan, the movement of Pataria (from the word *patee*, which meant rags, indicating the humble origins of its followers) stirred the lower strata of the population against the rich clergy, rejecting any sacrament given by priests who committed simony.

These impulses for religious reform were already present north of the Alps, with a centre at the abbey at Cluny in the tenth century; but how did they reach Rome? They were initiated by Emperor Henry III, who liberated the Papacy from the local aristocracy so that it could be brought under the Emperor's control; at the same time, the changes attracted those who wanted to be active in the reform of the Church. Gregory VII was thus able to re-establish papal authority between 1073 and 1085, igniting a conflict around the question of investiture (both the Pope and the Emperor believed they had the right to 'make' bishops), which concluded with the Concordat of Worms in 1122 (which established that emperors had the right to invest bishops with secular, but not sacred authority in the territories they governed). The ancient ecclesiastical system, founded on close collaboration between the Papacy and the Empire, was therefore drawing to a close. In such a period of uncertainty and division among the clergy (for example, in Lombardy there were often two bishops in one city, one on the side of the Pope and one on the side of the Emperor), ecclesiastical institutions were sometimes too weak to be able to absorb the protest movements, which were generally led by charismatic preachers.

New types of religious life based on the renunciation of material possessions, but which did not provoke radical challenges to the Papacy, were absorbed by the Church, among them the mendicant orders of Dominicans and Franciscans. The core of the religious experience for Dominican preachers was study; every convent had a theology teacher

---

Box 2.1   Arnaldo of Brescia

Born around the year 1100, Arnaldo became known in his hometown from 1138 for his criticism of the clergy's wealth and lifestyle, and for leading a popular insurrection against the bishop Manfredo, who was supported by Pope Innocent II. Condemned by the Pope, he fled to Paris and then to Zurich, where he led more anti-clerical protests. After Innocent's death, he returned to Italy where he was absolved by the new pope, Eugenius III, and moved to Rome just as the city was witnessing a popular revolt for a communal republic, which forced the Pope out in 1146. During the insurrection, Arnaldo preached that the clergy should abandon temporal power, and that the Church should return to apostolic life. He believed that the Pope's rule over Rome was illegitimate, and that the only suitable government for the city was a communal republic with the ancient city as its point of reference. With the return of Pope Hadrian IV in 1155, Arnaldo was expelled by conservative elements in the senate who felt threatened by his democratic speeches. The Pope condemned Arnaldo to death in Rome in June that same year, his body was burnt and his ashes scattered in the River Tiber.

---

and the time there was spent praying, preaching and studying. The Franciscans had a similar educational structure, and believed in the evangelical power of example, the life of St Francis having been one of sacrifice and penitence, in imitation of Christ's experience. The city populations, which had been growing for a century, were fertile ground for the new orders. These new missionaries were welcomed by people worried by the lifestyles of the new city bourgeoisie. One of the most famous Dominican preachers, Giordano of Pisa, wrote at the start of the fourteenth century: 'It is so difficult to live in cities, just as it is difficult to stay in a fire without burning, or to walk in the mud without getting dirty.'

The Dominicans, adopting a life of apostolic poverty and stressing the value of obedience, presented the Church with few problems. The immense following and legacy of St Francis was at first more difficult to deal with. Franciscans identified wealth with evil, a stance clearly unacceptable to the immensely rich Church. However, it was not difficult for the Papacy to find allies within the Franciscan order, who needed the Papacy as the formal owner of religious houses. Remaining dissenters, inspired by the writings of Joachim of Fiore and St Francis, referred to themselves as 'spirituals', because they felt the Church had lost its spirituality. The Dominican and Franciscan orders generally appeared at the margins of the populated areas of cities. For example, in Florence, the Franciscan Church of St Croce and the Dominican Church of St Maria Novella were built outside the second circle of city walls but within the third. The mendicant orders left a magnificent architectural legacy for many cities. While in accordance with the orders' constitutions the construction of churches had to avoid the use of precious materials and any form of luxury, some of their churches are examples of exceptional dimensions and wealth. The best examples are perhaps the Basilica at Assisi – further embellished in later years by some of the greatest painters of the thirteenth and fourteenth centuries, such as Cimabue and Giotto – and the Church of St Dominic in Bologna. Despite their beauty, the materials chosen were generally poor and local, though the orders often received magnificent works of art as gifts from rich followers. Franciscan art was typical for the diffusion of plates bearing images of St Francis and his life. These, along with frescoes, acquired a remarkable propagandistic value.

In 1053–4, a final break occurred between the Western Church and Constantinople, when Pope Leo IX and the Patriarch excommunicated each other and split the Church into Roman and Orthodox, a separation that still exists today. At the root of the schism were the Pope's claim to be the only representative of the universal Church, and the theological issue surrounding the Filioque clause in the Creed (which was added at the First Council of Constantinople in 381, and emphasized that the Son, Jesus, was an equal divinity with the Father), which was not accepted by Greek orthodoxy. Leo IX also began to confront the Normans in southern Italy but, when defeated militarily by them, decided to forge an alliance. Their kingdom was founded in 1130 by Roger II and included the whole of southern Italy and Sicily (taken from the Arabs). The Normans became the principal allies of the Papacy in the twelfth-century conflicts with the Empire.

From the eleventh century, the Papacy concentrated its efforts mainly on international politics – the conflict with both Eastern and Western Empires for the control, respectively, of Christianity and of Italy; and the Crusades. The Crusades were wars to recover Christian holy places from Islamic occupation, though one of them was waged against the Orthodox Byzantine Empire. They often had economic and political motives, but the religious motive was used in order to justify the attacks and to mobilize

---

Box 2.2   The Normans

The Normans were descendants of the Vikings, who moved from Scandinavia at the end of the eighth century and settled first in the northern part of France, consequently called Normandy, during the ninth and tenth centuries. The Normans converted to Christianity and spoke French. They arrived in Italy in small numbers, and employed local people in the construction of the new state. The adjective 'Norman' was largely a dynastic label, and they mixed, through marriage, with the southern Italian aristocracy. Apart from their personal names, they slowly lost their links with their duchy in Normandy.

---

participants; however, this religious motivation, of seeking to rescue holy places, and to earn spiritual benefits (such as the remission of pain in purgatory), was very real and forceful for many of those who took part. The Crusades were started by the Christians in the name of the Cross – despite the fact that Christianity had been born as a non-violent religion (though it had not been so since Constantine's time) – against Islam which, in contrast, had never rejected war and had incorporated the idea of the *jihad* into its doctrine. The first Crusade was preached by Pope Urban II in 1095, and its justification was at least consistent with eleventh-century thought; the Church decided to accept St Augustine's concept of a 'just war', as a war to defend and expand Christianity. From the conflict against Islam, the Crusade concept was later extended to the persecution of any form of religious dissent in the West. Through political alliances, Crusades and the repression of dissent, the Church strengthened its role remarkably during the twelfth century, becoming increasingly able to function as a spiritual government over the Western world. The Papacy's wars were described as religious missions, glorified and made sacred. The Pope persuaded other Italian and European states to take part in them; the maritime cities, for example, saw the wars as ways of improving their commercial control over the Mediterranean coasts. Genoa, Pisa and Venice took part in the first Crusade, even though at the time they were fighting each other for control of the seas – the conflict between Venice and Genoa continued until the fourteenth century. For the maritime cities, the crusades were a source of wealth; for the Pope, the republics' participation was crucial, since their naval superiority was unassailable by the Muslims, and they were responsible for the transportation of soldiers.

In 1145, Pope Eugenius III established, in the bull *Quantum Praedecessores,* that the Crusaders would be granted a remission of their sins. More bulls by subsequent Popes confirmed what came to be called *indulgentia peccatorum* (indulgences). As the philosopher, theologian and saint Thomas Aquinas (1224–74) underlined, throughout the thirteenth century participation in the Crusades remained the only way to obtain plenary indulgence (forgiveness for all sins) (*Quodlibet,* II, 14–16). The Papacy reached an age of triumph under Innocent III (1198–1216). In 1204, a Crusade took place, supported by a number of Western rulers, against the Christian Empire of Byzantium, considered schismatic since 1054. The Latin occupation of Constantinople was short-lived (lasting until 1261) but was long enough to allow the Roman Church to export and impose its institutions despite the steady resistance of the local clergy. Innocent III became famous also for his endeavours to suppress any form of religious dissent, underlining the link between the Crusades and the fight against heresy. Lay movements that criticized the Church for its wealth and corruption were condemned. Many of these movements expressed dissatisfaction with the existing political and social order, and heterodox religious doctrines spread widely among the marginal and the poor, often acquiring an explicit political character and becoming the object of the Church's condemnation and repression. The Church expected secular authorities to collaborate and repress heretics after they had been denounced by the Church: political and religious dissent were thus united under the same label and exposed to repression by the authorities, both secular or religious. However, this happened mainly outside Italy, as Italian movements critical of the existing society (Pataria, Franciscans, and the followers of Joachim) were not at the same time heretical.

The Church established a tighter control on the faithful by imposing compulsory communion and confession in 1215, and by creating the first structures of the tribunal of Inquisition. The latter was responsible for searching out and condemning heretics before delivering them to the political authorities, who carried out the verdicts, many of which were death penalties. The tribunal of the Inquisition became increasingly efficient during the thirteenth century – and perfecting itself in subsequent centuries – with the publication of instruction manuals for inquisitors, the regular use of torture in order to force confessions, and by involving the new Franciscan and Dominican monastic orders in the process, both of which gave valuable help. In 1215, Innocent III opened the Fourth Lateran Council, which specified various ways of repressing heresy, including measures to persecute Jews, who were forced to wear visible signs of recognition whenever they were among Christians.

However, in the twelfth and thirteenth centuries, the Church was not seriously threatened by popular heresy; but a more intellectually sophisticated attack came from translations of Greek and Arabic philosophy, which introduced to Italy the writings of pagans such as Aristotle, and neo-Platonic, Hebrew and Muslim philosophers. The Papacy sought to forbid the reading of these texts, and Gregory IX decided in 1231 that they could only be diffused in expurgated versions. However, it soon became clear that it was impossible to prevent their use at universities, since they were among the most important and stimulating texts of ancient philosophy. It was necessary to answer some of the theological questions posed by those books, something the Dominicans, particularly St Thomas Aquinas, began to address in earnest.

The other threat to the Papacy came from the German Empire. The conflict between the two powers was reinforced on both sides by reference to the rhetoric of Roman universal authority and tradition, and was prompted each time by the emperors' claims that their own power came directly from God, without the Pope's intercession. That theoretical offensive accompanied the military attacks against northern Italy by Frederick I Barbarossa, who began the first campaign for the control of Italian cities and destroyed Milan in 1161. The Pope, Hadrian IV, responded by reinforcing his alliance with William, the Norman king of Sicily. The next Pope, Alexander III, arranged an alliance with a league of Italian cities, which defeated Barbarossa at the famous battle of Legnano in 1176.

The final conflict between the two powers was declared inevitable by Pope Gregory IX (Pope in 1227–41) in the following century. The Pope alleged that Frederick II, king of both Germany and Sicily, who was crowned Emperor in 1220, had shown little interest in the Crusades, and decided to excommunicate him. The Papacy invaded Neapolitan territory, but was defeated by Frederick II. The Papacy represented Frederick II as a murderer and a heretic, the personification of the anti-Christ; for his part, the Emperor laid claim to the Roman imperial tradition, proposing Rome and Italy as the authentic centres of imperial power and claiming his right to them. Gregory died in 1241; a few years later, the new Pope Innocent IV decided to find a new military ally and protector. He moved to France and, after a Council at Lyon in 1245, persuaded King Louis IX of France to wage a Crusade against the Emperor, by now defeated in two major battles in Italy by the cities of Parma and Bologna.

The French prince, Charles of Anjou, brother of Louis IX, defeated Manfred (Frederick's son and successor) at Benevento in 1266, marking the end of the German imperial dream of restoring power in Italy, and placing the south under French dominion. The Papacy had finally triumphed over the emperors, but, as we shall see, only to find itself held hostage by the French king, and being forced some fifty years later to move its seat from Rome to Avignon.

THE MARITIME REPUBLICS

A European economic recovery manifested itself in the coastal cities even before the eleventh century; even in difficult times, these had been able to maintain a relative vitality thanks to their relationship with the Eastern Empire. During the Germanic migrations of the sixth and seventh centuries, inhabitants of the mainland around the area that is now Venice moved out on to small islands, divided between them by canals and protected by the sandy belt of a lagoon. When Constantine became the first Christian Roman Emperor, the conversion of Venetia was assured by the establishment of an Episcopal see in Aquileia. In 403, Aquileia was attacked and destroyed by the Goths, and its inhabitants found refuge on the islands along the coast. According to later Venetian legends, this event marked the foundation of Venice on the islands of the Rivo Alto in 421. In fact, the presence of Venetians on the islands of the lagoon was not permanent at that time; many still lived on the mainland and continued to seek to repopulate Aquileia.

Having no land to cultivate, and with fish and salt as their only resources, the Venetians dedicated themselves to commerce under Byzantine protection. The islands of the lagoon had an amazing effect on visitors. The intellectual Cassiodorus, minister of the Ostrogoth King Theodoric, wrote in the sixth century: 'Your houses are similar to the nests of sea birds, one moment they are resting on the earth and the next they are gently rolling on water.' A similar amazement was still evident in the thirteenth century; when Crusaders from all over Europe gathered in Venice in 1202, they were astonished to see a city where people lived without working in the fields and walked among canals and bridges.

The maritime cities were the most technologically advanced communes and realized the first forms of self-government (hence the term Maritime Republics used by historians). Their merchants undertook long journeys by land and sea – most famously, Marco Polo

---

Box 2.3 Commerce with the East

The Maritime Republics provided the East with slaves (captured in what is currently Germany and Poland, and in other Slav countries), wood and weapons, woollen cloth and linen. The Venetians sold glass and gems produced and fashioned by Venice's own artisans. From the East they brought spices (pepper, cinnamon, nutmeg, ginger, cloves), which were used in the preparation of foods, in pharmacy and for beauty products. They also brought perfumes, grey amber, and musk and incense, balm, ivory and precious stones (emeralds, rubies, turquoise, jade), carpets, silk, ceramics and dye products.

(1254–1324), who journeyed to the court of Kublai Khan in China. In memory of this maritime tradition, the current flag of the Italian navy has at its centre the symbols of the four Maritime Republics. The first Italian Maritime Republic was Amalfi, which had trade arrangements with the Eastern Empire and the Arabs of Tunisia, Spain and Egypt by the tenth century. The Amalfi merchants bought luxury goods to sell to the rest of Europe. They also wrote the first code of maritime navigation, the *Tavole amalfitane*, which remained in use for centuries. The city was ruled by independent dukes until 1039, then by the Normans under Robert Guiscard, and was finally annexed to the Kingdom of Sicily in 1131.

In Mediterranean Italy, navigation experienced technical improvements in the eleventh and twelfth centuries with the diffusion of the compass, the wind rose, the *portolano* (a book of sailing directions, charts and harbours), the astrolabe, and the triangular sail (called the 'Latin sail', though it was originally discovered in the East in the seventh century). In the thirteenth century, the rudder fixed at the stern of the boat replaced the simple oars that could easily be broken by violent waves. There were two types of ships: *galea* (galleys) and cargo ships. The first were used for military purposes; they were slim, fast, up to fifty metres long, and propelled by many oars. Cargo ships were mainly powered by sails. Later, from *galea*, the term '*galeotto*' originated, which means 'condemned to stay on the *galea*', often for life, chained to the oars.

Pisa, linked to the sea by the River Arno, grew by fighting the Saracens (Muslims, principally from north Africa) and conquering the islands of Elba, Corsica and Sardinia. However, defeated by Genoa in 1284, it began a rapid decline. Like Pisa, Genoa successfully fought the

Saracens, but from the early thirteenth century it was governed by an oligarchy that was in continuous conflict with the population. From the fifteenth century, the oligarchy often allowed other powers to govern the city, such as the Visconti family of Milan; or France or Spain. After many wars against Venice up to the fourteenth century, Genoa was finally defeated by its rival, which became the master of the Mediterranean (though Genoa kept many eastern Mediterranean ports).

The superiority of Venice came largely from a special relationship with Byzantium. The first steps towards the independence of Venice from Byzantium came partly as a consequence of the religious struggle between the East and West of the Empire in the eighth century. In 726, a Byzantine decree by Emperor Leo III declared the official religion to be iconoclastic, prohibited the veneration of religious images and ordered that existing ones be destroyed. In Constantinople and in the eastern provinces this decree was imposed by the Emperor's representatives and was generally observed. In the West, and particularly in Italy, it caused wide distress and proved to be unenforceable. The Pope challenged the decree, and all Italian cities rallied around him as a rumour was spread that he would be arrested and killed by the Emperor if he refused to obey. Encouraged by the Lombards, a rebellion against Byzantium spread all over Italy, and the Venetians joined the revolt. Though the rebellion was swiftly and cruelly repressed, the Emperor conceded a certain local autonomy to Venice, and recognized Orso (as recent historiography has suggested) as the first governor, or local *dux* – known as a *'doge'* in Venice. The doge, at first an imperial functionary, became the *signore* of the city in the following centuries, surrounded by a general assembly and by counsellors who represented the nobility and limited his power. From the ninth century, the Venetian doges continued to act as Byzantine functionaries, when in fact they created their own form of republican government, generally run by members of local powerful families. The republic therefore owed very little to the Eastern Empire from a political point of view. At the end of the ninth century, Venice had become the liveliest site of commercial exchange between East and West. The converging interests of Venice and Byzantium kept the Adriatic free from Slav and Arab pirates.

The full sovereignty of Venice as a city-state is generally considered to have begun at the time of the doge Pietro Tribuno (888–912), though the independence of the city was not the result of any violent or dramatic event, and no precise date can be attributed to the phenomenon, which happened progressively during the ninth century. Independence was based on an ambiguous attitude on both sides: Venice continued formally to recognize Byzantine supremacy, and Constantinople considered the city its subject. Venice's birth as an independent city-state did not change its relationship with Byzantium. Its so-called *bizantinismo* continued well into the twelfth century, illustrated by its involvement in joint military actions (in the name of common strategic interests) and the many signs of Byzantine cultural influence on Venetian institutions, art and society.

In the eleventh century, the balance of European power began to shift from East to West. At the beginning of the century, the Byzantine Empire under Basil II was the vastest and richest, but by the end of the century the German emperors appeared superior to it, the Pope had declared the Patriarch of Constantinople to be schismatic and virtually a heretic, and the Normans were threatening from southern Italy. However, Venice needed, for important material reasons, to continue its relationship with Byzantium – the Byzantine ports of the eastern Mediterranean were crucial areas for Venetian commerce, and Byzantine art and culture was admired and imitated to make Venice more splendid. The most magnificent monument to Byzantine influence on Venice is the Basilica of St Mark, built in the eleventh century on the foundation of a church erected in the ninth century and destroyed by a fire in 976. The monument was a public demonstration and celebration of Venice's new wealth and power, but the architects and decorators took their inspiration from Byzantium. The church was structured along the lines of St Sophia at Constantinople, and St Mark's principal architect was a Greek from Constantinople.

This special relationship was based on the fascination that Byzantium exerted over Venice – its lifestyle as much as its art and architecture. Members of the Venetian aristocracy and doges went on occasion to find wives in Constantinople and brought them back to Venice, importing as they did so ways of life and manners typical of the Byzantine elite. In 1004, the son of Doge Pietro II Orseolo, Giovanni, married Maria, who was, according to Venetian chroniclers, the niece of Basil II of Constantinople. A contemporary account by Peter Damian, a hermit from Ravenna and later Bishop of Ostia, reports the extremely sophisticated habits of the 'lady from Constantinople', who caused a scandal for refusing to wash in common water, eating with golden forks and using perfumed incense in her bedroom. These habits were clearly unknown in the Venetian society of the time and were the expression of a more sophisticated court. From the eighth to the eleventh centuries,

Byzantium granted the Venetian doges their noble titles, a privilege shared by dukes in Naples, Amalfi and Gaeta, all of which had been ruled originally by Byzantium. These titles were quite independent of political subordination, and reinforced the political and personal prestige of these Italian rulers, a further indication of the importance that Byzantium had for Italy's collective imagery. Byzantium granted these titles in gratitude for services rendered (which, in the case of Venice, were often military), and the Italian dukes increased the influence of their families as a result.

The military support that Venice provided to Byzantium continued until Venice was in a position to assert genuine independence. In 1071, the port of Bari, the last Byzantine stronghold in southern Italy, fell to the Normans. When the Normans attacked Dalmatia three years later, it became evident that Byzantium was no longer able to defend the Adriatic coast. Venice took the initiative, triumphantly defeating the Normans and boosting its already impressive naval superiority. Consequently, Doge Silvio summoned the representatives of the Dalmatian cities and asked them to take an oath that never again would they allow Normans on to their land. The document that records this event shows the changed attitude of Venice, which could now act as a new Byzantium. As a result, Venice obtained full freedom of commerce with the Eastern Empire in 1082, with complete exemption from customs duties, and permission to trade in Asia Minor, Greece, Syria and Constantinople. The city's symbol became the lion, representing its patron saint, Mark the evangelist, whose body, according to legend, had been stolen by some Venetian sailors from Alexandria where it had been buried.

Once it became powerful, Venice did not hesitate to take part in the fourth Crusade, which ended in the sacking of Constantinople. On that occasion, the Venetians stole many treasures, among them the famous golden horses that today adorn the Basilica of St Mark. When Constantinople reverted back to Byzantium in 1261 it was no more than a shadow of its former magnificence and power, as large parts of the Empire remained under Western control. Genoa and Venice continued to fight each other for the remains of the Empire. Venice came to control most of the eastern Adriatic, including crucial ports in Dalmatia such as Zara, Split, Dubrovnik and Durazzo. Venice celebrated its control of the Adriatic on Ascension Day with the feast of the 'marriage with the sea' (*sposalizio del mare*), when the doge, arriving on a luxurious boat at the entrance of the port, threw a ring into the sea and proclaimed: 'We marry you, our sea, as a sign of our true and everlasting domination.'

From the first half of the thirteenth century, the Mediterranean balance of power was threatened by the Turks, who caused the final collapse of Constantinople in 1453. As the Turks also represented a threat to Venice, the city sent its fleet to defend Constantinople, but it arrived too late. Many Venetians (as well as other Westerners) were in Constantinople and fought to defend the city until the end. A great deal of the Byzantine legacy lived on in Venice; for example, in the colonies in the Levante, or in the conservation and promotion of a Greek culture in the city, among the vast Greek community of refugees.

The plain and fertile Venetian mainland, very different from the harsh lands around Amalfi and Genoa, allowed the city, from the fifteenth century, to conquer a vast territory that extended westwards to the River Adda, east of Milan, building an important agricultural and commercial base. Its ships could navigate the River Po to Pavia, where goods were sourced and transported to central and northern Europe. The Republic of Venice had a long life, which ended only with the Austrian occupation of 1797.

LANDSCAPE, CITIES AND COUNTRYSIDE

Inevitably, the economic development centred on Venice expanded through trade to the cities beyond the lagoon: Venice imported wine and wheat from them, and exported Eastern products in return. Through the River Po, it made contact with Pavia, which benefited from Venice's vitality. Lombardy and Tuscany also experienced a period of commercial reawakening. In the south, Bari, Taranto, Naples and above all Amalfi maintained similar relationships with Constantinople to those held by Venice. They were commercially very active, and, like Venice, did not mind conducting business with Muslim ports, though they took part in Crusades with the aim of freeing the Mediterranean from the Muslims and restoring it as a 'Western' sea. Pisa and Genoa, in particular, presented themselves as soldiers of Christ and of the Church, and brought back immense wealth from their triumphs. Pisa Cathedral, built after the sack of Palermo in 1064, symbolizes both the mysticism of the victors and the wealth that maritime trade could bring.

The Risorgimento historian, Carlo Cattaneo, argued that the 'ideal principle' of Italian history in any age was the city; that Italy's history was an urban history. From the mid-thirteenth century onwards, the government of cities often switched between Guelph (supporters of the Pope) and Ghibelline (on the side of the Emperor), however, as Cattaneo explained, the difference between the two was not enough to have an impact on the long-term development of Italian communal life, just as 'the wind and the tides of the sea are not the principle that makes the ship float and cleave the waves, nor are they the motive of the journey'.

Naturally there were many 'Italies', and the 'Italy of cities' presented many varieties. First of all, the history of the Italian city was not purely an urban history; the countryside penetrated the city, and the city embraced the countryside. In Cattaneo's words, 'the city formed with its territory an inseparable body', 'a political person, an elementary state, permanent, indissoluble'. The general framework of Italy's Middle Ages is therefore constituted by the binary concept 'city–countryside', within which historians have explored the complex and shifting relationships between commerce and land, aristocracy and democracy, 'feudalism' and 'capitalism'. North of the Alps, European cities developed in contrast to, rather than in unification with, the countryside. In Italy, the evolution developed in the opposite way. The ancient community of the *civitas* was not separated into city and surrounding territory, and the cities were not classified merely as mercantile corporations. In Italy, culture and society were more 'civil' and 'urban-centred' than in the rest of Europe.

North and central Italy was, alongside Flanders, the most urbanized region of Europe, because of the number, dimension and complexity of its urban communities. Because of Italy's unique position in the post-Roman world, and its role as the frontier between East and West, many cities began to act as commercial and international centres of exchange. From Lombardy to Sicily, the landed aristocracy preferred not to be confined to the countryside, and the cities remained under their political control. In the fifteenth century, the Tuscan Renaissance poet, Cristoforo Landino (describing Florence), affirmed that it was primarily the re-urbanization of the nobility that revived Italian cities after the decline of the post-Roman period. Indeed, the class of merchants and artisans, the so-called 'bourgeois', was only one of the urban social classes, and commerce and manufacture represented only a fraction of city activities. Urbanization was not simply synonymous with commerce; even in commercial cities, aristocracy and land continued to prevail over other classes and activities. This was also true at a political level; in the history

---

Box 2.4   The peasant world and cities in the Po Valley

Outside the Roman world it was possible for the peasantry to live without contact with cities, which were few and could be located hundreds of kilometres apart. But in the Po Valley, even when cities were degraded and depopulated, like under the Lombards and Charlemagne, no peasant ever lived more than one day's walk from one, and often even two or three cities . . . In the age of deforestation and the Crusades, cities began to grow again, and occupy a greater presence in the peasants' horizon. Cities had markets, where everyone went to sell, and more rarely to buy, products; cities consecrated the priests who served mass for the peasants and baptized their children; cities were where nobles and monks went to settle their litigations; cities conserved the precious relics that everyone, when possible, went to worship.

(Barbero, 2007, p. 14)

---

and fortunes of the cities, their control and the defence of their freedom was in the hands of the landed aristocracy – the *possessores*.

It was precisely that aristocratic class and its lifestyle, rather than the merchants, that gave rise to a new, peculiarly Italian, urban landscape characterized by palaces (*case gentilizie*) and towers built within the city; it was the nobility that led the movement towards city autonomy, to the rebirth of the city-state and the foundation of the commune. Like its ancient predecessor, the new city-state was, first, an aggregation of important families, though socially mixed. Therefore, as Philip Jones has argued, Italian cities did not develop as 'non feudal islands within feudal seas', as in the north. They were hybrids, bringing together two traditions, the ancient and the medieval, and reuniting two identities, the political and the economic – as much aristocratic as bourgeois, a double character recently emphasized also by other historians.

Another aspect of the central Middle Ages was the deforestation of woodlands to create space for agriculture. In the early medieval period, the parts of the Po Valley closest to the river were covered in forest. Wood was fundamental to the life of medieval humankind – the aristocracy used the forests for hunting, cut wood was used to heat dwellings, to create peasant tools, building materials, weapons and other items; and until the early modern period, animals – mainly cattle and horses, but also pigs, sheep and goats – were pastured in forests. Between the fifth

45

and the eleventh centuries, saints were believed to spend most of their time in the forests, away from the cities for prolonged periods, while nobles spent most of the day hunting. One of the most venerated saints from the late Middle Ages was St Eustachio, who was a supposedly stubborn and ferocious hunter before his conversion. According to legend, while hunting, he met a deer with a lit cross between its horns and immediately dropped his weapons. This changed his life completely – he never hunted again and became an illustrious saint. Today, he is the patron saint of hunters and game wardens. The aristocrats obviously did not follow his example: to be able to continue their favourite hobby, they recreated woodland where it had been eliminated in favour of cultivated land. But from the twelfth century, northern and central Italian cities grew in number and population, and the inhabitants began to reduce the woods drastically and replace them with cultivated land, thus replacing a pastoral economy with agriculture.

The extension of agricultural land in this way brought dramatic consequences. When forests could still be fully exploited by human beings, food was more varied and there was a wider range of foods available. This is probably why, according to Massimo Montanari, famines were mentioned less frequently, and with less dramatic results, in the early than in the late Middle Ages (although we must remember that we have much more evidence for the later period). In the earlier times, even if the production of cereals fell below the norm, there were more alternatives than there were later, when bread and flour, soup and (in the early modern period) polenta had become the principal ingredients of the diet of rural populations. The peasant diet became poorer, reaching its lowest levels in the modern age, when a diet based mainly on maize undermined the health of the population of the northern countryside right up to the early twentieth century.

Moreover, during the central Middle Ages, new relationships of property and production emerged that excluded peasants from the use of forests. Before the eleventh century, uncultivated land was common, but after that, the propertied classes began to prevent its free use. For this reason, meat, or at least some types of meat, became a kind of status symbol, a sign of social distinction. Most of the rural population suffered from the progressive expropriation of previously held rights. Production increased, but only to the advantage of a few people, and the population also increased. There were more people, fewer areas in which to look for food, and a more limited diet. All these changes occurred progressively and slowly across the Middle Ages, rather than through abrupt changes.

The Po Valley area was at that time, and right up to the nineteenth century, an area rich in water. Towns and cities were criss-crossed by rivers and artificial canals that were navigated intensively and presented an alternative and effective transport system to the roads. In the thirteenth and fourteenth centuries, cities gave an unprecedented impetus to the construction of canals, as the growth of commerce required quick and safe means of transport. Canals were safer than natural rivers because they were less affected by the weather, and were constructed in a rational way to allow for easy navigation. Boats and barges enabled the transportation of people, animals and goods in much larger quantities than did carts drawn by horses or oxen. Boats were also easier to defend from raiders' attacks. As early as the time of the Canossa dynasty (from Mantua) in the eleventh century, Boniface, and later his daughter Matilda, made the waters of the Po safer by creating a kind of armed fleet which kept the river free from pirates.

The Po Valley in the Middle Ages was also characterized by a flourishing of cities. Mantua was chosen by the powerful Canossa family as the capital of their state, which controlled most of the lower Po Valley, from Piacenza to the Adriatic Sea below Ferrara. Boniface, who created one of the first shipways of the Po Valley (called *Fossa Bonifacia* and uniting the Po with the Tartaro at Ostiglia), also became Duke of Tuscany and therefore controlled all the traffic between northern and central Italy towards Rome. This created problems for the Emperor, who regarded Boniface's control as an interference with his traditional route into Italy and the Pope's city.

The long-term prosperity of the Po Valley cities began on the basis of artisan, financial and agricultural activities that were both prompted and improved by the availability of a vast commercial outlet, of which waterways were a fundamental feature. From a political point of view, cities were able to unite in a league called the Lombard League in the twelfth and again the in thirteenth centuries against the German emperors. The second half of the twelfth century was the 'golden age' of the Lombard communes, first at Milan, which defeated the Germanic Empire militarily and became the hegemonic city on Lombard territory. It was in this period (1177–9) that Milan built the Naviglio Grande (great canal) outside the city.

Monasteries played a crucial role, alongside cities, in both politics and the economy during the Middle Ages. From the time of the Lombard communes, monks implemented important agricultural changes; cultivated lands bordered, and at times moved inside, city walls. All cities had at least a partially rural aspect, for agriculture was also an urban phenomenon. The monastic orders had an impact on this too, as they were self-sufficient and planted large vegetable gardens and vineyards. Consumption of wine was not only justified by the churchmen's liturgical needs, but also by a belief in its therapeutic, or at least invigorating, quality. Franciscans and Dominicans integrated easily with the urban environment: instead of retreating into open and quiet areas, they founded their religious homes among the streets, participating in the lives of the poor and the artisans with the aim of providing spiritual direction.

CITY-STATES

The phenomenon of city-states is more than just a medieval experience; as historian Mario Ascheri has recently recognized, it was a founding event of Italian history. Despite the fact that the communes created allegiances to cities rather than regions, Cattaneo described them as the first step towards a possible (though never realized) federalism: 'the Communes,' he wrote, 'are the Nation: the Nation in the most intimate asylum of its liberty'. The relationship between cities was generally one of competition; once a city had 'conquered' the surrounding territory, it came into contact with the next nearest city, which was involved in a similar operation to control rivers and road access to expand commercial activity. Unable to forge a common front against traditional powers – with the important exception of the experience of a number of leagues between the twelfth and the fifteenth centuries – the city-states illustrated as early as in the eleventh century the reasons for the failure of federalism in Italy. Many lively ports in southern Italy ensured communication and exchange with both Italian and other ports around the Mediterranean. However, conflicts in the south between Byzantines, Muslims and Normans brought southern cities to their final incorporation into the Norman kingdom of Sicily from 1130. In the centuries that followed, links between the north and south of the peninsula were mainly those of culture, through the development of an Italian language and literature, which originated in Sicily and then moved to Tuscany, and of religion, in the form of the power of the Roman Church and the cult of saints.

Despite being ruled formally by the German Empire, cities began to create forms of self-government, motivated by the strength of their dynamic economy and society. Conscious of their uniqueness, cities began to use the term *commune* in the last decades of the twelfth century. Juridically, the city-state included people of both Roman and Lombard laws and habits; from the twelfth century onwards cities began increasingly to use Roman law, which they thought was more appropriate to contemporary conditions. It began to be studied at universities, which were founded in many cities in imitation of the University of Bologna (the oldest university in the Western world, founded in the early twelfth century). But ancient law was not enough, and new decisions had to be taken that arose from the contemporary situation: cities, for example, needed to decide what attitude to take regarding the representatives of the Papacy, the Emperor, or the nearest city that might create obstacles to, or impose taxes on, the circulation of goods. To address such problems, cities needed to exercise full political and legislative power. During the wars against Emperor Barbarossa it became evident that both the representatives of the commune and significant numbers of young men were ready to serve and sacrifice their lives, and that they understood that the freedom of the city lay in the hands of its citizens. The Roman concept of being a citizen (*civis*) became central once more. Citizens were all those who habitually resided in the city, independent of their social role and position. They identified themselves with their city, not with the Empire, which was far away, evanescent, and at times even an enemy.

The Roman tradition played an important cultural role. Every city could do as Rome had done. Once they had begun the process of creating forms of self-government, the promulgation of laws, the construction of walls, how could cities accept the impositions of an emperor who was considered unresponsive to local needs? Cities began to refuse interference in their government and their relationship with the surrounding territory. The sense of identity was transmitted not only through universities, but also to the wider public, through public ceremonies that were normally organized by the Church, such as processions dedicated to local saints. We have evidence of this mature urban civilization thanks to internal sources (city statutes and chronicles) and reports by foreigners, who described the Italian cities of the twelfth and thirteenth centuries as wonderful places, rich in goods and beautiful churches, palaces, roads and other public investments, all realized under the local public authority. Very few similar examples could be found abroad, apart from great cities to the east on the scale of Constantinople.

In the mid-twelfth century, Bishop Otto of Freising, Barbarossa's uncle, observed that what most distinguished Italian cities was the absence of kings, who were only found on the other side of the Alps. The

German bishop also complained that Italian cities did not observe the Emperor's laws, welcomed the Emperor coldly whenever he passed by, and only obeyed him when they had no choice – for example, when he defeated them in war, as in the 1161 imperial destruction of Milan and the imposition of royal rights (*regalia* – the 'regalian rights', mainly fiscal rights, that had been usurped by the communes). With the *regalia*, Barbarossa sought to prevent the northern cities from creating leagues, and to restore normal rule over the region. The creation of leagues did not guarantee that all cities allied against the Emperor; since the main loyalty was to the city and not the region, cities whose survival was threatened by larger cities nearby – as, for example, were Como, Lodi or Cremona by the aggressive expansion of Milan – could ally themselves with the Emperor in the hope of maintaining their independence. None the less, most northern cities were able to reach a common political and diplomatic policy on the basis of parity, which was impossible in the alliance between small cities and the Empire. Created in 1167, the Lombard League, the *Societas Lombardie*, was the best known of the leagues. It included most of the largest and strongest cities in Piedmont, Lombardy and Venetia. The Lombard League defeated the Emperor at the legendary battle of Legnano in 1176, and in 1183 agreed a peace at Constance, where it obtained a charter of liberties for the Italian communes. Constance established the formal foundation of communal autonomy; for example, the cities' freedom to elect their own consuls and make local laws. These leagues never became stable political federations, however. After the battle of Legnano, the Milanese wrote to the commune of Bologna (which had supported the league):

> We announce that we have triumphed over our enemies. The dead, the drowned and the prisoners are countless. We have taken the shield, the ensign, the cross and the spear of the Emperor. In his chests we have found gold and silver. It is impossible to evaluate the booty. It goes without saying that we do not consider it our own stuff, but the common inheritance of the Pope and of the Italians.
>
> (Dean, 2000)

The perception of having fought an Italian war was not only because of the support received from other cities and the Papacy, but also because the enemy was a king who spoke a different language, and was therefore felt to be external to Italy. As the historian Girolamo Arnaldi has observed, the struggles of the communes against a foreign king

Map 2.1 The cities of the Lombard League

Source: adapted from Daniel Waley, *The Italian City-Republics* (London: Weidenfeld & Nicolson), p. 129.

contributed to the creation of a common sense of belonging, which was later interpreted (particularly during the Risorgimento, and even more by the neo-Guelphs, who wanted a united Italy under the control of the Papacy) as the birth of an Italian sentiment.

Among the city-states, Rome was a special case: having ceased to be the 'capital of the world', abandoned for Ravenna and for Constantinople, it had been left to the Pope by the Emperors. By continuing to reside in Rome, the Pope had made it his own city. However, the image of a passive city entirely dependent on the Pope is misleading, particularly in the twelfth and thirteenth centuries, when Rome engaged in the world of the cities and communes. The commune was active in international commerce, forging many treaties – particularly with Pisa and Genoa – and controlling a large part of the central Tyrrhenian coast. Roman merchants could be found at trade fairs in England and Ireland, and in what are now Belgium, Switzerland and France. The Papacy gave financial support to the most powerful and dynamic social groups. The shift towards closer control by the Papacy and the local aristocracy came during the thirteenth century, with the formation of a powerful restricted elite of around fifteen families, who had accumulated unprecedented possessions and power.

The Papacy had to acknowledge that the new political class that governed the cities made a distinction between the temporal and the spiritual, which had always been intertwined in people's daily lives. As Lauro Martines has observed, 'the more political discourse avoided religious metaphors and diction, the more it made a new track for itself'. While this process took centuries to complete, the first steps of 'secular political feeling' were taken in thirteenth-century Italy, rooted in the strong local patriotism of the time. A lay urban culture continued to develop, particularly at the level of universities and schools for notaries, and a lay written language was becoming increasingly important in the age of commercial expansion. The resulting conflict between Church and laity saw the emergence of great poets such as St Francis, Cecco Angiolieri and Dante in the cities – the spread of their ideas being made possible by a rich cultural background and critical tradition. Many complex questions provoked controversial debates: Who is the good citizen? The good merchant? The good Christian? This culture had an impact on both civil and religious architecture, particularly in the examples of Romanesque style in the cities and countryside in Lombardy and Emilia. According to Daniel Waley, the achievements of Italian communes in art and thought 'was to prove hardly less influential than that of ancient Greece'.

Cities in the north-western region of Piedmont were the first to develop into a regional state. The rulers of the *Pedemontana* (literally 'at the feet of the mountains') were either foreign *signori* who occupied the region from time to time (such as the Anjou, or *signori* from Milan), or local *signori* (for example, the Saluzzo and Monferrato families) who did not possess sufficient strength to create an interregional power until the House of Savoy, of external origin but well integrated south of the

Alps, was able to create a regional state. The House of Savoy arrived on the Italian side of the Alps as a result of marriage arrangements in 1045. Their expansionist policy was particularly successful under Thomas I (1189–1233), who obtained many declarations of vassal-like loyalty from important Piedmontese families by offering them military protection. The success of the House of Savoy in Piedmont as a regional state was unusual compared with others who took power in parts of the peninsula only in the fourteenth and fifteenth centuries – perhaps with the exception of Milan, which already had a strong regional presence before the Visconti came to power at the end of the thirteenth century. Cities such as Verona (under the Della Scala) or Ferrara (under the Este) built a city *signoria* (the control of the city by a powerful family, which became a typical phenomenon in central–northern Italy from the mid-thirteenth century) and only later a regional one, which had consequences for the relationship between city and countryside, as new rules were imposed on the people living in conquered areas. The House of Savoy, also because its members came from outside, did not chose one city as their centre, and the relationship between urban and rural citizens was more equal. Chambéry, in what is now France, was the headquarters of the administration, but there were no dominant cities.

In the twelfth century, Italian city governments were led by consuls (the number of whom varied) and by a general assembly. Everywhere, the government of cities was under the influence of a few important families, and the nobility dominated the consulate, though notaries and jurists (in the thirteenth century generally holding university degrees) also participated in the assemblies. The culture of lawyers and notaries in Lombard and Tuscan cities reached a sufficiently high level of professional preparation to allow them to have a say in the cities' politics, which contributed to the idea that politics had to be conducted by lay rather than religious authorities. Rich merchants also had an influence in the government of communal cities, though they were an elite within the middle classes. In order to nominate consuls, or, for example, to support the outbreak of war, the whole citizenship was gathered to approve the measures, usually in the cathedral square. This was not a form of conscious participation in decision-making, but it nevertheless maintained the principle of popular entitlement to power. Consuls changed rapidly, normally every year, and some of them were not aristocrats but had distinguished themselves in some way – for example, through a military career. Even though the general assembly continued to gather, cities soon evolved a council structure, with which the consuls conferred. When it became difficult, by the end of the twelfth century, to maintain peace between powerful rival families, executive power was transferred to a single individual external to the city, the *podestà*, who was generally trained in law and could only hold office for six months or a year. At the beginning of the thirteenth century, the power of the *podestà* was no longer exceptional but had replaced the consuls in most communes. However, the *podestà* was not a political ruler but an administrator, at the head of the judiciary and with police powers, whose initiatives had to follow city council decisions. The position of *podestà* became a regular profession, with its own manuals of conduct, and legal administrators spent their lives moving from city to city to do their job.

Particularly in the first half of the thirteenth century, intellectuals imbued with classical culture began to shape the political science of the communes. At the same time, literature regarding the government of the city was developed under the active patronage of Frederick II in Sicily. The city was described as a fatherland, a *patria* for whose freedom it was possible, noble and normal to give one's life. Linked with this ideology of 'good government' was the legislation against luxury imposed on many Italian cities from the thirteenth century onwards. This was needed to reduce the private ostentation that came from greater material wealth. Rules were established regarding exaggerated expenditure on clothes, banquets and jewellery, and fines were introduced against those who did not comply. In this way, the city-state reaffirmed the primacy of public over individual interests, even when it entailed the use of illiberal behaviour and interference in the private sphere. The first law to limit banquets appeared in Bologna in 1288, with the intention of limiting excessive spending on food. There was also an international context, as a similar law was introduced at the same time in France, and a century later in England (though Italian cities legislated more often and in greater detail than elsewhere), demonstrating the circulation of ideas and problem-solving that transcended frontiers – a feature that became more evident during the Renaissance, when manuals of social behaviour published in Italy became models for other European countries. The study of anti-luxury legislation allows historians to understand what rich people liked to do (for example, how they dressed), because what was condemned was what people evidently wanted. Laws on dresses and jewellery also concerned the artisans who produced them – as stated, for example, in this decision taken by the commune of Parma in 1258:

From this time forward women's garments are to be made as long only as to reach the ground, plus a quarter of a *braccio*, and no more; and tailors are to be held under oath to observe this and not to cut longer robes; and if they transgress, they are to pay L3 on each occasion.

(Dean, 2000)

These proscriptions did not always work, as many rich people could afford to pay the fines. Also, the magnificence displayed during public celebrations did not correspond to the discipline that cities sought to impose at the private level.

SOUTHERN ITALY

As Cattaneo observed, 'the whole nation did not take part in the heroic age of cities'. The experience of southern cities, and particularly the Mediterranean republics, initially shared many similarities with that of northern communes, but was made different by foreign invasions. However, the invaders did not destroy local culture and its links with the rest of Italy, and their political dominion left some space for local initiative, as ruling families in cities such as Salerno or Palermo still remained relatively powerful. The Normans in Sicily, though they favoured the Roman Church, respected the Greek Church (which still survives there), Islam and the Jews. Norman culture coexisted with the various, pre-existing cultures on the island.

Emperor Frederick II (1194–1250), son of a German (Swabian) father and a Sicilian–Norman mother, considered himself a Sicilian. He described Sicily and southern Italy as his own 'country', and Italy as his own 'cultural inheritance'. He was horrified by Germany with its morbid landscapes, long winters, 'muddy cities' and 'primitive' castles. Frederick invited poets from different Italian regions to his court. Dante later acknowledged, in *Literature in the Vernacular*, the importance of the national literary and linguistic network created by this court, and recognized that 'everything our predecessors have produced in vernacular must be called Sicilian'. As soon as he became Emperor, Frederick sought to extend his rule to the communes of northern Italy. This reigniting of the conflict with the communes resulted in victory for Frederick in 1237, but this was followed by the communes' revenge in 1248 at Parma. Frederick died two years after his defeat.

Encouraged by Pope Clement IV, the French Charles of Anjou moved to Italy in 1266, defeated Frederick's successor, Manfred, and began the period of the Anjou dynasty in southern Italy. The capital of the Sicilian kingdom moved from Palermo to Naples, which became one of the major centres for the dissemination of (French) Gothic art in Italy: the churches of S. Lorenzo and S. Chiara, with the tombs of the Angevin kings, are testimony of that first phase in the history of Naples as the capital of southern Italy. Charles of Anjou brought some improvements to southern Italy – namely, road building, ports and agriculture. However, these developments benefited mainly merchants and bankers from outside the region, particularly those from Tuscany, largely because of Charles' refusal to develop local financial initiatives. Rather than encourage the local economy, he imposed heavy taxation, and regarded Sicily and southern Italy as a bottomless money-pit. This provoked a revolt among the Sicilian population. The spark was a row between Sicilian men and some French soldiers, who harassed a Sicilian woman in 1282 in a church square in Palermo, where the population was waiting for the religious service at Vespers. The woman's husband stabbed to death one of the soldiers and the crowd began ferociously to attack the others while the bells were ringing for Vespers. French soldiers and women who had married Frenchmen were killed without mercy. However, Charles of Anjou repressed the revolt, and the Pope rejected a project for supporting a Sicilian federation of communes under his sovereignty. The Sicilians, who would have preferred anything to remaining under French rule, had no choice but to ask another foreign power for help, and they turned to Peter of Aragón for assistance. Peter had married Constance, daughter of Manfred, and could therefore lay claim to Sicily. He moved to Sicily in 1282 and remained there for the rest of his life. The Vespers has remained one of the major moments in the collective memory of Sicilians, as it expressed the population's desire for autonomy for the island. In July 1943, in order to mobilize the Sicilians against the Anglo-Americans, the Fascist government sought, unsuccessfully, to promote the formation of 'volunteers of the Vespers'. Post-1945 Sicilian separatism also made reference to the medieval event.

The settlement of the Aragonese in Sicily was aided by the Treaty of Anagni of 1295, a papal initiative, after which Boniface VIII appointed James of Aragón as king of Sardinia and Corsica. While this was not substantiated by any legal right, James II began a series of diplomatic moves to impose his control on Sardinia, whose politics and culture would be influenced increasingly by Spain in the following centuries. The history of Sardinia, both prior to and following James' coronation, had many connections with the rest of Italy, in particular with Pisa, Genoa and the Papacy, which were constantly involved in efforts to keep the island free from the Muslims and to 'latinize' its Church.

LITERARY TEXTS, MUSIC AND ART

The work of Francis of Assisi, with the *Canticle of the Sun*, is one of the first examples of Italian literature. It was written around 1226, in Umbrian vernacular, to celebrate God through His creatures, the sun, moon, stars, wind, fine weather (*sereno*), water, fire, earth and death:

> Be praised, Thou, my Lord,/With all Thy creatures,/Especially my lord the Sun:/He gives us the day/And he is beautiful and shines/With great splendor./Of Thee, Most High, he is the sign.//Be praised, Thou, my Lord,/For Sister Moon and the stars:/In the sky Thou hast created them,/Clear, precious, and beautiful.//Be praised, Thou, my Lord,/For Brother Wind/And for the air and the clouds/And for the sky serene and all the weather/Through which Thou givest sustenance/To Thy creatures.//Be praised, Thou, my Lord,/For Sister Water/Who is very useful and humble/And precious and chaste.//Be praised, Thou, my Lord,/For Brother Fire/By which Thou lightest the night:/And he is beautiful and joyous/And hardy and strong.//Be praised, Thou, my Lord,/For our sister and mother, the earth,/Who sustains and nurtures us:/She brings forth the various fruits/With coloured flowers and greenery.// . . . //Be praised, Thou, my Lord,/For our sister bodily death,/From which no living human can escape:/Woe to them who die/In mortal sin.

> (Francis of Assisi, 2002)

This poem, an example of the *lauda* (from Latin *laus*), expresses the happiness of humankind throwing itself into God's arms, in contrast to apocalyptic medieval pessimism, and celebrates the relationship between earthly and divine realities. The *lauda* was created as a litany or lamentation in biblical style. It was the fruit of the collective mysticism of popular religious manifestations, and was influenced by the climate of renewal from below in the Church. The *lauda* was one of the most ancient musical expressions in the vernacular, a devotional canto sung by the faithful in the streets. It was a simple chant in syllabic style, intoned by a soloist friar who was joined by a chorus of children, and it used methods from both liturgical and secular music. The canto was accompanied by musical instruments: the *viella* and the *ribeca* (ancestors of the violin), the organ, the trumpet, the lute and the horn.

With Jacopone of Todi (1236–1306) the *lauda* evolved into sacred drama. Unfortunately, the music of his *laudi* (roughly ninety in number), as well as that of Francis's *Canticle of the Sun*, has been lost. The passionate character of Jacopone, 'mad with the love of God' (*impazzato d'amore di Dio*), bearer of an exasperated and aggressive mysticism (he was imprisoned by Boniface VIII for several years), found its expression in a mixture of cultured and popular words, raw images and broken syntax, all of which give his poetry a passionate and violent intonation:

> O heart's jubilation, love and song,/Joy and joy unceasing,/The stuttering of the unutterable –/How can the heart but sing?//Joy shooting upward uncontrollably,/Where is the heart to contain it?/O shouting and singing oblivious of all,/Joy brimmed to overflowing!//O jubilant joy and somersaults of happiness,/Pray, learn to be prudent:/Sensible people with sensible smiles/Cannot understand the wildness of your ecstasy!//Learn to conceal the bliss/Throbbing thickly beneath the surface:/There is meaning all unknown to sensible people/In the joyous gyrations of the wounded heart.

> (Jacopone da Todi, 1982, pp. 227–8)

While Francis and Jacopone gave birth to the *lauda* in central Italy, a fundamental contribution to the birth of an Italian literary language arrived from the south of the country: Sicilian poetry. As noted above, the context was the court of Emperor Frederick II in Palermo, and its origins can be found in the European troubadour tradition. One of the earliest European literary movements was created in southern France at the beginning of the twelfth century; the word *trobar* meant the act of composing verses, probably from the popular Latin *trovare* (from *tropa*, a rhetorical figure, and signifying melody, aria or canto in the language of music). Poetry in the vernacular with musical accompaniment thus came into being: indeed, its most common form was the *canzone* (song). Miniatures of the time depict troubadours singing accompanied by an instrument. The names of about 400 troubadours are known, some of whom were members of the aristocracy, and two were female poets: Azalais di Porcoiragues and the Countess Beatrice di Dia. The troubadours lived at the feudal courts, and they performed idealized songs of court life. At the centre of that life was love for a lady, to whom the knight submitted in order to improve himself as a man. The service of love to a lady was elaborated by Andreas Cappellanus at the court of Marie de Champagne. According to Cappellano, real love could only be adulterous, because it had to be free, while married love was a compulsory relationship. Therefore, real love could only be imagined or dreamed. In *Lancelot*, by Chrétien de Troyes, adulterous love drives the knight to treason when Lancelot betrays his oath to King Arthur, whom he was sworn to serve, because of his love for Arthur's queen. Dante was attracted to the ambiguity of this tale, and in *The Divine Comedy* narrated the story of Paolo and Francesca (*Inferno*, V), the adulterous sister and brother-in-law (*cognati*) who were led astray by the reading of *Lancelot* and ended up in hell among the lascivious.

Troubadour poetry had great importance in Italy, particularly when the southern courts of France were wrecked by Innocent III's violent crusade against the Albigensians (1208–29) and many troubadours found refuge in Italy. Provençal poetry in Italy, and several of its authors, are celebrated by Dante in *Inferno* (XXVIII, 118–42), *Purgatorio* (XXVI, 117), and in *Literature in the Vernacular* (II, ii, 9; vi, 6; x, 2; xiii, 2), and had an influence, as noted above, on the Sicilian school. Frederick II encouraged the fusion of different cultures. His German father had been a poet, his mother was Norman and he had been educated in both French and German. Beginning in 1220, he encouraged the birth of lyric poetry in the vernacular in Italy, modelled on the Provençal poets and the German *Minnesänger* (romantic poets). The 'Sicilian school' was a group of about twenty-five poets active between 1230 and 1266. The most famous of these were Giacomo da Lentini, Rinaldo d'Aquino, Giacomino Pugliese, Stefano Protonotaro and Pier delle Vigne, the latter remembered by Dante in *Inferno* among the suicides. However, there were fundamental differences between them and the Provençal poets. First, these authors were not aristocrats or knights, but came from the bourgeois world of the professions, law in particular. They did not compose music; therefore their poetry was destined only to be read. Their world was at court but it was no longer a feudal world; vassalage had receded into the background. The emphasis of their poetry was no longer on the lady but on the nature and effects of love. The experience of love thus became analysed through psychological introspection. This phenomenology of love is evident in one of the first sonnets written by the notary and poet Giacomo da Lentini, who invented this poetic form. This is the first quatrain, based around the polarity of eyes and heart:

Love is a desire coming from the heart
Through intense delight;
and it is the eyes that first engender Love,
and the heart that feeds it.

(Giacomo da Lentini, 1915)

The metrical and rhetorical structures of Sicilian poetry influenced the entire Italian lyric tradition, as its original model. The Sicilian poets were rooted in Provençal poetry, but made no reference to daily chronicles or political struggles, since the imperial regime did not encourage the climate of freedom and political argument that had often been the setting of Provençal poetry. The hendecasyllabic line became the fundamental metrical structure of Italian poetry; it originated in the ancient Franco-Provençal lyric, but had fewer rules and created many different rhythms.

Until the end of the thirteenth century, Florentine literature did not show any expansionist tendency, as Florence was not yet a political or economic capital. As Carlo Dionisotti has argued, 'in the first half of the thirteenth century a current of new poetry ran from Sicily to the Tyrrhenian area and Tuscany, crossed the Apennines and grew, but also stopped, at Bologna'. It was as a result of the relationship between Frederick II's imperial functionaries and the communes of central Italy that this occurred, but also because many of Frederick's functionaries came from the law faculty of the University of Bologna, where many Emilian and Tuscan intellectuals had also studied. In this way, Sicilian poetry spread to Tuscany and Bologna. The new poets took from the Sicilians the *canzone* and the sonnet, but also experimented with the ballad and the political song. Among the most original Sicilian–Tuscan poets were Bonagiunta Orbicciani from Lucca (ca.1220–90) and Guittone d'Arezzo (ca.1235–94). In *Purgatorio* (XXIV, 49–63), Dante conversed with Orbicciani, who conferred on the poet the honour of having created the *stil novo* (new style).

Popular poetry and music was transmitted by minstrels, who performed in squares, in front of churches and in the streets. As Piero Camporesi argues, their jokes were often obscene and were sometimes condemned by the Church, but they were extremely popular – at their performances, 'the meaning of life seemed to change rhythm and dimension, farce replaced drama, the *joculator*, the *comicus*, dethroned the *tragicus*'. Not only did minstrels become a central feature in popular culture, but they also came to play a fundamental mediatory role between clerical and vernacular cultures. Indeed, while the Church hierarchy was opposed to them, there was often collaboration between local clergy and minstrels.

In all Italian provinces, the thirteenth century was a time of renovation and transformation of styles, in art as well as literature. The extraordinary success of St Francis's preaching had an impact on both – Assisi became a pictorial laboratory – and the same was true for the activities of Frederick II (St Francis died in 1226 and Frederick in 1250). Iconoclasm never took root in Italy, and the movements for the reformation of the Church which began by preaching austerity soon became reconciled to the use of artistic resources, which were eventually vigorously exploited. When Cistercian reform spread from France through Italy in the twelfth century, during St Bernard's journeys to Rome, a new type of monastic architecture was disseminated and adopted by the mendicant orders, but a comparison of Cistercian austerity and the decorative wealth and numerous paintings dedicated to Franciscans and Dominicans showed how discretion and caution in the use of images did not suit the Italians. The emphasis on icons continued through the centuries; after the Reformation in the sixteenth century (which had little effect in Italy), the Church persisted in demonstrating its loyalty to the cult of images, echoed in this by the ornamental variety of Italian luxurious dwellings, public palaces and squares – a constant cross-fertilization between the secular and the sacred continued to characterize Italian art.

Late-thirteenth-century Italian art was a reaction to two major artistic 'invasions': those of Byzantine art, which arrived mainly through Venice after its conquest of Constantinople in 1204 made possible contact with Greek decorators and mosaicists; and of French Gothic. At the end of the century, mosaic art developed in particular in Rome, which became a major centre of innovation. The vitality of Venice and Rome was matched by a kind of 'southern Renaissance', with the building of castles in Apulia and Sicily under Frederick, such as the Castel del Monte near Barletta, or the castles of Syracuse and Catania. These buildings, which bring together the Gothic experience of the Cistercians, Arabic architecture and Byzantine influence, demonstrate the cosmopolitanism of Frederick's reign, while Assisi, Siena and Rome, in central Italy – home to artists such as Giotto and Cimabue – became a beacon for artists from all over the peninsula.

SELECTED FURTHER READING

For an overview of this period, see D. Abulafia, *Italy in the Central Middle Ages, 1000–1300* (Oxford: Oxford University Press, 2004). Two indispensable surveys of the Italian city states are P. Jones, *The Italian City-State: from Commune to Signoria* (Oxford: Clarendon Press, 1997) and D. Waley, *The Italian City-Republics* (London: Weidenfeld and Nicolson, 1969). T. Dean, *Crime and Justice in Late Medieval Italy* (Cambridge: Cambridge University Press, 2007) provides important insights on Italian criminal justice from the mid-thirteenth to the end of the fifteenth century. A concise and authoritative study of the relationship between Venice and Constantinople is D. M. Nicol, *Byzantium and Venice: A Study in Diplomatic and Cultural Relations* (Cambridge: Cambridge University Press, 1988). D. Webb, *Patrons and Defenders: The Saints in the Italian City-States* (London: Tauris, 1996) is an interesting study of the cult of saints in the political life of Italian Medieval city states.

3

The Middle Ages of the Courts

CHRONOLOGY

REBIRTH AFTER PLAGUE: THE AGE OF THE SIGNORIE

In the fourteenth century a terrible plague, known as the 'Black Death', hit Italy. It arrived during a period of dynamic commercial exchange between East and West on ships from the eastern Mediterranean; ships which also brought the rats carrying the plague bacillus. In Italy, the plague attacked first in Sicily, originating from contaminated Genoese ships arriving at Messina from Constantinople in 1347. From there, the epidemic spread across most of Italy and into the rest of Europe. The population of Europe was approximately 80 million people at that time, around 25 million of whom died of the plague. Its effects on Italy were worse than elsewhere because of the degree of urbanization; the peninsula had more than 150 cities of over 5,000 inhabitants, and the disease spread more easily where contact between people was closer. In many cities, the plague killed citizens a small number at a time, reappearing often after 1348. The population reached its lowest point in the first decades of the fifteenth century, by which time Florence, for example, had lost two-thirds of its population (down from 100–120,000 to 37,000). While cities organized defence measures (medicinal remedies and forms of social control, as well as processions and rituals invoking God and the patron saints), many inhabitants moved temporarily to the countryside, where the plague was less prevalent. At the end of the fourteenth century, the population of Italy had fallen to 8 million – from 11 million in 1300 and 9.5 million in 1350. Seeing the many empty dwellings, built during the thirteenth and fourteenth centuries, when the population was increasing, must have had a profound impact on contemporaries.

Only after a full century did the peninsula recover its lost population. By the end of the fifteenth century, Italy once more had the most populous cities in Europe. Milan, Venice and Naples each had more than 100,000 inhabitants, matched in Europe only by Paris, and even small centres were comparable to cities of international importance abroad. Calabria, for example, had around ten centres with about 2,000–7,000 inhabitants. Verona, in the Venetian Republic, had 25,000 inhabitants and a bustling port on the River Adige. The population of Messina, at the time one of the busiest ports in the Mediterranean, also stood at 25,000 – as did that of Rome. Very few non-Italians lived on the peninsula or in Sicily at the time; the most mixed regions were the Savoy state in Piedmont, which was still characterized by its interests on both sides of the Alps, and Sardinia, where the Catalan–Aragonese presence was stronger than in the rest of the south.

By the mid-fourteenth century, the Italy of communes had turned into the Italy of despotism, with the rule of dynastic city lords (*signorie*). Before the *signorie*, the communes experienced the period of *podestà* rule noted in Chapter 2. The role of the *podestà* in the thirteenth century, which emerged from the conflicts between powerful families, did not in itself lead to peace, but it did create more stable governments. The *podestà* was responsible to the citizens for the results of his work, and at the end of his mandate his activity was judged by a group of *sindici* (the procedure was called *sindicatus*). Their duty was one of control, in accordance with the Roman figure of the *sindicus-procurator*. The *podestarile* government brought about an explosion in the official registration of documents and their conservation, with the first archival rules. The fact that today we have so many written documents with which to study the detailed history of every city is thanks to this (medieval) need to demonstrate everything in a juridically precise manner. While archives had begun to be collected in the eighth century, their volume increased in this period, thus enabling Italy to preserve an unusually large quantity of documents in comparison with other countries. As John Larner explains, by contemporary European standards, medieval Italy was indeed 'an immensely literate, legalistic, and bureaucratic society in which a great deal was written'. Written source material is today still distributed over more than ninety state archives, reflecting the pattern of local governments as they existed during the late medieval period.

Created as a way to solve conflicts, the *podestà* government was challenged from its early years, as the nobility constantly sought to control it. The *signorie* of the fourteenth century were rooted in a period of conflict – between populations and noble families, or between the Guelph and the Ghibelline parties for control of the city – during which time the *podestà* became an increasingly permanent figure. Unlike the *podestà*, the *signorie* were hereditary lordships. The Guelph–Ghibelline antagonism no longer represented the factions involved in the struggle between Popes and emperors as it had during the thirteenth century, but merely tended to mask new divisions. As John Kenneth Hyde has put it, by the second half of the fourteenth century Italians 'were ceasing to think in the traditional papal–imperialist terms and were beginning to see the parties as local groups in competition for power'.

The evolution of city-states into *signorie* was not abrupt or violent, though the actual moments of transition could indeed be violent, or at least involve the threat of violence; more often, local powerful families increased their control over cities to the point that they were being run by these narrow oligarchies. As shown in Chapter 2, the countryside continued to influence the city, and feudal families always had a strong influence on city politics. As Daniel Waley underlines, 'the essence of the *signoria* was the victory of landed power'; city-states dominated the surrounding territory, but at the same time, the communes struggled to maintain independence from the rural lords. In this sense, the feudal system was never overthrown in Italy, but persisted alongside urban culture.

Conflicts between aristocratic families stimulated academic debates on the nature of political power: Giovanni of Viterbo and Brunetto Latini (Dante's teacher and later chancellor of the Republic in Florence) wrote about *res publica* in reference to the city-states; Ptolemy of Lucca underlined the significance of giving people the chance to choose their representatives, as opposed to the arbitrary choices of kings, and considered it appropriate and opportune to change rulers frequently, since the best government was one made by the wise and the virtuous. These figures were writing at a time when monarchical rule was the dominant form of government in Europe, when people measured their lives by the monarchs who ruled them, and, as Marc Bloch has demonstrated, where English and French kings were believed to be thaumaturgic. However, in the Italian cities, governments were generally anonymous – years were marked with reference to a particular *podestà*, and by their succession; and the history of the cities was becoming largely a 'human' history, in which the divine dimension was accorded relatively little importance. Divine intervention was used to explain what was external to questions of government, such as inexplicable events like epidemics or floods. Government was no longer received, wanted or decided by God.

However, religion still played an important part in the ritual and action of governments, and was not entirely excluded from city government, as Church and state shared in the practice of 'civic religion' – a set of religious ceremonies and activities that reinforced civic solidarities, such as the cult of patron saints, or processions on important festival days to commemorate political turning points or military victories. Moreover, daily life in the fourteenth and fifteenth centuries was ruled by religious imperatives. During religious festivities it was forbidden to work, and cities added civic festivities to the religious ones, which were not holidays (which did not exist for the vast majority in society), but were days dedicated to social events related to the family, group or city. Each city had its own feast days, but some of these feasts were common to the whole country: St Valentine, for example, was celebrated everywhere on

14 February, and carnivals took place throughout the whole peninsula; the use of masks (often mocking famous people) and carnival floats was already present, from Mantua to Venice, and from Milan to Florence and Rome. Carnivals celebrated ancient Roman events as well as contemporary ones. Feasts for patron saints could last more than two weeks, with rituals, horse races, hunts and tournaments. Particularly in Venice, which was beginning to acquire the natural appearance of a theatrical stage, secular traditions and patriotism involved most of the citizens.

With the emergence of a new class of entrepreneurs and lawyers in the fourteenth century, lay communal schools began to replace ecclesiastical ones. It was clear that the latter were orientated towards a classical and religious culture, which was not satisfactory for men of action, who needed a more technical and scientific training. Initially, these lay schools were private, but the communal authorities quickly began to institute city schools, choosing teachers, and deciding salaries and holiday times. Education was considered to be a public service that should benefit the whole collective, though in fact only rich families could take advantage of it. Schools were not only created for business purposes but also to meet the needs of the city administration, so communal schools insisted on the centrality of classical culture – education was the foundation of the common good, and the study of Latin remained essential.

Italian cities were riven by internal disputes as well as by rivalries with other cities. From an artistic point of view, these rivalries expressed themselves in the construction of great monumental works, on which cities spent huge sums of money. With a few exceptions, the fourteenth century persisted as a century of cities, but no longer of communes and republics. In Florence, all attempts to turn the government into a dictatorship were unsuccessful until the sixteenth century, as the final defeat of the popular revolt of the Ciompi in the second half of the fourteenth century confirmed the bourgeoisie in government. The other major republics were Venice, Siena and Lucca, governed by a nobility that had close ties with the bourgeoisie and was involved in commerce. In most other provinces, feudal or aristocratic *signori* succeeded in imposing their power.

Architecture had already expressed city patriotism during the communal age; during the age of the *signorie* it expressed dynastic assertion. In Milan and other Lombard cities, the Visconti family left visible traces of its long dominion from the fourteenth century. The Sforza family, which followed the Visconti after a brief attempt to return to republican

---

Box 3.1   The tumult of the Ciompi

The revolt of the Ciompi is one of the first examples of economic and social protest in European history. The Ciompi were wool workers, and one of the lowest social classes in Florence. They were excluded from political representation and their salary was at subsistence level in normal times. In 1378, following a time of economic crisis resulting from the devaluation of the currency and the consequences of the plague, they occupied the Priori Palace, asking for political rights and to be able to create their own corporation. The revolt, described by Machiavelli in *The Florentine Histories* a century and a half later, met with temporary success, but was defeated by 1382. The Ciompi brought together social protest and mystical beliefs – a reflection of the apocalyptic period of anxiety that followed the plague. This mixture of social rebellion and apocalyptic views, typical of the lower classes at the time, was considered by governments to be a threat to order.

---

government in 1447–50 (the *repubblica ambrosiana*), continued in the Visconti's footsteps by building, for example, the colossal Sforzesco castle within the walls of the city centre. Similar activity was carried out by the Este family at Ferrara, the Gonzaga at Mantua, and the Montefeltro family at Urbino, all of whom constructed beautiful urban monuments. In line with these other princes, the Popes felt the need to improve Rome, not only for reasons of civic pride but also to raise the city's prestige in the Western religious world. Links between city *signorie* and the Popes were close: cardinals could become Popes and all the families mentioned above had members who were cardinals. Venice extended its architectural works to the whole area of the republic as well as within the city, where important families, including those of the doges, built many new palaces during the fifteenth century, particularly alongside the Grand Canal.

The establishment of the *signorie* reduced civil strife, but not immediately or completely. Civil instability could still cause the movement of entire social groups from one city to another. For example, when Florence conquered Pisa at the beginning of the fifteenth century, many business families who had previously developed commercial links with Sicilian cities moved to the island and made it their home. Family struggles for the control of Florence, particularly between the Albizzi and the

Medici in the fifteenth century, forced aristocratic families and individuals to move to Venice, Ferrara, Naples or Rome.

To embellish their cities, governments produced guidelines for the construction of squares, gardens and palaces to make them worthy of honouring the city, which was to be respected as if it were a person. The construction of Milan's Duomo began under Gian Galeazzo Visconti at the end of the fourteenth century, the same time as other famous Lombard cathedrals, such as the Certosa of Pavia or the Cathedral of Monza, were built. The architects were persuaded that they had to triumph over the French Gothic style with spectacular and flamboyant churches. A similar attitude was held in Venice, where the works for the S. Maria dei Frari began in 1340 and took a century to complete. As contemporary artists observed, there was in Italian cities a taste for oral criticism and public discussion on artistic matters; people generally demonstrated a curiosity about architecture, which was often related to their daily activities. As the art historian André Chastel noted, 'everyone believed themselves to be an artist' and interfered with the artists' work by giving their opinions. This was also a way in which people expressed their municipal loyalty, often in competition with the nearest city: 'the instinctive and joyful affection of the Italian for the celebrity of his province and village, that *campanilismo* . . . contributed to keep [municipal loyalty] alive'. This did not change with the slow regional unification achieved by the most powerful city-states during the fifteenth century (Lombardy, the Venetian Republic, Florence, the Papal States, and the Kingdom of Naples). The feudal system and the power of the aristocracy were particularly strong in southern Italy and Sicily because, as was seen in Chapter 2, the city movement there had been halted by foreign occupation, principally, after the age of Frederick II, by French and Spanish conquest.

In Sicily, the instability and war that followed the Vespers in the thirteenth century, and economic and trade decline as a result of the plague in the fourteenth century brought further periods of instability and weak government, which allowed the feudal aristocracy to expand its privileges. In the fifteenth century, Sicily became increasingly isolated, subject to the Aragonese monarchy and governed by viceroys. The separation from Naples continued until the 1430s, when the Anjou had no more successors and the Aragonese took control of both regions. As Palermo declined, Naples enjoyed a period of splendour from the fourteenth century, connected to the cultural and economic life of the other Italian cities despite foreign domination. The best writers and artists (including Petrarch, Boccaccio and Giotto) worked there temporarily. King Alfonso V, who ruled from 1416, made a deal with the aristocracy, allowing them to strengthen their power over the local vassal populations. He often, however, summoned parliament in the hope of controlling them. As in the rest of Europe, the parliament included representatives of the nobility, the clergy and the cities – the latter being called on to balance the power of the nobility. While Sicily and most of the south was left at the mercy of local barons, Naples emerged as one of the largest and most culturally progressive cities in Europe, giving rise, as will be seen in the next chapter, to extraordinary Renaissance architecture and music.

THE PAPACY BETWEEN ROME AND AVIGNON

With the establishment of the Inquisition, the Church created a fully-developed system of persecution. In the minds of the persecutors, violence was justified by the belief that heresy would lead to eternal punishment. Civil society, however, did not always receive these ideas favourably, and many cities did not reject the possibility of pluralism, just as many people did not like what was seen to be gratuitous violence. The inquisitors were called 'rapacious wolves' and the population often protested against their activity, particularly in the thirteenth and fourteenth centuries. The Waldensian movement, condemned as heretical by the third Lateran council in 1179, was organized to defend itself successfully and even killed some inquisitors; the Ghibellines often opposed inquisitors across Italy; armed families in Florence, Piacenza and Cremona confronted Dominicans. The Inquisition achieved the expulsion of the religious movement of the Cathars, or Albigensians, from Venetia and Emilia; sixty of its members were burned alive at Treviso in 1233, and around 200 met the same fate in Sirmione a few years after the inquisitors' arrival in the town in 1273. At Parma, the burning of two women in 1279 sparked a popular revolt, and for eight years the inquisitors could not even enter the city, which was subject to an interdict imposed by the Pope. In Lombardy, the Dominican inquisitors had many heretics burned, and persuaded the Pope to place an interdict on the Ghibelline Bergamo, declaring the city to be an 'accomplice' of the heretics. The spiral of violence led the inquisitors to create proper armies from the mid-thirteenth century onwards, a development that further escalated the brutality; for example, in 1259 a crusade was organized against a Ghibelline ruler from north-eastern Italy, Ezzelino of Romano, which resulted in his death in battle and the murder of his relatives.

From the thirteenth century onwards, the Papacy was confronted in Europe (though not in Italy) by the growth of national states, and by societies that were developing a 'bourgeoisie' of merchants, artisans, bureaucrats and professionals which favoured the diffusion of a lay culture, rather than a culture that was, as it had been in the early Middle Ages, the preserve of the clergy. At this politically and culturally difficult time for the Church, the Popes sought to increase the number of pilgrimages to Rome by offering indulgences (partial remission of temporal punishment for sins) to pilgrims. The value of these was steadily enhanced, culminating in the plenary indulgence proclaimed by Boniface VIII for those who took part in the jubilee of 1300. This was the first jubilee in the history of the Papacy, and granted indulgence to all those who went to Rome and followed a specific itinerary of various sacred sites. Guglielmo Ventura, a Piedmontese chronicler in Rome for the jubilee, described the economic advantage that the Papacy enjoyed as a result of the pilgrimage:

> Bread, wine, meat, fish and oats were cheap; but hay was very expensive; and so were hotels ... Leaving Rome on Christmas Eve I saw a huge crowd, which no one could have counted ... Several times I saw men and women trampled under other people's feet. I managed to escape that danger several times. The Pope received countless sums of money, because day and night two clergymen stayed at the altars of St Paul with rakes in their hands, raking up endless sums.

In 1305 a French Pope, Clement V, was elected, and in 1309 he moved from Rome to southern France. His successor, John XXII also lived in Avignon, and the French city remained the new capital of the Papacy until 1374, during which period Avignon underwent remarkable architectural and economic development, beginning with the construction of a new palace as the Popes' residence. There were a total of seven Avignon Popes, all French, a fact that cast doubts on the idea of the universality of the Church – the Papacy simply appeared to be under French control.

As Avignon prospered, Rome declined economically, since the regular flow of money resulting from the presence of the Papacy stopped. Respected intellectuals, poets and charismatic religious figures criticized (though in very different ways) the Church for its corruption and avidity:

Box 3.2   Dante and Rome

Dante was fascinated by the double function of the city, as both capital of the Empire and of Christianity. With the election of Clement V and his departure for France, Rome was widowed. The city had already been transformed from a city of saints and martyrs to a city of corruption and intrigue, beginning with the Constantine donation and reaching a climax with Boniface VIII (1295–1303). The Emperors had also abandoned the city; and Dante, who was a convinced Ghibelline and supporter of the autonomy of temporal power, hoped to see the capital of the Empire on the banks of the River Tiber. However, even if the two powers were never going to return to Rome, he thought the city had to remain at the centre of world civilization, towards which men would continue to turn ('And looks at Rome as if it were his mirror', *Inferno*, XIV, 105).

---

for example, the philosopher Marsilius of Padua (1275–1342) in *Defensor Pacis*, William of Ockham, Catherine of Siena, Dante Alighieri in *De Monarchia*, and Francesco Petrarch. Catherine of Siena, born in 1347, dedicated her life to the care of the sick and the poor, and addressed letters to important politicians of the time from the position of a defender of the peace between the Italian states and the Papacy. After many letters to Gregory XI, she went to Avignon in 1376 to persuade him to return to Rome.

Petrarch described Rome as an ancient matron, still fascinating in her old splendour but worn out by the Pope's distance. In the middle of the fourteenth century, Boccaccio and other chroniclers (such as Giovanni Villani) declared that Rome, from being the 'head' of the world, had become the 'tail'. This was a result of the interruption of architectural commissions by Popes and cardinals, and of the diminished stream of pilgrims. Commercial activities declined as the struggle between aristocratic families for control of the city and its countryside revived, and Tuscan banks and companies decided to close their Roman headquarters. A considerable number of the rural population left the villages, which gradually reverted to pasture, inhabited only by shepherds and bandits. The Roman countryside remained poor and rife with malaria until the modern age. The relationship between city and countryside, so important elsewhere in Italy, dissolved and was only re-established with difficulty after the return of the Popes. Regular attempts by Roman citizens to

---

Box 3.3   Letters from Catherine of Siena to Pope Gregory XI

Letter imploring him to cure the 'plagues' of the Church and to persuade him to return to Rome:
O father, sweet Christ on earth, please follow the path of that sweet Gregory [Gregory the Great] . . . Please be no longer occupied with friends or relatives, nor with your temporal activity; but only with virtue and with the exaltation of spiritual things . . . I heard that you have made some cardinals. I believe that it would be God's honour, and better for us, if you always chose virtuous men. If the opposite occurred, it will be an insult to God, and a ruin for the holy Church. No surprise, then, if God sends punishments and calamities to us.

Letter again imploring his return to Rome:
Alas, father, I am dying from the pain, and still cannot die. Please, please, do come, and stop resisting God's will, which is calling you. And the eager sheep of your flock are waiting for you to come and hold the seat of your predecessor and champion, Peter the apostle. Because you, as Christ's vicar, must rest in your own place. Therefore please come, and hesitate no longer; and be comforted, and do not fear anything that could happen, because God will be with you.

(Boccardi, 2003, p. 92, letter 185; p. 94, letter 196).

---

establish communal governments up to the end of the fourteenth century were finally halted by the full return of the Papacy, which first abolished the commune's political autonomy in 1398 after arresting and killing the organizers of a rebellion against Boniface IX, and then began to operate a form of absolutism subsequently extended to the entire Papal States.

Before the return of the Popes, however, some political projects aimed to restore the greatness of Rome. Cola di Rienzo (1313–54), a notary and great orator of humble origin, sought to recreate the republic against the interests and struggles of Popes and the aristocracy. He gained the support of many men of letters, Petrarch among them, who saw in his strivings the restoration of Cicero's republic, an earlier medieval dream of returning to the Roman age.

Di Rienzo's was not the first attempt to re-found a Roman Republic. As early as the twelfth century, a republican representation of the city had begun to emerge, in contrast with the existing ecclesiastical and imperial conceptions of Rome. As a result of the conflicts between Emperors and Popes, sections of the population became aware of their ability to play a greater political role – for example, through dependence on the Emperors with the object of reinforcing autonomist claims against the Popes. Between 1144 and 1149 an emancipation movement led to the establishment of a bourgeois elite at the council, which asked the Pope to leave the administration of the city to a communal institution called the *Senato*, which met symbolically at the Campidoglio. That civic republican ideal revived again in the fourteenth century, when Cola di Rienzo seized power in Rome in 1347. He assumed the title of tribune and was supported by the middle classes against the aristocracy. He commissioned a painting in the Colosseum in which Rome was represented as a mourning female figure in black on a ship surrounded by waves in a storm, alongside other women, each representing a different Italian city, whose ships had already sunk. Cola di Rienzo extended his proposal of renovating Rome and limiting the power of the aristocracy in the whole of Italy in an attempt to found a federation of cities under Rome's leadership. He summoned a successful assembly of the cities' representatives, where he put forward the idea of a renewed Roman republic delimited by the Alpine frontier; and that Italian cities were Rome's sisters and all Italians were Roman citizens. However, the time was not ripe for republican solutions, either in Rome or in the Italian city-states, which rejected limitations on their autonomy. Cola di Rienzo, though defeated, and killed by a mob in 1354, nevertheless left a permanent mark on the collective memory of Rome and Italy as the first figure to recognize the end of the imperial dream and to claim that Rome's salvation lay in the creation of a political structure based on the cultural and linguistic unity of the Italian people.

Many of the revolts that spread to Rome during the Avignon years were sparked by powerful Italian states such as Milan, Naples and Florence, all of which sought to expand into Papal territory, taking advantage of the Popes' absence and the resulting political instability. Faced with these territorial challenges, Pope Gregory XI decided to return to Rome, and in 1378 an Italian Pope was elected once more – the Neapolitan Urban VI. The French cardinals, however, refused to recognize the new Pope, claiming that he had been imposed by the Roman mob, and proclaimed a different Pope, Clement VII, who moved to Avignon. This move created a new schism, with two Popes at the same time, one in Italy and the other in France, who excommunicated each other. The schism was formally resolved only in 1418 at the Council of

Constance, where a sole new Pope, Martin V of the Colonna family, was elected. He was the first of an almost uninterrupted succession of Italian Popes, a pattern that was only broken in recent years. During the schism period, new expressions of religious opposition appeared, some with origins in the previous heretical movements, and all criticizing the Church for its wealth, corruption and temporal power. One famous heretic was the Bohemian theologian and religious reformer, Jan Hus, who was burnt at the stake in 1415.

SAINTS AND CITIES

Italian cities were full of images: icons and paintings of saints and the Virgin Mary were mixed with those of political and military heroes, celebrating both supernatural and civil achievements. During the eleventh century, at the time of Popes Gregory VII and Urban II, the cult of the Virgin Mary had acquired great importance; the image of the divine mother developed from the emergence of an increased focus on the humanity of Christ. The cult of the Virgin enjoyed huge success from that period onwards.

Urbanization in the twelfth century favoured the spread of cults of local patron saints. Before that time, a saint was essentially a body, or a fragment of a body, animated – because of the saint's conformity with Christ's life – by supernatural powers that could heal and protect those who prayed and asked for the saint's intercession. The collection and circulation of relics increased the number of altars in cathedrals, for it was there that relics were deposited once they had been consecrated, a custom that evolved from the eighth century onwards. Looting of relics often occurred, particularly by French and German travellers, as their countries had fewer relics than Italy. Many saints' bodies were stolen; for example, the remains of St Severo were taken from Ravenna to Germany in 836, and in 1162 the relics of the Magi were sent from Milan to Frederick Barbarossa in Cologne. Throughout the early Middle Ages, Italy remained a sort of hallowed country for the Western world, where it was possible to acquire sacred relics cheaply and easily, sometimes with the help of unscrupulous clergymen.

The cult of patron saints in Italian cities began at the time of the transition from the ancient to the medieval age. Roman cities that were transformed into medieval cities in the period of the barbarian invasions were always centred on the cathedral. Particularly during the

Byzantine–Gothic wars, in an atmosphere of fear and uncertainty, the bishop became the principal reference point, and the patron saint the main element of unity. Of all the interpretations of the Italian commune, the most acceptable is perhaps the one that emphasizes the convergence of the needs of the city aristocracy, the new bourgeoisie and the bishop. The aristocracy governing the cities often played a crucial role in establishing the cult of new local saints. For example, in Mantua, the cult of a saint clearly connected to the powerful was that of St Anselm, disseminated by Matilda of Canossa. Anselm II, Bishop of Lucca, was expelled by the Lucchesi, Henry IV's supporters, and found refuge with Matilda, subsequently becoming Bishop of Reggio and then of Mantua, where he died in 1086. His biography, detailing the miracles he performed both while alive and after his death, was written during Matilda's reign.

However, saints were not always made by the powerful, because sometimes it was the population who sought proof of miracles. A popular religiosity emerged that required miracles and manifest signs, such as, for example, the power of healing. In many cases the mendicant orders played an important role as they were close to marginal people, and the latter wanted saints who defended the poor. The Church was very wary in these cases, since requests were sometimes made for people who could be considered heretic. For example, in mid-thirteenth-century Mantua, the Church decided not to make Giovanni Bono a saint, despite a great many requests from the people who continued to make pilgrimages to his grave, because the powerful were uninterested in him and considered him to be a non-conformist. The Church was also cautious because, towards the mid-thirteenth century, there was a great proliferation of cults.

The cult of a local saint could also acquire political meaning. For example, the image of St Ambrose of Milan was present on the city *carroccio* (chariot) at the battle of Legnano and, two centuries later, a legend retold by fourteenth-century Milanese chronicler Galvano Fiamma stated that St Ambrose led the troops of Luchino Visconti against the predominantly German and Swiss army of Lodrisio (who wanted to succeed Galeazzo I and sought to usurp the throne) at the battle of Parabiago in 1339. Ambrose had allegedly been seen driving away the enemies, and the victory was attributed to him; a statue of St Ambrose of Victory was built at Parabiago as a result. The use of *carrocci* with images of patron saints is an example of how city pride and popular religiosity were intertwined. The *carroccio* symbolized the unity of the city, and its departure to war was accompanied by popular processions, important elements in the construction of civic religion. In

Visconti Milan, one of the most famous Lombard medieval poets, Bonvesin de La Riva, demonstrated the strong bond between defence of the city and religion in a book dedicated to his city:

> Many foreign tyrants have tried to install here the seat of their tyranny, yet the divine goodness, with the constant intercession of the blessed mother of our Lord Jesus Christ, in whose honour our cathedral is built . . . together with that of our patron St Ambrose . . . has often defended the city from tyrannical rage.
>
> (Dean, 2000)

Cults revering the same saint could be found in different parts of Italy; for example, the cult of St Pilgrim was followed in villages on both sides of the Apennines. This was the case with a number of saints, showing that the mountains were not a barrier between the populations who lived on either side of them in the Middle Ages, but on the contrary united them, becoming geographical mediators through which encounters and exchanges of various kind occurred.

SAINTS, WITCHES, OR MOTHERS: IMAGES OF WOMEN BETWEEN THE MIDDLE AGES AND THE RENAISSANCE

Matilda of Canossa was probably the most powerful woman of Italy's Middle Ages. In 1664, her corpse was transferred from Castel Sant'Angelo in Rome to the Basilica of St Peter, where it remains today. She had died five centuries earlier, but she became a heroine in the collective memory because of the role she had played as the ally of Pope Gregory VII, when she allegedly helped him defeat the Emperor. When she died (aged 69) in 1115 in a village near Mantua, her body was preserved, testimony to the idea that the terrible events of her own time had not defeated her. On the one hand, she was a rare example of a female warrior and head of state who had competed with the most powerful men of the age; yet on the other, she was a medieval woman who shared the fears and beliefs typical of her time. She gave substantial gifts to churches and monasteries, and spent her political life fighting the Emperor (Henry IV) and serving the interests of the Church. She sought to maintain a large state under feudal control, though with difficulty, since the cities were beginning the process leading towards communal autonomy. Despite her many defeats, her final military victories were largely a result of the establishment of a chain of castles, which constituted an invincible barrier from the Apennines to the Po Valley, and which the Emperor never succeeded in seizing entirely. Matilda's memory was particularly valued in the seventeenth century, as she was a model heroine for a time when the Church needed new allies in the fight against the Reformation; her monument in St Peter's was therefore commissioned from the most distinguished architect of the time, Gian Lorenzo Bernini (1598–1680). Her wars against the Emperors had been wars on the side of Christ, crusades that the Church needed to repeat against heresy. Despite her two marriages, her image remained, in the paintings of the time, of a lonely, isolated woman married only to God. This image was also depicted in literature; literary critics argue that Dante described her in *Purgatorio* (especially XXVIII and XXXIII) using the name Matelda. In his account she walked alone with only flowers for company, to represent a life spent in loneliness and courage, having confronted without external help events that would have discouraged many men. Three centuries later, in the *Gerusalemme liberata,* the poet Torquato Tasso (1544–95) emphasized her role as a female warrior who fought and won using her own stratagems. Matilda's fame had been so vast that she reappeared in the chivalric romances of the sixteenth century; at around same time as Tasso's poem, the artist Paolo Farinati (1524–1606) depicted her alone on horseback, at the site where she was later buried at San Benedetto sul Po.

Matilda's life was exceptional among medieval women. In medieval society, ordinary women were marginal and considered to be on a par with children. Women authors of literary texts were rare, so their views could not be propagated, and almost everything written about women came from men. The only women who left written testimony were a few *cortese* poetesses, some important saints or nuns (who wrote mainly about mystical experiences), and some female aristocrats and the wives of merchants. Though their number increased, in the main they did not defy the poetic and ethical conventions of their time. Aristocratic and ecclesiastical theories of women were challenged only with difficulty by the new commercial classes, and were transmitted to subsequent generations, therefore continuing to have a profound impact in successive centuries even under changed social conditions. For example, many commune statutes specified that husbands were allowed physically to punish their wives as long as it was done *sine sanguinis effusione* (without spilling blood). Women's lives were limited in terms of property ownership, inheritance and freedom within marriage, and all these limitations were scrupulously drawn up in the statutes. Male privilege in succession was overtly emphasized from the first communal *consuetudines* onwards. The twentieth-century English medievalist, Eileen Power, observed the paradox that, among the lower classes, women worked with men in the fields or the workshops every day, but when they went to mass on Sunday they were told that, while the Virgin Mary was the gateway to heaven, women in general were the gateway to hell.

In fifteenth-century aristocratic family books, women appear as wives and daughters, but especially as mothers – in the physical sense of being procreators. Data from the Florentine census from 1427 makes it clear that the middle classes and, to a greater degree, the lower classes, used forms of birth control, but that among the economic elite, female fertility was the maximum possible in the biological cycle. Explanations for the high birth-rate must take into account the high mortality rates: for example, out of twenty children born to the aristocratic Corsini family in Florence, only ten survived for one year, while only five lived for more than twenty-four years. Love was excluded from the marriage practices of the elite, and was considered at the time to be something for poets and the lower classes. Sentimental expressions were not common in family correspondence. Evidence of passion and love were absent, for example, from the bourgeois family investigated by Renaissance architect, poet and mathematician, Leon Battista Alberti (1404–72), who was interested in the study of the mercantile classes. While Boccaccio celebrated passion as a force of nature, Alberti described it as a 'fury' and the 'vice of an unstable soul'. In its place, the new bourgeoisie was meant to live by values of reason and utility.

The Church's ideas on marriage and family spread across the Western Christian world, but they were mainly influenced by the Italian social context. Among the basic rules were that monogamy was right and divorce was wrong, that incest was a sin, and that marriage between close kin was forbidden. Although the Church began to develop a Christian doctrine for marriage in the twelfth century, it was only at the Council of Trent in the sixteenth century that theologians made the marriage contract binding. Before Trent, the Church permitted the expression of mutual consent between partners as the only requisite for valid marriage.

In medieval society, the typical aversion and distrust towards women continued despite the increased number of female saints: women were allegedly weak and prone to sin, and therefore needed to be controlled and corrected. They needed to be admonished and disciplined more than men because they were more susceptible to the demon lust, which explains, for example, why cosmetics were condemned with such great insistence. Sex played a central role in the Christian idea of sin, and as a result women were regarded as a major cause for concern. They were exhorted to surpass themselves by imitating abstract models of sanctity or, when that was not possible, to accept marital control and discipline – in either case, to give themselves up. Nor did the humanist period bring substantial changes. As Christopher Celenza has noted, the Renaissance remained a 'fundamentally misogynistic era'. Women's virtues (modesty, humility, obedience to man) were still private and maternal – the virtues that had denied women active participation in public life for centuries both before and after the Renaissance. Indeed, humanists such as Alberti were intellectuals but also social creatures, inevitably influenced by the habits and the ideals they lived by.

Some historians suggested that, from the twelfth century onwards, and gathering pace in the thirteenth, heresy became more accessible to women. However, this has been questioned by recent historiography, and the participation of women in religious life does not seem generally to have followed unorthodox ways. In Italian cities, groups of women gathered at the margins to live by preaching and begging as Christ's followers – the most famous example was that of Chiara of Assisi; but they were not heretics. Many chroniclers of the first jubilee in 1300 described a high female participation, and it is now believed that at least a third of the pilgrims were women. The gathering of women in pilgrimages had been witnessed long before 1300, and it increased from that time and included women drawn from different social classes. For this reason, cities began to organize associations to welcome and act as hosts for women who travelled on their own. Women did this for many reasons, not only from religious devotion: a pilgrimage in which they travelled on their own or in groups, sometimes facing long and hazardous journeys, provided them with moments of freedom they could otherwise rarely experience.

Some pious women became famous for their roles in important political events. In Italy, the most famous was Catherine of Siena, who hoped to end the schism in the Papacy, but she was not the only one; those who followed her included Angela of Foligno and Chiara of Montefalco. These women attained a real significance in the political–religious field; the percentage of canonized women had never been as high as it was during the last three centuries of the Middle Ages, when about a quarter of all the new saints were female, and many of them even wives and mothers. However, their exclusion from serving mass and the sacraments within the official Church was never seriously challenged.

In the fifteenth century, the fixation with magic phenomena that had followed the plague began slowly to be replaced by a more specific obsession – that of the Devil and his power over human beings. Miracles and the desire for miracles, though accepted by the Church's official culture, had already begun to raise suspicions in the thirteenth century, as the work of Jean-Claude Schmitt shows. While these concerns existed in every medieval century, in 1232, under Pope Gregory IX, enquiries over sanctity began to include official questions designed to verify that the miracle was not the work of the Devil, while women who devoted themselves to magic or spells were accused of being possessed by the Devil. The beginning of witch-hunting, which raged through Europe from the fifteenth to the seventeenth centuries (though it was never strong in Italy), can be traced back to the equation of magic with heresy established by Pope John XXII in the fourteenth century with the bull *Super Illius Specula* of 1326, though it was officially promoted only in 1484–6 with Innocent VIII's bull *Malleus Maleficarum*. At the same time, magic and astrology continued to prosper. This was partly for political reasons in Italian cities, where both communes and *signorie* paid magicians and astrologers to cast evil spells on rival cities, and between the fourteenth and sixteenth centuries, astrology was very popular in universities and courts all over Italy.

By the sixteenth century, the spirituality and prestige of female sanctity had lost its importance. As a consequence of the Reformation and Counter-Reformation, facts, arguments and theological preparation became more important than divine inspiration. In the seventeenth century, as female spirituality continued to be regarded, as always, with suspicion, the place of women was no longer the altar but the torture chamber of the Inquisition and the stake. The nocturnal excursions of witches had replaced the inspired ecstasy of spiritual women as an image of womanhood.

THE ITALIAN LANGUAGE IN THE AGE OF DANTE AND PETRARCH

The culture of the Italian communes reached its highest point with the poetry of Dante Alighieri. All the aspects of medieval life (social, philosophical, religious, political, artistic and scientific) converge in his work.

Born in Florence in 1265 to a family from the minor Guelph nobility, he studied rhetoric with Brunetto Latini and became friends with *Stil Novo* (New Style) poets such as Guido Cavalcanti. Married, as was normally the case, according to his father's will, he instead loved Beatrice, who was married to another man and who died in 1290. To this love he dedicated many New Style sonnets – for example, *Rime* and *Vita Nuova* – a book which contains some of his most beautiful poems, such as *Tanto gentile e tanto onesta pare*. He took an active part in Florentine political life, which was characterized at the time by the aggression between two alliances: the Bianchi, who maintained the need for autonomy, and the Neri, linked to the Papacy by mercantile interests. Dante sided with the Bianchi, and had to leave the city after the ferocious repression that followed the Neri victory under Pope Boniface VIII. He lived in exile at the courts of northern Italian cities such as Verona (with Bartolomeo Della Scala), Treviso and in Lunigiana, and it was as an exile that he wrote *The Divine Comedy*, the *Convivio*, and *Literature in the Vernacular*.

With *Vita Nuova*, Dante created the first text of Italian literature to contain love poems as well as political and philosophical rhymes, all of which took the lyric tradition to its highest level; in the *Convivio*, he offered one of the first models of scientific–philosophical prose in the vernacular, and in the *Divine Comedy* an unparalleled example of poetry and narration. Finally, in *Literature in the Vernacular*, he defended the vernacular and determined its literary tradition. *The Divine Comedy* in particular constituted an element of Italian identity that involved all social classes, and it remained a watershed of moral and political judgement as well as artistic expression in the centuries that followed.

The theme of *Literature in the Vernacular*, written in Latin, is the definition of a literary vernacular, bringing Latin and other forms of expression together, as well as a review of rhetorical forms (metrics and style) to be used in the new Italian language. The work, written in 1303/4, was unfinished (it was intended to be divided into four volumes, but Dante did not complete even the second). In it, Dante demonstrates the nobility of vernacular, which he regarded as superior even to classical Latin, which in his view was an artificial language:

> We shall hasten on to define the vernacular as that which children learn from those around them, when they first begin to distinguish words; or, more briefly, that which we acquire without any rule, by imitating our nurses. From this we have another, secondary language, which the Romans called 'grammar' ... Now of these two the nobler is the vernacular, first

because it was the first type to be used by the human race; secondly because the whole world employs it, albeit divided into different pronunciations and forms of expression; finally because it is natural to us, while the latter is more an artificial creation.

(Alighieri, 1981, Book I, p. 15)

After acknowledging the formation in southern Europe of three languages, *oc*, *oïl* and *sì*, Dante turned his attention to the vernacular of *sì*, which was spoken in Italy. He analysed fourteen varieties of vernacular on a linguistic and geographical basis, none of which corresponded to the illustrious vernacular used by writers. Consequently, it became necessary to define it in its ideal characteristics, which could not be found in any specific region but in the work of the best writers:

> Now we have hunted over the glades and pastures of Italy without finding the panther we are tracking, let us pursue it in a more rational way, that we may with diligent care trap in our nets this creature whose scent is everywhere and whose person nowhere . . . And so having reached our goal, we may say that it is an illustrious, cardinal, courtly and curial vernacular in Italy, which belongs to every city in Italy and is not seen to be the property of any one, by and against which the vernaculars of all Italian towns are measured and weighed and compared.

(Alighieri, 1981, Book I, pp. 33–4)

According to Dionisotti, *Literature in the Vernacular* proposed an ideal linguistic and literary unity, a unity that could be based on existing varieties of language, but could at the same time surpass them.

In the nineteenth century, when Italian intellectuals supported the idea of a united nation, they looked on Dante, Petrarch, Boccaccio and the Renaissance humanists as the founders of the language. They believed that only a common native language could become the true vehicle for the transmission of a national culture; as a result, as Christopher Celenza has emphasized, the study of Renaissance Latin was doomed. Despite the importance of the first examples of Italian vernacular (and despite these nineteenth-century preferences), it is indeed necessary to remember that, during the Renaissance, Latin remained a universal language, and all humanists, just like medieval writers, were bilingual.

More than any other work of Italian literature, Dante's *Divine Comedy* was disseminated immediately and extensively. It was promptly transcribed and commented on, read among the nobility, studied in intellectual circles, and sung by people in the streets. Its spread took it to differing cultural and social milieux and to a wide geographical area. Multiple copies were made in response to popular demand, produced by fourteenth-century amanuenses and writers as well as by simple workers in Florentine copyist shops, all of which helped to increase commercial circulation. In the sixteenth century, by which time printing was well established, the philologist Vincenzo Borghini wrote that Florentine copyists 'were mainly people who had a shop and earned their living by copying and selling books; and it is said that one of them married off I don't know how many daughters by producing one hundred copies of Dante'.

The fantastic journey through the afterlife of hell, purgatory and heaven described in the book (a typical motif of both classical and medieval literature) was intended as a liberation from sin. Dante's work is divided into 100 cantos grouped into three parts: the 34 *Inferno* cantos, one of which is an introduction to the work in its entirety, and two further parts of 33 cantos each. Virgil leads Dante through hell and purgatory, and Beatrice, the dead woman he loved, leads him to heaven, completing a journey from the knowledge of evil to the experience of the sacred good. It is striking that Dante's afterlife, particularly in *Inferno*, is connected to and determined by life on earth. In the episode of Farinata and Cavalcante (*Inferno*, X), Dante is led by Virgil to the heretics' and atheists' circle, where he converses with Farinata, the head of the Ghibelline in Florence, who died shortly after Dante's birth, and with Cavalcante de' Cavalcanti, the poet and father of Dante's friend, Guido Cavalcanti. Despite being condemned to live in hell, Farinata has not changed his views, and his chief thoughts are for the political conflict in Florence. Erich Auerbach has argued that the same is true for Cavalcante, entirely absorbed by the passions of his earthly life, prima-rily by his love and concerns for his son. Similarly, Guido da Montefeltro asks of the poet: 'Say, if the Romagnouls have peace or war' (*Inferno*, XXVII). Gradually, interpretation of the *Comedy* also assumed a metaphorical character. Sandro Botticelli (1445–1510), the greatest Florentine painter of the late fifteenth century, produced a long series of paintings of the *Comedy*. But, in Botticelli's representation, *Inferno* is peopled with writhing and contorted human beings, a depiction intensi-fied in *Purgatory*, while *Paradise* has images of the saved in various states of ecstasy, surrounded by a sumptuous and unreal landscape.

The success of *The Divine Comedy* decided the question of the language: it signified the ascendancy of Tuscan and the beginning of the decline to the status of dialect of the other Italian spoken languages. *The Divine Comedy* was followed by Petrarch's *Canzoniere* and Boccaccio's

Decameron, both written in Tuscan and adopted as models elsewhere shortly afterwards. As Dante acknowledged, this new Italian language was based on the Sicilian tradition of the thirteenth century, disseminated in Tuscany and transcribed in Tuscan versions. With Florentine merchants trading all over Italy, and with the nomadic life of many intellectuals who, like Petrarch and Boccaccio, went into exile because of internal political struggles, the superiority of Tuscan was established by the end of the fourteenth century. It was then that a unitary literary language was established throughout urban Italy. Dante, Petrarch and Boccaccio were imitated in every centre of high culture in both northern and southern Italy. The Venetian publisher, Aldus Manutius, played a fundamental role in the spread of the language by publishing accessible copies of Dante's and Petrarch's works in 1501–2.

Another of Dante's historical and political concerns was the destiny of Rome, which appears at a number of points in *The Divine Comedy* and forms the main theme of the third part of his treatise *De Monarchia*. This was written in Latin and consisted of three books; in the first, Dante argued, with reference to ancient writers such as Homer and Aristotle, that universal monarchy was necessary for the wellbeing of humankind; in the second, that supreme authority belonged to the Roman people; and in the third, that the Emperor, as the titular head of the Roman monarchy, and the Pope, as the head of Christianity, were independent of each other, and that both received their authority from God. The right of the Romans to dominate the world, wrote Dante, came from both earthly and divine sources. The Roman people, he argued, had been the most noble and virtuous, and power should be a prize awarded to the virtuous. Perfection could also be attained with the aid of miracles, and, as miracles pleased God, they were clear signs of His will; since the Roman Empire had also reached its perfection with the help of miracles, then its perfection must be desired by Providence. Stories of these miracles, like the Capitoline geese that saved Rome from the Gauls, or the hail that stopped the Carthaginians, were reported by Livy and other ancient writers. Dante mixed these points with more rational ones, in particular the history of Roman law and the thoughts of Cicero. The most significant and modern part of the work is in the third book, where Dante denies that the authority of the Empire depended on that of the Church, 'as a labourer depends on the architect'. Anticipating the scientific and philological work of the humanists, he proclaimed that the Constantine donation must be a forgery, on the grounds that the Emperor could not donate territory to the Church since it would contravene the duty entrusted to him to maintain undivided rule over his subjects ('it is illegal for the Emperor to divide the Empire'); and the Church could not accept it because Christ had refused temporal power ('my kingdom is not of this world'). The figure of Dante pervaded Tuscan culture even before the poet's death in 1321, and continued to do so long after that date.

Giovanni Boccaccio was born in 1313 in Tuscany, the illegitimate son of an unknown mother who was brought up by his father, a merchant and member of the Neapolitan Banco de' Bardi. While very young, he was sent to work in Naples with the Bardi, the bank of the Anjou court. There he came into contact with merchants, sailors and members of the lower classes as well as the nobility, and acquired a knowledge of the habits of the different social classes of the Mediterranean, of which Naples was a major economic and political centre. After this experience, he lived partly in Florence and partly in the Romagna, and it was in Florence in 1348 that he witnessed the terrible plague described in the introduction to the *Decameron*, which he began writing the following year. The background to the work is the plague, an event that disrupted the daily life and habits of ordinary people in extreme ways; many of the characters in the novellas were still living, or had died only recently. The action is set in precisely defined places, generally the cities of Italy's merchant and bourgeois class such as Venice, Naples or Siena. The reader of *Decameron* will not find wars, knights, heroes, or conflicts between Church and Empire in its pages, but rather the active bourgeoisie of the Italian communes, with its convictions, tastes and daily existence. Only after it had been described by Boccaccio did the merchant class begin to be part of Italian literature.

Descriptions of the experience of love in *Decameron* categorically abandoned the court tradition and became characterized by everyday gossip. Love in the *Decameron* is wholly human and physical. Boccaccio also described the erotic adventures of churchmen, generally priests who made love to married women and organized diversions to keep their husbands away. However, the *Decameron* distinguished between the clergy and the sacred: only the former was mocked. This was typical of society at that time, when criticism and mockery of the Church was widespread, but never entailed a lack of respect for the traditional Christian heritage.

Following the principles of *De Vulgari Eloquentia*, Boccaccio explored a spoken vernacular with idioms from different Italian dialects (literary critics refer to his 'multilingualism'): some novellas are characterized by

---

Box 3.4   Frate Alberto (Decameron)

In *Frate Alberto* (the second novella of day IV), a priest persuades a gullible Venetian *popolana* that an angel has fallen in love with her and wishes to visit her at night while her husband is busy in Flanders on merchant business. For several nights, the priest disguises himself as an angel and enjoys intimate encounters, which the *popolana* appears to like. He is finally exposed through the gossip between her and other Venetian women, who do not believe the story of the angel. The dialogues, as in many of the novellas, include both popular language and the use of dialect.

---

typical expressions from Bologna, Genoa, Pisa, Naples, Sicily and so on. Building on Dante's work, he therefore realized in the *Decameron* a linguistic geography of fourteenth-century Italy. As critics have pointed out, the *Decameron* could never have been written without Dante's *Divine Comedy*; Boccaccio brought Dante's lively world and language to a stylistic level that was less scholarly and more popular. However, it is important to notice that, after writing the *Decameron*, Boccaccio continued to write in Latin. The evolution towards the vernacular was indeed not considered inevitable by his contemporaries. Moreover, Latin could communicate to an international audience, it was more linguistically stable, and had a long tradition (which was linked to the history of ancient Rome, symbol of the glorious origin of Italy).

In contrast with Dante and Boccaccio, Petrarch created a new type of intellectual – the 'pure' scholar, detached from social commitment and devoted only to his inner life and his poetry. In a country torn for centuries by tyranny, internal wars and foreign domination (and later by the Catholic Counter-Reformation from the sixteenth century) this attitude became both convenient and dominant. Much more than Dante, whose political horizon was that of the universal powers and the city-states, Petrarch had a precise idea of an Italy to which he dedicated the famous *canzone, Italia mia, benché 'l parlar sia indarno*. This poem deplores the continuous civil wars in Italy and the use of German armies, themes that were later taken up by Machiavelli and Guicciardini. The conclusion asks of the arrogant lords who ruled the courts and made the wars:

Who will defend me?
I cry out with pain: Peace, peace, peace.

Box 3.5   Petrarchism

The renewal of vernacular poetry in the second half of the fifteenth century was based on the imitation of Petrarch. In 1501, the Venetian humanist Pietro Bembo edited the *Canzoniere*, which became a fashionable book that was reprinted 167 times over the century. Since then, Petrarchism has become the compulsory precept of Italian and some European lyric poetry, expressing a taste for an elaborate and affected form much used by lesser poets. Its decline began with the rise of romanticism, and the return of sincerity and 'inspiration' as central poetic concerns. In *Zibaldone* (1817–32), the poet Giacomo Leopardi observed that Petrarch had been imitated so much 'that we have heard each of his sentences a thousand times, to the point where he himself seems to be an imitator'.

Francesco Petrarch was born in 1304 in Arezzo, where his father, a notary, had moved two years previously after being exiled from Florence when the Neri faction prevailed over the Bianchi. He moved between different parts of Italy and France, particularly Avignon (during the time of the Popes), where he met Laura, the inspiration for his poetry, as Beatrice had been for Dante. In 1350, on his way to Rome to take part in that year's jubilee, he met Boccaccio in Florence, and subsequently exchanged many letters with him that are revealing about both his personality and his poetry. A typical problem for Italian intellectuals was the sense of having a divided identity, caused by the physical presence of the Roman Church. Petrarch was torn between his love for literature and admiration for classical culture, and his religious sense of guilt. In the last year of his life, he denounced his love for Laura, an act that stimulated him to write the *Canzoniere*, his principal poetic work. Women became, for Petrarch too, a source of corruption.

Dante, Petrarch and Boccaccio all dedicated verses to Italy, representing the country as a wounded and defiled woman. For example, in *Literature in the Vernacular*, Dante counterposed German political unity (which existed in his imagination rather than in reality) with Italian cultural unity: 'although we lack a Prince, it would be false to say that the Italians have no Court, since we have one indeed, albeit spatially dispersed'. Later in the sixteenth century, at the end of *The Prince*, Machiavelli called on the Medici to liberate all Italy, rather than just Florence. From the thirteenth to the eighteenth centuries, long before the

Risorgimento, there was a sense of belonging to an Italian literary community, founded on the civilization of the courts as the rich literary heritage of the age of Dante.

THE BIRTH OF AN ITALIAN CUISINE

Recipes for food also cultivated links between different parts of Italy. From the thirteenth century, dried pasta was widely used in Liguria; before that, its production was restricted to Sicily, where it had probably been brought by the Arabs, who had known the technique from the early Middle Ages. The term 'macaroni' was used for the first time in Liguria in the thirteenth century for dried pasta, drawn into long strips with a hole through the middle, which could be preserved for some time. In the fourteenth century, documents from Genoa mention 'lasagna makers' and show that dried pasta had become part of the rations on ships. Other regions, beginning with Apulia, started producing long-life dried pasta in the fifteenth century, and it became popular, first in Naples and then throughout Italy, from the seventeenth century. A science of gastronomy was developed from the fourteenth century, anticipating the culinary boom during the Renaissance.

The Renaissance was the golden age of Italian cuisine, a model much imitated abroad – at least among the elite. The development of regional recipes began to spread, creating a Po Valley tradition, a Roman–Tuscan tradition and so on. Their European hegemony continued until the beginning of the seventeenth century, when Italian cuisine fell from favour and was replaced in elite fashion by French cooking. One of the most famous cookery books of the late Middle Ages was the Sicilian *Liber de Coquina*, written in a form of spoken Latin full of vernacular terms. It was the progenitor of a number of gastronomic treatises written in vernacular throughout Italy in the fourteenth century. The Tuscan *Libro di cucina* was largely a translation of the *Liber* into vernacular, and the Venetian *Libro del cuoco* also carried recipes from the *Liber* in Venetian dialect. These works circulated throughout Italy, in large numbers, in the most sophisticated circles, some of them being destined for professional cooks. The first culinary expansion, from Frederick II's territory to the rest of Italy, occurred initially in those areas that were politically connected with the Emperor; for example, through Ghibelline governments. Historians have emphasized the connection between the birth of Tuscan poetry and the Ghibelline environment. Among the elite of the

---

Box 3.6 Culture at the court of Frederick II

At the time of Frederick II . . . men in Italy were almost primitive and lived in the most miserable and shabby way. And this Frederick renewed and refined and instructed everything, and, among all emperors, was gifted with beautiful, noble and adorned habits.

(Thirteenth-century chronicler Jacopo D'Acqui, in De Stefano, 2007, p. 10)

---

thirteenth century there was an aspiration towards a more sophisticated and sumptuous way of life, and Frederick II was seen as a model among Italy's elite. With the end of the Norman domination in the south and the arrival of the Anjou, the tradition of dietary treatises and gastronomic literature continued in other parts of Italy, particularly in Tuscany, the region that had been closest to Frederick II. The new culinary writing in the vernacular traced a similar route from Sicily to the north that had earlier been taken by Sicilian poetry.

Like most contemporary novels, Boccaccio's *Decameron* made numerous references to food (for example, VIII, 3; IV, 9; V, 9). The fourteenth-century aspirations to luxury and a comfortable life pervaded literature and also found expression in minor poetry. For example, the poet Folgore of San Giminiano described groups of people who shared a love of banquets and the pleasures of life without vulgarity and with good taste, sustained by the virtue of generosity and free of religious restraint. However, in *Esposizioni sopra la Comedia di Dante,* Boccaccio later condemned the excesses of food consumption and the proliferation of banquets among both laymen and the clergy. At the same time, new social figures emerged around the culture of food, with the stable employment of professional cooks in aristocratic families. In the mid-thirteenth century it was evident how luxurious Sicilian cuisine had become fashionable at rich people's banquets in Florence: ravioli, lasagne, macaroni, citrus fruits, dates, almonds and spices, as well as medicinal products such as the Arab-influenced syrups.

As Anna Martellotti has observed, 'cooks travelled and gourmands were everywhere': among the Popes' chefs at Avignon there was a Florentine; and the chef Chichibio, protagonist of one of Boccaccio's most famous novels, set in Florence, was Venetian. Written treatises as well as oral tradition brought Sicilian cuisine to the whole of northern

Italy; Venetian cookery books reproduced Sicilian dishes, and Tuscan cookery books strongly influenced by Sicily appeared in Bologna. As Sicilian poetry became Tuscan, and Tuscan literature in turn became Italian, so Sicilian cuisine was transmitted to the whole of Italy, showing that dietary fashions developed alongside other cultural and scientific developments.

SELECTED FURTHER READING

J. Larner, *Italy in the Age of Dante and Petrarch, 1216–1380* (London: Longman, 1980) is a recommended introduction, which should be followed by T. Dean (ed.), *The Towns of Italy in the Later Middle Ages* (Manchester: Manchester University Press, 2000), an immensely useful selection of primary sources, which have been introduced and contextualized. First published in Italy in 1979, G. Tabacco, *The Struggle for Power in Medieval Italy: Structures of Political Rule* (Cambridge: Cambridge University Press, 1989) covers the political and social history of Italy from the early Middle Ages to the Renaissance. L. Martines, *Power and Imagination: City-States in Renaissance Italy* (London: Pimlico, 2002) is a lively and thought-provoking work on the nature of the Italian city states from the origins of the communes to the high Renaissance. Two important books on Italian society, family and gender relations are D. D'Avray, *Medieval Marriage: Symbolism and Society* (Oxford: Oxford University Press, 2005) and P. Skinner, *Women in Medieval Italian Society, 500–1200* (Harlow: Longman, 2001).

4

· · · · · · · ·

Renaissance Italy:
From the European Model
to the 'End of Italy'?

CHRONOLOGY

ITALIAN POLITICS IN THE FIFTEENTH AND SIXTEENTH CENTURIES

For European monarchies in possession of solid armies and finances, Italy was a kind of promised land. The peninsula's political fragmentation encouraged ambitions for conquest. Italian states attempted to avert foreign occupation with the constitution of an Italian League in 1454, in the hope of maintaining a balance by avoiding internal wars and in defence of what they publicly called 'Italian liberty'. This balance was, however, very fragile, and the period between the end of the fifteenth century and 1559 is known as that of the 'Italian wars', during which France, Spain and the Germanic Empire fought each other on Italian territory. Paradoxically, it was during this terrible period that Italy experienced the period of the high Renaissance. Historian and politician Francesco Guicciardini (1483–1540) observed that the multiplicity of capital cities and princely courts in the regional states guaranteed Italy's political and cultural polycentrism, without which the Renaissance would probably have been impossible. He therefore concluded that the absence of a unified monarchy had perhaps been an advantage for Italy:

> But the misfortunes of Italy . . . tended to stir up men's minds with all the more displeasure and dread inasmuch as things in general were at that time most favorable and felicitous . . . Not only did Italy abound in inhabitants, merchandise and riches, but she was also highly renowned for the magnificence of many princes, for the splendour of so many most noble and beautiful cities, as the seat and majesty of religion, and flourishing with men most skillful in the administration of public affairs and most nobly talented in all disciplines and distinguished and industrious in all the arts.
>
> (Guicciardini, 1969, Book I, pp. 3–4)

The fifteenth and the sixteenth centuries in Europe were a time of cultural dynamism, confessional struggles and religious wars. The Renaissance and the Reformation were the result of a deep crisis in European civilization – they represented perhaps the greatest historical shifts since the beginning of the Middle Ages and before the Enlightenment in the eighteenth century. They brought about the revolutionary affirmation of rational thought and the crisis of religious authority. The Renaissance aspired to new intellectual and political forms, which suggested the need to wrest power from clerics in religious matters and give it to the people; often, this meant the subjection of religious to secular power. The Reformation was powered by a deep religious feeling, and aimed at breaking the compromises that had made the Church a temporal power.

One aspect common to the whole of Italy in the fifteenth and sixteenth centuries was a unique way of conducting politics, characterized by a complicated network of alliances, with relationships based on dependence and the need for protection. This complex web was constantly changing, as the desire for the expansion of larger powers and the need for protection of smaller ones could set off minor, or even major, local political 'earthquakes'. It was difficult, and at times impossible, for foreigners to understand the rules that maintained and periodically altered this complicated balance; in particular, it was a challenge for foreign diplomats, as the French ambassador Philippe de Commynes (1447–1511) mentioned in his *Mémoirs*.

As we saw in the previous chapter, the world of the central and northern Italian city-states came to an end in the fifteenth century, when dominant cities were able to control their surrounding territory and create a small number of regional states. Some Italian states remained republics, at least in name: Venice, Florence, Genoa, Siena and Lucca. The republican institution had been praised by humanists such as Leonardo Bruni (1369–1444), who defended freedom of speech and the right of the virtuous to power. Republics did not hamper the control by aristocratic families of city and regional state governments, which continued to strengthen themselves throughout the Renaissance period. In Venice, the elites remained quite distinct from the middle classes, and aristocratic life continued to prosper, as elsewhere.

The only city in which political participation was widely extended to the middle classes was Florence, when the city underwent moments of political crisis. In the second half of the fourteenth century, Milan under the Visconti embarked on a campaign of expansion, conquering most of Lombardy, Verona, Vicenza and Padua, Genoa, and parts of Piedmont and of Emilia (including Bologna). After the conquest of Carrara at the end of the 1380s, poets from different Italian cities (such as Antonio Loschi from Vicenza, Francesco di Vannozzo from Padua, and Saviano of Siena) celebrated Gian Galeazzo Visconti (1351–1402) as a new ruler for the whole peninsula, who could unify Italy and bring peace. Florence remained the only city to oppose Milan. However, in 1402, a devastating plague ravaged northern Italy, killing Gian Galeazzo. While the Milanese expansion would probably have been halted in any case by the economic exhaustion of the Visconti state (which, after new conflicts with Venice and Florence, had already lost most of its territory by 1433), as Hans Baron has suggested, this event was interpreted by the Florentines as though they had resisted Milan – the victory of a city-republic against a tyranny. The Milanese–Florentine confrontation demonstrated how Italian politics had become secularized: the medieval divergence of Guelphs and Ghibellines – of Papacy and Empire – had been replaced by one between dynastic expansion and the ideal of free city-state. Conflict between Italian states seemed to be resolved in 1454 with the Peace of Lodi, when the border between Milan (then under the Sforza dynasty) and Venice was fixed at the River Adda, and a non-aggression pact, named *Lega Italica*, confirmed the division of Italy into the five major states of Milan, Venice, Florence, Rome and Naples.

At the end of the fifteenth century, another moment of crisis for Florence arose as a result of the revolutionary preaching of the Dominican writer and politician Girolamo Savonarola (1452–98), who argued that artisans and shopkeepers were the morally healthy section of society, and attacked the privileges of the Church, for which his writings were later listed in the Index of prohibited books; his radical message could not last long, and political pressure both inside and outside Florence (in the Papacy in particular) led to his arrest in 1498; he was tortured and then hanged, and his body was burnt in the Signoria square according to the will of Pope Alexander VI. In the fifteenth century, Florence saw the rise of the Medici dynasty, with Cosimo the Old (1389–1464) and Lorenzo the Magnificent (1449–92, whose life coincided with the golden age of the Florentine Renaissance), although only with Cosimo I (1519–74) did it turn into a despotic state; by then, Florence had extended its territory to most of the Tuscan region (including Pisa, Siena, Pistoia and Arezzo, but not Lucca), and Cosimo was given the title of Grand Duke of Tuscany in 1569 by Pope Pius V.

The other major republic of the fifteenth century, Venice, was a state whose control expanded from the Po Valley to the Dalmatian coast, and even to parts of Greece. Its mainland possessions extended to Padua, Vicenza and Verona (incorporated between 1404 and 1406), the Veneto, Friuli and Dalmatia (between 1414 and 1423), and Brescia and Bergamo (in 1428), up to the border with the province of Milan. The republic had been established without external help, and remained independent even when, from the seventeenth century, most of Italy was conquered or under foreign control. The republic controlled the Church by subordinating it to the government: the Patriarch, head of the Venetian Church, was elected by the senate rather than imposed by Rome; in order to fight the Reformation and at the same time prevent excessive Papal interference, Venice established its own Inquisition. By the beginning of the eighteenth century, the population of the republic numbered more than 2 million, 1.7 million of whom lived in mainland Italy. Venice was still governed by an assembly of citizens, the Grand Council, though its members were drawn mainly from prestigious families. The Venetian aristocracy was so proud of the city's independence and power that it never accepted fiefs and honours from any king, a common practice in the rest of Italy. Venice was the first state to use permanent embassies at foreign courts; and the ambassadors' reports are one of the most important sources for the study of contemporary European society. As the capital of a Renaissance state, in 1600 Venice was still one of the largest cities in Western Europe, despite the spread of the terrible plague during 1575–7.

The control of Venice's mainland possessions was based on a balance between oligarchic rule and local autonomy. Friuli maintained a regional parliament, which decided on financial and military matters. Local councils maintained power in Verona, Vicenza, Treviso and Brescia. A study of the Brescian case has demonstrated how Venetian attempts to increase control coexisted with the survival of a plurality of powers. To a certain extent, the Venetians relied on local aristocratic families to govern; Venetian and local aristocracies were therefore not antithetical but complementary. Ruling families, with their network of allies constructed through marriage ties, everywhere maintained strong economic links with the countryside on which their power continued to be based, even while they controlled urban institutions.

In 1512, the Medici family, which had been in exile after a popular revolt in 1494, returned to Florence, and began its inexorable march towards hereditary rule, establishing itself definitively as a dukedom under Cosimo I; principalities also existed in Ferrara under the Este, Mantua under the Gonzaga, and Urbino under the Montefeltro. These were prosperous states and very lively centres of humanism and the arts. The Papal State continued the medieval, nepotistic style of rule into the sixteenth century. In an Italy divided by rival families, the Roman Church was always a fundamental ally, the point 'of departure and of arrival of each group, the aim and often the instrument of court loyalty, the synthesis of any other court's activity', as Walter Barberis has remarked. Court intellectuals sometimes chose ecclesiastical careers in order to best serve their patron family, so strong was the bond between powerful families and the politics of the Church. Guicciardini, as a humanist and a republican Florentine, ultimately hoped for the ruin of the Papal State; nevertheless, he was entrusted with such important roles by the Medici popes (Leo X and Clement VII) that his personal cause and that of the Popes eventually coincided.

Italian *signorie* and regional states appear to historians as the most modern of their time because of their economic and cultural vitality, but also because they were not bound as vassals to the medieval monarchies to the same extent as in the rest of Europe. However, as Niccolò Machiavelli (1469–1527) lamented, Italian states were weak and separated; the strong state of the future was clearly going to be born abroad. The unified monarchies of Castile and Aragón was the first example of a modern state able to dominate the conscience of its subjects. The re-establishment of the Spanish Inquisition in 1478 served to maintain unity of race and faith by persecuting the Jews, who were expelled from the country in their hundreds of thousands in the last decade of the fifteenth century. Repression then extended to the Muslim communities and political dissenters. The Inquisition acted to crush all internal opposition to the monarchy.

While Spain forged national unity under one crown, Italy remained politically disunited, as well as the focus of both Spanish and French expansionist policy. After the death of Alphonso of Aragón in 1458, the French and Spanish monarchies fought several wars for possession of Naples. In addition, in 1499, the French King Louis XII occupied Milan on the basis that his grandmother was a Visconti. After various vicissitudes, wars and shifting alliances, the French gained control, though never a secure hold, over part of the Po Valley, while the Spanish took the south – and ruled it from 1504 until the eighteenth century.

A third great power returned to expand in Italy: the German Empire. From 1356, the rules for electing emperors had changed in Germany, to a system in which the seven leading vassal states in Germany elected the Emperor, who retained the title 'Emperor of the Romans' although the tradition of coronations in Rome had ended and the Empire had become mainly Germanic, confined to Central and Eastern Europe. However, when Ferdinand of Aragón died in 1516, he was succeeded by his grandson, Charles V, whose mother had been married to a Habsburg. Charles had been brought up in the Habsburg court, and found himself in control of Spain, Naples, Sicily and Sardinia, as well as of the German Habsburg possessions – the widest-controlled area in Europe since the Roman Empire. Wars for the control of northern Italy between the Empire and France followed; and when, in 1527, the Papacy backed the French King Francis I, the imperial army besieged and sacked Rome. The ferocity of the imperial mercenary soldiers (mainly Spanish, as well as many Lutheran Germans) who killed innocent people, took hostages and burnt books, provoked horror and outrage among Italian intellectuals, who lamented the destruction caused by the 'new barbarians'. However, the sack of Rome did not leave long-term scars on the city – which continued to augment its population, reaching about 125,000 inhabitants by the seventeenth century – or interrupt the flourishing of Renaissance culture. For example, the autobiography of the Florentine artist Benvenuto Cellini (1500–571), goldsmith and metalworker, who helped to defend Rome before moving to Florence and then Mantua, shows the capacity of artists to continue to work and travel around Italy at a time of plague and war:

> Because I have always taken great pleasure in seeing the world and had never been to Mantua . . . I departed with my father's blessing, mounted my fine horse, and rode on him to Mantua . . . Since the world was under the clouds of pestilence and war, I travelled to Mantua with the greatest difficulty; when I arrived I sought to begin working; then I was put to work by a certain Milanese master named Niccolò, who was the goldsmith of the Duke of Mantua.
>
> (Cellini, 2002, Book I, 40, p. 71)

On his abdication in 1556, Charles V divided his huge territory into two kingdoms: the western and southern territories, including the Italian possessions, were to be ruled by Philip II; and the German territories (including Austria, Bohemia and Hungary) were to be controlled by Ferdinand I. The year 1527 marked the beginning of Spain's political predominance in Italy. Under Charles V, baronial power in Sicily and in the mainland south remained undisturbed. Many Spanish aristocrats moved to Palermo, and Sicilian noble families spent time in Madrid; these moves facilitated mixed marriages and a blending of the political elites and their interests. The viceroy government of Sicily had Castilian as its official language, though communication with the population had to be in either Sicilian dialect or Italian. Naples was a centre of major interest for the Spanish regime, as it was a huge city with an important market in both luxury and standard goods. Controlling the city was never easy – mainly, as Chapter 5 will show, because of revolts (provoked by economic conditions) among the lower strata of the population.

By 1600, Spain controlled 5 million of Italy's 13 million inhabitants. Both Charles V and Philip II continued to grant fiefs to Italy's powerful families; they also increased control over the Papacy, as many barons

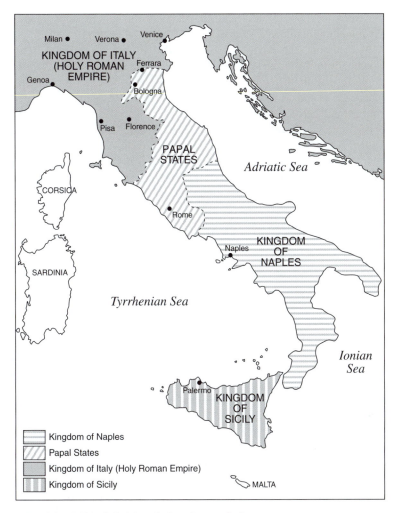

Map 4.1 Political divisions in Renaissance Italy

Source: adapted from Denis Hay and John Law, *Italy in the Age of the Renaissance, 1380–1530* (London: Longman, 1993), p. 352.

from those families became cardinals. The Papacy collaborated with Spain in its plans for an anti-Turkish *reconquista* – Crusades sanctified by the Church against the Ottoman Empire. Under the Spanish regime, Italy enjoyed an age of peace; but its control lacked deep roots: Italian princes often sought to regain the country's freedom, with the major dynasties (of Este, Medici and Gonzaga) being largely autonomous, Piedmont unreliable and Venice always a potential enemy.

In Piedmont, the Savoy dynasty decided to move its capital from Chambéry to Turin, under Duke Emmanuel Filiberto, in 1564. During the Reformation, the House of Savoy had begun to lose territory on the other side of the Alps, and in 1533 Geneva rebelled against Savoyard control and became a beacon of Calvinism. This led the dynasty to concentrate its interests south of the Alps, towards the sea and the Po Valley, where they controlled the duchy of Aosta, Piedmont, and the county of Nice (nevertheless, in standard sixteenth-century works, such as those of the Bolognese historian Leandro Alberti, the Savoy dynasty was considered to be French and not Italian). During the French occupation between 1536 and 1562, Turin's municipal authorities exercised more control over civil and religious life than they had under the House of Savoy. The return of Emmanuel Filiberto to Turin after the peace of Cateau-Cambrésis was followed in 1564 by the nomination of a new Archbishop, Girolamo Della Rovere, which re-established in the city a stable and long-lasting religious–political axis. While the rest of the peninsula was characterized by a very intense urbanization, Piedmont contained only a small group of cities. At the end of the sixteenth century, only Turin and Mondovì had more than 10,000 inhabitants, and very few towns had more than 5,000, and the weakness of this urban fabric favoured the dynasty's policy of centralization. The House of Savoy began to create a civil religion by promoting court ceremonies that were not restricted to the cathedral but rather centred on different churches, as a sign that they could 'assimilate the entire religious topography of the city', as Paolo Cozzo has demonstrated. On the one hand, some important municipal cults were transformed into state cults; while on the other, the city incorporated the sacred elements (*sacralità*) of the Savoy dynasty.

During the Renaissance, the Papal Court had become one of the richest and worldliest in Europe; the scandalous and luxurious lifestyle of many of its Popes and cardinals continued to provoke protest among European intellectuals. The nepotistic system reached its climax, and the city became one of the major centres of cultural patronage. The 1498 alliance between Pope Alexander VI and the French King Louis XII against the Milanese Sforza helped the Pope to extend control over the Romagna. The military campaign against that region, described by Machiavelli in *The Prince*, has been defined by Volker Reinhardt as akin to a war of extermination. When the Sforza family line died out in 1535, the Duchy of Milan passed to the Empire and thence to Philip II, though the French only relinquished official control over Lombardy in 1559, with the peace of Cateau-Cambrésis.

In the sixteenth century, it therefore seemed that Italy's destiny was to be decided by foreign powers. Contemporary intellectuals debated whether Italy was finished: did it have to end that way? Guicciardini replied in the negative: after many extraordinary cultural, political and economic achievements, the country could not simply go backwards. Indeed, during the sixteenth century, Italy continued to be at the front-line of commercial expansion. Italian cities were still the most advanced economies in Europe; Republican Venice was as rich as absolutist Paris, with new palaces being built beside the Grand Canal, and an amazing concentration of luxury shops between the Rialto Bridge and St Mark's Square. From Piedmont to Venice, Naples and Salerno, Italian cities produced high-quality luxury goods that were sold all over Europe. Their products were of outstanding design, made with rare materials and highly worked by skilled artisans. Foreign visitors were impressed by the intense level of horticultural cultivation near the cities, with the intro-duction of exotic products such as tomatoes, and began to consider Italy as a land of plenty. This was true only of the upper classes, as most Italians ate mainly bread and pasta. The frugality of their diet was evident when compared with the larger, meat-eating northern European travellers. As in the previous centuries, the relationship between city and countryside continued to be very close. Peasant families could not ignore the urban world of commerce and exchange, and when they were not in the fields the peasants often took part in work as, for example, black-smiths, shoemakers and woodcutters.

Despite foreign political control, Italy was not subject to foreign domination: its local institutions continued to exist; its elites continued to exercise control over their territory and its administration; its cultural achievements and way of life continued to develop as singularly Italian, and the Italian ruling class continued to be involved in commerce, banking and textile production. The transfer of foreign elites into south-ern Italy was limited by the need to maintain a good relationship with the local barons, and the Aragonese court was already largely Italianized by the mid-fifteenth century.

The four most influential Renaissance writers: Machiavelli, Jacopo Sannazzaro (1457–1530), Baldassarre Castiglione (1478–1529) and Ludovico Ariosto (1474–1533), chose to write their books in Italian rather than in Latin. Their works had a profound influence abroad, only surpassed by Petrarch's love poems and Boccaccio's *Decameron*. The fact that their work was not in Latin – still an internationally understood language – but in Italian was no obstacle at a time when foreign students studied at Italian universities and educated travellers visited Italian cities. Italian was in this period the best-known foreign language, as French was to be from the seventeenth century onwards.

RENAISSANCE AND HUMANISM

The dominant social groups in the city-states produced one of the liveliest intellectual movements of the time: humanism. It appeared initially in Florence and spread to the rest of the country, mobilizing an intellectual elite in central and northern Italian cities and in Naples. Humanists were part of (and addressed) the urban ruling classes – noblemen, rich bourgeois, princes, prelates, professionals. They were concerned with the study of classical Roman and (to a lesser extent) Greek culture, embracing all fields of knowledge, but with a particular interest in the humanities and in the study of society. They taught public men the art of rhetoric, intended as the art of persuasion in both speaking and writing. From the middle of the fourteenth century, they began to use the word 'Renaissance', creating an imagery of renewal to mark their sense of living in an age of regeneration, of 're-emergence into light after what they were the first to call "dark ages"', as Peter Burke has noted. By studying ancient urban history, they identified 'civilization' with urbanism and classicism. Everything that came between the Roman age and the Renaissance was described as 'barbarism'. To the medieval mentality, the classical age had been too far in the past, but at the same time still too present, to be considered as a historical phenomenon. On the one hand, there was the continuity of tradition; for example, the Germanic Emperor was considered to be a direct successor to Caesar and Augustus; but on the other hand, there was an unbridgeable abyss between pagan and Christian civilizations. Those two opposed tendencies were not yet sufficiently balanced to allow an attitude of historical detachment, which humanists thought they now possessed. Believing that their own cities were the renewal of classical cities, humanists praised their own time too – and their own ruling classes.

Classicism also involved the study of the language. Latin was considered to be the only lively sign of Roman domination, as it was still known throughout Europe. The attempt to study Latin texts in their historical context prompted the application of fine philological techniques, and the birth of classical scholarship. Early Florentine humanists, at the beginning of the fifteenth century, despised vernacular writers and considered even Dante and Petrarch to be inferior to ancient writers. However, by studying Latin, they began to explore its development and different stages, just as Dante had done, coming to recognize, as Martines puts it, 'the historicity of language'. In a study of the crisis of the early Renaissance, Hans Baron has demonstrated how humanists in their first (Latin) phase, tended to become detached from their own age – particularly in Florence during the period of political crisis in the fourteenth and the fifteenth centuries. In the following decades, when the threat of a Milanese invasion had been overcome, the city humanists began to see Florence as a new Rome, and recognized that classical ideals 'could serve as an ethic of social engagement for citizens in their own modern states': civic humanism strengthened local city patriotism. This development coincided with a new appreciation of Dante's theories of the vernacular. Also, humanists began to consider Petrarch as an example of both an expert in, and an enthusiast about classicism, as he had assembled the greatest collection of Latin classics known at the time, even surpassing the Papal library. Both Dante and Petrarch had seen Rome as the exemplar of Italy's glories and virtues.

In the second half of the fifteenth century, the libraries of Lorenzo the Magnificent and Pope Nicholas V had become the main custodians of Greek texts, and Greek began to be taught in the most important Italian universities, though it only became common for Italian humanists to understand Greek in the sixteenth century. The belief was that the study of classical texts could be the basis for the creation of a political science suited to the present times, and this was often linked to a need to secularize politics. Serious study of ancient texts resulted in the discovery, by the Roman humanist Lorenzo Valla (1407–57), that the Constantine donation was a forgery. He demonstrated that the donation was full of anachronisms, including the fact that it was written in a Latin so crude that it did not conform to that of Constantine's time, and that it cited towns that in Constantine's time had not yet been founded. Valla's work was reprinted in 1518, a year after Martin Luther's reformation programme, and contributed to the spread of hatred against the Church. The question of the fake donation at the beginning of the modern age made it clear that the false document, the testimony of Papal temporal power, was an Italian question, inextricably linked to the country that hosted what the bishops believed to be St Peter's heirs. Places and monuments mentioned in medieval literature in relation to Constantine and Pope Sylvester happened to be in Rome and in other Italian cities, from the north-east (Grado and Aquileia) to the north-west (Tortona in Piedmont) to the centre and centre–south (Ostia, Tivoli, Capua and Naples), to the extreme south and Sardinia. Ariosto mentioned the donation, recalling Dante's scepticism, in his *Orlando Furioso*. Machiavelli, who was passionate about Dante and interested in the religious question, was no longer concerned with the donation, which had for him, at that point, no meaning, but with the substantial problem of the presence of the Papacy on Italian territory.

In the fourth book of the *Storia d'Italia*, Guicciardini provided a synthesis of the donation question, using it as a pretext for a long digression on the origins and the history of the papal temporal power:

> On these foundations and by these means, raised to secular power, little by little forgetting about the salvation of souls and divine precepts, and turning all their thoughts to worldly greatness, and no longer using their spiritual authority except as an instrument and minister of temporal power, they began to appear rather more like secular princes than popes.
>
> (Guicciardini, 1969, Book IV, p. 149)

The work was not published until 1561, more than twenty years after Guicciardini's death, and various parts were censored. The first unabridged version was only published in the second half of the eighteenth century. At the beginning of the seventeenth century, the Calabrian philosopher Tommaso Campanella (1569–1639) defended the Pope against Machiavelli, supporting an anachronistic vision of the Pope's superiority over state power. By then, the debate on the donation had been replaced by a debate on Papal power, and had assumed the marked characteristic of a primarily Italian question.

Alongside the religious problem, both Machiavelli and Guicciardini investigated the history of Italy and the reasons for its divisions. Machiavelli, who revolutionized political thought, came from a noble Florentine family and received some education in the humanities. In 1494, after Charles VIII of France had invaded Italy and entered Florence, Piero de' Medici was expelled, accused of having accepted the king's conditions, and the Florentines proclaimed the republic. Machiavelli proposed his own candidature as secretary of the republic, but was defeated by a candidate supported by Savonarola. Machiavelli, who considered religion only in its external forms (institutions) and not for its moral values, had no understanding of the mystical character of Savonarola's preaching, and despised him as an ecclesiastical man: only a politician, not a prophet, could lead a republic.

After Savonarola had been accused of heresy and executed, Machiavelli became secretary of the republic and began his missions to Italian and European states to gather information for the city about other governments' policies. In 1506 he followed Julius II's campaign against Perugia and Bologna as an observer, and from there he developed some of the ideas he later presented in *The Prince*; in particular, that 'good' and 'bad' policies did not exist, but only policies that could be either useful or damaging to the security of the state. In 1509, when Julius II acquired the Romagna, Machiavelli understood the risk that Papal expansionism posed to the Florentine republic, and described the Pope's political and military activity as a 'disastrous fury'.

In 1513, the Medici returned to power and Machiavelli was imprisoned, tortured and confined to a villa in the countryside, where he began to work on his most famous treatise, *The Prince*. When his relationship with the Medici improved, in 1520 Pope Clement VII commissioned from him a history of Florence (*Istorie fiorentine*), in which Machiavelli illustrated the advantages of a national army over mercenary troops. He had already addressed this question in the *Discourses on Livy* (1512–19), in which he argued that the modern state ought to imitate the ancient Roman citizen militia.

The Prince consists of twenty-six chapters, which can be divided into four parts. In the first (I–XI) Machiavelli described how to gain and maintain a new state; in the second (XII–XIV) he examined the art of war; in the third (XV–XXIV) – the most important part of the treatise – he analysed the qualities necessary in the art of government, concluding with the idea that the Prince should ignore traditional moral requirements, as these often do not correspond to political necessity; and in the final part, chapter XXV discusses the role of 'fortune' – the obstacles that could hinder the realization of the state – while chapter XXVI concludes with a call to Lorenzo de' Medici to take up arms against foreign rule and liberate Italy. Having seen at first hand how other European states functioned, Machiavelli began to raise the question of Italian unity as a political necessity. The chapter ends with the final verses of Petrarch's poem *Italia mia*. Machiavelli freed politics from the moralistic aspects of medieval theology, and his Prince symbolized humanistic individualism. However, as Chabod suggested, even more than unification, Machiavelli called for a state that could 'defend Italy from the barbarians'. In 1521, Machiavelli met Guicciardini, a Florentine humanist from a family very close to the Medici, with whom he began an intense correspondence. Though Guicciardini did not believe in formulating universal laws for politics, he did regard history as an entirely earthly variable, which had to be freed from Papal and medieval religion.

ARTISTS AND ARCHITECTS

Humanists were not only political thinkers or historians, but also artists, architects and inventors. They observed that the medieval city was not constructed organically; its Romanesque and Gothic monuments were spread around cities in no order, mixed with houses and other buildings. Renaissance artists developed a system of representation based on linear perspective between the 1420s and 1440s, and began preparing plans to redesign cities to make them more symmetrical and geometric. The first Italian writers on art and art theory, such as Lorenzo Ghiberti (1378–1455), Leon Battista Alberti (1404–72) and Giorgio Vasari (1511–74), believed that classical art had been destroyed at the beginning of the Christian age, as a result of the barbarian invasions and the hostility of the Church, but had been reborn as the mainstay of the Renaissance style.

Traditional classical themes were utilized in a variety of Christian images, so that classical mythology was revived, but incorporated simultaneously into Christian allegories. In the early Renaissance, Boccaccio had been the first to return to ancient sources and to demonstrate a critical and scientific approach to classical art; some of his writings, such as *Genealogia deorum*, define him as the precursor of scientific Renaissance treatises. However, the revival of classicism was most evident in architecture; this was not surprising in Italy, where numerous classical buildings had survived almost intact. The Rome that Filippo Brunelleschi (1377–1446) visited at the beginning of the fifteenth century was a complex and disordered urban area; from then on, the Popes began to reorganize it, making it a centre for the study of ancient archaeology and of the trade in antiquities, up to that point dominated by Padua and Venice. Generations of architects visited Rome to study the Pantheon, the Colosseum, the Arch of Constantine and the Theatre of Marcellus, with the intention of following the principles upon which they were built.

Box 4.1 Vasari's Lives of the Artists

Giorgio Vasari became famous for his treatise *Lives of the Painters, Sculptors and Architects*, first published in 1550. The first edition was dedicated to the Grand Duke Cosimo I de' Medici, and was rewritten and enriched with portraits of artists in 1568, an edition that was published many times in Italy and abroad. He described the lives and works of Italian artists since Cimabue, maintaining that Tuscan artists had brought Italy out of the Middle Ages. However, his *Lives* also included non-Tuscan artists and provided an extraordinary history of Italian art between the Middle Ages and the Renaissance. Indeed, his life is proof of the anti-parochialism of humanist artists: he lived and worked between Florence, Arezzo, Modena, Bologna, Rome, Camaldoli (in Romagna), Parma, Mantua, Venice, Lucca, Naples, Rimini, Ravenna, Urbino and Cortona (near Arezzo). His work is considered as the birth of art criticism in Italy. In the foreword to the first part, he explained how the barbarian invasions had ruined Italian art: that they could not have been more distant from ancient Roman values, and they 'had no longer any good customs or ways of life. Nay more, there had been lost at one and the same time all true men and every sort of virtue, and laws, habits, names, and tongues had been changed; and all these things together and each by itself had caused every lovely mind and lofty intellect to become most brutish and most base'. From the fourteenth century in Tuscany, however, new artists were born who restored art and custom to the beauty and values of Roman times: 'discerning well enough the good from the bad and abandoning the old manners, turned to imitating the ancient'; and specified, 'the ancient were the works made before Constantine'. (Vasari, 1996, Vol. I, pp. 37, 45).

With Alberti, architecture became concerned with all the questions posed by humanistic culture. Alberti belonged to a rich Florentine family, but was born in Genoa, brought up in Venice and studied law and science in Padua, moving to Florence in his thirties, though returning only for short visits as he began work at the Papal court. He was a writer, thinker and technician as well as an architect, who only began working on monumental art in his forties, and writing his famous critical and modern interpretation of Vitruvius's art, entitled *On the Art of Building*, in 1450.

Alberti raised architecture to the level of the liberal arts, separating conceptual from manual work, the artist's idea from its execution. As a result of his knowledge of Italy, Alberti was not limited by Florentine culture, and set architectural rules and models to which Italian artists were bound for a long time.

One of the Florentine sculptors who had a major influence on Italian painters, decorators, architects and sculptors was Donato de' Bardi, called Donatello (1386–1466), who worked not only in Florence but also in other cities, particularly Padua. Another Florentine, Tommaso Cassai (1401–28), known as Masaccio, proposed a new form of painting which, like Donatello's, left Gothic behind and created a solid, heroic humanity based on the representation of powerful figures; he pioneered linear perspective, particularly with his Trinity in S. Maria Novella in Florence. These new forms, elaborated in Tuscany, spread rapidly, as demonstrated by Paolo Uccello and Donatello in Padua; new schools challenged Tuscan hegemony in Milan, Padua, Urbino and Ferrara, and artists moved between different cities, so that by the second half of the fifteenth century Florence was no longer at the centre of Italy's artistic topography. Piero della Francesca (circa 1416–92), for example, having spent his youth in Florence, was active mainly in small towns near his birthplace, San Sepolcro (Arezzo) and the princely courts at Ferrara and Urbino. His painting was at the same time both peasant-like and rustic, and aristocratic and heroic: the meeting between these two aspects gave an epic character to his work. For example, the group of frescoes entitled *Storia della Croce* ('History of the Cross') at the Church of S. Francis in Arezzo harked back to the climate of the Crusades at the time of Pius II, with complex battle scenes, illuminated landscapes and fortified towers set high on hills; the *Polittico* for the Church of S. Augustine at San Sepolcro represents several saints of giant stature with grave expressions, after Masaccio. At that time, under Federico of Montefeltro, Urbino became one of the major centres of modern culture.

In southern Italy under Spanish rule, Naples and Palermo functioned as cosmopolitan centres, where Italian artists met and formed their own style, including Antonello of Messina and painters from the Marche and from Spain. Their style cannot be defined as typical of a certain area because of the mixture of styles from all over Italy and beyond, an international culture that informed the work of artists in Sicily and in the kingdom of Naples.

In northern Italy, Andrea Mantegna (1431–1506) surpassed the Tuscan painters by creating images using perspective that had never been seen before; nature was represented by an architectonic system of blocks and slabs of stone, and he depicted human beings living among ruins dressed as ancient Romans. In Mantua, he worked for the Gonzaga family and decorated the famous *Camera degli Sposi*. As a friend to many humanists, he placed images of the Gospels and of saints' lives in Roman history. Donato di Pascuccio d'Antonio (1444–1514), known as Bramante, was the most influential artist in Lombardy; born near Pesaro and educated in Urbino, he worked as a painter in Bergamo. From 1480 to 1499 he worked for Ludovico Sforza, called Il Moro, in Milan, where he created his first masterpiece, at the Church of S. Maria at San Satiro, where he used perspective for the first time to create the illusion of an apse.

Pupil of the Florentine sculptor, painter and goldsmith, Andrea del Verrocchio (1434/7–88), Leonardo da Vinci (1452–1519) was heir to all the aspirations of fifteenth-century Florence. He lived and worked between Florence, Milan, Rome and Touraine in France, and grappled with questions of sculptural form – for example, in the equestrian statue of Francesco Sforza; of order and symmetry and *chiaroscuro* in painting – as seen in *The Last Supper* and the *Mona Lisa*; and in architecture, taking part in discussions about the cupola of the cathedral at Pavia. In Milan, he decided to give a theoretical basis to his doctrine by writing a series of treatises on perspective, anatomy and mechanics. During the last years of the century, humanists such as Leonardo produced many sketches that studied human anatomy and analysed natural phenomena such as water and wind.

While most artists worked collaboratively in workshops under the strict control of the commissioning patron, figures such as Leonardo and Michelangelo acquired personal fame. As André Chastel has observed, these artists became almost 'directors of social life', and they had a role and a prestige unimaginable abroad, linked to a comprehensive, universal idea of art: before Leonardo, who was at one and the same time painter, sculptor, architect, engraver, writer, poet and musician, this was true of Giotto (painter, head of the monuments and fine arts office, architect and town-planner); Verrocchio (painter, engraver and sculptor); Michelangelo Buonarroti (1475–1564), who could handle any artistic technique; Vasari; and Gian Lorenzo Bernini (1598–1680), the last example of these great, comprehensively artistic, figures.

The typical Italian relationship between city and countryside fostered links between artistic work and the construction of landscape; close links between water engineers, botanists, gardeners and landscape designers were common. During the Renaissance, Italian technique in these areas had an international dissemination as important as that of painting and the decorative arts. The numerous villas outside Italian cities from Piedmont to Sicily are witness to the relationship between art and nature during and after this period, with endless variations around country estates and the development of the typical Italian garden. However, the Renaissance was fundamentally urban and not rural; even the authors of pastoral literary works lived in towns, though they often retired to country villas in the summer. Fourteenth- and fifteenth-century paintings exemplify this relationship between city and countryside, as many of the landscapes have a geometrical aspect that recalls city architecture, and reflect the fact that artists were required to make statements about their city.

The manners of Italian aristocrats were imitated in Europe, and nobility of talent was regarded as seriously as nobility of blood: artists such as Raphael Sanzio, Michelangelo and Titian lived like princes, as they were in demand by monarchs all over Europe. One development that was exported was the extensive use of mass communication and propaganda. The princes and elites of the Italian states did not limit propaganda to the written word, but relied also on the persuasive power of images, statues and buildings. The court, in particular, became a theatre, a spectacle of luxury through which princes sought to extend their influence and prestige both within and outside the state, and to maintain control over the local ruling classes. The lifestyle of court society evolved, establishing new norms of beauty and aesthetic conceptions. Despite being a minority movement, during the sixteenth century the Renaissance influenced a large section of the population, in part a result of the invention of the printing press: teachers, artisans and shopkeepers, and a considerable number of women, were involved alongside sections of the elite.

COURTIERS

The nineteenth-century historian, Jacob Burckhardt, argued that the achievement in fifteenth-century Italy of such high levels of civilization and elegance served to justify belief in the perfect courtier, not as an ideal but as a reality. The most famous courtier's manual, by Baldassare Castiglione, *Il Cortegiano* (The Book of the Courtier), is indeed set in a real court, that of Urbino in 1507, where he lived and began a successful diplomatic career. Born in Mantua province, Castiglione studied

Latin and Greek in Milan, where he was educated as a gentleman at the court of Ludovico il Moro; he moved between the courts of Mantua, Milan, Urbino and Rome (with Pope Leo X). When his book was published in 1528, it was already famous at courts throughout the whole of Italy, such was the interest among the Renaissance aristocracy for the subject. It was subsequently translated and disseminated throughout educated European society during the sixteenth and seventeenth centuries. Some thirty years later, another work on etiquette became a European bestseller: *Galateo* by Giovanni Della Casa (1503–56). Born in Tuscany, Della Casa studied in Florence and continued his humanistic education in Padua. He then chose an ecclesiastical career, protected by Alexander Farnese in Rome. Della Casa became Archbishop of Benevento near Naples, and finally became Papal Nuncio in Venice, where he also worked for the Inquisition.

While Castiglione's interest was focused on the relationship between courtier and prince, and more generally on court life, *Galateo* was aimed more widely at the urban Renaissance gentleman. As Machiavelli had done for politics, Della Casa intended to create a set of manners, and, again like Machiavelli, he sought to establish a form of obedience to a common law: not the law of power, but the law of custom and practice, of *come si fa* ('how to do things'). In this sense, *Galateo* can be considered as one of the first hymns to the 'modern man', as Carlo Ossola has observed in his Introduction to a recent edition (2000) of the text. It was also a hymn of praise to urban life, for 'anyone who chose to live not in solitude or in a hermitage, but in cities and among men'.

The attempt to create an etiquette for the perfect gentleman was softened by an accent on spontaneity and modesty. The sixteenth-century gentleman was well aware of the time in which he was living and knew that, despite the importance of classical models, he had to adapt to the practical needs of the present. This was particularly true with regard to language, and the need to opt for a solution that was not strictly Tuscan but tolerated cautiously neologisms of Spanish or French origin. At the same time, a gentleman was supposed to assimilate as much Latin as was considered compatible with the needs of modern prose. The perfect courtier had to be a skilled knight and warrior, but also to be able to moderate these qualities with a touch of *dilettantismo* (amateurism), to appear graceful and natural with it. The Renaissance court was his natural environment as the ideal place for the development of the *sereno equilibrio* (serene balance) preached by fifteenth-century humanism in imitation of the ancient Greek and Roman civilizations. As Alberti wrote in *Iciarchia*, to do things well meant 'to behave with modesty, gracefulness and a refined attitude which should delight those who observe you'. The sense of measure and discretion was also a feature of the ideal state – one founded neither on extreme wealth, nor mired in poverty, but based on a majority of 'mediocre' citizens.

Della Casa's work continued to be an influence well into the eighteenth century, when the poet Giacomo Leopardi, who was very interested in the 'customs of the Italians', pointed in *Crestomazia italiana* to 'the kindness, the grace and the amiableness of manners'. Leopardi assigned the *Galateo* to the category of 'practical philosophy', thus anticipating its interpretation during the Enlightenment and throughout the nineteenth century, with the publication of a *Nuovo Galateo* by Melchiorre Gioia, a philosopher from Piacenza, which shifted the emphasis from 'conversation' to 'social reason'. The tradition of the etiquette manual therefore continued, but in the context of new and different ideas and tastes. The 'cleaning up' of 'customs' also meant 'civilization', a civilization that depended on the use of reason and on what was practically 'useful': for Gioia, 'civilization thus consists of the victories obtained by the principles of social reason on the disordered impulses of nature'. The 'new' *Galateo* was handed down to subsequent generations of educated Italians, this time in a united Italy to writers who no longer lived in a court society.

Despite their attempts to free themselves from the Middle Ages, sixteenth-century humanists were still 'rather medieval'. Castiglione's *Courtier* drew on medieval traditions of courtly behaviour and love as well as on Plato and Cicero, and even Machiavelli's *Prince* was part of the medieval genre of books of advice for rulers. The humanists' attention was not limited to the classical texts, but ranged restlessly from antiquity to the present, and even Machiavelli and Guicciardini recognized some value in medieval prophetic literature, which continued to be very popular through *cantastorie* (story tellers and singers) in Italian cities until the Counter Reformation. According to Guicciardini (in a letter to Goro Gheri of 1518), 'today just like in the past ... great things have been anticipated by great prodigies'; and Machiavelli admitted in his *Discourses on Livy* that 'no grave accident in a city or in a province ever comes unless it has been foretold either by diviners or by revelations'. Ariosto's most famous book, *Orlando Furioso* (first published in 1516) shows the result of the author's study of classical epics, and in particular his knowledge of medieval romance. It is neither an imitation of the classical epics nor of medieval romances: he had, as Burke has described, 'a foot in both camps'. Both Ariosto's and Castiglione's works could only have been written by writers with a thorough knowledge of both ancient and medieval traditions. Humanists were divorced from the classical age by the legacy of Christianity and could only achieve a classicism that was tempered by the beliefs and aspirations of the Christian society they inhabited. Nevertheless, the humanist movement was secular, just as Italian culture in the Middle Ages had been fundamentally the work of laymen.

THE COUNTER-REFORMATION, THE NEW ROME AND ITALY IN THE SIXTEENTH CENTURY

The development of the Papacy in the second half of the fifteenth century also meant social, economic and cultural progress for Rome. The triumphant classicism of that period had its reference point in an idealized image of ancient Rome, which the Papacy believed itself destined to recreate. This idea had been sustained by humanists in the previous centuries; for example, historian and humanist Flavio Biondo (1392–1463), born and educated in Romagna, moved to Rome where he worked for the Popes, and analysed the institutions of ancient Rome in his last work, *Roma Triumphans*, arguing that the Church was the true heir of Roman universality.

However, the increasing worldly power of the Church continued to provoke protests from both laymen and local churches who proposed reform, protests that converged in the preaching of Savonarola and his followers. Once the communes had become regional states led by principalities, the families who aspired to power gained great advantage through Papal investment and recognition. Cardinals drawn from powerful Italian families strengthened the 'Italianness' of the Papacy. The fortunes of the Popes therefore ran parallel to those of the Italian political and social elite.

The ideas of the Reformation reached humanist intellectuals in Italy who were trying to free the country from popular superstition. When Luther's ideas became known they were rejected by the Papacy, particularly because of their appeal against both Papal hierarchy and the sacramental system of salvation, essential to which is the centrality of good works. Luther's books began to be read in Italy following the ninety-five theses of 1517, and his doctrines became intertwined with existing religious tensions in Italian cities: an anti-clerical culture, ancient millennarian and prophetic anxieties, humanistic Renaissance thought and wide-spread desire for a return to the origins of Christianity. It was difficult for the Papacy to forbid the reading of books that entered the country from the other side of the Alps, because there was a clandestine book market fed by flourishing commerce and by the flood of foreign students who came to study at the universities of Padua and Bologna; books appeared anonymously, with fake authors or nicknames. In addition, Venetian printers, who always welcomed novelties and had contacts with printers all over Europe, made it possible to buy Luther's books in Venice.

After the imperial army's sack of Rome in 1527, the Papacy launched a powerful and organized reaction. Protestant groups had begun to appear in cities that had links with France, such as Lucca, Ferrara, Modena and Siena, and a prompt Papal response was necessary. Under Paul III Farnese, Ignatius Loyola created the Jesuit order, and Cardinal Gian Pietro Carafa reorganized the Inquisition. Carafa became Archbishop of Naples and head of the Inquisition, and went on to become Pope with the name Paul IV. He sent so many people to prison that when he died in 1559, the Roman crowd attacked and burned the Inquisition palace, and freed its prisoners. By 1570 there was almost no active Protestantism in Italy.

The Papacy could not act through repression alone; it had to challenge Protestant doctrine ideologically. This was carried out officially at the Council of Trent, which lasted from 1545 to 1563. The need for a Catholic reform was not prompted merely by Luther, though. There was continuity between the many requests for reform since the Middle Ages (as seen in previous chapters) and attempts to renew religious life in the sixteenth century. The episode of Savonarola had been anticipated by a number of less-well-known attempts by preachers and mystics (many of whom were women) to reinvigorate Italian religious life. As John Martin has observed, the introduction of printing led to the diffusion of books in the vernacular and of devotional texts among the urban lower middle classes, further stimulating the need for new spiritual models and a deeper religiosity. Indeed, new initiatives developed before the Council of Trent, particularly centred on charity (the Theatines, the Barnabites, the Capuchins, and, among female groups, the Angeliche and the Ursulines), concerned with the spiritual and material help of the poor and the marginalized. Trent was therefore principally, but not solely, a response to Protestantism.

The city of Trent was located within the Empire but was ethnically Italian and therefore influenced by both the Emperor and the Pope. The council was not a democratic meeting where doctrine was discussed, but was dominated by leading Spanish Jesuits, who imposed their definition of orthodoxy. It legitimized purgatory and therefore the possibility of mediation; it confirmed the mediation through good works and Papal indulgences, and therefore penitence and pilgrimages; it re-established the need for the administration of sacraments by priests, and enshrined the doctrine of transubstantiation denied by Luther. Church control over books extended to ancient and early Christian classics, which were often censored, corrected or abridged, helping to create a generalized mistrust of Italian-text editions among Italians and foreigners alike. A gap persisted between the decisions taken at Trent and the variety of religious experiences that demanded reform in Italy, and it was not easy for the Church to impose uniform religious practices on the whole country. From Trent onwards, the relationship between the Papacy, religious groups and popular beliefs continued to be one of negotiation and resistance, not simply one of repression.

Architecture continued to be one of the means of propagating Catholicism, as revealed by Papal biographies, which remarked on the importance of the 'zeal for God's house'. According to a biography by the humanist Giannozzo Manetti, Pope Nicholas V (1447–55) recommended on his deathbed that St Peter's basilica and other religious buildings be renovated. The new Basilica of St Peter was the major work begun by Julius II (Pope 1503–13), who decided to transform Rome into the capital of the Renaissance. Bramante, Michelangelo and Raphael were among the artists who worked for him. The movement promoted by Julius II intensified under his successors, particularly Cardinal Giovanni de' Medici, Lorenzo's son, who became Pope as Leo X (1513–21). The decision taken at the Council of Trent sustained these efforts by reiterating the veneration of images in close connection with the cult of saints and relics – just as the Council of Nicea had done eight centuries before. Images were not only artistic expressions, but useful instruments of propaganda, as they illustrated religious 'stories' and Christian history.

Roman culture was characterized by a passion for archaeology, and Rome became a city of excavations and new constructions, full of ruins with many empty spaces, where beautiful gardens were created and many discoveries were made, such as the Apollo of Anzio and the Laocoon of Aquilino. In April 1506, the first stone of one pillar of the new St Peter's cupola was laid. Julius II's tomb was entrusted to Michelangelo, and the new basilica was to preserve the tomb of St Peter and the mausoleum of Julius II. After the deaths of Julius II and

Bramante, the original plan came to a halt, and both lack of money and much discussion postponed the completion of the basilica until 1626: 120 years, twenty Popes and ten architects later. This meant that the final result was an essentially composite design. The work of Bernini placed the Renaissance construction within a Baroque landscape, with an oval piazza encircled by columns. By walking inside through the huge porch, visitors take a journey through the labour of generations. Only at the cupola, at the centre of all the differing perspectives, is it possible to have a sense of Bramante's and Julius II's great project.

In 1508, following Bramante's suggestion, the Pope called a young artist from Urbino, Raphael Sanzio (1483–1520), to Rome. His father was a painter and he had been educated within the extraordinary culture of the Montefeltro family (which had ruled in Urbino since the thirteenth century), so well described by Castiglione in *The Courtier*. Before moving to Rome, Raphael had worked in Perugia and Siena, revealing his genius in his depictions of portraits and facial expressions. He incorporated into his balanced and peaceful art elements of Leonardo, of Michelangelo's force and of Titian's use of colour. In the Vatican, Raphael worked on frescoes for Julius II's apartment, showing himself to be a natural interpreter of the humanistic aspiration for a reconciled and serene humanity; his art originated in a mature and rich culture, together with a conception of ancient times as a golden age. His images of the Virgin illustrate the perfection of his art, which achieved its pinnacle in the *Madonna Sistina* of 1513.

While Leonardo placed painting above all arts, Michelangelo considered sculpture to be the supreme artistic form. He worked for the Pope in Rome, as did Bramante and Raphael, contributing to the debate on St Peter's, and moved between Rome, Venice, Bologna and Florence, in which city he sculpted a gigantic David in marble, which appeared in the Signoria square in 1504 and used for the first time the anatomical concept of *contrapposto* (the weighting of the body on the right-hand side). The following year, Michelangelo worked on Julius II's tomb and mausoleum in Rome, which was completed in 1512. The latter was a synthesis of fourteenth- and fifteenth-century themes, brought together and inspired by ancient art, Greek beauty and triumphant Roman style. He subsequently returned to Florence and worked in the Medicis' sanctuary of San Lorenzo. The new Pope Paul III brought him back to Rome, commissioning him to paint the Last Judgement in the Sistine Chapel on a wall measuring 17 by 13 metres. Michelangelo's composition was conceived and executed as a fearsome rotation of figures, ascending on the left-hand side, and descending on the right-hand side; brown bodies whirled on a background of deep blue, above the sinister red of the inferno beneath, around the central figure of Christ, who appeared as a Hercules or a Jupiter.

What was achieved in Rome in the first half of the sixteenth century in the fields of architecture, sculpture and painting marked out Italy from the rest of the West, giving the peninsula a classic style that had no equivalent in France, the Netherlands or Germany. The fifteenth-century experience had anticipated aspects of that art, but the new Roman classicism overtook what had existed previously: these artists considered ancient art with equanimity; they relied on it but were never intimidated by it. There is no Renaissance church that is simply a copy of a Roman building; there are no art works that merely imitate Greek or Roman compositions: however, they all convey the same air of dignity, clarity and idealization. Sixteenth-century Roman art thus became the expression of a new culture, which developed from within the wider humanistic culture of the time and soon expanded to other parts of Italy, beginning with Tuscany and Lombardy.

Parts of what is now defined as Lombardy were at the time under the rule of the Venetian republic, and were influenced by Venetian art as well as by the new Roman style. At the end of the fifteenth century, Philippe de Commynes defined the Grand Canal as 'the most beautiful road in the world, and the most adorned with houses'. Venice's religious and civil ceremonies were magnificent, performed as naval parades. The city's decline, as a result of the voyages of discovery and the increasing advance of the Ottoman Empire following the conquest of Constantinople in 1453, was not yet apparent between the sixteenth and the seventeenth centuries. It had, however, become evident that Venice was now primarily a mainland Italian power. In a rich city, with a sophisticated taste for exoticism and a cultural heritage that looked to Byzantium more than to Rome, humanism developed differently from the way it did in Rome and Tuscany. With the new century came a passion for building villas on the mainland, where gentlemen and ladies found a natural environment in which to discuss love and culture; an example of which can be found in literature in the *Asolani* by Venetian writer and humanist, Pietro Bembo (1470–1547). Around 1530, Venice rivalled Rome in stature and defined a new phase of classical art, which was rapidly followed by the complex so-called Mannerism. The works around St Mark's Square continued with the bell tower *loggetta*, the first modern addition to the square, in 1537–40. Venice contributed to the fifteenth-century artistic revolution with the transformation of painting through a new use of colour, which generated new forms of light and tone, in the work of Giovanni Bellini, Titian and Giorgione.

Among Giorgione's (1477–1510) pupils was Titian Vecellio (1485–1576), whose influence spread during the sixteenth century across the whole of northern and central Italy. He became an artistic authority both in Italy and internationally; strongly connected to Venice, he maintained beneficial relationships with princes at Ferrara and Mantua, with Pope Paul III, and the Emperors Francis I and Charles V. Titian's work for Paul III exemplifies both the relationship between Popes and artists in the age of artistic patronage (*mecenatismo*) and that between Popes and their relatives in the age of nepotism (the papal practice of making their nephews cardinals). In particular, the painting *Paolo III con i nipoti* is an expression of the vicissitudes that propelled the Farnese family among the Olympians of Italy's ruling elite. Painted a few months after the Pope had made his son, Pier Luigi, Duke of Parma and Piacenza, it was a difficult picture to construct, taking into consideration, as it had to, the Pope's will and the struggle between his nephews; and indeed it remained unfinished. In the painting, Paul III is seated, flanked by cardinal Alexander Farnese standing and Duke Ottavio bowing in the act of reverence. The act of reverence was the Pope's due when greeted by all mortals and consisted of them bowing three times, ending with the kissing of the Pope's foot. Cardinals were required to show reverence, but the painting shows only the layman bowing, about to kiss the foot stretching from the papal gown. The portrait therefore reflects the Pope's habit of nominating his nephews as cardinals (even if they did not have the required qualifications) in order to enhance the power of the family, and responds to an apparent desire for immortality in projecting present dynastic power into the future.

In the mid-sixteenth century, a new Italian form of art, called Mannerism, spread across Europe. The building of aristocratic villas, already a feature in the Venetian republic, spread to other parts of Italy; and one of the palaces that most influenced Europeans was the *Palazzo del Tè* in Mantua. Artists moved around Italy as before, bringing with them new styles to other regions and in turn learning and absorbing new regional experiences. The new Duchy in Tuscany enlarged public buildings, adding parks and gardens in order to create grandiose surroundings for court ceremonies. Cellini was a typical exponent of the new art form, his sophisticated formalism and his complex and bizarre taste becoming typical of the age. Florentine Mannerist art was expressed mainly in its monumental fountains – complex compositions on several levels in which statues were distributed elegantly around stretches of water that graced aristocratic gardens. Indeed, Mannerism was at its finest in the design of gardens and grottoes (which produced the word 'grotesque') as in, for example, the Boboli Gardens in Florence.

Venetian Mannerism was mostly evident in the area around Vicenza, where Andrea Palladio (1508–80) modelled villas with increasingly animated façades. In painting, Jacopo Robusti (1518–94), known as Tintoretto, began to accumulate or disperse figures with dramatic effects of light and shadow, distributing figures in all directions across the whole area of the picture – as evident, for example, in his *Last Supper* of 1564–87. Tintoretto was entrusted with important commissions at the Doge's Palace in Venice; in 1588, he completed the theatrical and disproportionate *Paradiso* in the salon of the Grand Council. The art of Paolo Caliari (1528–88), known as Veronese, who also worked in Venice, was less exaggerated; at the *Sala dei Dieci*, in the Doge's Palace, Veronese's more harmonious style demonstrated the persistent influence of Bellini and Mantegna when Mannerism was in vogue. The phenomenon of counter-classicism, or counter-Renaissance (a concept developed by Hiram Haydn in the post-war years), or Mannerism, was already present at the time of the Renaissance. Mannerism can be seen as a constant in European literature, and as a complementary phenomenon to classicism in any age. However, Burke has suggested that rather than an anti- or counter-Renaissance, Mannerism should be described as a late phase of the Renaissance, born of the crisis engendered by the Reformation, the French invasions in Italy and the sack of Rome. At the end of the century, like Rome and Florence before it, Venice began to exhibit a sense of weariness. With a few exceptions, the seventeenth century was a period of stasis, when little new was created, and patrons of the arts were content with the great works of the previous period, enhanced by their success throughout Europe.

LITERATURE AND ITALIAN LANGUAGE IN THE SIXTEENTH CENTURY

The development of a common Italian literary language, which intensified during the fifteenth and sixteenth centuries, was not restricted to intellectual circles, but extended to the chancelleries of Italian states. At the beginning of the sixteenth century, the Neapolitan writer Jacopo Sannazzaro corrected the southern elements in the first draft of his *Arcadia* (in prose and verse) according to the rules of literary Florentine; in a similar way, the Ferrarese Ludovico Ariosto (1474–1533) modified the Po Valley characteristics of his *Orlando Furioso*, following rules established by Pietro Bembo, as was evident in the third and definitive edition of the poem in 1532; Baldassarre Castiglione, also in the third and final edition of his *Courtier* of 1524, replaced various expressions influenced by Latin and local dialects with a veneer of *toscanità*. A later edition from 1528 increased the Tuscan emphases after editing by the Venetian aristocrat, Giovan Francesco Valerio, with Bembo as consultant.

Leon Battista Alberti helped to boost the vernacular language in the mid-fifteenth century by according equal weight to vernacular and Latin in his book *The Family in Renaissance Florence*, and by launching a competition of vernacular poetry in 1441 entitled *Certame coronario*. Lorenzo the Magnificent in Florence promoted the vernacular as the official language of culture and the court. As a result, a courtly language emerged, founded on a vernacular influenced by Latin and purged of dialect elements. The literary language was also unified throughout Italy with the development of Petrarchism in the second half of the century. However, this was a very refined vernacular, different from that in common usage. The type of intellectual, often of the court, defined by Petrarch was also responsible for the linguistic choices made in the sixteenth century. However, the prevalence of Tuscan and the final victory of vernacular over Latin still required linguistic unity, a demand that also came with the development of the press, which needed uniform rules of vocabulary, orthography, grammar and punctuation. Intellectuals such as Pietro Bembo collaborated with printers in introducing norms – for example, the apostrophe and the semi-colon – and in proposing a new principle of style. The son of a successful diplomat, Bembo belonged to an ancient Venetian aristocratic family, which educated him in humanist studies and particularly in the cult of Petrarch. While his father was ambassador to Florence he met Lorenzo the Magnificent. When he returned to Venice, the prestigious publisher Aldus Manutius commissioned from him a new edition of the *Canzoniere*, which appeared in 1501. Bembo subsequently became the major exponent of Italian literature, establishing the norms of the vernacular and championing a renewed Petrarchist tradition.

Venice was the European capital of printing, and it was there that the 'language question' exploded. As the literary critic, Romano Luperini, has suggested, the central contested issue was: 'Which should be the linguistic norm capable of unifying the written and spoken vernacular of Italy's educated people?' There were three main positions in the ensuing debate:

1 Bembo, in *Prose della volgar lingua* ('Proses in the vernacular', 1525) proposed a language based on Petrarch for poetry and Boccaccio for prose, which represented a return to the fourteenth century.
2 Baldassarre Castiglione and Giangiorgio Trissino were among supporters of a common language that used the language of Italian courts as a model to create a mixed idiom on the basis of Tuscan.
3 Nicolò Machiavelli, in *Discorso sulla lingua* ('Essay on the language', 1515), proposed the use of contemporary vernacular Florentine.

Bembo's proposal, for a language that responded to the needs of an aristocratic culture separated from daily life and founded on the cult of the past, prevailed. To take inspiration from a language of two centuries earlier meant choosing the separation of a written from a spoken language, a classicism reserved for the elite: a limitation of language creativity, reduced to imitating a fixed norm, anachronistic and ahistorical. By the mid-sixteenth century, high literature throughout Italy was unified through classicist language, while the decisions taken at the Council of Trent regarding the exclusion of the use of vernacular in the liturgy (1513) was another example of language distancing the elites from the lives of ordinary people.

In prose, the link with Boccaccio's language was less rigid, though the use of a language that was continually being superseded served to remove literature from accessibility to the general public and turned it into rhetoric, often unable to express the immediacy of life. Only in the nineteenth century did the 'language question' start to find appropriate answers. The inadequacy of the language 'solution' in the sixteenth century was evident from the emergence of a new language alongside that of culture: a literary language that exalted the grotesque, the realistic and comic, the expressionistic. The anti-classicist revolt took shape around Teofilo Folengo (1491–1544). In his mock-heroic poem *Baldus*, an Italian dialect lexicon is grafted on to a Latin morphological–grammatical and metrical structure. At the same time, in Venice, the comedies of Angelo Beloco (1496–1542), nicknamed Ruzante, became very

---

Box 4.2   The *Index of Forbidden Books*

In 1559, the Roman Church, confronting the huge production of books in Lutheran Germany (around 180,000 books during the sixteenth century) and fearing their diffusion in Italy, published the first *Index of Forbidden Books*, under Pope Paul IV. The main casualty was the Bible: all translations in the vernacular and in Latin were censored, apart from St Jerome's *Vulgata*. The first Italian translation of the Bible appeared in 1848, at the time of Mazzini's Roman Republic. Almost all printed works were prohibited to the public, among them Dante's *De monarchia*, Boccaccio's *Decameron*, the writings of Machiavelli and Erasmus, as well as almost all Greek and Latin classics. In 1571, the Congregation of the Index was created to control publishing activity and to keep the catalogue of forbidden books updated. Books that appeared on the Index were burned, and their authors and publishers subject to trial.

---

popular. Their protagonist was generally a poor peasant who lived an upside-down reality compared to 'official' reality. The peasant only understood a vital reality linked to the material needs of existence, food and sex, and his language was a dialect from Padua. Through these authors, the most realistic expressions of Italian literature took revenge on the language and concerns of the elite.

During the Renaissance, tensions originated by the dualism caused by the physical presence and control of the Roman Church over society were expressed, in particular in the centre of humanism, Florence, at the court of the Medici. On the one hand, humanist and poet Angelo Ambrogini (1454–94), known as Poliziano, was hedonistically exalting a love for earthly life and encouraging all to enjoy it. On the other hand, the Dominican priest and popular preacher Savonarola insisted that life ought to be lived in preparation for a 'good end'. For the humanists, time had an earthly duration which should be exploited in order to improve human life, while for the faithful, still bound to the medieval mentality, time spent on earth served as a preparation for the afterlife. The devastating plague of the mid-fourteenth century, together with recurrent epidemics, had strengthened the mendicant orders and spread their written expositions of the art of dying well. Lorenzo the Magnificent, a shrewd politician, expressed both tendencies: he wrote religious *laudi* as well as carnival songs.

The most illustrious victim of the climate of Counter-Reformation was Torquato Tasso (1544–95), author of an epic narrative of the final phase of the first Crusade, *Gerusalemme Liberata* (1575), who, concerned to find himself outside Catholic orthodoxy, sent his poem to theologians and denounced himself to the Bologna Inquisition; in 1577, he submitted his poem to the Ferrara Inquisition, which absolved it. However, oppressed by a sense of guilt, he accepted all requests for revision and cut out important parts of the poem in a self-destructive rage. He worked for the Este family (which ruled Ferrara from the thirteenth century), a difficult environment, given their historic practice of not challenging the Papacy. Tasso eventually spent seven years in a mental asylum, while his poem was published without his approval and enjoyed great success. In 1592, he radically rewrote the poem and retitled it *Gerusalemme Conquistata*, a work that critics consider to be infinitely inferior to the earlier version. Tasso's drama is perhaps the best-known example of the climate of censorship that the Counter-Reformation imposed on intellectuals.

SELECTED FURTHER READING

Recommended introductions are D. Hay and J. Law, *Italy in the Age of the Renaissance, 1380–1530* (London: Longman, 1989), C. Black, *Early Modern Italy. A Social History* (London: Routledge, 2001) and P. Burke, *The Italian Renaissance: Culture and Society in Italy* (London: Polity, 1999). H. Baron, *The Crisis of the Early Italian Renaissance: Civic Humanism and Republican Liberty in an Age of Classicism and Tyranny* (Princeton, NJ: Princeton University Press, 1966) is an essential examination of classicism and civic humanism in Renaissance thought, and this should be followed by C. Celenza, *The Lost Italian Renaissance: Humanists, Historians, and Latin Legacy* (Baltimore, Md.: Johns Hopkins University Press, 2004). O. Niccoli, *Prophecy and People in Renaissance Italy* (Princeton, NJ, Princeton University Press: 1990) is a thought-provoking and highly readable study of popular culture during the traumatic age of foreign invasions.

5

Under Popes and Distant Kings: Italy in the Age of the Baroque

CHRONOLOGY

ITALIAN POLITICS IN THE SEVENTEENTH AND EIGHTEENTH CENTURIES

While reflecting on the age that followed the Counter-Reformation, the early-twentieth-century historian, Benedetto Croce, observed that, while Italy's rejection of Protestantism had kept the country in one sense united, it had done so at the price of a kind of cultural hibernation, cut off from the movement of ideas that spread across the rest of Europe, because of the domination of the Papacy and Spain. Italy, he claimed, 'was resting, tired; and it is a beautiful and wishful metaphor, to say that she was not completely finished and dead'. These views were typical of a historiography that saw the seventeenth century and the first half of the eighteenth century as a period of decline between two glorious ages – the Renaissance and the Risorgimento. This was a reading influenced by nineteenth-century nationalism, which hoped that the Risorgimento marked a break with an era considered hostile to the 'modern age', in which Italy was disunited and subject to the will of foreign powers. This chapter explores the common threads of Italy's culture and society in the period between the Counter-Reformation and the Enlightenment, a long period which left important legacies for modern Italy, in terms of social discipline (as a result of the Council of Trent), of scientific discoveries, and of achievements in art, architecture, music and literature. As John Marino has remarked, while the French and Spanish invasions conquered Italy politically, Italy continued to export its culture to France and Spain, as well as to the rest of early modern Europe.

From 1618, Europe was shaken by the Thirty Years' War, caused by the French–Habsburg confrontation over pre-eminence in Europe. The Italian states were affected indirectly, mainly in the economic field; the Venetian republic in particular suffered disruption of some of its northern markets (mainly in textiles, glass and luxury goods). The worst moment came in 1627, when Duke Vincent II Gonzaga of Mantua died leaving no heirs. This precipitated a crisis of succession (the Duchy interested the Habsburgs, the French and Piedmontese alike), which led to war and the sack of the city by the imperial army in 1630. Mantua and the Monferrat were fiefs of the Empire, but were claimed by Vincent II's nearest male relative, the French Duke of Nevers. After a period of war between France and Spain, the Duchy of Milan had become the first *signoria* to be subject to a foreign power – and it remained under Spanish control for 170 years, from 1535. When the Mantuan crisis occurred, the Spanish governor of Milan warned Madrid about the threat a French domination of Mantua would bring to the Spanish position in Italy. This led to a direct confrontation on Italian territory, when, in 1629, Louis XIII's army crossed the Alps and defeated Charles Emmanuel of Savoy. In 1630, the French and the Spanish negotiated a truce and confirmed Charles Nevers as Duke of Mantua. The war was devastating for parts of northern Italy, and coincided with an epidemic of the plague. As the Thirty Years' War continued, the Spanish increased taxation in Naples to support and sustain Milan, provoking moments of high social tension in the city. After the end of the war, Italy experienced a period of relative political peace for the rest of the century, though it was one also marked by economic stagnation until around 1680. Culturally, there was still artistic vitality, particularly with the boom in Italian Baroque architecture in Piedmont, Rome, Campania, Apulia and Sicily.

Political turmoil returned at the beginning of the new century with the Spanish succession crisis of 1700, sparked when Charles II died with no direct heirs. The fate of Naples, Sicily, Lombardy and Sardinia was therefore at stake, until the peace of Utrecht in 1713 left the Austrian Habsburgs in control of Naples and Lombardy, and the House of Savoy in control of Sicily. This arrangement lasted only a few years, until 1720 when, for geographical convenience, an exchange assigned Sardinia to the House of Savoy, and Sicily, reunited with Naples, to Austria. This changed again in 1735, after a war over the Polish succession, when Austria ceded Naples and Sicily to a Spanish Bourbon. The regular succession crises of this period were clearly destabilizing for Italian states. However, while Italy was still politically divided, a specific Italian culture continued to develop, particularly through the production of new literary, artistic and musical forms, which kept alive a sense of identity and geographical integrity. As Chapter 6 will illustrate, the Enlightenment and the impact of the French Revolution together provided the foundation for a movement towards Italian independence, but in the seventeenth and eighteenth centuries Italian states were still a long way from devising solutions for political unification.

During this period, the *Serenissima* ('Most Serene') Republic of Venice was menaced increasingly by international encirclement, not only from the Adriatic but also from the mainland, where the Habsburg Empire expanded to Venice's western, eastern and northern borders. Military expenditure and arms production increased – the latter concentrated mainly at the Venice Arsenal and in Brescia, the republic's armaments capital. Moreover, Venice's relations with its Italian neighbour, the Church, were strained. Venetian aristocrats criticized Papal nepotism and opulence, Venice did not accept the Papal Inquisition, and the University of Padua recruited Protestant students. When Pope Paul V imposed an interdict on the republic, hoping to incite the clergy to rebel against its rulers, Venice expelled the Jesuits and imprisoned clerics who sided with the Pope. The Venetian monk and theologian Paolo Sarpi (1552–1623) wrote a pamphlet in favour of limiting Church power to the spiritual sphere and advocated the birth of national churches along the lines of the Anglican Church in England under Henry VIII. During the war for the succession of Mantua in 1627–30, Venice came close to entering the war on the side of France and Piedmont against Spain and Austria, but the Venetian senate preferred to remain defensive. The republic's only Italian military adventure was its participation, along with Parma, Tuscany and Modena, in an anti-Papal league in 1642, which resulted in the Pope's devastation of the Polesine (the countryside of lower Venetia on the Po Valley), and demonstrated that there was little to be gained from war. Despite continued conflict with the Ottoman Empire between 1645 and 1718 reducing its overseas territory to the island of Corfu and the Dalmatian coast, in 1700, Venice was still the most dynamic port in the Mediterranean; only later in the eighteenth century was it overtaken by Marseilles. At the time Napoleon Bonaparte invaded Venice in 1796, however, the city chose to offer no resistance – by this stage war was no longer considered an option. During the seventeenth and eighteenth centuries, Venice continued to invest in prestigious buildings – palaces, churches, hospitals and mainland villas – which helped to produce a new source of wealth: tourism. Like Rome, Venice was visited by European aristocrats who wished to improve their education and artistic taste. By the mid-eighteenth century, about 30,000 of the city's 140,000 inhabitants were foreigners, many of them English, which made Venice a cosmopolitan cultural centre.

At the opposite end of the peninsula, the southern regions were particularly affected by dynastic changes, which saw Sicily initially under the French Philip V, then the Piedmontese Victor Amedeo II, followed by the Austrian Charles VI, and the Spanish Charles III; this constant change caused the Sicilian nobility to suffer problems of identity, because their traditional links with their Spanish allies were broken. New strategies and alliances had to be created within the new courts to enable the barons to maintain political control over the island. Feudal lords controlled commerce and built castles all over southern Italy. The Spanish regime simply maintained the existing baronial power, but, in order to limit corruption, viceroys tended to employ foreigners.

However, regal powers were limited to command of the army and rule within pre-existing legal systems. In Sicily, unlike the rest of Italy, the King of Spain was also an apostolic delegate, because the Spanish Inquisition had replaced the Roman Inquisition for the investigation of heresy. Sicily had a parliament composed of representatives of the barons, the clergy and the towns, whose duty it was to confirm the king's tax requests. Naples retained the Roman Inquisition after the Spanish Inquisition was rejected following two riots, in 1510 and 1547. Spanish viceroys notwithstanding, the southern mainland was a Papal fief, like Ferrara and Urbino, in which the Church taxed the clergy. As in Naples, Milan under the rule of Spain also rejected the Spanish Inquisition, not through popular riots but because of the governor's advisers: the governor was the representative of Spanish power in Milan, and 40 per cent of his political advisers were from Milan or other Lombard provinces.

The viceroy's position had been weakened in the past because he was always considered a foreigner: the local aristocracy and city representatives, and the parliament in Naples, had the right to petition the king directly and therefore tended to ignore the viceroys. The viceroy who gained the most influence, Pedro Toledo, had done so in part through the 1539 marriage of his daughter Eleonora to Cosimo de Medici, who was Duke of Florence in the years 1537–74. Toledo had therefore increased his power by linking his family with Italian elite families (though this was a mutual affair, with power and prestige also flowing in the opposite direction, as Cosimo was propped up by Spanish power); two of his sons also married members of the Neapolitan aristocracy, which helped to root his power in the local context. Despite these moves, Toledo's power diminished as he ventured further from the capital. The attempts to introduce the Spanish Inquisition, which would have strengthened royal power, failed as a result of aristocratic opposition and popular riots. From the age of Toledo onwards, viceroys learnt well that Spanish rule was limited: they must appease the local nobility and accommodate the Church's interests, as well as watch the lower classes constantly, to guard against revolt. A joint Spanish–Italian Council of Italy was created in Madrid in 1558 to supervise Naples, Sicily and Milan (under Spain from 1535), but in effect Spanish power continued to decrease during the following century.

Unrest in Naples continued throughout the sixteenth and seventeenth centuries, usually provoked by hunger, and illustrative of the city's lack of loyalty towards the Spanish government. Two major events that shook many contemporaries, one at the end of the sixteenth century and the other in the mid-seventeenth century, produced similar problems and displayed similar patterns of popular revenge against centuries of aristocratic repression and violence.

The first occurred in 1585, when a grain shortage provoked hunger riots in Naples. One of the representatives of the people in the Neapolitan parliament, Giovan Vincenzo Starace, the son of a silk merchant, was brought by the mob, sitting backwards on a chair, to the traditional site of popular government in the city at St Augustin, where he was killed. This was simultaneously an example of a leader's reversed status and a parody of execution rituals in which the condemned – usually elements of the lower classes – were paraded through the city. During the march, shops were closed, and the crowd of onlookers insulted Starace and armed themselves. He was eventually lynched by a furious crowd and his corpse was mutilated and dragged through the poorest areas of the city. The urban masses participated in large numbers, included artisans and shopkeepers, and the riot horrified contemporary observers all over Europe. The crowds were only subdued when the viceroy imported grain and sold it cheaply, but a savage and large-scale repression followed: about 800 people were tried, 270 tortured, and 12,000 Neapolitans fled the city. In all, 31 rioters were condemned to death, 430 jailed, 71 sent to ships' galleys and 300 exiled.

A second revolt took place in 1647, when a new tax on flour and fruit caused the poorer areas of Naples to riot, under the leadership of a young fish-seller from Amalfi, Tommaso Aniello, known as Masaniello. Crowds occupied the royal palace, forcing the Viceroy to retreat to Castel Nuovo, which was placed under siege. As in the previous century, artisans and shopkeepers joined the revolt and the houses of rich government officials, nobles, tax farmers and creditors were attacked by the hungry multitude. The aristocrats hired bandits to kill Masaniello, but the attempt failed and further infuriated the masses: bandits and aristocrats alike were killed, and more palaces were attacked. The Viceroy had no choice but to abolish the new taxes and grant the people more power within the city council. By treating with the Viceroy, Masaniello lost popular support, he was killed and his corpse dragged around the city in a similar gruesome ritual to the one Starace had suffered. Tommaso Astarita has shown that other rituals were evident in the riots: goods from sacked palaces were distributed to the poor, and parts cut from the bodies of dead aristocrats were put on display. Once the government imposed its rule again, it increased the price of bread once more, and Masaniello's corpse was reassembled and given a saint's funeral, in which he was honoured by hundreds of people.

In January 1648, the Spanish government promised an amnesty to rebels and a tax reduction but, as anti-feudal rebellion spread into the countryside, it sent a fleet to bombard the city, while the aristocrats began a ferocious repression in the provinces, hiring bandits to kill rebels and peasants; as the government gradually took control of the situation, rebel leaders were executed. While food riots and rebellions were endemic in early modern Europe, these events illustrated the relatively weak control the Spanish had over southern Italy; the viceroys were powerless against angry mobs, though the monarchy could always send troops to crush revolts. Masaniello remained a romantic hero in European public memory, and characters based on him appeared in operas and paintings during the following two centuries.

In 1647, a similar revolt broke out in Palermo over the rising price of bread, and then spread to other cities and towns. The popular cry against taxes and bad government (*fora gabelle e malo governo*) was evidence of the centrality of the taxation issue at the time, but like the Masaniello rebellion in Naples it was also a political revolt against the municipal aristocratic form of government. Once again, the Sicilian aristocracy's loyalty to the Spanish government facilitated the violent restoration of power. It was not just a shortage of food that created revolt. Indeed, the principal attitude towards famine in the seventeenth century was one of expiation and deference to God's will: famine was seen as a divine punishment for people's sins, and a food crisis normally produced orderly religious processions rather than protests. For example, the Palermo revolt began early in May 1647, with the people walking backwards while praying in the streets of the city asking God for rain to save the harvest. Sensibility towards moral lapses increased during a time of famine, when sinners were invited to confess as an act of redemption. Instead of disturbing the traditional order, famine at first reinforced it. It was only when the viceroys and the public administration increased the price of bread even after the coming of the rain that devotion turned to anger, and bread replaced the images of saints on the spears carried in processions. Revolts occurred whenever political divisions and antagonisms combined with popular hardships that had been provoked by food shortages and economic pressures. In the case of the Sicilian revolt of 1647, the result was the condemnation of government policies coupled with a loss of popular identification with the fortunes of the Catholic monarchy.

The two centuries of the viceroys were characterized by high taxation, foreign domination, popular revolts, and famines. They also witnessed regular natural catastrophes – earthquakes, eruptions of Vesuvius, and epidemics. There were also, however, important cultural achievements in philosophy, such as the work of Giambattista Vico (born in 1668) and Pietro Giannone (born 1676 in Puglia), and in literature, with the work of the Neapolitan Giambattista Marino (1569–1625), whose poetry also influenced Baroque music. Naples in particular was one of Italy's cultural capitals in the seventeenth and eighteenth centuries; it was the only large port in the southern kingdom, it boasted the only university and was the site of most of the banking facilities to meet the financial needs of the kingdom's elite. Many Italian communities lived there: Genoese, Florentine, Venetian and Milanese. By the seventeenth century, Naples had become an exporter of *maccheroni*. One Neapolitan obsession was gambling, which provided the government with revenue, so the viceroys' few attempts to suppress it were resisted successfully. When, in the eighteenth century, illegal gambling houses began to prosper, gambling became linked with urban organized crime – subsequently named the *camorra* – though, in general, life in Naples was no more dangerous than in any other large European city of the time.

The high quality of the work of the many painters who lived in Naples made the city the only one in Italy truly comparable to Rome in terms of the number and quality of its artists. New churches, private palaces, convents and cloisters appeared in the city throughout the two centuries of viceroyal rule. The urban planning of Naples changed with the building of the most important city artery by Viceroy Toledo, which still bears his name. However, the real masterpiece of viceroyal architecture was the royal palace created by architect Domenico Fontana, which in 1600 replaced the old palace.

The Austrian viceroys in the first half of the eighteenth century sought to import reform and to reorganize the Sicilian economy, improving transport safety and fighting banditry in the countryside. However, Austrian weakness during Habsburg involvement in the Polish war of succession increased the Empire's financial requirements from the island, making the Habsburgs dependent on the local elite. The latter was thus able to regain control, in exchange for its financial support, and to block reform that was deemed harmful to the rulers' secular privileges.

In the Papal States, strong city identities developed in the Marche and Umbria, though no individual city prevailed over the others, which made it difficult for the Popes to control the area whenever anti-Papal revolts occurred. From 1598, following the end of the Este dynasty, the area around Ferrara came under Papal control; there, as in Bologna and Romagna, the Pope was represented by a legate, a cardinal who ran the provinces on behalf of the Pope, and the areas were known as the Legacies. The legate controlled the clergy, the administration of justice, and the investigation of heresy through arrest, capture and execution.

The major political problem in the Papal States was the maintenance of Papal control over the nobles in the neighbouring provinces, who used banditry to retain and expand their territorial control. Papal justice often used exile as a punishment to deal with this phenomenon, but banditry continued to flourish. The local clergy often coexisted with banditry, and sometimes even favoured it.

THE POST-TRIDENTINE SOCIAL WORLD

Population growth in Italy continued in the eighteenth century (reaching 18 million in 1800), but at a much lower pace than in other European countries, indicating a relative decline. However, Italy continued to be Europe's most urbanized country, with the greatest number of cities and the highest density of population. By 1770, Turin had 82,000 inhabitants; Milan recovered from the devastating plague of 1630, which had halved its population, claimed 126,000 inhabitants by the end of the seventeenth century, and became a cosmopolitan and intellectual centre in Europe, under Austrian control from 1715.

The urbanization of the nobility continued to distinguish Italy from northern Europe. City aristocracies were constituted from bankers, military nobles and bureaucrats, all of whom possessed land. Land brought prestige, economic stability and the dependency of the peasants who lived in the surrounding countryside and worked for them. As Christopher Black has shown, there was extensive mobility between city and countryside in the early modern period, which often involved travelling long distances throughout the peninsula. Ambassadors moved from city to city; and shepherds travelled to different parts of the country across mountain ranges. Wealthy women moved for matrimonial reasons; and the poor relocated from the countryside to the cities for work as servants or prostitutes. Seasonal workers journeyed according to the harvest; state officials went to collect taxes or rent money within state boundaries, or to administer justice; merchants, patrons and artists or musicians travelled the whole country; and members of any state could be sentenced to temporary exile in another state. Baroque and pastoral literature and music frequently idealized the urban image of the rural world, and the concept of the villa in the country continued to expand its appeal. Commerce was constantly connecting cities with countryside, and mills in particular were a common point of contact between peasants and townspeople, with the miller often serving as a communicator of urban culture and new ideas – as in the case of the Friulian miller Menocchio (studied by Carlo Ginzburg), who questioned religious orthodoxy in the Venetian republic.

In urban society, many were employed as servants – an occupation for both males and females; people generally worked as servants while they were young (as teenagers or in their early twenties). Prostitution was an important and recognized aspect of Italian city life. While at times (particularly in the case of epidemics), lay and religious authorities viewed it more strictly, as long as it did not create a public scandal it was usually tolerated; in some cities, prostitutes were confined to specific districts; for example in Venice near the Rialto Bridge, or in Florence around the Mercato Vecchio. Elite prostitutes enjoyed good lifestyles, were educated, dressed elegantly and posed nude for important painters. At the lower levels, prostitutes also provided other, non-sexual, services: they practised magic and were consulted for spells to bind loved ones or defeat love rivals. Their magic, like that of witches, included the treatment of illnesses or the recovery of lost fortunes.

From the second half of the sixteenth century in both northern and southern Italy, women's lives were influenced, particularly at the level of the aristocracy, by the fact that aristocratic families adopted an increasingly marked patrilinear structure, characterized by male primogeniture, excluding daughters and younger sons from inheritance. Marriage was therefore only encouraged for the eldest son, while the others had to remain celibate and choose a military or ecclesiastical career. This reduced the collateral lines of elite families and resulted, in the long term, in a demographic decline of the aristocracy. Control over the family as a constituent cell of society led religious authorities to try to discipline behaviour and any transgression that violated the model imposed by the Council of Trent. Indeed, as a part of the wider attempt to reassert the Church's power over European society, the Council also took decisions that were to affect aspects of domestic life. As the sacred aspect of marriage had been declared, polygamy became a crime punishable by the Inquisition. Those who ignored the sacred aspect of marriage were treated as heretics: men could be condemned to between five and ten years in the *galea* (ships' galleys), and women sent to prison. As Irene Fosi has demonstrated, family morality could be policed with the help of neighbours and relatives:

Domestic walls were not impenetrable. The eyes and ears of neighbours were ready to detect gestures, noises, shouting: the home and its rooms formed an indivisible unity with the street, nullifying any distinction between public and private.

However, there were exceptions in the indissolubility of marriage, as separations were allowed in the case, for example, of adultery or extreme cruelty. The Tridentine Council established that marital disputes had to be brought before the ecclesiastical court. As Joanne Ferraro has demonstrated in research on the Venetian case, much reluctance remained with regard to the observation of the new rules, which frequently clashed with individual desire. Women who had been forced into marriage when very young, for example, later used Tridentine definitions of marriage to prove that their unions were not valid.

Painting reflected the changes in society. Following Petrarch's love poems, painters before Titian had portrayed images of gentlemen's lovers which combined love, passion and sexuality outside marriage. The *cortese* adoration of the ideal woman had been replaced by an attempt to bring together love and sexual passion, bridging a separation that had existed throughout the Middle Ages. This process was obstructed by the mid-sixteenth-century Church, which strengthened its control over people's habits, and made it difficult to continue the tradition of love portraits. Only German romanticism at the end of the eighteenth century returned to combining both kinds of love; however, it did so within the revaluation of marriage, something that had largely been ignored by the more innovative idea of free, extra-conjugal, love of the Italian Renaissance. Family and public morality became inextricably linked; family reputation and honour were important resources that required confirmation by an extra-familiar context of social relations. The concept of honour was related to the family mainly with regard to vigilance over female sexuality; in all patrilinear societies it was necessary for children to be legitimate, so that property did not pass to those of different blood from the husband's. Surveillance of women's sexual honour was therefore crucial to safeguard the continuity and strength of the lineage. However, there were many ways of establishing, losing and reconstituting the honour of women, men and families. As Giovanna Fiume's research has shown, forms of compensation existed that meant honour was not always irreparably lost and could be renegotiated. Religious and lay institutions for orphans and abandoned women served to protect them from falling prey to 'dangers of honour'. Such women could create a new reputation and even prepare a dowry that could put them back in the marriage market. The image of the Sicilian woman imprisoned within the walls of the family was also a stereotype that emerged only later. Indeed, as demonstrated by Jane Schneider, only women from rich families could afford not to go to work in the countryside; instead, they stayed at home for long years preparing complicated sets of white embroideries that came to symbolize female sexual purity and economic wealth. For the majority of the female population in both cities and countryside, reality consisted of a combination of housework and agricultural work, child care and various urban jobs such as laundress or maid.

As Guido Ruggiero's research shows, the moralists of the time, even those educated in a humanistic environment, seemed more influenced by Christian values than by contemporary practice. The ruling classes worried about maintaining a public standard of morality to a greater degree than did the common people. Indeed, for the lower classes, honour and shame were elastic and malleable concepts. As elsewhere in the early modern period, the number of illegitimate children in Italy was very high; weddings celebrated after years of cohabitation were commonplace, as was prostitution, which was a common profession, as noted earlier, particularly in cities, for which women had only to register and pay for a licence. Only in the nineteenth century, when the state became stronger, did private behaviour become a matter of public regulation.

A VIOLENT COUNTRY?

By Western European standards, Italy has always had a reputation for being a violent society, a reputation that extended from the time of the Renaissance to the 1970s. In biographies such as Cellini's, violence was constantly present, and later historians, including Burckhardt, confirmed his view of the sixteenth century. There were factors that favoured lawlessness in Italian society, starting with its geography: the presence of many remote mountain areas facilitated escape for bandits and criminals, and central authority was always threatened by the surrounding hilltop baronial fortresses. The high population density of cities made social control very difficult. Male servants with a bad reputation were called *bravi*, and they provided an armed service to landowners and the aristocracy. Generally criminals who escorted the elite and intimidated their enemies, they were particularly brutal in rural areas, where they

---

Box 5.1 Description of the *bravi* in Manzoni's *The Betrothed*

Here is Alessandro Manzoni's description, from the early 1800s, of two *bravi* hired, during the Spanish domination of Milan, by an arrogant nobleman, Don Rodrigo, in order to threaten the priest Don Abbondio and discourage him from celebrating the marriage of two young lovers, Renzo and Lucia, who are workers in the silk industry in a village near Lecco on Lake Como:

> As he turned the corner the priest glanced towards the shrine in his usual way, and saw something that was both unexpected and unwelcome. Opposite each other where the paths flowed, as it were, together, were two men: one of them was astride the low wall, with one leg dangling outwards and the other on the path; his companion was standing leaning against the wall, with his arms crossed on his chest. Their dress and manner, and what the priest from where he was could see of their faces, left no room for doubt as to their profession. On his head each wore a green net hanging over the left shoulder and ending in a large tassel; from this net a heavy lock of hair fell over their foreheads. They had long mustachios curled up at the ends; shining leather belts on which hung a brace of pistols; a small powder-horn dangled like a locket on their chest; the handle of a knife showed from a pocket of their loose, wide breeches; they had rapiers with big, gleaming, furbished hilts of pierced brass, worked in monograms. It was obvious at first glance that they were men of the class known as *bravi*. This class, now quite extinct, was then flourishing in Lombardy, and was already of considerable antiquity.

(Manzoni, 1997)

---

threatened peasants on behalf of the landowners. *Bravi* also settled personal vendettas and at times enjoyed the exciting life of the city, taking part in gambling activities and frequenting brothels.

Banditry was seen as politically strategic in landowner–peasant relations; bandits were much feared but also mythologized. Some bandits were forced to live in hiding most of the time, though they could be pardoned if they helped to capture other dangerous bandits. Some bandits carried out vendettas on behalf of rival families, and were employed indiscriminately as criminals or soldiers – serving in the army or forming part of a criminal band were interchangeable ways of finding employment. This situation existed all over Italy, but was stronger in the south because the viceroys' power was not strong enough to control the local barons who employed bandits.

In a pamphlet on the brigands in Italy, the French writer Stendhal (Marie Henri Beyle) (1783–1842) – who arrived in Milan with Napoleon's army in 1800 and then travelled extensively around the country – noticed that, while in France and every other European country, people who lived by stealing and killing were universally condemned, in Italy they were respected by the public. Italians were, of course, terrified by brigands, but they also felt sympathy for them when they were punished. Short poems narrating the lives of famous brigands were extremely popular, and the public regarded them as heroes, feeling an admiration for them 'very close to the feeling that, in ancient times, the Greeks felt for some of their semi-gods'. Like Manzoni, Stendhal also commented on the *bravi* in Lombardy:

> In 1580, in the heart of Lombardy emerged a very feared corporation of assassins: that of the *bravi*. Many rich lords hired them and used them to satisfy all their fancies, whether caused by hatred, vendetta, or love. The *bravi* performed with an incomparable ability and audacity the most difficult missions: even the authorities feared them. From 1583 the Spanish governor in Milan made vain efforts to destroy such a dangerous corporation: he issued endless edicts, which did not prevent the *bravi* from continuing to be employed. In 1628 their category was particularly flourishing and they had the most daunting reputation for murder and kidnapping.
>
> (Stendhal, 2004)

Brigandage had existed in Italy, as Stendhal affirmed, from time immemorial, but its wide diffusion began in the mid-sixteenth century. Government weakness meant that brigands were often granted impunity, and such an adventurous life fascinated many young people, who longed to escape the tyranny of a feudal lord or the Church authorities. While the whole of Italy was infested by brigands, they were strongest in the Papal States and the Kingdom of Naples. After describing the way the brigands dressed, Stendhal noticed that their equipment was a mixture of the religious and the military: together with weapons they carried images of saints, Jesus, and especially the Virgin Mary, which were considered necessary to save their souls: 'nothing more dreadful than this mixture of cruelty and superstition!'. They believed that dying at the stake, following absolution by a priest, would ensure a place in heaven. Even when killed by the police, these brigands remained heroes in the eyes of the public, who attributed more genius and courage to them than to regular military leaders.

AN AGE OF HUNGER

As Massimo Montanari's research has shown, early modern Europe was an age of hunger, one in which the gap between the patterns of consumption of rich and poor widened. The global enrichment of urban societies, the increasing products offered by an expanding market, and the role of money, all contributed to the concentration of wealth and power, and to extreme levels of misery and deprivation.

The Renaissance had introduced into gastronomy a similar aesthetic attention to that informing etiquette and the arts, from the adornments that accompanied dishes to the convivial scenery, the presentation of food, the gestures that attended service and, as treatises such as the one by Della Casa discussed above, the relationship between eating and manners, from the correct use of cutlery to rules about chewing. This aesthetic attention distinguished elite food consumption. The early-seventeenth-century literary work that most defined the class divide in terms of food was *Bertoldo*, by Giulio Cesare Croce (1550–1609), first published in 1606. Croce was a self-taught blacksmith from Romagna who found great success as a popular writer and a *cantastorie*, accompanying his stories on the violin in village squares and at city festivals – though he had no patrons and eventually died in poverty. The Bertoldo of Croce's work was a peasant who fell ill and was treated by court doctors, who gave him the most sophisticated foods of the time, which were totally unsuited to his coarse stomach. He continued to ask for a pot of beans and onion, the only food he was used to, but to no avail. Having to eat the food of the rich, he died in terrible pain. The book reflects many medical treatises of the time; Giacomo Albini, doctor of the House of Savoy, for example, warned that pain and illness would come to those who did not eat according to their social status. For the peasants, this meant they must continue eating flour products or cereals. Flour became a crucial part of their lives – in the form of bread, *focacce* and polenta. In 1630, Cesare Righettini wrote a 'heroic poem' entitled *La Polenta*, a parody of Ariosto's *Orlando Furioso*, in which the heroic champion

Orlando, after four days of abstinence from food because of his search for Angelica, ate a giant dish of polenta and died.

Consumption was entirely dependent on the results of the harvest, which caused not only nutritional but also psychological imbalances, as anxieties about food became totally ingrained into daily life. Similar literature, with different outcomes from *Bertoldo*, can be found in Spain, where the best literary example was Don Quixote's Sancho Panza, constantly preoccupied with the need to eat, in contrast to the dreamy mental world of Don Quixote, and always eager to take part in banquets whenever his master's adventures gave him the chance. Literary works provide us with knowledge of what the urban middle classes and aristocracy ate in Italy between the sixteenth and eighteenth centuries. Much correspondence throughout this period confirms the use of and praise for vegetables and various types of herbs, an attitude that was typically Mediterranean and bore little comparison with the other side of the Alps.

One of the last examples of the creative era of Renaissance and Baroque gastronomy (subsequently displaced by French supremacy) was a treatise on *L'arte di ben cucinare* ('The art of cooking well') published in 1662 by Bartolomeo Stefani, the main chef at the Gonzaga court. In his writing he described a banquet he organized for the visiting Queen Christine of Sweden, who abdicated and moved to Italy in 1655 after converting to Catholicism. The most prominent part of Stefani's description, besides the dishes, was the amazing architectural scenery of the lunch: a theatrical representation intended to impress the eyes even more than the stomach.

Food was also very important during the feasts in honour of patron saints, especially in a peasant society that suffered from hunger for most of the year. The feast was the moment when dreams of abundance came true, albeit briefly; it was the moment of communal sharing of food in a mood of solidarity. The preparation and distribution of food were central aspects of this collective activity, and many typical products and recipes of Italian cuisine originated in the festive cycle linked with recurrent patronal celebrations. The succession of saints' days therefore became what Marino Niola has called the sacralization of the economic cycle.

PHILOSOPHY, SCIENCE AND RELIGION

In 1600, after a trial that lasted seven years, the Inquisition had the philosopher Giordano Bruno burned at the stake in Rome. The other

---

Box 5.2   A sixteenth-century Italian gastronomic itinerary

The doctor and writer, Ortensio Lando, wrote a *Commentario delle più notabili e mostrouse cose d'Italia e d'altri luoghi* ('Commentary on the most remarkable and monstrous things of Italy and of other places' – first published in 1548), in which he pretended to recommend to an improbable Aramaic tourist in Italy what and where to eat in each region. He therefore described the typical food and wine of various parts of Italy, making a sort of oeno-gastronomic guide of the country:

> Within one month, if the wind is favourable, you will arrive in the wealthy island of Sicily and you will eat such maccheroni . . . If it is convenient to spend Lent in Taranto, you will become larger than longer, such is the tastiness of fish cooked with oil and vinegar, and with certain fragrant herbs and some flavour of whole nuts, garlic and almonds . . . In Naples you will eat . . . fish, mushrooms . . . almond cakes . . . In Siena you will eat excellent marzipan, exquisite apricots, and tasty *ravagiuoli* [portions of fresh cheese] . . . Not far from Pisa, in a place called Val Caci, you will eat the best and most beautiful ricotta that was ever seen from East to West . . . I do not want to forget to warn you that in Bologna they make the best sausages that were ever eaten . . . If you have a sudden desire to eat a perfect quince jam you must go to Reggio, Mirandola and Correggio, but lucky you if you get to that cheese from Piacenza . . . In Piacenza they also make a dish called *gnocchi* with garlic, which would resuscitate the appetite of a dead man . . . In Padua you will find excellent bread, *berzamino* wine, small pike . . . Should I not tell you about the fish from Chioggia? About the Venetian plaice, gilthead, oyster, scallop and grey mullet? . . . You will find good wine in Friuli and even better in Vicenza, where you will also eat the most perfect baby goat. Shall I not tell you about the large carp of Lake Garda? . . . As you arrive in Brescia I want you to go on my behalf to mister Giovan Battista Luzago . . . and ask him to give you to drink that *vernaccia* wine . . . the Brescians have, apart from the *vernaccia* of Cellatica, superior muscatel . . . As I am sure that you will not return to your beloved fatherland without visiting Genoa, I warn you that they make cakes called *gattafure* . . . Oh the muscatel pears! You will drink such a good muscatel from Tagia that if I drowned in a barrel of that wine I would feel like dying the happiest death.

important philosopher of that time, Tommaso Campanella (1568–1639), was tried and imprisoned many times (the longest term being between 1599 and 1626) accused of being a heretic, but managed to escape the death penalty by pretending to be mad and enduring torture. After publishing the *Apologia pro Galileo* and the political utopian work *Sun City*, he was arrested again, but persuaded the judges of his faith and subsequently fled to France. Another example was that of Galileo Galilei from Pisa (1564–1642), forced to renounce his scientific discoveries because they conflicted with Aristotelian physics and with the Papal beliefs supported by the Jesuits.

The habit of living with a dual truth and a dual morality, the tendency towards pretence and the need to mask one's deepest ideas and feelings were theorized by Torquato Accetto in the treatise *Della dissimulazione onesta* ('On honest dissimulation', 1641): 'I carry the mask, but only because I have no choice, because no one can live in Italy without it.' He praised the cautious life, which, according to him, 'went well with the soul's purity'; indeed, he argued, 'the rose appears so beautiful because at first sight it conceals that it will be so short-lived'. The difference between philosophers' attitude in Italy and in other countries is evident in John Locke's *Letter Concerning Toleration* (1689), written while he was exiled in Holland after the defeat of the Whig party in England:

> although the magistrate's opinion in religion be sound, and the way that he appoints be truly evangelical, yet if I be not thoroughly persuaded thereof in my own mind, there will be no safety for me in following it. No way whatsoever that I shall walk in against the dictates of my conscience, will ever bring me to the mansions of the blessed.
>
> (Locke, 2003, p. 232)

Like the Roman Church, the Spanish ruling class sought in southern Italy to control the cultural centres that had been created during the Renaissance, closing down academies, and persecuting the southern Italian philosopher-scientists Giordano Bruno, Giambattista Della Porta and Bernardino Telesio; however, rebel intellectuals did emerge, even from monasteries, as the cases of Giordano Bruno and Tommaso Campanella demonstrated. Educated within Catholic culture and religion, these authors had to face not only the drama of persecution, but also internal dilemmas of choosing to operate outside an established tradition.

Bruno was an industrious writer and teacher from Nola in Campania. As a Dominican novice at the Naples seminary, he read forbidden books by Erasmus and Lucretius and, after being summoned to Rome, he escaped to Geneva, where he converted to Calvinism. He moved between France, Germany and England where, in London, he published a book which argued that the universe comprised a number of different worlds all rotating around their own sun, therefore dismissing the Christian theory of the Creation. Homesick for Italy, he returned to Venice in 1591, where the republic charged him with heresy and handed him over to Rome, where he was burned by the Inquisition.

Campanella was born in Stilo, in Calabria, in 1568, of a peasant family. He became a Dominican as his only option to be able to study, and came into contact with Telesio's work. From 1589 he began travelling: he left Calabria and moved to Naples, where he met Della Porta and became interested in the scientific study of magic. In 1591, he published the *Philosophia sensibus demonstrata* ('Philosophy of the senses demonstrated'), clearly influenced by Telesio, and the following year was summoned by the Dominican Order, which ordered that he abandon his ideas and return immediately to Calabria. He disobeyed and moved to Florence, then to Bologna, where the Inquisition confiscated all his manuscripts, and on to Padua, where he wrote various works. In 1593–4, in a treatise entitled *Della monarchia dei cristiani* ('On the monarchy of the Christians'), he expressed his fundamental political conception: the unification of all peoples of the world under one common law, which was both civil and religious.

In 1594 he was arrested and tortured for the first time and extradited to Rome, where he shared a prison with Bruno. In 1595, he was forced publicly to renounce his ideas and to live in a monastery on the Aventine Hill, where he wrote an operetta on *Lutherans, Calvinists and other heretics*. Subsequently sent back to Calabria, Campanella organized an anti-clerical, anti-Spanish conspiracy, with the aim of establishing a republic. The conspiracy was discovered and he was arrested and condemned to life imprisonment. In prison in Naples until 1626, Campanella wrote some of his major works, including *Sun City* (1602). He was then transferred to the Roman prisons of the Inquisition and liberated on the personal decision of Pope Urban VIII, who hoped to use him in the supervision of the Inquisition. But Campanella intervened in 1633 in Galileo's Inquisition trial in favour of the scientist and was therefore forced to flee to France, where he died in 1639.

Sun City is the idealized programme of the failed Calabrian insurrection. It appears that the literary stimulus for the work came from Diodoro Siculo, who, in the second book of his *Histories*, told a merchant about the habits of the inhabitants of an island in the Indian Ocean. The chief of the City of the Sun was both a religious and a civil leader, helped by three princes, Pon, Sin and Mor, symbolizing *Potenza* (power), *Sapienza* (knowledge) and *Amore* (love). The first of these princes oversaw military affairs, the second had charge of the liberal and mechanical arts (governing with as many officials as there were sciences), and the third was responsible for human development, education, medicine, feeding and clothing. The basis of life in the City of the Sun was the communal nature of property, including women. Education began at three years of age and there were no class distinctions. Children were brought up by the whole community and the lack of personal interest that resulted from dedication to every art meant that there was no crime. *Sun City* is in the form of a dialogue, in which an Hospitaller (a knight of the order of the Hospitallers at St John in Jerusalem) asks questions of a Genoese boatswain in the service of Christopher Columbus. One of the questions was: 'Are the inhabitants of the City of the Sun Christians?', to which the boatswain answers that they only followed the law of nature, which brought them close to Christianity. Christian religion could be defined as the law of nature plus the sacraments: by bringing it back to its natural state, it would become 'mistress of the world'. As Eugenio Garin has explained, political reform and religious renovation were very closely linked, and this is why Campanella was strongly opposed to Machiavelli and his 'reason of state'. While Machiavelli wanted to distinguish state and religious power from each other, for Campanella the two remained strictly intertwined. Both the religious aspect and Campanella's social demands must be understood within the historical context in which he lived: his City of the Sun reflected the widespread misery among the population of southern Italy; the desire for an egalitarian and communal society being derived from the unbearable conditions imposed by the feudal society in which the Catholic Church was an instrument of power.

Counter-Reformation Italy was in part an anti-clerical country, full of atheists who were lively intellectuals and prolific writers. Academies, which were to expand rapidly in the eighteenth century, were, according to Hanlon, the 'breeding ground for atheism', but atheism was also a feature among the common people: village disbelievers such as Menocchio, the miller described by Carlo Ginzburg, whose research has demonstrated how the orthodox views imposed by the Inquisition were challenged not only by forbidden literature but also by a rich traditional popular culture that had existed for centuries. The fact that most Italians in the early modern period were illiterate does not mean that they had no culture. As shown by Ginzburg's example of Menocchio, literary and traditional oral cultures were mixed. Also, peasant oral culture was transmitted by popular writers and sung in villages by the *cantastorie*, while the majority of the working urban population had a basic knowledge of reading and writing for practical purposes. Taken together, this culture facilitated the spread of unorthodox ideas.

By the late sixteenth century, the problem of controlling knowledge had become particularly pressing, and the Inquisition more active in prosecuting heresies concerning the interpretation of the natural world, including mathematics. Initially regarded as inferior to philosophy, it was taught increasingly at Italian universities, principally in Padua, where the first European observatory was built, housing a huge telescope. The same university became the leading European academy for medicine, through the study of the work of Galen of Pergamum: specialist chairs were created in surgery, anatomy, paediatrics and geriatrics. These advances led to Catholic orthodox beliefs being questioned increasingly. One of the teachers at Padua University was, from 1592, the Florentine mathematician Galileo Galilei, who developed the world's most powerful telescope in the first decade of the new century, and which he donated to the Republic of Venice. After this, Galileo moved to Florence, where he was offered a highly paid job as mathematician and philosopher at the court of Grand Duke Cosimo II. In 1614, he declared that religious and scientific truths should be separated, a theory contrary to Catholic belief, which brought him into conflict with the Inquisition. The latter put him on trial and placed Nicolaus Copernicus's work on the Index. Absolved at the trial, Galileo persevered and published a pro-Copernican pamphlet, the *Dialogues on Two World Systems*, in 1632. Pope Urban VIII summoned him to Rome and, despite Galileo's work being in translation and having a wide influence abroad, he was held by the Inquisition in a palace in Tuscany. He retained many disciples in Italy, especially among scientists who continued to experiment with the telescope, tasks made easier by the fact that Italian workshops crafted the world's finest glass lenses. Nevertheless, the condemnation of Galileo warned Italian scientists to be careful and not to reveal their true beliefs; most scientists in Italy until the eighteenth century were Jesuits (the Company of Jesus had been founded in 1534 by the Spaniard Ignatius of Loyola), and Galileo's work remained on the Index until the 1740s. The heliocentric view of the universe was not accepted by the Catholic Church until 1822. However, Galileo's legacy was not erased by the

Inquisition, and persisted in the work of advocates of Copernicanism, who continued to use the telescope – some of them were Jesuits, such as the German astronomer, Christopher Clavius. Indeed, many Catholic scholars had begun to question the Ptolemaic system and did not expect such a strong intervention from the Church. As Paula Findlen has remarked, observational astronomy continued to advance in Italy. Though many scholars continued to write in Latin, scientific works appeared increasingly in Italian (most of Galileo's works had been accessible to anyone literate, as they were in Tuscan), broadening the interest of society in scientific discoveries.

CLERGY, SAINTS AND MAGIC

As Gregory Hanlon has remarked, Italian cities were 'arsenals filled with relics accumulated over centuries'. Italy was also crammed with dioceses, each of which had a bishop: in 1600 they numbered 315, compared with 130 in France – a much larger and more populous country. Bishops were selected by the Pope, with the exception of Sicily, where that privilege lay with the Spanish king. Bishops confirmed children, consecrated new churches, ordained the clergy and reported suspicions of heresy to the Papacy. They could also grant licences and dispensations – for example, to married people who wanted to separate, or to relatives who wanted to get married – and they also had a central role in deciding on new devotions and pilgrimages.

The secular clergy lived among the people, administered the sacraments and, if ordained, were supported by an income that was not subject to state taxation. For this reason, many aristocratic families tended to have one son who was a priest, and placed some of their property in his name: as Hanlon has described, 'obtaining a good benefice was often the point of departure for the social rise of a whole family'. Many of these priests did not respect canonical regulations. However, this did not usually create problems within their local parishes; people tolerated priests' sexual activity as long as this did not create scandal by involving virgins or married women of the community, and as long as they looked after their children, administered the sacraments and did not ask for high donations. When communities denounced members of the clergy to the bishop it was because the priests had offended community morals; for example, by gambling, practising usury, carrying weapons or being involved in magic and carnival activities.

The secular clergy grew in part as a result of the assistance of the Jesuits, who organized schools throughout Italy, the number of which increased from eighteen in 1556 to eighty in 1630 and to 111 in 1700. Numbers of churchmen continued to expand more generally in the late sixteenth and the seventeenth centuries. Around 1625, for example, clergymen made up 12 per cent of the population of Lecce in Apulia. The abundance of clerics contributed to the building of new churches, which made Lecce a centre of Baroque architecture in Italy, developing a very distinctive urban landscape. A northern city, Ferrara in Emilia, with 20,000 inhabitants, contained ninety-six churches and fifty monasteries, convents or other types of religious institution. Religious events, particularly when they involved the transportation of relics, were spectacles to which ordinary citizens contributed by hanging flags and banners at their windows and producing street paintings. People were obsessed with giving pious donations, and with the idea of purgatory.

In contrast to the secular clergy, the regular clergy took vows of chastity, poverty and obedience. They were segregated from the population at the margins of towns and lived according to the *regula* (rule). As mentioned in Chapter 4, during the early modern age female orders experienced the same growth as male orders. By mid-century, noble families suffering economic difficulties placed daughters in convents to avoid the dowry problem. In 1589, the use of grilles in churches was introduced, hiding nuns from all visitors, however close the relationship; nuns were forbidden from keeping servants or pets, and their correspondence was checked by the abbesses. These laws, even if only partially observed in many cases, were resented by nuns of noble birth, who were not used to such strict rules of life and had previously thought of convents as akin to congregations of ladies.

People expected priests to help placate divine anger, believing that they had the capacity to summon supernatural powers. Many rituals were forms of exorcism, protection against evil forces, while others were used to invoke God's help – when, for example, there was a bad harvest, a drought, or there were plagues and natural disasters. People took part in processions, following the priests and carrying images of saints, often barefoot and whipping themselves to show God they were begging for mercy for their sins. Saints interceded between the people and God, and belief in miracles was much stronger at that time than belief in medicine. The most important intercessor continued to be the Virgin Mary, whose shrine in Loreto, near Ancona, became the most famous in Catholic Europe. Loreto is located a few kilometres from the Adriatic coast near

Recanati in the Marche, and contains the most important Marian relic: the walls of the house where the holy family lived in Nazareth and where Mary brought up God's son. The house is contained within a marble edifice constructed by the architect and sculptor Andrea Sansovino (1467–1529) from a design by Bramante. According to legend, the walls flew from Palestine to Loreto, transported by angels, in order to escape Islamic occupation. Having decided to approve this fantastic story, the Roman Church supported Bramante's project for reconstructing the sanctuary, first under Julius II, then under Leo X, who entrusted Sansovino with its completion. Since then, while its fame declined from the eighteenth century, Loreto has remained an essential stop on the pilgrimage to Rome.

The Jesuits looked after the wellbeing of pilgrims between the sixteenth and eighteenth centuries. The *Compagnia di Gesù* (Society of Jesus), officially approved by Pope Paul III's bull *Regimini militantis ecclesiae* of 1540, was one of the most effective instruments of the Church's renovation. In addition to the three traditional vows of poverty, chastity and obedience, the Jesuits established a fourth one of obedience to the Pope's orders, which had to be the willing and total obedience of a lifeless body (*'perinde ac cadaver'*). It was the Jesuits who defended Loreto from the attacks of the Reformation. Not only heretics, but also intellectuals who wanted Church reform believed a more 'moral' and inner religiosity was needed, which would not propagate superstitions based on such irrational miraculous stories. The Jesuits were able to save the pilgrimage to Loreto and indeed to reinforce devotion to the shrine, assisted by the fact that such devotion was shared by thousands of pilgrims and was deeply rooted among the masses. Loreto therefore became a symbol of the Counter-Reformation.

Loreto is not the only Marian shrine in Italy: the country is filled with them – from the twelfth century to the present day, more than one shrine a year has been dedicated to the Madonna. In 1982, there were 1,539 Marian sanctuaries out of a total of 1,763. They can be found all over the peninsula, but are concentrated mainly in the north, the highest number being in Liguria. After the later unification of Italy, Loreto became a key site of national memory and identity, chosen by Catholics as a centre of religious pilgrimage to counter the civil–political pilgrimages of the time (as, for example, that of 1884 at the King's tomb in the Pantheon or, in 1895, the 25th anniversary of the seizure of Rome by the Italian army). Later still, in 1891, Leo XIII conceded full indulgence to those who made the pilgrimage to Loreto. With Mary's help, Italy's Catholics had to fight a new crusade: against atheism and liberalism. Felice Cavallotti, the radical and anti-clerical member of parliament, in a speech to the chamber in the 1870s, called Loreto the 'sacred business of fraud'. The coexistence of civil and religious influences, which underpinned the cult of protector saints, surfaced particularly during the feasts dedicated to them. In 1642, with the note *Pro observatione festorum*, Urban VIII made the celebration of the patron saint an obligatory feast, therefore a day on which work was forbidden. Civil influence over the patronal choices brought about a kind of cohabitation between saints, that, as Niola (2007) has observed, 'made the patronal pantheon in Italian cities particularly crowded, especially during the Baroque age'.

After the Council of Trent, discipline tightened on the practices and representations of sanctity, and the gap widened between Roman central-ization and local patronal practices. The autonomous role of local churches and city governments in the creation of new saints had gradu-ally been reduced from the twelfth century onwards, but it was the process of canonization that principally became centralized during the sixteenth and seventeenth centuries. In an attempt to de-localize saints, the 1630 Papal decree *Pro patronis in posterum eligendis* placed the patronage system under the direct control of the Roman Church; it also established that only previously canonized saints could be chosen as protectors.

One of the most enduring cults from the seventeenth century is that of St Gennaro in Naples; already a feature in the sixteenth century (particu-larly after Gennaro's help had been sought during a plague epidemic in 1527), the cult soared to new heights in 1631, when Gennaro's relics were considered to have rescued the city from a devastating eruption of Vesuvius, by halting the flow of lava. The eruption had already killed over 3,000 Neapolitans when the bishop decided to take Gennaro's head outside the Cathedral, at which point the saint's dried blood became liquid. The miracle has continued to occur almost every year since then, and has become the major saintly event in the city; on the few occasions when the blood failed to flow, it was commonly believed that great evil would be visited on the city. The bleeding of saints' bodies has been a recurrent phenomenon since the Middle Ages and has continued until recent times (with the success of the cult of Padre Pio, an early twenti-eth-century capuchin from Puglia who allegedly developed stigmata on his body and whose devotion has spread, and still persists, all over Italy). Saints could develop stigmata during their lifetime, or could spill fresh blood when dead. A study by Giulio Sodano on the case of Naples in the seventeenth century has explained how the aristocracy sustained the belief in miracles that involved the spilling of blood. In the early modern period, the glory of prestigious families was considered to depend on the nobility of their blood, which had been transmitted down the centuries. Both nobles and saints possessed a virtuous and exceptional blood, the first thanks to their predecessors, and the second as a result of divine intervention.

The belief in saints had much in common with the belief in witches. Many lay people, mostly women, simply imitated priests and learnt how to practise exorcism. With the bull *Coeli et terrae* of 1586, Sixtus V unleashed the harshest attack ever against magic and astrology, both of which became heresies and were no longer tolerated. The main victims were the thousands of women accused of being witches, who were brought to Inquisition tribunals. However, the job of a witch was not dissimilar to that of a priest: they cured illnesses, and used amulets and images, including those of saints and crosses. This could be one reason why Italy, where magic proliferated more than in other European country, did not witness the same level of furious and bloody repression of witches experienced on the other side of the Alps. The Italian Inquisition was not as worried by female magic as by the new male interest in science; indeed, magic persisted well into the modern age. Research carried out by the Neapolitan anthropologist Ernesto De Martino (1908–65) illustrates the continuation of such beliefs into the twentieth century.

While the Spanish Inquisition helped Spain to create a nation of Spaniards by repressing Muslims and Jews, the same was not possible in Italy, which had no centralized state. Nevertheless, Popes decreed that Jews had to live in ghettos created in Italian cities. The Roman Inquisition, while responsible for executing about 300 people, did not reach the murderous levels achieved by the Spanish Inquisition; instead, it focused increasingly on the repression of thought, using the Index and creating a climate of fear that any unorthodox behaviour could be reported to Rome.

ART, ARCHITECTURE, LITERATURE AND MUSIC IN THE BAROQUE AGE

The use of painting by noble families to display their status continued from the Renaissance into the Baroque period. However, a fundamental novelty was introduced by a young Lombard artist, Michelangelo Merisi (1573–1609), known as Caravaggio after the name of his town near Bergamo, who began painting the common people: card-sharps, soldiers, fortune-tellers and lute-players. This underworld appeared even in his paintings of sacred subjects, which often shocked his contemporaries. Caravaggio moved between Lombardy, Rome, Naples and Messina. Between 1597 and 1602 he worked in Rome in the Church of S. Luigi dei Francesi, producing some of his most beautiful works: *St Matthew and the Angel*, the *Vocation of St Matthew*, and the *Martyrdom of St Matthew*. He knew the life of the lower classes and had a tormented life himself, constantly tangling with the law because of violent quarrels and unorthodox habits. After being wounded in a fight on his way to Rome, he caught malaria and died near Porto Ercole in Tuscany in 1610, at only 37 years of age. He hated Mannerist art, its allegories and conventional forms. His realism was based on the Brescian Renaissance painters Girolamo Savoldo (1480–1548), Girolamo Romanino (1484–1562), Alessandro Bonvicino, known as Moretto (1498–1554), and on Leonardo and the early-sixteenth-century Venetian painters. His choice of disreputable and ambiguous models to represent the apostles brought religious art down to a more human level.

His revolutionary innovation, one of the most important in Italian painting, was the invention of *chiaroscuro*: the use of shadow by casting light only on the most dramatic part of the painting. Caravaggio's studies of light took advantage of the scientific discoveries of his time, a time when the work of the scientist and the artist were closer than in previous periods. He created a sort of *camera obscura* in his studio, as described by a 1620 biographer:

> A unified light which came from above without reflection, as might happen in a room with the walls painted black; in this way lights and shadows would be very bright and very dark, and they would have a non-natural impact on painting, something which was never realised or thought of by any painter in any previous century.

> (Parronchi, 2002)

The contribution of the Neapolitan scientist Della Porta was especially important for Caravaggio. Della Porta wrote a treatise on optics entitled *De refractione* (1593) after the invention of binoculars, which publicized the *camera obscura* beyond its use in optical laboratories. During the eighteenth century, painting was also given new vigour with the work of artists from Venice: Francesco Guardi, Antonio Canale (known as Canaletto), and Giambattista Tiepolo whose mythological and historical paintings decorated palaces in northern Italy and Spain.

As was the case during the Renaissance, in the Baroque era Italian cities were the location for processions and festivities, and the importance of building façades continued to increase. The key word was 'rhetoric': the art of persuasion through images that were subordinate to the aims of orthodoxy and absolutism. The corresponding Baroque musical style was that of sensual and spectacular melodrama, which contrasted with the more classical experiences of the theatre (comedy and tragedy) in other parts of Europe. Baroque art dominated from the early seventeenth to the mid-eighteenth centuries and represented a resurgence of previously less productive regions of Italy, particularly Piedmont and Sicily.

New architecture was also prompted by population growth. Early in the seventeenth century, Rome had 100,000 inhabitants. The problem of overpopulation (and the consequent spread of epidemics) was confronted by undertaking public works in the areas just outside the city centre. Already by the end of the sixteenth century, Pope Sixtus V and his chief architect Domenico Fontana had begun to enlarge the city by creating around 10 kilometres of new roads furnished with aqueducts and fountains. Citizens were encouraged to build houses with the offer of tax relief, and rich villas with gardens began to appear at the edges of these areas.

Rome was also expanding because of increases in the number of pious tourists during the Counter-Reformation period. At every jubilee (every twenty-five years) hundreds of thousands of visitors flocked to the city (reaching a total of 700,000 in 1650). In the interest of maintaining such an inflow, the Papacy spent money on the creation of new monuments, thus diverting attention from the needs of Rome's citizens to the beautification of the capital. Italian architecture's main concern, as before, was to create a *bella figura*, and religious orders, aristocrats and cardinals all contributed. To a greater extent than previously, Italian Catholicism in this period rejected the evangelical and reform model of unadorned churches. Over-decorated buildings were to reflect God's splendour and to fix Counter-Reformation precepts in peoples' minds. Papal tombs became monuments rich with ornament and portraying stories of saints and martyrs – symbols of a militant optimism that accompanied the spectacular style of the Baroque period. Ceiling painting became very fashionable in aristocratic palaces, depicting triumphal

allegories drawn from classical and mythological examples that celebrated the glory of famous families. This fashion extended from palaces
to churches.

Roman Baroque architecture was spearheaded by three artists: the
Neapolitan painter Pietro da Cortona (1596–1669), the Lombard architect Francesco Borromini (1599–1667), and the Tuscan architect and
sculptor Gian Lorenzo Bernini (1598–1680). The 'artistic director' of
Baroque Rome was Bernini, the designer of the colonnade of St Peter's
Square, which made it possible for the Pope to receive 100,000 pilgrims
at a time. Bernini sculpted theatrical scenes on to fountains such as the
Triton and the 'fountain of the rivers' in Piazza Navona. On the latter, a
large obelisk has at its base a rock inhabited by river gods, all huge
statues in complex poses. Other major architectural achievements were
the Villa Borghese, an opulent building created by a cardinal – the
nephew of Innocent X, the Barberini Theatre, and the Palazzo Farnese
by Antonio Sangallo. Pope Alexander VII (1655–67) rebuilt Rome with
the needs of tourists in view, creating wide roads for both practical and
aesthetic reasons, which eased traffic problems and facilitated the age of
the Grand Tour, during which, particularly in the eighteenth century, the
European educated elite travelled to Italy to learn good manners and the
art of conversation, and to improve their knowledge of art and architecture. Public building was also a response to the problems posed by
unemployment and begging. Seventeenth-century Rome was full of
beggars: in 1660, there were around 10,000, a tenth of the population,
assisted by hospices, charities and various church activities.

Pilgrims could also approach St Peter's by crossing the S. Angelo
bridge, which Bernini decorated with ten statues of angels holding the
instruments of Christ's Crucifixion. The Pantheon, an ancient pagan
temple, was restored and consecrated as a church, adjacent palaces were
removed and a square created around it. The city's expansion came to a
halt in the eighteenth century when, as a result of huge debts accumulated over the previous century and the general economic crisis, there
were no longer sufficient funds for new works. In the eighteenth century,
Rome's population climbed to 130,000, making it the third largest city in
Italy after Naples and Venice, but the figure remained unaltered during
the following two centuries as Rome rested in its existing splendour with
an economy based almost exclusively on tourism.

In 1684 and 1693, Sicily was hit by devastating earthquakes and some
of its cities had to be entirely reconstructed. One of the masterpieces of
European eighteenth-century urban theatricality is the town of Noto, in

the Iblei hills near Syracuse in the south-west of the island, rebuilt in just a few years based on a herringbone pattern, and conceived by local architects as a vast theatre that provides amazing perspectives over the higher part of the city. Another capital of Baroque art was Turin under the House of Savoy, a result of the work of Guarino Guarini (1624–83), a member of the Theatine order, who had lived in Rome (where he was a student of Francesco Borromini), Sicily, Paris, and finally arriving in Turin in 1666. There he built the Palazzo Carignano with its elliptical entrance in an undulating façade and, among his religious buildings, the Chapel of the Sacred Shroud in Turin Cathedral, and San Lorenzo dei Teatini. In 1715, Victor Amedeo II employed Filippo Juvara (1678–1736), born in Messina and educated in Rome, to build the Basilica of Superga, the mausoleum of the Savoy family, on a hill overlooking the city. Among the artists influenced by Juvara was Luigi Vanvitelli (1700–73), the son of a Dutch painter who worked in Ancona and Rome, and was called to Naples in 1751 by Charles III, who entrusted him with the construction of the Royal Palace of Caserta, considered to be the Italian Versailles, a building whose classical influence is subverted by its enormous proportions and its immense garden that represented a masterpiece of Italian landscaping. A huge central staircase, flanked by two smaller ones, opens on to a dramatic perspective of arches and marble columns.

In the seventeenth and eighteenth centuries, Italy provided two original contributions in the field of theatre: the drama, which evolved into melodrama, and the improvised form of Commedia dell'Arte. A theatrical vision of life was portrayed through complex and spectacular scenarios which created a sense of power designed to overawe the audience; the opposite of Shakespeare's declaration in England at the time that the whole world was a stage, and men and women merely actors. Pastoral drama had already become successful in the late sixteenth century with Tasso's *Aminta* (1573) and Battista Guarini's *Pastor Fido* (1590), which portrayed an idealization of court life and were shown across Europe. They describe the love-lives of shepherds, with hints of tragedy and comedy in a fairytale atmosphere. Pastoral drama has four musical intervals between the acts and the chorus enters the scene at the end of each act, sometimes interrupting the action. In the seventeenth century, the poetry of Giambattista Marino (1569–1625), particularly *Poems* (1602) and *Adonis* (1623), brought together theatre and music in literature: the literary text had to be both seen and heard, with the aim of creating a surprise effect. Other arts followed the example (painting, sculpture and music) in the attempt to seduce the public with surprising metaphors – the new style was called *Marinismo*.

The Commedia dell'Arte first appeared in Venice as the comedy of the 'zanni'. Zanni (the name Giovanni in Venetian dialect) was a harlequin-like figure portraying a servant in conflict with his master, a merchant. Actors were professionals who earned their living by giving recitals. For the first time, actresses appeared on the scene, although the Church opposed this and made things difficult for theatrical companies in cities where it had influence. When comedians arrived in cities, they had to obtain permission to play from both the civil and religious authorities. As plots were often improvised, the Church could not easily exercise effective preventive censorship. In Commedia dell'Arte, standard characters could be identified by their masks, a form of theatrical symbolism that later spread from Italy to the rest of Europe. The form became successful beyond the court and moved from city to city; it was improvised and open to anyone who could buy a ticket, therefore playing mainly to a bourgeois public.

Italians called Commedia dell'Arte 'sudden' or 'improvised' comedy, while contemporary foreigners called it 'Italian-style comedy'. Theatre moved beyond the courts, and actors with little money and no patrons travelled around the Italian states. They invented masks that corresponded to non-heroic characters of daily Italian village and city life and spoke in different dialects, creating protagonists with whom most of their public could identify: no heroes, but poor and cunning people, cuckolded husbands, deceived old men, and shrewd, unscrupulous servants, each of whom represented the precise characteristics of a particular city: Bergamasco, Neapolitan, Milanese and Venetian. Once it was clear that sex and the mockery of powerful people were successful themes, female characters were staged alongside the stock character of the bullied aristocrat. The image of Italians presented by comedians was of a cunning and unreliable people, full of ideas and genius but at the same time ignorant and incoherent, never prepared to make a stand and constantly avoiding commitment to principles. This image can find its way back to the characters in Boccaccio, where craftiness, luck and love take centre stage as motivating factors and themes. Another interpretation explained these characters as anti-government, anti-nationalist sceptics of power and authority from above, where only taking matters in one's own hands gets them done. By taking regional masks on stage across Italy, comedians helped to create an Italian identity long before it was thought of by national revolutionaries.

> **Box 5.3   Carlo Goldoni and Venetian theatre**
>
> Carlo Goldoni was born in Venice in 1707, when the city was in a state of what Marvin Carlson has called 'its long and luxurious decline' as the 'pleasure capital of Europe' (Carlson, 1981). Government attempts to restrict expenditure on parties, extravagant dresses and jewellery had little chance of success, and masked figures in street theatre as well as opera were well received by the public, which included many tourists as well as residents. In Goldoni's time, opera was performed in Venice in at least eight theatres, compared with two in both London and Paris. With Goldoni, masks stopped being called Pantalone, Arlecchino, Bighella and Colombina and took on the names of the Venetian bourgeoisie and lower classes. They began to be characterized by the peculiar conditions of their social class and lifestyle: gentlewomen, sharp-tongued females, travelling merchants, soldiers and lovers.

At the end of the sixteenth century the *Camerata dei Bardi*, an academy of Florentine scholars and musicians, decided to reintroduce song into theatre, as in the ancient Greek tragedies. At the Florentine court, Jacopo Corsi, the poet Ottavio Rinuccini and the composer Giacinto Peri produced the first operas, *Dafne* and *Euridice*, in 1598 and 1600, respectively. Both had pastoral subjects, following the poetic fashion of the time. They were presented at the Pitti Palace for the wedding of Maria de' Medici and the future king of France, Henry IV, and are considered to be the first melodramas. *Euridice* is a pastoral fairytale with a mythological theme, characterized by a style of singing akin to talking known as *recitar cantando* (performance singing), a dialogue sung by single voices in which the text was lifted by the music. *Recitar cantando* was interrupted by arias – verses which alternated with instrumental refrains in which the character expressed his or her feelings. Inspired by these examples, the Cremonese Claudio Monteverdi (1547–1643), who became the most important musician of the time, wrote *Orfeo*, first performed in Mantua in 1607. Opera, as it came to be called, continued to develop in Mantua, Rome, Venice and Naples, initially intended as a court spectacle for the celebration of extraordinary events. In Mantua, a theatre with 6,000 seats was built for the wedding of Francesco Gonzaga, in which Monteverdi's *Arianna* was performed. The melodrama elegantly brought together different artistic forms: literature, music, the figurative arts and architecture. It met with extraordinary success in the European courts and its popularity has continued to the present day.

The term Baroque is used in music to indicate the period between the early seventeenth and mid-eighteenth centuries, when music adopted a fundamental role among the arts, through its theatrical contribution. Instrumental music increasingly acquired a more independent role, no longer restricted to accompaniment for songs and dances. New musical forms included sonatas, which brought together the harpsichord with two string instruments; the solo violin concerto; and the concerto grosso, in which a small group of musicians (called a *concertino*) play with a larger group (called a *ripieno*). Through these new forms, musicians exhibited a virtuosity that took Baroque poetic exuberance to new heights. Until the mid-seventeenth century, Italy was the unqualified leader in European musical innovation, and Italian was the *lingua franca* of musical Europe. Italian musicians were sought for courts all over Europe, and Italian was considered to be the ideal language for singing; Italian courts were centres of musical life, in terms of both theatrical performance and the construction of instruments.

Churches increased their use of music during liturgical celebrations, and music began to accompany theatre through madrigals, which brought music and poetry together. Indeed, poets began to write madrigal verses, as in, for example, the *Rime* by Giambattista Marino. *Intermezzi*, musical interludes between the acts, punctuated theatrical performances. By the end of the century, with the work of great composers such as Arcangelo Corelli (1653–1713), Alessandro Scarlatti (1660–1725), Antonio Vivaldi (1678–1741) and Tomaso Albinoni (1671–1751), opera and Baroque music had become popular throughout Italy (essential, for example, to Venice's carnival) as well as abroad.

While singing and recitals were already present in the Italian literary tradition, as we have seen, and had been encouraged by the Renaissance interest in beautiful manners (for example, Castiglione wrote in *Cortegiano* about the beauty of singing literary texts), the common opinion of Monteverdi's contemporaries was that *Orfeo*'s singularity lay in its actors singing rather than speaking. The apparently unnecessary *intermedio*, which often introduced decorative fantasy elements but also surprising *coups de théâtre* marking the formal organization of the story, was also typical of the opera. *Orfeo* was also a success because it conformed perfectly to the conventions of pastoral themes: the mythological final scene, where Orpheus is destroyed by the bacchantes, was only suggested, while the hero was lifted skywards by a singing Apollo emerging from a cloud. The rescue and apotheosis of the hero, in a clear personification of the prince figure, conformed well to the demands of court eulogy. For its return to classical and mythological themes, as well as for its echoes of Dante and Petrarch, *Orfeo* is seen as a great Renaissance work, though the recited solos and dialogue were characteristic of the Baroque period.

THE CONTINUING LANGUAGE DEBATE

A network of academies developed in Italy from the mid-sixteenth century and into the seventeenth, with the aim of expanding literary culture beyond the courts. The most influential was the Arcadia, created in Rome in 1690, which sought to weaken the impact of *Marinismo*, proposing the return to classical themes. However, by the early eighteenth century, Italian poetry had begun to lose its pre-eminence in Europe, surpassed by the development of English and French national literature. In this as in other fields, Italy began to import foreign models. The influence of the European Enlightenment on Italian literature is evident in Giuseppe Parini (1729–99), a neo-classical Milanese writer and a member of the Arcadia, whose work *The Day* was a satirical poem on the social codes of the aristocracy.

As Chapter 6 will demonstrate, late-eighteenth-century writers regarded literature as the art that could bring Italy closer to the movement of ideas that already characterized other European countries – the 'age of Enlightenment' – a stance that led eventually to support for the struggle for independence and unification. Manzoni's poetry in the nineteenth century was a fundamental contribution in the debate on the birth of a national language. Before that, the most progressive intellectuals of the Italian Enlightenment sought to close the gap between written and spoken language, and debated the problem of the links between the linguistic and cultural unity of what they began to call 'the nation'. The scholar Alessandro Verri (1741–1816) introduced the Milanese newspaper *Il Caffè* (1764–6) by proclaiming that it was the founders' intention to avoid 'vain display of rare and delicate terms', and to write so as to be 'understood throughout the whole world'. The prose of this period was characterized by the introduction of French words and by the simplification of syntax. The Latin model, full of subordinate clauses with the verbs at the end of sentences, was replaced by simpler and more straightforward structures. The Milanese Enlightenment thinkers of *Il Caffè* upheld their right to invent new words and to Italianize foreign terms.

The jurist and scholar Cesare Beccaria (1738–94), in his *Ricerche intorno alla natura dello stile* ('Researches around the nature of style', 1770), asserted that literary works should make stylistic choices based on holding the reader's attention and communicating sensations. Melchiorre Cesarotti, in *Saggio sulla filosofia delle lingue* ('Essay on the philosophy of languages', 1785), stated that language was a living organism which evolved alongside changing historical and social situations; he therefore proposed a balance between innovations in vocabulary and syntax, and examples from earlier authors. The *Accademia della Crusca*, one of Italy's most prestigious and conservative intellectual academies, which was opposed to these new proposals, continued to defend the fourteenth-century Florentine model. In 1612, the first edition of the dictionary of the Crusca Academy had been published in Venice, based entirely on fourteenth-century authors. Only in its third edition, in 1691, did it include some sixteenth-century writers, such as Tasso. This Florentine model was finally defeated in 1783, when Grand Duke Leopold of Tuscany suppressed the academy. Around the same time, a new dictionary appeared – the *Dizionario universale critico enciclopedico della lingua italiana* ('Critical universal encyclopaedic dictionary of the Italian language', 1797–1805) by the abbot Francesco D'Alberti of Villanuova, which welcomed technical neologisms, foreign words and the living language spoken by the Florentine people. The debate, however, continued: the poet and scholar Vincenzo Monti (1754–1828) led a current of classicists in criticizing Enlightenment writers for their uninhibited use of foreign words, and argued the need for the retention of a noble language from the later medieval period separate from the language of the common people, although even these classicists were open to some innovation and did reject exaggerated archaisms. The purist current, led by the Veronese Antonio Cesari and the Neapolitan Basilio Puoti, was the most conservative, preferring a return to the pure language of the fourteenth century. Puoti later wrote the chief grammatical work of purism, *Regole elementari della lingua italiana* ('Elementary rules of the Italian language', 1833), and founded a school at which Francesco De Sanctis (1817–1883), one of the most important Italian literary critics, studied. De Sanctis recalled of his school days that pupils studied fourteenth- and sixteenth-century authors and were then required to practise their writing 'according to a certain choice of solemn and noble words, not worn-out from usage and not too obsolete, and by constructing sentences that were not too complicated or in the manner of Boccaccio, but elevated, solemn and abundant'.

The purist tradition would finally be defeated with the arrival of Romanticism in the nineteenth century. One of Romanticism's precursors was the Piedmontese Vittorio Alfieri, born in Asti in 1749. Alfieri supported not only the diffusion of a language close to the needs of the people, but also the freedom of intellectuals from political elites. In a book entitled *The Prince and Letters*, he made reference to Machiavelli as one of the last examples of a free author who did not defer to any prince. His heroic interpretation of Machiavelli was based on the idea that, by outlining the ruthless qualities princes should possess, the Florentine writer was expounding the qualities of the free writer; that is, the complete independence from political power, allowing freedom of judgement and the search for truth that was the supreme duty of an intellectual. Alfieri's work therefore became a heroic denunciation of the absolutism and oppression of eighteenth-century political power, and his praise of Machiavelli was later approved by the poet Ugo Foscolo (1778–1827) in *The Sepulchres*. It was in the prince's interest to be a patron of writers in order to make them write formally elegant and pleasing books that did not challenge his power and were empty of content. Among modern writers, Alfieri recalled Tasso and Ariosto who, during the Counter-Reformation had become flatterers in order to be protected by their princes and had therefore produced an art inferior to the one they would have produced in an atmosphere of intellectual freedom. As for many eighteenth-century writers, Alfieri's all-time hero was Homer, the poet of the Greek people who worked without political protection, in exile and poor, yet was a superior poet to Virgil, who had been protected by Augustus, who was rich and praised by his contemporaries. Alfieri exalted literature as the only art that could challenge absolutism, providing the first of many reflections on the relationship between the intellectual and power, which continued into the twentieth century in the work of Antonio Gramsci and Alberto Asor Rosa. The final attack on seventeenth-century literature came from Francesco De Sanctis in the nineteenth century. De Sanctis, in his history of Italian literature, demonstrated how taste had changed: he hated allegories and witty remarks, the ceremonies of rhetoric – the seventeenth century was for him a corrupted age, the underworld of Italian literature. Only in the context of the nineteenth century could Italian literature be returned to

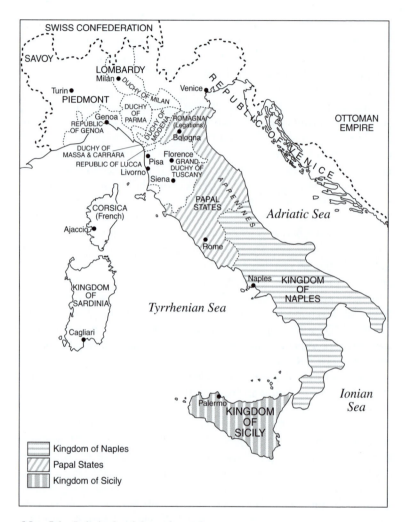

Map 5.1 Italy in the eighteenth century

Source: adapted from John Marino, *Early Modern Italy, 1550–1796* (Oxford: Oxford University Press), p. 287.

its former splendour: 'literature could only be reborn through the resurrection of the national conscience'.

As the next chapter will illustrate, it was the Enlightenment at the end of the eighteenth century that provoked the re-emergence of the idea of Italy's unification. Early-eighteenth-century authors such as Vico, whose

Scienza nuova, published in 1744, was later seen as the basis of natural law; Antonio Genovesi, a professor at the university of Naples, who confronted the issue of the landless peasantry in southern Italy, proposing that all Church land should be converted into peasant leaseholds; Ludovico Antonio Muratori, who sought to reform the curricula of Catholic schools and universities; and Giannone, who argued that legal punishment against heresy should be meted out by the state and not the Church, were important influences. However, these intellectuals did not insist on the idea of Italian unification, in part because it seemed politically unrealistic, and in part because they believed that the loss of Italy's cultural prestige was all too evident when Italian cities were compared with the lively centres of Paris, London and Amsterdam during what historians define as the European 'Age of Reason'.

SELECTED FURTHER READING

J. Marino (ed.), *Early Modern Italy, 1550–1796* (Oxford: Oxford University Press, 2002) and D. Sella, *Italy in the Seventeenth Century* (London: Longman, 1997) are excellent overviews of the period. T. Astarita, *Between Salt Water and Holy Water. A History of Southern Italy* (London: W. W. Norton, 2005) provides an interesting and readable insight on the southern regions. The Spanish social, religious and political influence on Italy is covered by the authoritative study by T. Dandelet and J. Marino (eds), *Spain in Italy: Politics, Society and Religion, 1500–1700* (Leiden: Brill, 2007). J. O'Malley (ed.), *The Jesuits: Culture, Sciences, and the Arts, 1540–1773* (Toronto: University of Toronto Press, 1999) provides a nuanced examination of the impact of the Jesuits on Italian culture. The ideas of the precursors of the Italian Enlightenment in the early modern period are examined by V. Ferrone, *The Intellectual Roots of the Italian Enlightenment* (New York: Humanity Books, 1995).

6

A National Melodrama:
The Epic of the *Risorgimento*

CHRONOLOGY

1861	First election of the Italian parliament; Victor Emmanuel II becomes the King of Italy; Turin capital of Italy
1865	Florence capital of Italy
1866	Third war of independence: Italian forces defeated; Prussian forces defeat Austria; Venetia to Italy
1870	Napoleon III defeated by Prussia; Italian troops enter Rome; Rome becomes the capital of Italy.

THE ITALIAN ENLIGHTENMENT

Towards the end of the eighteenth century, most of Italy was living under famine conditions, which encouraged rulers to implement 'Enlightened' policies of reform. To confront both economic crisis and relative cultural decline, Italian intellectuals began to promote a sense of revival, or *risorgimento*. The movement was initiated in Naples and Milan, influenced by a wider European Enlightenment culture. For late-eighteenth-century thinkers who took part in the Enlightenment, famine and disease were no longer signs of God's will, but the result of poor government policies. Debates on the best form of government had continued from the post-Renaissance period. Political thought in this earlier period had been inspired by the publication of Machiavelli's *Discourses* and *The Prince* in 1531–32, and Guicciardini's *History of Italy* in 1561–4 (previously circulated in manuscript); these works formed the basis for the subsequent analysis by the Piedmontese priest and political thinker Giovanni Botero (1544–1617), author of *The Reason of State*, and of Paolo Sarpi. As seen in the previous chapter, the political movements of the Renaissance and post-Renaissance were revived by the work of early Enlightenment thinkers such as Ludovico Antonio Muratori, Giambattista Vico and Pietro Giannone, and, in the second half of the eighteenth century, by reformers such as the Milanese Pietro Verri (1728–97) and Cesare Beccaria.

Famine and epidemics also provoked new interest in ways of tackling poverty and living conditions, both in cities and on large rural estates. While 'enlightened' European rulers were as paternalistic as the absolutist rulers before them, they now had secular interests to protect, and began an assault on the privileges of the Church. The Jesuits, in particular, were targeted for their wealth and their interference in education, and were expelled from most states, until the Papacy finally dissolved the order in 1773. In Piedmont, Charles Emmanuel III eliminated tax exemptions for the clergy, expanded the army and brought education and poor relief under the control of the state; he also abolished serfdom and promoted agrarian reform in Sardinia. In Lombardy under the Habsburg Empress Maria Theresa, local intellectuals such as Verri and Beccaria took part in discussions about reform. In Tuscany, the government undertook land and ecclesiastical reform, reducing the number of feast days and suppressing monasteries. However, reforms aimed against religion met with popular opposition everywhere. When common land was divided and sold, it was bought by rich landowners, so the situation for the peasant masses remained unchanged, thus exacerbating social tension. This kind of land reform, like the religious reforms, was not welcomed by the lower classes. By 1789, the year of the French Revolution, many reformers were also unhappy with the limited results obtained so far by the reform programme, and were drawn to the events in France. The cry 'liberté, egalité, fraternité' resounded all across Italy, as it did in the rest of continental Europe. The new ideas also spread to the Papal States; as in the rest of Italy, the Enlightenment attracted young aristocrats and bourgeois intellectuals, who gathered in the salons of private palaces or in public cafés and began discussing ideas that were in marked contrast to orthodox Catholicism and its associated morality.

The idea of nation (which implied the concept of an Italian struggle for independence and unification) did not become a realistic goal supported by writers until the nineteenth century; however, during the eighteenth century, a number of histories of Italy and Italian literature indicated a will to overcome the era's sense of decline, and to reconsider the concept of Italy, by harking back to the centuries between Dante and Machiavelli. For example, in 1723, Giacinto Gimma from Bari had published an innovative history of Italian literature entitled *Idea della storia dell'Italia letterata* ('Idea of the history of literary Italy'), which focused on prose as well as poetry, and incorporated the history of Italian literature into the wider history of Italian culture. Gimma was animated by patriotic fervour; when mentioning the word 'nation', he indicated not a political outcome but a cultural condition common to all the peoples between the Alps and Sicily, which had extended from the time of Dante to the seventeenth century. The absence of a political strategy marked the gap between his work and De Sanctis's famous history of Italian literature a century later; however, Gimma's perspective anticipated the arguments of the Italian Enlightenment patriots. Other works followed along these lines: *Della poesia italiana* ('On Italian poetry') by Francesco Saverio Quadrio, first published in Venice in 1734; *Storia della letteratura italiana* ('History of Italian literature') by Girolamo Tiraboschi, first published in Modena between 1772 and 1782; and *Del Risorgimento d'Italia negli studi, nelle arti e nei consumi dopo il Mille* ('On the renaissance of Italy in the studies, the arts and consumption after the year 1000') by Saverio Bettinelli, published in Bassano in 1773, which interpreted Italy's history of literary production as having alternated between moments of glory and of decline.

The Enlightenment intellectual Pietro Verri, influenced by both Machiavelli and Montesquieu, founded the Academia dei Pugni in Milan, a group which included his brother Alessandro and Cesare Beccaria, among others. They published the most renowned newspaper of the Italian Enlightenment, *Il Caffè* (1764–6), first issued the same year as Beccaria's *On Crimes and Punishments*, an influential work throughout Europe, which argued that the aim of punishment had to be re-education rather than vengeance, and proposed the abolition of the death penalty. Both Beccaria and *Il Caffè* debated the problems of penal justice in eighteenth-century Lombardy; the writers wanted not merely to reform the judicial system, but to replace it with a new system based on the equality of law and the separation of powers – in which they were influenced principally by Montesquieu and Voltaire. This debate was instrumental at the time in bringing about the abolition of torture in most of Europe; between 1770 and 1777, Pietro Verri contributed by writing a pamphlet on torture, *Osservazioni sulla tortura* ('Observations on torture'), which was published posthumously in 1804, when torture was abolished in Lombardy by Joseph II. However, this was simply the final act of the struggle against torture in the Italian states; the first condemnations of the practice had come from the humanists at the end of the fifteenth century, moved by the inhumane treatment meted out to witches throughout Europe. Verri had previously written a pamphlet against torture in 1763, the *Orazione panegirica sulla giurisprudenza milanese* ('Panegyric speech on the Milanese judiciary'), in the sarcastic tone often used by these intellectuals against their adversaries. In this work, a conservative supporter of torture, infuriated by the enlightened reforms in Prussia and France, demonstrated the irrefutable necessity of torture:

> If innocent citizens must not be subject to torture, then we must conclude that innocent citizens must never become victims of headaches or fever … but innocent citizens do suffer from these illnesses; it is therefore false that innocent citizens must not be exposed to torture.

Similarly ironic was the praise for the Milanese assembly of judges, the Senate:

> In Milan there is a body of judges who are the lords of law, and this is the Senate, which is entrusted with judging the material possessions, the life and the reputation of citizens, either according to the law, or against the law, or outside the law.

The three possibilities were listed as if there were no differences between them. Verri's *Osservazioni* became a key text, followed in 1842 by *Storia della colonna infame* ('History of the infamous column') by the Milanese poet and novelist Alessandro Manzoni (1785–1873), which represented an attack on the vast power of judges and supported the distinction between legislative and judicial powers. According to Giulio Carnazzi, Enlightenment thinkers can be seen as the precursors of the defence of civil rights in Italy.

News circulation was widespread and rapid throughout Europe in the second half of the eighteenth century. Italian gazettes revealed the existence of a public opinion that was well-informed about, for example, the violent reactions in the Netherlands to Joseph II's despotism, the heroic idealism of republicans such as Pasquale Paoli in Corsica, or the outbreak of the American Revolution. Terms such as 'virtue', 'patriotism', 'republic', 'democracy' and, increasingly, 'revolution' became well-known across the peninsula, while a new generation of intellectuals developed under the influence of Diderot and d'Alembert's *Encyclopaedia*. With Milan, Naples was an important and dynamic centre during the Enlightenment period, where intellectuals from all over Europe gathered. Many of these intellectuals tried, with difficulty, to pose an alternative to the Counter-Reformation culture that had strengthened the popular belief in saints and supernatural powers. In order to fight against superstition, popular publications such as the widely-read almanacs were employed to attack the world of magic. In Piedmont in the 1780s, over 200,000 copies of Enlightenment almanacs were published each year. These were designed to be read in public, and both propagated the latest scientific progress and attacked religious superstitions, including, for example, the belief in saintly power and the fanaticism surrounding events such as the liquefaction of St Gennaro's blood.

Milanese Enlightenment thinkers depicted their city as a centre of progress, in contrast to Papal Rome which was described, for example,

---

Box 6.1   Cafés and revolution

The discussion of new ideas and the diffusion of Enlightenment gazettes was encouraged by the new fashion for coffee houses, which appeared in Europe following the arrival of coffee from the Middle East. According to Etienne François, the first European city to open a coffee house was Venice around 1647. The fashion exploded in the eighteenth century, when it became linked with the intellectual life of Enlightenment thinkers and, later, the revolutionaries of the *Risorgimento*. Cafés were places of liberty, where the intellectual middle classes could converse about art, politics, economics and literature without the restrictions of the formal society of aristocratic salons. However, as a play by Goldoni in Venice of 1750 showed, café culture had also started to permeate the lower classes:

> *Trappola*:   It is really something that makes you die of laughter, to see even porters coming to drink their coffee.
>
> *Ridolfo*:   Everyone seeks to do what everybody does. Once grappa was fashionable, now it is coffee.

(Goldoni, 2004, Act I, p. 85)

According to Maria Malatesta, during the eighteenth and nineteenth centuries even prestigious coffee bars such as Florian in Venice were frequented, at different times of the day, by different social classes.

(Malatesta, 1997, p. 59)

---

in the correspondence from Pietro to Alessandro Verri, as the epitome of intellectual degradation, a city interesting only for its art and architecture. Together with Naples and Milan, Venice witnessed the flourishing of scholarly initiatives with a number of Enlightenment publications such as the *Giornale dei letterati d'Italia* ('Newspaper of the Italian literati'); the Venetian Arcadia academy played an important role in emancipating Italy from the marginal forms of Baroque literature and facilitating the discussion of themes receptive to European rationalism.

THE LEGACY OF THE FRENCH REVOLUTION AND NAPOLEON

In 1796, French troops led by the young Corsican general Napoleon Bonaparte founded short-lived, French-dominated republics in Italy. Italian supporters of the French Revolution welcomed Napoleon and fought in his Italian Army. After crossing the River Po at Piacenza and defeating the Austrians at Lodi, Napoleon entered Milan. The patriot Francesco Melzi d'Eril (1753–1816) was an eyewitness to the event, which coincided with the Pentecostal celebrations:

> There is a warning that Bonaparte is arriving today. The whole city is going to welcome him outside Porta Romana . . . He passed through it at a gallop . . . The people followed in happy celebration; but in the sense of a feast day, rather than of a new order of things which we were not imagining yet.

The Milanese people then received a bilingual proclamation:

> The French Republic, which has sworn hatred to tyrants, has also sworn fraternity to all peoples. The tyrant who oppressed Lombardy for so long has caused much evil to France; but the French know that the king's cause is not the cause of the people. Respect for property, for individuals; respect for the religion of the peoples: these are the feelings of the French Republic and of the victorious Italian army.

Bonaparte subsequently established a provisional administration for the city which included some local patriots and aristocrats, among them Pietro Verri.

In 1798, the French army entered the Papal States and declared the end of Papal rule in Rome; in 1799, they arrived in Naples and Tuscany and in 1797 invaded the entire territory of the *Serenissima*, including Venice. The book on the statue of the lion of St Mark in the city's main square, which had carried the inscription: *Pax tibi Marce, Evangelista meus*, was replaced by the declaration of human rights. Venetian patriots interpreted this as a sign of new times – democracy replacing religion – but their hopes were soon crushed: the French signed the treaty of Campoformio with the Habsburgs and, in exchange for Austrian renunciation of Lombardy, Belgium and Modena, the Habsburgs were given Venetia. No one expressed the bitter disappointment with Napoleon better than Foscolo in *Last Letters of Jacopo Ortis*. With the exception of Venetia, all of mainland Italy was under the control of 'revolutionary'

Map 6.1   Italy after the Napoleonic invasion (1797)

Source: from John A. Davis, *Italy in the Nineteenth Century, 1796–1900* (Oxford: Oxford University Press), p. 289, by permission of Oxford University Press.

French authorities imposing French laws and administrative systems, and French attitudes to property and religion.

Napoleon's conquest of Italy brought major changes in the political condition of the country, with the formation of 'sister republics'. The *Repubblica Cisalpina* included Lombardy and the former Po Valley duchies; the *Repubblica Ligure* revived the old aristocratic Genoese Republic; the Roman Republic replaced the Papal States; the *Repubblica Partenopea* in the continental south replaced the Bourbon monarchy; and the *Repubblica Cispadana* was established in the Emilia Romagna region. These republican experiences of the 'Jacobin triennial' of 1796–9 did not last long, dependent as they were on Napoleon's military fortunes, but were nevertheless crucial in providing the practice of democracy for a new political class that would later set in motion the national *risorgimento*. The constitutions created in these years demonstrated the interest of revolutionaries in the relationship between state and citizens: they explained in detail the duties and rights of citizens, and the functions of members of parliament – who had to express the general will and not just the needs of electors. The concepts of nation, equality and freedom began to be interpreted as rights among large sections of Italian public opinion.

The French claimed to bring liberation, and some Italians believed them. These young, educated, urban, middle-class men and women called themselves patriots and expressed a genuine enthusiasm for liberty, equality and progress; they hated the Church and the privileges of the aristocracy; they had republican ideals and were great propagandists. Many of them from across Italy flocked to Milan, considered to be the centre of the French presence, thereby enlarging the ranks of the Milanese bourgeoisie. As a result, Napoleon began to rely increasingly on the moderate elements to govern the city. Some patriots wanted the unification and independence of Italy, but had little hope of that at the time; instead, they had to depend on the French and be content with the French constitution which, in theory, granted freedom of the press, of association and worship, equality before the law and legislative assemblies.

With the arrival of the French, Rome, more than any other Italian city, was overwhelmed with revolutionary words and imagery. The break with Papal domination and an exaltation of the republican past increased the already lively interest in ancient history and uncovered the existence of another secular and republican Rome obscured for centuries by clerical dominion. Memories of ancient Rome and the Rome of Arnaldo, Cola di Rienzo and Giordano Bruno had not disappeared. One of the

---

Box 6.2   The birth of the Italian flag

In Milan in 1796, the French established a militia called the Lombard legion, whose flag was white and red – inherited from the Milanese coat of arms, and green. The cities of Modena, Ferrara, Bologna and Reggio Emilia, which together constituted the *Repubblica Cispadana*, decided to use the same flag of green, white and red. Subsequently, the flag became a symbol of freedom. During the Restoration, the flag appeared only clandestinely, and was waved by patriots during attempted revolutions before 1848. The wide use of the tricolour during the five days of Milan in 1848 persuaded the Piedmontese King Charles Albert to adopt it as a 'national' flag, with the coat of arms of the House of Savoy at its centre.

---

revolutionaries, Nicola Corona, addressed people among the ruins of the Forum, vowing that Rome 'begins to resume its ancient decorum, its honour and glory; and the fathers of the *patria*, who have been groaning under the yoke of ignorance and fanaticism, are now reborn to imitate the ancestors who triumphed and proclaimed laws'. As research by Francesco Bartolini has shown, a new political language came into circulation, founded on the explicit use of ancient history as a means of constructing a new urban identity. While they were more progressive than the states of the old regime, the French republics did not really respect the Jacobin ideals they claimed to support. Indeed, despite the efforts of the Italian revolutionaries, within a short time the power vacuum created by the departure of the old monarchs was filled by the leaders of the French army. The main aim of the French governors was to keep order and to tax the population in order to maintain the army. They ruled through the army and used minor nobles as local administrators, excluding the patriots. Moreover, high taxation and requisitions led to anti-French rebellions. The peasants hated the French and so did the Church, since the invaders had confiscated Church properties and banned religious pilgrimages and the cult of local saints. Anti-French revolts continued to spread, often causing local civil wars. For example, in 1799, Cardinal Ruffo marched with the peasantry from Calabria to Naples to 'fight the Godless French'; in Naples, 7,000 members of the enlightened middle classes were massacred as Jacobins; this slaughter of intellectuals highlighted the problem of the relationship between intellectuals and the peasantry that would be a major question during the

Risorgimento. In Tuscany, peasants rebelled under the slogan 'viva Maria'. Other forms of protest included disregard for French laws and the continued observation of religious practices, as republican institutions had demonstrated no sensibility towards the problems of the peasant masses. The Neapolitan writer Vincenzo Cuoco (1770–1823) analysed the reasons for the republican defeat and the return of the Bourbons in Naples in 1799 in a famous book, *Saggio storico sulla rivoluzione napoletana del 1799* ('Historical essay on the 1799 Neapolitan revolution') written a few years later when Cuoco was exiled in Paris, and first published anonymously in Milan in 1801. Revolutions, he explained, could be active or passive: active revolutions were sparked by the precise needs of the majority of the population, while passive revolutions marched with a foreign army under whose domination the national elite was unable to involve the popular masses. Clearly, the *partenopea* revolution belonged to the second category. The Bourbons returned to power and unleashed a ferocious repression against the republicans that lasted until 1806, when the French army returned to establish a new French regime, this time no longer republican in nature.

The French regimes persisted in Italy until Napoleon's defeat in 1814, though with some changes that reflected the shift in France from republic to empire, and the consequent transfer of political power into the hands of moderates all over Italy. In 1805, the Cisalpine Republic, which included part of Venetia (to the west of the River Adige), became the 'Kingdom of Italy', with its capital in Milan and Napoleon as its king. Piedmont was annexed to France, and the Kingdom of Naples was governed by Napoleon's brother, Joseph Bonaparte (1806–8) and later by Napoleon's brother-in-law, Joachim Murat (1808–15). By 1809, the Papal States had also been annexed, by which time French rule had become more imperial than republican, and many patriots had become disillusioned. The press was censored and representative assemblies represented only the elite. Popular revolts continued, with bloody risings and land occupations, mainly against taxation and conscription. In this period, Italy's principal secret society, the *Carbonari,* was created in the south. Secret societies had elaborate oaths and rituals, organized conspiracies and plots and, with the departure of the French, believed their time had come in the fight for Italian unification.

The French left Italy an important legacy – their legal and administrative systems. Under French rule, decisions were taken by state officials who, as urban and educated lawyers, acted according to fixed rules and modern legal codes: they were appointed by the French and stayed in their positions when the French left. But perhaps more important was the legacy of ideas and mentalities. Italy had taken part in the eighteenth-century Enlightenment, its intellectuals favouring rational decision-making, legal rights, economic progress and general education, and despising Catholic superstition. After Napoleonic rule their beliefs had become more rooted, as the French had unleashed serious attacks on the Church, made state schools compulsory, and espoused values that were patriotic rather than religious. All this brought about a clash between incompatible ideals. Some Italians embraced this legacy and even those who did not were still exposed to the ideas.

Despite the disillusionment Italian patriots felt with Napoleon, he also left a legacy. The most famous of the many odes to Napoleon after his death in 1821 was Manzoni's *Fifth of May* (translated by Goethe into German), which conveyed dramatic intensity and emotion, illustrating that Napoleon was still regarded differently from the absolutist rulers of the Restoration. The poem exalted his geographical conquests, lauded him as the arbiter between the spirits of absolutism and liberalism, and emphasized the contrast between his glory and his downfall – he remained a romantic hero who inspired intense love and equally intense hatred.

Following Napoleon's defeat and the Congress of Vienna in 1815, Austria governed most of Italy. Italy remained 'used' by foreigners as it had been since the sixteenth century; Piedmont alone remained independent, out of the necessity of keeping the French away from the peninsula.

Austrian-dominated northern Italy was governed without a constitution and did not rely on the Italian middle classes. The aspiration for a constitution was thus another fundamental legacy of the French period. Austria recovered possession of Lombardy-Venetia, dominated Tuscany (through family ties) and central Italy, and had a great influence on the Papal States, as the Pope welcomed the Restoration and saw Austria as a Catholic ally. However, in the Papal States, the middle classes had no intention of simply accepting the Restoration, as revolution in Romagna in 1830 demonstrated. In the south, Ferdinand I of the Two Sicilies was also allied to Austria; Sicily was discontented about the return to governance from Naples, and revolts broke out continually on the island. Indeed, between 1805 and 1815, Sicily was occupied by the British fleet, which had been there to fight the French and remained under the pretext of protecting the Bourbon family, which had been forced to flee Naples. Under the 1812 constitution the British abolished feudalism in Sicily and encouraged commerce in land and property so it would no longer be a privilege of the nobility and the Church. When Sicily returned to being

Map 6.2 Italy after the Congress of Vienna (1815)

Source: from John A. Davis, *Italy in the Nineteenth Century, 1796–1900* (Oxford: Oxford University Press), p. 291, by permission of Oxford University Press.

ruled by Naples, its parliament was dissolved and no attempt was made to involve the middle classes in the government of the island. The poverty of the rural masses, and the disappearance of common land that had followed the privatization of fiefs, was a persistent problem that continued to provoke revolts throughout the Risorgimento period, to the extent that peasant violence represented the most feared aspect of the revolutions of 1820, 1848–9 and 1860. Piedmont and Liguria were the only potential anti-Austrian regions in Italy. The Piedmontese House of Savoy sought to reverse the French experience and restore the past by refusing to grant a constitution, and reinstating the privileges of the aristocracy and the Church.

In Venice, despite the fact that many had welcomed the Austrians as liberators against the tyrannical French in 1797, the young nobles and professional middle classes had absorbed French revolutionary ideas and wanted a constitutional regime. Intellectuals began organizing throughout Lombardy-Venetia, where top jobs in the civil service and administration went to Austrians or to those who spoke German, where universities and schools had to follow the Viennese curriculum, and where the Austrian legal code was introduced. Italians saw this as a Germanic invasion – competent but foreign. Many northern landowners had properties in both Lombardy and Piedmont, and chose loyalty to Piedmont, often moving there and becoming officers in the Piedmontese army that would later wage war on Austria.

Secret societies continued to organize and ferment local revolutions in the 1820s and 1830s. One famous society, the 'Perfect Sublime Masters', was created by the Tuscan revolutionary Filippo Buonarroti (1761–1837) in northern Italy and, like the Carbonari in the south, it attracted thousands of former Napoleonic officers. A *carbonaro* from Genoa, Giuseppe Mazzini (1805–72), who dedicated his entire life to what the historian Mario Isenghi has described as his 'rigorous and extremely demanding idea of nation' based on the three principles of independence, unity and republic, addressed Italian youth in particular: in exile in Marseilles in 1831, he founded the clandestine organization, 'Young Italy'.

LANGUAGE AND NATION

After the Enlightenment, Romanticism came to dominate literature and philosophy, initially in Germany and England, and then in the rest of

---

Box 6.3   Buonarroti on secret societies and Mazzini's Young Italy

Buonarroti on secret societies:
The secret society . . . is a democratic institution in its principles and in its end; but its forms and its organisation cannot be those of a democracy. With respect to doctrines, which one assumes are held in a pure form by the leaders, they would be better preserved and transmitted by them . . . With respect to action . . . it is absolutely necessary that the impulse come from above and that all the rest obey. This society is nothing else but a secret army, destined to fight a powerful enemy.

(Eisenstein, 1959)

From the manifesto of Mazzini's Young Italy (1931):
Love of the country, abhorrence of Austria, and a burning desire to throw off her yoke, are passions now universally diffused, and the compromises inculcated by fear, or a mistaken notion of tactics and diplomacy, will be abandoned . . . Italy does know that there is no true war without the masses . . . that the secret of power is faith; that true virtue is sacrifice . . . We swear it by the thousands of victims that have fallen during the last ten years to prove that persecutions do not crush, but fortify conviction; we swear it by the human soul that aspires to progress.

(Mazzini, 1955)

Europe. It may seem contradictory, but the most original discussions on romanticism in Italy came from classicists such as Giacomo Leopardi, from Recanati in the Marche (1798–1837) and the Greek–Venetian Ugo Foscolo (1778–1827). The Piedmontese patriotic writer Silvio Pellico (1788–1854) argued that, while the apparent aim of these poets was romantic drama, the real aim was the development of Enlightenment ideas, which were at the heart of the Risorgimento. Italian poets of the time did not accept the appellation of 'romantic', regarding romanticism as having a 'barbarian' and Protestant origin.

Alfieri's message of national re-awakening from the end of the eighteenth century was taken up by Foscolo, who wrote a poem entitled *The Sepulchres* (later a classic reading for generations of Italians), introduced by a verse that sounds like a call to action: 'To great things the urns of the strong inflame strong souls.' The subject was the relationship between the tombs of Italy's dead greats and the best among the living, the latter needing inspiration to emulate past glories. Foscolo showed how, for centuries, Italy had lived with the problem of the comparison with its glorious past; the travellers of the Grand Tour always remarked on the contrast between past splendours, visible in Italy's ruins and architecture, and the present inferiority of a country of peasants, priests and bandits, divided into many small states. As the French clergyman and ambassador Dufour De Pradt wrote in a book on the Congress of Vienna, Italy had been transformed into a picture gallery that everyone wanted to visit. Foscolo's cry, 'Italians, I exhort you to histories', was a call to the inhabitants of Italy to feel part of one nation, by looking back at their history.

However, a nation needed a national literature and a national language, and the first political attempts to unify Italy developed alongside discussions on language and identity. In the first decades of the nineteenth century, Italy had still not achieved linguistic unity; and the written language was not that of spoken expression. In 1817, Stendhal remarked:

> The written language is only spoken in Florence and Rome. Everywhere else people continue to use the ancient local dialect, and speaking Florentine in ordinary conversation is considered ridiculous. A man who writes a letter opens the dictionary, and words are never emphatic or pompous enough. As a result spontaneity, simplicity, and a nuanced prose are unknown things in Italian. If one needs to express those feelings, one has to write in Venetian or in Milanese.
>
> (Stendhal, 1817)

In 1806, Manzoni wrote to the French scholar Claude Fauriel: 'The state of Italy divided in fragments, and the almost general laziness and ignorance have posed so much distance between the spoken and the written language, that the latter can be almost be defined as a dead language.' In *Zibaldone*, in 1821, Giacomo Leopardi wrote: 'in order to put the Italian language really on its feet, it is, in short, necessary to put Italy and the Italians on their feet'. Apart from Leopardi, one of the greatest Italian poets of all times, the most genuine language was expressed by two poets who wrote in dialect: Carlo Porta (1775–1821) in Milan, and Giuseppe Gioacchino Belli (1791–1863) in Rome. Both provided lively descriptions of popular life in their cities.

Leopardi lived in the Papal States and recalled Italy's past glory, denouncing both Austrian and French rule. His patriotic poems were not his best ones, but they created a bridge between Italian poetry and the Risorgimento. In an essay entitled *Discorso sopra lo stato presente dei costumi degli italiani* ('Reflection on the current state of Italians' habits'), written in 1824 but published for the first time in 1906, Leopardi investigated the causes of weak Italian identity, putting together an identikit picture that is in large part still valid today. In other European countries (apart from Spain, the only country Leopardi considered to be more backward than Italy) a social bond was maintained by the role of elites in the practice of good manners and habits, which were then disseminated among the lower classes; in Italy, however, there was no recognizable elite with which the whole of the society could identify. This led to problems of indifference, selfishness, apathy, cynicism, misanthropy, obtuseness and a short-sighted outlook among the Italians. Not only did Italy lack a political centre, it also lacked a sense of society:

> I leave out that the nation, not having a centre, does not have a truly Italian public; I leave out the lack of national theatre, and of a truly national and modern literature . . . But even leaving all this out, and focusing only on the lack of society, the natural result is that Italy does not have a manner, a specific Italian habit. Either there is no habit at all, or it is such a vague and indefinite concept that leaves the discretion of deciding how to act on any occasion almost entirely to each individual. Not only each city, but even each Italian has their own habit and manner.
>
> (Leopardi, 2001)

In *Zibaldone*, Leopardi emphasized the need to reinsert Italian intellectual life into the great circuit of European ideas. First, it was necessary to update the language in order to bring to life a civil society. The principal author of this reform was Manzoni, through his novel *The Betrothed*. In a letter to Fauriel in 1821, Manzoni wrote that the difficulty in dealing with historical subjects came principally from the poverty of the language:

> An Italian writes, if he is not Tuscan, in a language that he has almost never spoken, and (even if he was born in the privileged region) writes in another language which is spoken only by a small number of Italy's inhabitants . . . This poor writer completely lacks the feeling, so to speak, of communion with the reader, the certainty of managing an instrument equally known by both.

Against classicists and purists, Manzoni argued for the primacy of usage over literary tradition: 'usage is the arbiter, the master of languages', he wrote in *Sentir messa* ('To hear mass', 1835–6), a thesis he developed in the later works *Sulla lingua italiana* ('On the Italian language', 1847), *Saggio sul vocabolario italiano secondo l'uso di Firenze* ('Essay on the Italian vocabulary according to Florentine usage', 1856), and in the report *Dell'unità della lingua e dei mezzi di diffonderla* ('On the unity of the language and on the means to propagate it', 1868) produced when he was in his eighties and presiding over a commission for the study of the diffusion of 'good language and pronunciation' under the new state. The only written language that was both in use and understood all over Italy was Tuscan. The Tuscan language, spoken by educated people, therefore ought to become, according to Manzoni, the Italian language; between the national but unpopular solution of a literary language, and the popular but non-national solution of the dialects, Manzoni highlighted a third way: the living and spoken Florentine language.

Political unity was also to have consequences for language. According to the 1861 census, Italians who could read and write made up less than a quarter of the population, and that included even those who could only sign their names. In southern Italy in particular, 90 per cent of the population was illiterate. The percentage of these who could express themselves in Tuscan Italian varied from 2.5 per cent (according to Tullio De Mauro) to 9.5 per cent (according to Arrigo Castellani). Primary education was particularly in crisis: as Enrico Malato has observed, in the Kingdom of the Two Sicilies, the law authorized illiterate women to teach, and in Piedmont, one of the most advanced regions, teachers always spoke dialect, 'under the pretext that children would not otherwise understand'. Catholic opposition to mass education, based on the idea that education, without the support of religion, was an instrument that led to atheism and social disorder, contributed to the maintenance of ignorance.

ROMANTICISM AND RISORGIMENTO

Romantic literature arrived in Italy in the shape of an article by the French Romantic writer Madame de Staël, called '*Sulla maniera e la utilità delle traduzioni*' ('On the manner and utility of translations'), published by the periodical *Biblioteca italiana*. Italian Romanticism rejected the symbolism typical of the English and German variants and engaged with the rationalism of the Lombard Enlightenment, opening up the latter to the concept of 'the people'. In *Lettera semiseria di Grisostomo al suo figliuolo* ('Semi-serious letter from Grisostomo to his son', 1816), the Milanese poet and patriot Giovanni Berchet (1783–1851) wrote that the poet had to be understood by the people, the only class of individuals that was prone to emotion: 'The only true poetry should be popular poetry'. For this reason, writers needed to use a common language that was suited to the literate bourgeois public.

The years between the Restoration and Unification were those of the Risorgimento. In Italy, Romanticism became identified with the struggle for national independence. Romantic–Risorgimento literature was therefore politically engaged and was characterized by a strong educational strain, particularly regarding the bourgeois class, the 'people' that had to become a 'nation'. At the root of the flourishing patriotism was the Mazzinian Romantic idea of popularization. Mazzini's slogan was 'thought and action' and, at the time, 'action' meant illegal activity and could lead to prison, shooting, hanging or, in the Papal States, despite the Pope's hostility to the French Revolution, even the guillotine. Many followed Mazzini's example and went into exile (a path already trodden by Foscolo, the first Romantic exile). Condemned to death in Piedmont, a 27-year-old Mazzinian called Giuseppe Garibaldi fled Italy and began an adventure that made him the 'hero of the two worlds'; he took up arms in Latin America (where there are still streets and squares named after him today) until it was possible, in 1848, to return to fight in Italy. Another young Mazzinian, Jacopo Ruffini, sentenced to imprisonment at the same time as Garibaldi was sentenced to death, failed to escape and instead committed suicide for fear of not resisting interrogation. His two brothers followed Mazzini to England, where one of them, Giovanni Ruffini, wrote an autobiographical novel entitled *Lorenzo Benoni, or Passages in the Life of an Italian* (first published in Edinburgh in 1853). It narrates the vicissitudes of a young patriot who took part in the first Mazzinian conspiracies while at the same time living a romantic love story. All the elements of Risorgimento romanticism are present: autobiography, condemnation by the authorities, exile in England, and love. Ruffini also wrote a story, *Doctor Antonio*, which concerned an Italian exile who returned to Italy to fight and, forced to choose between love for a woman – an English lady who had challenged the social conventions of her society to follow him – and love for the *patria*, chose the latter. In an ending typical of Risorgimento romantic novels, he was imprisoned and the woman he loved died gazing at his prison from a castle in southern Italy. For many young men, death was associated with 'making history' – a violent self-sacrifice in the name of a higher ideal. In 1860, before leaving Genoa for Sicily, Garibaldi wrote to a relative: 'I have no other desire: to die for Italy.' In Federico De Roberto's master-piece *The Viceroys* (1894), set in Sicily just after Garibaldi's landing, one of the characters, Lorenzo, decides to become a *garibaldino* and sends a letter to his fiancée, Lucrezia, in which he announces his aim of joining Garibaldi to accomplish his duty to the Fatherland, and begs her not to cry should the great destiny of dying for Italy befall him.

Many attempts to continue the fight ignited by Mazzini were defeated. Failure created martyrs, and the sacrifice of the martyrs consciously fed Mazzini's civil 'religion' (the religion of the *patria*). The most famous of these sacrifices were made by the Bandiera brothers and by Carlo Pisacane, the former executed in 1844 and the latter lynched in 1857 after trying to organize revolutions in southern Italy and finding no support among the peasantry – both cases illustrating the lack of interest in the national cause.

A typical Italian genre of the time was the patriotic poetry that cele-brated the myth of the fallen hero. One of the first such poets was Alessandro Poerio (1802–48), a Neapolitan patriot who lived mostly in exile and died during the revolution in Venice. Poerio wrote the song *Risorgimento* (1836) and books of poetry full of comments on the martyrs for the Italian cause, on Italy's past glories and on the resting place of great Italians. Luigi Mercantini, author of a *Hymn to Garibaldi*, wrote refined poetry, particularly in *La Spigolatrice di Sapri* ('The gleaner of Sapri'), on the unfortunate expedition of Pisacane to Southern Italy (1857). In this poem, a peasant woman simply but movingly remembered:

> I was on my way to glean one morning/When I saw a ship in the middle of the sea/it was a steam ship,/and it carried a tricolour flag.

The story is alternated by the refrain: 'They were three hundred,/they were young and strong,/and they are dead'. Another famous refrain was that composed by Arnaldo Fusinato in the poem *A Venezia* ('To Venice', 1849), dedicated to the city's surrender to the Austrians after the long resistance that followed the 1848 revolution:

> The epidemic rages,/bread is lacking,/on the bridge /the white flag waves!

It was intended that the reader should be absorbed by the strong images of a myth that became legend. Many of these poems were written to be set to music and so were more widely diffused. The most famous was the

---

Box 6.4   Italy's national anthem (1847)

The anthem brings together glorious events from the Italian past (the battle of Legnano of 1176; the Sicilian Vespers; Ferruccio – Francesco Ferrucci, who defended Florence against Charles V in the sixteenth century; the child named Balilla who threw a stone at the Habsburg army, starting a popular revolt in Genoa in 1746); it also makes references to ancient Rome and to a Mazzinian religiosity:

> Italian brothers,/Italy has awakened,/And is wearing the helmet/Of Scipio on her head./Where is Victory?/Let her bow her head,/ Because God made her/Rome's slave.//*Let us join in legions,/We are ready to die!/Italy summoned us!*///For centuries we have/Been trampled on and derided,/Because we are not a people,/Because we are divided./Let it be that one flag,/One hope bind us together;/The hour has come/For us to join forces.//*Let us join in legions . . .*//Let us unite and love one another;/For unity and love/Show to peoples/The ways of the Lord/Let us swear to liberate/Our native soil;/If united under God,/Who can conquer us?//*Let us join in legions . . .*//From the Alps to Sicily,/Legnano is everywhere;/Every man has the heart/and hand of Ferruccio./The children of Italy/Are called Balilla;/The sound of every trumpet/Sounded the Vespers.// *Let us join in legions . . .*//The sold swords/are reeds that bend;/The Austrian eagle/Has already lost its feathers/Together with the Cossack/It drank Italian blood/And Polish blood/But its heart burned.//*Let us join in legions,/We are ready to die/Italy summoned us!*

march by Goffredo Mameli, with music by Michele Novaro, which later became Italy's national anthem, taking the title from its first line, *Fratelli d'Italia* ('Brothers of Italy', 1847). Born in Genoa in 1827 and educated in university Mazzinian circles within a strongly Romantic culture (including writers such as Victor Hugo, Lord Byron, Foscolo and Manzoni), Mameli died aged 22 in the defence of Rome alongside Garibaldi. In his songs, he embodied the Mazzinian ideal of poet-prophet, who translated thought into action through his literature.

A common thread running through this kind of literature was the repetitive character of the narrated events, in which the experience of the suffering of the national community was constantly renewed, with its natural continuity unchanged. The recurrent elements were: the oppression of Italy by foreign populations or tyrants; the internal division among the Italians, which favoured that oppression; the threat to the national honour caused by such oppression; and the unlucky but heroic attempts at redemption/liberation. The Risorgimento was therefore represented as the awakening of a people as it acquired consciousness of its past and of forgotten values, but it was also a proper resurrection – a cancellation of an original sin, a redemption from a political and ethical fall.

There was no European model for patriotic poetry. In Italy, it influenced people through songs played by bands or sung in cafés, and by resuming popular rhythmical structures. The opera (born, as was seen in Chapter 5, in the early seventeenth century) was extremely popular in the nineteenth century, and became a patriotic weapon, disguising its message to elude censorship. Gioachino Rossini in *William Tell* (1829) told the Swiss story of heroic resistance to oppression with allusions to the Italian case; Vincenzo Bellini, in *I puritani* (1835) described the hardship of exile (common to many Italian patriots in the 1820s and 1830s) and concluded the opera with the idea that it was beautiful to die shouting 'liberty'. In 1889, the poet Giosuè Carducci wrote that the composer Giuseppe Verdi (1813–1901) 'presaged the revival of the Fatherland'; his songs were 'unforgettable and sacred to anyone born before 1848'. Carducci was mainly referring to *Nabucco*, which became the most significant opera in its expression of the Risorgimento mood. *Nabucco* is set in Jerusalem and Babylon in 586 BC, but reminded the public of the Italian situation:

> Go, my thought, on golden wings/Go, alight upon the slopes, the hills,/where, soft and warm, the sweet breezes/of our native land are fragrant!/Greet the banks of the Jordan/ And Zion's razed towers. . ./Oh, my country so lovely and lost!/Oh, remembrance so dear and ill-fated!/Golden harp of the prophetic bards,/why do you hang mute on the willow?/Rekindle the memories in our breasts,/speak to us of the times of yore!/Just as for the cruel fate of Jerusalem,/intone a strain of bitter lamentation,/otherwise let the Lord inspire you with/a melody to give us strength to suffer!

The political effect of Verdi's opera can be attributed to the widespread popularity in Italy of the melodrama, which became the echo chamber of aspirations for national unity. Verdi's origins, a peasant family from the plain of Busseto near Parma, together with the fiery music of his early operas (*Rigoletto, Traviata* and *Trovatore*) were interpreted as a genuine expression of the soul of the Italian people. The public sometimes changed words to parts of his operas, to make the meaning more explicit: for example, in *Ernani* the 'lion of Castille' became the 'lion of St Mark'. According to Mazzini, Verdi's music inspired dramatic events and social faith, and became a universal language both for individuals and for the community. Mazzini also recognized a novelty in Rossini's choruses in a text of 1836 entitled *Philosophy of Music*. The historian Piero Brunello has interpreted the proclamation of the Venetian Republic by Daniele Manin in March 1848 as if it was modelled on Verdi's chorus of *Ernani* – as in an opera, in the squares of 1848 Italy patriots swore oaths, raising swords: ideas of brotherhood, oaths, proclamations of a fight against tyranny, the relationship between tenor and male chorus, all were elements typical of opera. In this sense, Verdi's operas can be seen as the 'soundtrack of 1848'.

Prison, exile, political battles and revolutions are the background to the extraordinary energy of the period, and to its literature. Exile was a key feature in the growth of the national and Romantic discourse. Italian intellectuals got together, especially in Paris and London, and produced a number of translations of French, English and German Romantic writers (including Honoré de Balzac, Hugo, Alphonse de Lamartine; William Shakespeare, Walter Scott, Byron; Johann von Goethe, Friedrich Schiller and Friedrich Klopstok). The Romantic spirit and national sentiment in Risorgimento literature combined in the historical novel, a popular genre at least until Unification; however, the most intense expressions are to be found in memoir writing, where literature expressed itself through history and politics. One of the most famous examples is *My Prisons* by Silvio Pellico; he was among the founders of *Il Conciliatore* in 1818, a Milanese newspaper that in many ways continued the experience of *Il Caffè*, but survived only briefly because of Austrian censorship. Pellico was arrested and sent to a harsh prison, an experience he described in his book, which is not directly political, but rather a narration of his intimate experience. *My Prisons* was edited many times and translated into other languages, making it the most-read Italian book of the nineteenth century – the Austrian Chancellor Prince von Metternich said that the book did more damage to Austria than a lost battle. The intellectual origins of *My Prisons* lay in the experience of Milanese journalism, and it can be seen as a product of eighteenth-century rationalism, in its problems with public dissemination, its distance from strictly literary interests, its pedagogic intentions and its civil passion.

Perhaps the most famous novel of Italian literature, Manzoni's *The Betrothed*, is a historical novel which tells the story of Renzo and Lucia, two lovers living in Spanish-dominated seventeenth-century Milan. The Spaniards were clearly associated with the Austrians in the nineteenth century, so the novel contains a patriotic message. A moderate Catholic, Manzoni also conveyed a religious message, intertwining large-scale and individual history; it is the story of an age seen through the eyes of the victims of high politics, and considers how individuals with faith in God can survive. Italy's history of the oppressed was one of dignified people who could withstand the pressured events. Manzoni wrote in beautiful literary Italian, which could be understood by the people without being provincial, and which contributed to its popularity.

Art, which over the previous two centuries had been more innovative than literature, was much less influential during the late eighteenth and early nineteenth centuries. Neo-classicism and the revival of archaeology were not as important as literature in the Risorgimento era. However, in sculpture, some world-class masterpieces were produced – in particular, the work of Antonio Canova (1757–1822), who produced, alongside busts of Napoleon (and the famous monument to the Emperor's sister, Pauline Bonaparte), the Tomb of Vittorio Alfieri in 1810; created before Napoleon's fall, this bore a crowned image representing Italy and was much discussed among his contemporaries, many of whom saw a patriotic message in it, despite Canova's commitment to the French Emperor.

THE DEVELOPMENT OF A NATIONAL DISCOURSE

Risorgimento thinkers and poets made reference to previous Italian thinkers and writers, establishing as they did so a cult of the 'fathers' of the nation – Dante, Petrarch, the Renaissance artists, Machiavelli and Galileo. Taken together, the reception of their ideas was the basis for the Risorgimento. The movement that led to the unification of Italy had many different souls – democratic, moderate, Catholic–liberal, anti-clerical, republican, monarchic. Early-twentieth-century anti-Fascist historians such as Gaetano Salvemini, Antonio Gramsci and Carlo Rosselli discussed the problems of the Risorgimento, convinced that its worst side (the most undemocratic forces) had triumphed. During the Resistance in the Second World War, there was an attempt to return to the democratic roots of the movement, the ones that had been repressed by Liberal Italy. Contradictions in the unification movement were evident as early as in 1848, however, particularly between a national–nationalist priority and the hope of a progressive and democratic solution. However, those divisions were not always apparent to all those men and women who, enthusiastically, in different ways and at different times, took part in revolutionary events. Indeed, the Risorgimento was not simply a movement of a narrow elite that rested on the actions of individual diplomats such as Count di Cavour or military leaders such as Garibaldi. As recently emphasized by Paul Ginsborg and Alberto Banti, despite the context of a largely illiterate society, tens of thousands of people took an active part as militants in political movements, while hundreds of thousands of others, often close to these militants, regarded the events of Unification with a mixture of trepidation and sympathy. The high numbers of those who became members of clandestine sects such as Young Italy, took part in revolts all over Italy in 1820–1, 1830–1 and 1848, participated in mass demonstrations, enrolled as volunteers in the wars for independence of 1849, 1859 and 1866, attempted insurrections in the 1850s, and fought alongside Garibaldi in 1860, constitute a highly significant aspect of Risorgimento history. The peasant participation in Sicily in 1860, the urban lower classes who fought behind the barricades with the bourgeois classes in 1848 in Milan and Venice, as well as the diffusion among all social classes of patriotic melodrama, are all elements that confirm the 'mass' dimension of the unification process. Moreover, the involvement of the 'people' was a conscious political aim for intellectuals who, despite the dangerous and illegal nature of their activity, sought to move large sections of the population to a militant commitment – to move 'people' to become a 'nation'.

Why did so many young men and women become patriots? Why did some decide to belong to secret societies, read forbidden books and think about subversive geopolitical transformation between 1796 and 1860? New Italian research, particularly by Alberto Banti, has begun to investigate what the national question meant for the men and women who saw it as an important part of their lives. The origins of the national discourse are to be found, once more, in the Enlightenment. In 1765, an article in *Il Caffè* entitled 'On the Fatherland of the Italians' imagined a conversation in a Milanese café. A newcomer arrives and mixes with a group of regular customers. One of the regulars enquires if he is a foreigner; the newcomer replies that he is not. He is asked if he is from Milan. Again, the answer is 'no'. The puzzled regular asks him where he is from, to which the stranger replies: 'I am Italian, and an Italian in Italy is never a foreigner, just as a Frenchman in France, or an Englishman in England.' They begin to converse and the newcomer outlines his views with reference to Italy's history: the origin of the Italian nation during the expansion of ancient Rome, when Rome extended its privileges to the whole country ('we were all similar at the beginning'); then the barbarians came, and for centuries Italians were disunited, but this had never altered those common origins – that uninterrupted continuity meant that all Italians should feel part of the same nation. The regular customer replies that differences between cities remained important; the newcomer agrees, adding that patriotism did not negate the legitimacy of Italy's ancient states and of their present institutional peculiarities. On a cultural level, they were all Italians and should contribute to Italy's artistic and scientific progress (which was what made a country into a nation), while politically it was natural to be loyal to one's own 'small Fatherland'.

Banti has demonstrated that this type of discourse was subject to a fundamental change from the 1790s. The impulse for that change came with Napoleon's Italian Army, through the pages of newspapers and leaflets, manifestos, books and prints, all of which were distributed around Italy in great quantity with astonishing speed. Unlike in previous decades, the *patria* no longer meant any kind of institutional system characterized by fair laws, but one single institutional unit: a republic with parliamentary representation. Patriotism, as writings of the time specified, was no longer just 'love for the *patria*' but 'love for the republican and democratic *patria*'. The authors of these writings were generally young intellectuals, journalists, writers, lawyers, doctors and former priests who had followed the events of the French Revolution with enthusiasm.

A decisive contribution to the discussion of a possible unitary Italian state came from Buonarroti. When the French were preparing the attack on Piedmont and Austrian Lombardy, he intensified contact with Italians living in Liguria and Nice in order to organize insurrectionary acts in support of the French. His speeches to the Italians in Nice (all Italians were brothers and sisters, all part of the same country and the same *patria*) influenced a proliferation of writing on the existence of a 'genius of the Italian nation', the principal characteristics of which derived from ancient Rome, a common blood and religion, common habits and language, and a precise and coherent geographical location. There was an imitation of France evident in many of these writings, in an attempt to eliminate the specific Italian history of cities and regions, and the complex variations this implied. This was difficult to sustain because, while it was true that

Italians had a common past, literary language and culture, the experiences of people who lived in different parts of the country varied along with environmental conditions, agricultural practices, and laws and institutions that had become stratified over the course of centuries.

After France compromised with Austria at Campoformio, the focus shifted from emulation of the French to a wholly Italian tradition. Foscolo, in the *Last Letters of Jacopo Ortis*, told of Jacopo's travels throughout Italy, including a visit to the Florentine church of St Croce, where he worshipped at the graves of Galileo, Machiavelli and Michelangelo. While contemplating these great Italians, Jacopo was 'overwhelmed by a sacred shiver'. By recognizing a common 'Italian genius', the story founded a new concept of militant nationalism independent of the French example. It was with this shift that the national discourse filtered into popular cultural expression such as poetry and opera – which reached the masses much more readily than did books or newspaper articles.

These emotional tempests were lived through by the younger generation – it was young people who discovered the nation and decided to fight for it. The Risorgimento was also a subversive phenomenon, which of course made it 'naturally' suited to the young. Ippolito Nievo's novel, *Le Confessioni di un italiano* (translated into English as *The Castle of Fratta*) contributed, perhaps even more than Manzoni's, to the construction of the national discourse. Nievo was born in Padua, and the characters of his novels moved mainly between Lombardy, Venetia and Friuli. He studied in the Lombardy-Venetian kingdom under the Habsburgs during the 1840s and 1850s, but was also involved in the political struggle against Austrian rule. In 1848, he was a Mazzinian and took part in the failed revolution in Mantua. He rejected the opportunity of following a judicial career, which would have entailed working for the Austrian administration, and instead became a writer and a radical journalist. In 1860, Nievo took part in Garibaldi's 'Thousand' expedition. During a journey from Palermo to Piedmont in 1861, charged with carrying some administrative documents for the expedition, he died when his ship went down. Nievo wrote his novel when he was still in his thirties, from the viewpoint of an 80-year-old man narrating his life spanning the eighteenth and nineteenth centuries. The novel included the typical ingredients of the nineteenth-century Romantic historical novel: castles, war, revolution (the protagonist takes part in the battles of the Risorgimento from the Napoleonic wars onwards), and a beautiful love story between the central character Carlino and his cousin Pisana, one of the most forceful female characters of Italian literature.

Women and families were also central to the national discourse. The family was expected to be the primary cell of the nation, educating and supporting the new generation of patriots. Foscolo, in exile in 1828, wrote an article, published by the *London Magazine* and entitled 'The Women of Italy', in which he condemned the practice of Church and aristocracy of keeping women locked away in convents; he thought that Italy could not have aspired to nationhood without the redefinition of women's role within the family. Mazzini also addressed Italian women as heads of the patriotic family – the heart of the *patria*. While Foscolo focused on the family of the elite, Mazzini sought to popularize a strong and classless image of the Italian family, which would produce citizens ready to sacrifice their lives. Many Risorgimento heroes were supported enthusiastically by their parents, particularly by their mothers, who at times appeared ready to sustain them even in the most self-destructive adventures. De Roberto described the patriotic character of Lorenzo (*The Viceroys*) thus: 'He was really a good young man, studious, a bit hot-headed, inflamed by the liberal ideas of his uncle, burning with love for Italy: when he wrote to his girlfriend he told her that he had three passions: herself, his mother, and the fatherland that needed to be redeemed.' Italian Risorgimento families therefore embodied a tension between familial love and the call of Romantic nationalism.

As Simonetta Soldani has demonstrated, many women became attracted to the national movement thorough the ideas of moderate Catholicism. Once involved, they made an important contribution to the success of patriotic–religious liturgies and the numerous ceremonies of mourning, thanksgiving and hope organized all over Italy in 1848. Once there were men killed, wounded and imprisoned for the cause, women in different parts of Italy began to exchange expressions of solidarity with one another. In 1848, Tuscan and Lombard newspapers published an 'address of gratitude from Tuscan women to Lombard women', for the help received by Tuscan patriots from Lombard women who sheltered, nursed and fed them during the first war of independence. Collective greetings, as signs of reciprocal recognition, continued to be exchanged after 1848 between women from Sicily, Tuscany, Lombardy, Venice, Genoa and Bologna.

THE REVOLUTION BEGINS: 1848

There were different ideas of nation, many *Italie in cammino* ('Italies in the making'): anti-clerical and neo-Guelph, democratic and moderate, republican and monarchist, unitarian and federalist. However, when the supporters of these views described the Italian nation in itself rather than specifically in relation to political outcomes, these differences disappeared – Banti calls this correspondence the 'elementary morphology of the national discourse'.

Mazzini took it for granted that Italy existed as a nation just like other European countries, because of its common literary culture, which justified the right to self-government and independence. His major enemy was the Papacy, since he favoured secular education and believed that only Rome could be the capital of Italy. As many before him, Mazzini wanted an end to Papal temporal power, but also the end of its power over the spiritual education of Italians. For many Risorgimento leaders, Catholic and anti-Catholic alike, the legacy of Rome was a central issue. For this reason, the unification of Italy was bound to produce a clash with the Papacy. However, Mazzini believed in God, and believed that Italian unification was God's will, and this provided a crucial aspect of his attempt to construct a civil religion.

Mazzini's belief in insurrection by the people – though by 'people' he meant urban intellectuals and the educated class, rather than the masses of peasants – was considered damaging by other, more moderate, supporters of the national cause. Among these was Vincenzo Gioberti (1801–52), a Catholic priest whose vision for the unification of Italy was as a confederation of states under the Pope's leadership – an idea that consciously recalled the Guelph factions of the Middle Ages, hence his programme was named 'neo-Guelph'. Gioberti reunited the history of Italy with the history of Rome, underlining the continuity between Latin and Catholic civilization, and asserting religion as the moral foundation of the Italian nation. He outlined his programme in an 1843 book entitled *On the Moral and Civil Primacy of the Italians*, in which he argued that only Rome expressed 'in embryo the unity of Italy and of the world'. These ideas influenced Pope Pius IX, newly elected in 1846, who became famous both in Italy and abroad as a 'liberal Pope'. However, there were many problems inherent in Gioberti's programme, not least the continued Austrian presence in northern Italy. Gioberti managed not to mention this anywhere in his book, because Austria was a key ally of the Pope. Moreover, he left open the question of why Italian states would want to be controlled by the Papacy.

Despite these contradictions (the title of 'liberal Pope' was itself an oxymoron), expectations rose that Pius IX would become the author of the future Italy proposed in Gioberti's *Primacy*. The image of Rome was turned upside-down, from the site of the past to the site of the future – no longer in Jacobin republican form, but now with an ecclesiastical focus. The idea of the Pope as a symbol of renewal assumed different meanings: a politico-national meaning for the liberals, and a religious–cultural meaning for those Catholics tired of the Church's traditionalism; for the Roman lower classes, the Pope represented a millennarian aspiration for a better life. These expectations were raised, often independently of the Pope's will, all over Italy, challenging the Restoration settlement. Between the Pope's declaration of an amnesty for political prisoners in 1846 and withdrawal from the war against Austria in 1848, Rome became the theatre for an impressive number of feasts and popular banquets, where the Pope was cheered and the rebirth of the city proclaimed, expressed, as Bartolini has described, with an 'impatient, almost revolutionary fervour'.

This fervour was met with bitter disappointment when the Pope made clear that he would not take part in an anti-Austrian war (and later withdrew all his 'liberal' concessions); in place of Papal leadership a moderate but secular programme gained ground, following the defeat of the revolutions. Led by Cavour and the House of Savoy in the 1850s, this proposal had first been presented by the Piedmontese Cesare Balbo (1789–1853) who, in *The Hopes of Italy*, argued for a federal union led by Piedmont. Balbo believed that King Charles Albert must take the initiative by waging war on Austria to unite Lombardy-Venetia with Piedmont. The problem with Balbo's programme was that he devoted little attention to the rest of Italy and focused on the north. These many and competing views all had a part to play in the revolutions that rocked the peninsula in 1848, and the first war of independence that followed.

The Italian revolution of 1848 began in Palermo, and forced the Bourbon monarchy to declare a provisional constitutional government. The fact that events occurred in Palermo before Milan has often been cited to counter the opinion that the Risorgimento was an imposition of the north against the south. The revolt started in the city of Palermo and immediately received help from the countryside (where armed gangs were organized), and extended to the surrounding areas and the continental south. The social unrest already present in the south, together with endemic unemployment in Naples and Palermo, brought about a temporary alliance between the urban lower classes, artisans, intellectuals and political activists. Anger was turned against the landowners of the big estates. Ferdinand II Bourbon was forced to concede a constitution, which inspired a temporary and enthusiastic political unity as well as liberal optimism; liberal and democratic newspapers flourished in the capital and provinces. A new government in Palermo was led by autonomists, who wanted a democratic constitution and separation from Naples. However, the Sicilian separatist movement was divided, as not all liberals agreed on the virtues of separation, and these tensions within the liberal movement weakened the revolution. Moderates wanted a stable compromise between the monarchy and parliament, afraid of mass political participation, while the democrats wanted to forge links with the masses through universal suffrage.

The revolution had a European dimension, and when a revolt broke out in Vienna, Italians answered with anti-Austrian risings in Milan and Venice. The patriot Daniele Manin (1804–57) led the Venetian revolution, which liberated prisoners and organized a Civil Guard. The Republic of St Mark was reborn. A day later, on 18 March 1848, the Milanese people began one of the most memorable events of the Risorgimento, the 'five days' of insurrection – a mass participation, including women, children and priests, that defeated the Austrian army. In the second day of the fighting, the Austrian general, Joseph Radetzky, admitted that there were more than 1,000 barricades in the city – which became symbols of collective defence against the weapons of power, an expression of the century's Romanticism. During these five days, Milan's image as victim of foreign occupation was replaced by that of a revolutionary city. On the first day, a manifesto appeared on the city walls that expressed the conviction that the future of Italy was at stake in Milan:

> People of Milan! The eyes of Europe are upon us considering whether our prolonged silence had been dictated by intelligent prudence or by fear. The provinces are waiting for a command from us. The destiny of Italy is in our hands. One day alone can decide the destiny of a whole century. Discipline! Unity! Courage!

Liberals and democrats returned to Milan from all over Italy. The celebration of the liberation from the Austrians revived memories of the history of the medieval commune; for example, by marking the anniversary of the battle of Legnano: 'Let the Germans come down again,' shouted the democrat, Pietro Perego, 'and we shall answer: to Legnano'; 'the sovereign people still remember those days ... and they are ready to renew them'.

Unity did not last long, as programmes for the Risorgimento continued to present a variety of proposals. Carlo Cattaneo, who played a primary role in the Milanese insurrection, supported the idea of a democratic republic (established successfully during the Venetian revolution), but he did not believe that it made sense for Italy to become a unified state with its capital in Rome, as the Mazzinians wanted; out of respect for Italy's regional traditions, Cattaneo advocated a democratic but federal solution. For him, Italy was not enslaved so much by foreigners as by its own leaders: freedom came before nationality. The solution he most despised was that of an Italy under the Piedmontese monarchy; his antipathy was such that when the moderates called Charles Albert to Milan, Cattaneo proclaimed that it had been useless to fight and defeat the Austrians only in order to be invaded by another (albeit Italian) monarchy.

Charles Albert decided to declare war on Austria, not to help the revolutionaries but, on the contrary, to take control of the situation to avoid the proclamation of a republic in Turin. He had been considering war against Austria with the aim of creating a kingdom of northern Italy and liberating the country from foreign occupation, but the war he imagined was a dynastic conflict supported by moderates, not a people's war provoked by insurrection in the wider context of a republican revolution. The Pope retreated, also worried by the political events, writing a document, called 'allocution', in which he restated his role as Pope of all Catholics, including Austrians. Volunteers from across the peninsula joined the Piedmontese army, transforming a war of the House of Savoy into the first war of Italian independence. After defeat at Custoza, the Piedmontese signed an armistice with Austria, but fought again a few months later, in March 1849, only to be defeated again, this time in Novara. Charles Albert was forced to abdicate and left the throne to his son, Victor Emmanuel II, under whose reign Italian unification was accomplished more than a decade later. Victor Emmanuel decided to maintain the constitution in Piedmont (the *Statuto*), in contrast to the other states, where rulers who returned to power after the defeat of the revolutions re-established their old regimes: for this reason, the 1850s are called the years of the 'second restoration'.

While in regular warfare the Italians had reinforced their reputation as a people incapable of fighting, the popular wars of the Risorgimento demonstrated the capacity of the popular masses to sacrifice and fight courageously in both defeat and victory. Shortly after the five days of Milan, the people of Brescia resisted the Austrian attack for ten days – days that ended in slaughter, and fixed two opposed images in the national memory: of the city as the 'lioness of Italy'; and of the Austrian general Julius von Haynau as 'the hyena of Brescia'. The defences of Rome and Venice would become mythologized to a greater extent, lasting, as they did, for months rather than days. The Roman Republic survived from February to June 1849, organized by Mazzini, Mameli and Garibaldi – the latter leading the military resistance against French troops summoned by the Pope to defend his temporal power. The Roman Republic was the most democratic (as demonstrated by its progressive constitution), reflecting the ideas of the radical current of the Risorgimento. More than 400 *garibaldini* died in one day during its defence. As Garibaldi moved north to fight in defence of the Venetian Republic, his wife Anita died, aged 31, an event that contributed to his cult as romantic hero of the Risorgimento. Patriots came to Venice from across the country, demonstrating the national significance of the struggle. In August the city surrendered in the face of Austrian bombs, hunger and cholera. The Venetian experience, like the Roman and the Milanese, took symbols of the city's past (St Mark, the republic) and united them with symbols of Italy's unification, such as the tricolour flag – even if it sometimes appeared with horizontal rather than vertical stripes.

THE IMPOSSIBLE RESTORATION

The second restoration was much more repressive than the first; Italy was still ruled by foreigners, now more overtly than before. French troops were stationed in Rome, Austria kept garrisons in Tuscany and central Italy, and placed Lombardy under military rule. However, the revolutions of 1848 had changed the situation fundamentally, and no real restoration was possible. The Bourbons never recovered their popularity; political stability could not be re-established in Sicily, as the island's economic problems and social discontent had not been addressed. The repressive aspects of the monarchy increased: the police state was strengthened, intellectuals were removed from administration, censorship was reintroduced, as was Church control over education; spies infiltrated the population, leading to arrests and trials, and bandits were recruited by the government to inform on political activists. Unsatisfied expectations were, however, still present. Middle-class discontent continued, as the government invested heavily in the army to the detriment of education and public works, and there were considerably more democrats and dissenters than before 1848. Many democratic and moderate exiles had moved to Piedmont, Switzerland, Britain and France. Austrian rule in Lombardy lost its reputation for efficient administration and acquired one for cruelty and tyranny. It was hated by the middle classes and even by the most influential aristocratic families. In Rome, the aristocracy welcomed the Pope's return, preferring stability over revolution and the republic, but the Pope had betrayed the expectations of the middle classes, which were now against him. Rome faced a financially disastrous situation and was not capable of military self-defence, being entirely dependent on the French.

Piedmont represented the only exception to the triumph of absolutism and reaction in Italy after 1848; it was the only state not dependent on Austrian influence or military power, and the only one to retain a constitution, with an elected parliament sharing governmental responsibilities with the monarchy. Victor Emmanuel believed the *Statuto* was important to keep democrats under control and to maintain the support of the moderates, which he needed because of his anti-Austrian stance. The *Statuto* (which became Italy's constitution on unification and remained so until the Republican constitution of 1948) was very moderate but its mere existence ensured a special role for Piedmont in Italy. It established the principle of judicial independence, the equality of citizens before the law, and rights of association. However, the aristocracy remained in control, property was declared inviolable, and the king remained the sole executive power and commander of the armed forces; and the alliance between throne and altar was confirmed, with Catholicism being declared the official state religion. Around 100,000 exiles moved from all over Italy to Piedmont, where they could meet, discuss publicly and promote the development and circulation of newspapers: they created an Italian culture in a single region. Some of them became deputies in the parliament and even ministers, since all Italians, though not foreigners, had the right to vote and stand for office. The constitution forced new behaviour on the aristocrats, as they now had to contest elections and persuade voters. The monarchy maintained control, but before long, intelligent politicians were able to influence parliament and public opinion. In addition, the constitution gave Piedmont the approval of foreign liberal states; it therefore acquired a new status, as a liberal national focal point.

Many exiles came from southern Italy. Some supported a return to Muratism (that is, they wanted to replace Ferdinand with Luciano Murat, the son of Joachim Murat, who had governed in Naples under Napoleon) in the hope of attracting French support, which they failed to achieve. Most of the liberal moderates championed Piedmontese leadership of a united Italy under Victor Emmanuel and looked to Cavour for assistance against Bourbon reaction. Many democratic exiles looked beyond a united Italy; a minority such as Carlo Pisacane, Rosolino Pilo and Pasquale Calvi opposed any compromise with the monarchy and sought to mobilize the rural poor of the South, placing social revolution before unification; others, such as Francesco Crispi (1819–1901), wanted the unity of Italy above all else, and were ready to compromise with the House of Savoy.

After the defeat of various Mazzinian and democratic attempts in the 1850s, unification under the House of Savoy seemed the only practical solution. Between 1849 and 1852, the Turin government was led by Massimo D'Azeglio (1798–1866); a Piedmontese patriot, an aristocrat and a liberal moderate politician, he was Balbo's cousin and married Manzoni's daughter. He was also a painter (of Italian Romantic–patriotic landscapes) and a novelist. The Piedmontese parliament was not made up of organized parties, but of groups named 'Right' and 'Left'. Neither group was disciplined, and deputies voted however they liked (as, for example, on anti-clerical reforms). Each government therefore sought to offer concessions and win MPs favour for each vote, a practice that has been interpreted as the beginnings of 'transformism' and corruption in the Italian political system. In 1852, Cavour replaced D'Azeglio as Prime Minister. Cavour was opposed both to the Mazzinians and to absolute monarchy, had edited *Il Risorgimento* with Balbo and had pressed for the constitution in 1848, when he entered parliament for the first time. After studying in France and Britain, he became a supporter of economic liberal systems and was responsible for the reforms of the army, administration and financial system that modernized Piedmont in the 1850s.

Cavour's diplomatic ability persuaded European powers, and Italian conservatives, that the choice was between revolution and Piedmont. A partial reconciliation took place between moderates and the defeated democrats, in the shape of the National Society (founded in 1856), led by Garibaldi with Manin as president, alongside a Sicilian, Giuseppe La Farina, who sought to promote an alliance between the House of Savoy and the national movement. The Society fomented national public opinion all over Italy and became an ideal instrument in Cavour's hands, particularly effective in the Romagna and the Papal States. The slogan was clarified: 'Italy and Victor Emmanuel'. In the name of this slogan, the Thousand (almost all of whom were republican democrats) defeated the Bourbons in Sicily and Naples in 1860. However, before the success of this popular conflict, a second war of independence in 1859 had already seen Cavour's efforts crowned with triumph, thanks in part to a French alliance and British benevolence.

The battles against the Austrians (Magenta, S. Martino and Solferino) were won mainly by the French army and ended with an armistice at Villafranca that only ceded Lombardy to Piedmont. The main Italian contribution to the war came from the mass desertion of Italian soldiers from the Austrian army. The popular element once more imposed itself, with protests in Tuscany, Emilia and Romagna, which led to the annexation of these regions to Piedmont, which the French Emperor Napoleon III accepted thanks to Cavour's persuasion and at the price of granting Nice and Savoy in exchange. The annexations were decided by plebiscites, the results of which can still be seen on the walls of municipal government buildings around Italy.

These plebiscites, which confirmed the annexation of parts of Italy to the House of Savoy – Lombardy in 1848 (although temporarily nullified by the Austrian re-conquest of the region in 1849), southern Italy in 1860, Venetia in 1866 and Rome in 1870 – have often been described as merely a manipulation of public opinion, well orchestrated by the National Society and controlled by the new rulers. They were not consultations similar to elections, as they took place once events had already occurred and served to celebrate the new situation; indeed, they were public and collective gatherings, generally with rulers at the head of processions and peasants following. However, new studies have begun to take them more seriously and explore what actually happened on occasions that represented, at least until Fascist mobilization in the following century, the highest point of popular participation in political consultation. The percentage of the votes in favour of Italian unification ranged from 92.6 per cent in the Marche to 99.9 percent in Mantua and Venetia. A number of paintings and drawings, many of which were produced by foreigners, illustrate the feeling of joy surrounding the voting procedure. The practicalities took place during feasts of a highly theatrical character involving not just voters but the whole of society, including women and children; the imperative of national unity eliminated divisions of class, party, generation and gender. During these patriotic moments, between 1848 and 1870, squares, streets, buildings and monuments were wrapped in tricolour flags, and men and women wore tricolour cockades on their hats and clothes.

WARS AND REVOLUTIONS FROM GENOA TO ROME – VIA PALERMO, NAPLES AND VENICE

Despite being blamed after unification for being an obstacle to Italian unity, southern Italy played a vital role in the process; it brought about the administrative collapse of the Bourbons, and the peasant revolt in Sicily enabled Garibaldi's successful campaign for Naples. When Ferdinand died in 1859, his successor, Francis II, continued the policy of neutrality towards Austria; when the people of Naples celebrated Piedmont's victory against Austria, he employed troops to crush popular demonstrations. In April 1860, a Mazzinian insurrection in Palermo was crushed by the police, but the execution of the conspirators had unfortunate consequences for the Bourbons; repression brought international condemnation and popular upheavals in the countryside. Peasants rebelled against taxes and carried the tricolour flag into the towns. Conspiracies continued despite the efforts to impose an apparent order by force. The exiles Pilo and Crispi returned to Sicily, the former to mobilize the countryside, and the latter to organize an expedition from the north to be led by Garibaldi. From Quarto near Genoa, one thousand *garibaldini*, students, intellectuals and manual workers, mainly from northern and central Italy, left in two ships, the Lombardo and the Piemonte. After stopping at Talamone on the Tuscan coast to stock up with arms, they reached Marsala in Sicily. In his memoirs, one of the *garibaldini*, Cesare Abba, wrote a description of the Sicilian exiles seeing the Sicilian coast as the ship approached it:

> How easy it is to recognize the Sicilian exiles among us! There they are, all crowding at the bows. They seem to concentrate their whole being in their eyes. There are about twenty of them, of all ages. It will be a miracle if Colonel Carini gets ashore alive, seeing that his heart is bursting with joy.

Once on the island, supported by the local peasant masses who were promised land if they fought with Garibaldi, the thousand now joined by other volunteers defeated the Bourbon army. By August they were in Calabria, and by September had reached Naples, unopposed and triumphant.

These events and their impact on Sicilian society have been recounted by Giuseppe Tomasi di Lampedusa (1896–1957) in his novel *The Leopard* (published posthumously in 1959), which described how the old elite managed to survive the events. Two episodes in the story are particularly revealing. Following Garibaldi's landing at Marsala, the brother-in-law of the aristocratic protagonist of the novel, the Prince of Salina, writes in a letter to the Prince: 'I am writing to you in a state of utter collapse ... The Piedmontese have landed. We are all lost.' However, the prince does not panic: 'the name of Garibaldi disturbed him a little. That adventurer all hair and beard was a pure Mazzinian'; nevertheless, he reflected, 'if that *Galantuomo* King of his has let him come down here it means they are sure of him. They'll curb him'. Indeed, the prince's nephew, Tancredi, who volunteers for Garibaldi's army, explains to him: 'unless we ourselves take a hand now, they'll foist a republic on us. If we want things to stay as they are, things will have to change'. The new liberal middle class, which many aristocrats feared would take power, soon begins to mix with the aristocracy, initially shocking the prince. When the liberal leader Don Calogero visits him wearing a tailcoat, the prince considers the fact that a non-aristocrat can climb the stairs of the palace dressed like that was a worse affront than the bulletin about Garibaldi's landing at Marsala. In the same way, the hatred for Cavour expressed by the reactionary priest Don Blasco in *The Viceroys* ('Don Blasco expressed himself violently against that Piedmontese polenta-eater') was soothed when a family member, the Duke of Oragua, is finally elected to the new Italian parliament; the duke's brother explaining to his young son: 'Can you see how much honour the uncle is bringing into our family? When we had the viceroys, our relatives were viceroys; now that we have a parliament, uncle is a member of parliament!'

Garibaldi's success forced Cavour to rethink Piedmont's role in Italy, not least because Garibaldi claimed the south in the name of Italy and the king, was a leader of the National Society and was more moderate than radical. The only way to control the south was for Cavour to choose annexation. In September, he sent troops to Rome to prevent Garibaldi's march on the city, which risked conflict with France and, in October, a plebiscite in the south favoured annexation. Expanding Piedmontese rule over the whole of Italy signified the final defeat of the democrats. Cavour succeeded because he exploited the divisions within the southern liberal movement, and because the opposition did not have a stronger alternative to Piedmont.

In 1861, when Turin became the capital of Italy, Venice was still under the Austrians and Papal Rome was protected by French control. The republicans accused the Piedmontese king of continual surrender, first at Villafranca, then in preventing Garibaldi from going to Rome. However,

Papal control of Rome was clearly precarious. Garibaldi's followers continued to prepare for attack, and Cavour finally declared that Rome must be Italy's capital city. By the time of his death in 1861, Cavour was one of the foremost architects of the unification of Italy, which could not have been brought about without the diplomatic successes he achieved during the second war of independence. Though it has often been argued that Cavour was interested only in the expansion of Piedmont, and he spoke and wrote mainly in French, he was a liberal moderate who took part in the culture of the Risorgimento, and eventually supported Garibaldi and the National Society. Cavour's legacy also continued in the area of anti-clericalism, as his laws limiting the power of the Church and his slogan of 'a free Church in a free state' became the basis for state–Church relations during Liberal Italy.

Establishing Rome as the capital of Italy took more years of struggle and diplomacy. In 1862, Garibaldi moved up from Sicily towards Rome with his volunteers. Diplomatic reaction to this alarmed the government, and the king moved to stop Garibaldi (the man who had liberated southern Italy in his name!), subsequently defeating him at the battle of Aspromonte. In 1864, a centre-right government led by the Bolognese Marco Minghetti (1818–86) treated with the French, who agreed to leave Rome within two years, while Italy promised not to attack the city; the capital was moved to Florence in 1865. The following year, the French duly left Rome, but when Garibaldi gathered another force, his 3,000 volunteers were defeated by a combination of Papal forces and the French, who had returned to protect Rome. At this point the situation was resolved by war rather than diplomacy or guerrilla action. The Prussian prime minister and later German Chancellor, Otto von Bismarck, who during the wars for German unification needed to open a front in Italy, proposed an alliance between Prussia and the Italian government against Austria; in the event of victory, Italy would be given Venice. The Italian army continued to demonstrate military incompetence with defeats at Custoza and Lissa, on the Adriatic, but Prussia won the war north of the Alps at Sadowa, and Venetia became part of Italy. The result of the plebiscites was 642,000 in favour and 69 against unification, though this last war of independence was a farce in comparison with the popular battles fought in the earlier struggle for independence. When Prussia fought another war against France in 1870, the French garrison was forced to leave Rome to move extra military forces to the Rhine. In September 1870, the Italian army finally entered Rome through a breach at Porta Pia, one of the gates in the walls surrounding the city that Michelangelo had created in the sixteenth century. The plebiscite resulted in 133,681 for and 1,507 against unification. Rome was finally proclaimed Italy's capital and Pius IX declared himself a 'prisoner in the Vatican', denouncing the new kingdom and the loss of his territories.

Various meanings were attributed to Porta Pia, as became clear from the annual celebrations that followed the liberation of Rome. From the start, the celebrations were spontaneous, involving different elements of the Roman population. Two distinct initiatives soon became evident, expressing the different moods of the Risorgimento: one came from the municipal authorities and was supported by the government, commemorating national unification under the banner of the monarchy with military parades, the distribution of medals and the illumination of public buildings. The other initiative came from political and civil associations such as workers' and anti-clerical societies, which organized demonstrations that were often republican and anti-government in nature. These unofficial celebrations were accompanied by feasting in the areas in Rome where the bulk of the ordinary people lived; these were the first secular mass festivals held in united Italy as they included potentially revolutionary ridicule directed both at clerics and at the government.

However, these divisions became apparent only after the first anniversary of unification. At the time, the celebrations united all factions in a solemn and joyful spectacle. Edmondo De Amicis, one of the most famous writers of Liberal Italy, described, in his *Impressions of Rome*, the overwhelming happiness of the patriots during the events of 20 September 1870 – the long-awaited moment:

> These big squares, these huge fountains, these giant monuments, these memories, this soil, this name of Rome, the soldiers, the tricolour flags, the prisoners, the people, the screams, the music, that secular majesty, this new joy, this reconciliation that memory brings between times, events and triumphs both ancient and modern; all this together is something that fascinates us, that strikes here, in the middle of our forehead, and seems to make reason dither; one would say that it is a dream; we almost cannot believe our eyes; it is a happiness that overwhelms the strengths of the heart. Rome! We cry out.

> (De Amicis, 1870)

Map 6.3   Unified Italy (1870)

Source: from John A. Davis, *Italy in the Nineteenth Century, 1796–1900* (Oxford: Oxford University Press), p. 293, by permission of Oxford University Press.

SELECTED FURTHER READING

D. Carpanetto and G. Ricuperati, *Italy in the Age of Reason, 1685–1789* (London: Longman, 1987) and J. Davis (ed.), *Italy in the Nineteenth Century, 1796–1900* (Oxford: Oxford University Press, 2000) are indispensable introductions to the period that led to Italian unification. An analysis of the challenges to the national project can be found in C. Duggan, *The Force of Destiny: A History of Italy since 1796* (London: Penguin, 2007). C. Lovett, *The Democratic Movement in Italy, 1830–1876* (Cambridge, Mass.: Harvard University Press, 1982) focuses on democratic nationalism in the Risorgimento process. A. R. Ascoli and K. von Hermeberg (eds), *Making and Remaking Italy: The Cultivation of National Identity around the Risorgimento* (Oxford: Berg, 2001) is a collection of valuable essays on the perception, implementation and contestation of Italian national identity, while L. Riall, *Garibaldi: Invention of a Hero* (New Haven, Conn.: Yale University Press, 2007) is a thorough examination of the myth-making that surrounded Garibaldi.

7

Liberal Italy

CHRONOLOGY

1878	Death of King Victor Emmanuel II; succession of Umberto I
1882	Triple Alliance between Italy, Austria-Hungary and Germany
1887	Francesco Crispi becomes prime minister
1892	Foundation of the Italian Socialist Party
1896	Italy defeated in colonial war at Adowa (Ethiopia); Crispi resigns
1898	Riots in Milan
1900	King Umberto I assassinated; succession of Victor Emmanuel III
1903	Giovanni Giolitti becomes prime minister
1910	Foundation of the Italian Nationalist Association
1912	Universal male suffrage
1914	'Red week' in June; Giolitti resigns; Antonio Salandra becomes prime minister; outbreak of First World War in August – Italy remains neutral; Pope Benedict XV succeeds Pius X
1915	Treaty of London with Britain, France and Russia; Italy declares war on Austria

CELEBRATING THE NEW NATION

In 1876, Pasquale Villari addressed the Italian parliament, reminding members that 'outside our narrow circle there is a numerous class to which Italy has never given a thought, and which it must finally take into consideration'. As early as 1843, in *On the Civil and Moral Primacy of the Italians*, Vincenzo Gioberti (1801–52) had argued that Italy existed on two levels: living and active for intellectuals and for some among the ruling classes, passive and 'vegetative' for the masses. Once unification had been achieved politically, the major question was, therefore, how to create an active loyalty to the new state among those who had hitherto been passive.

It was not solely in the new states such as Italy and Germany that nineteenth-century European post-revolutionary rulers confronted the problem of transforming people into citizens – as Eugen Weber has put it, regarding the French case, 'peasants into Frenchmen'. In a political democracy amid the constant threat of social revolution following the Paris Commune of 1871, it was necessary to find new methods of government and ways of creating loyalty; to invent a 'civil religion'. The symbol of Marianne in France was a unifying one, even though it was represented in different ways by radical Jacobins and moderates, as the monuments studied by Maurice Agulhon in radical and moderate local councils illustrated. In *The Invention of Tradition*, Eric Hobsbawm explained the two different levels – official and unofficial – involved in the construction of new traditions. The former is a 'political' level – institutional, organized by the state; while the latter is 'social', organized by associations and civil society. These two levels were evident in the case of the celebrations for Porta Pia, discussed in Chapter 6. However, historians should be cautious when using the term 'invention' in the case of the Italian Risorgimento; for example, an anti-clerical tradition was not *invented* in 1870 but had existed, albeit repressed, for centuries. Major steps towards the construction of a civil religion in Europe included the creation of a secular equivalent to the Church through state schooling, which promoted Republican values in France or monarchic values in Germany and Italy; the organization of public ceremonies; and the erection of public monuments representing both national and local heroes – for example, the statues of Victor Emmanuel, Garibaldi and Cavour to be found all over Italy, to which every city added its own local heroes, such as the statue erected to Manin in Venice.

The socialist movement, which began to grow towards the end of the century, was also aware that a nation-building process required the identification of *all* social classes, and the working class in particular, with the new state. With the foundation of an Italian Socialist Party in 1892, it became evident that socialism also acted within the boundaries of the nation – as a national section of the International. The most difficult goal for any political party was winning over the peasantry, which had only been involved actively in the Risorgimento on a few occasions. For the most part, the peasantry had local concerns, and was not yet educated in the cult of the nation; nevertheless, the new ruling class believed it to be possible to control the peasants because they were used to obeying traditional authorities such as the Church and the king. However, creating loyalty to the House of Savoy was another question: for centuries, the Savoy dynasty had meant little to those outside Piedmont, and, moreover, the Church (to which most of the peasant masses were loyal) opposed the new state. The decision to enfranchise only 2 per cent of Italians reflected these difficulties.

Having Rome as the new capital served the national myth. At its foundation as a state, Italy did not try to emulate ancient Rome but, on the contrary, seemed keen to free itself from that history. All that remained from the classical age was Rome's mission to civilize – for Gioberti, Catholic Rome; for Mazzini, Rome as the centre of the popular march towards fraternity and progress. The question of the new Rome was very important to the young nation, as is evident from the celebrations and buildings of the immediate post-1870 years. One crucial event was the welcoming ceremony for the king on his arrival in the capital. Until 1870 these ceremonies had been reserved for Popes, so it became necessary to create a new route around the city for civil processions, marked with new secular symbols. The Left deputy Benedetto Cairoli (1825–89) wrote about the need physically to create a new Rome, the symbol of Italian unification, alongside ancient Rome and the Rome of the Popes. Town planning became a vital part of this ambition. Piazza Venezia was chosen as the site for a huge monument to the unity and liberty of the nation, the 'Vittoriano'. Other monumental buildings included the new Court of Justice, the statue of Garibaldi on the Janiculum Hill overlooking the city centre, the statue of Cavour and Piazza Cavour, and (much later, in 1922, when republican ideas were no longer a threat) the statue of Mazzini on the Aventino, one of the ancient Roman hills. An ideal route was constructed that was nourished by a patriotic and national, rather than a religious, discourse. Alongside the remains of ancient Rome and confronting the monuments of Papal Rome, a new city therefore began to emerge as a symbol of a modern civilization and Italian unity. Driven by that impulse, the polycentric character of the Papal city, which had lasted for centuries, began to be replaced by monocentric town planning, in which streets radiated from a new centre at the foot of the ancient Capitoline Hill, or Campidoglio, in Piazza Venezia.

There, the Vittoriano monument to Victor Emmanuel II was to represent Italy's triumphal march into recent history as an 'opera', a complete and dramatic synthesis of all the different events and the emotional energy of the Risorgimento. The architect Camillo Boito explained that the monument had to express, 'like the symphony of a musical opera', 'the principal themes, concentrating the passions, the concepts, the colours of the wide dramatic picture in a short and powerful synthesis'; as historian Bruno Tobia has described it, the monument was a 'historical synthesis, a philosophy of history, incarnated in real and symbolic representations'. It had to provide both a metaphorical representation of the ideological content of the national revolution and a realistic depiction of the king. The huge statue of King Victor Emmanuel II is the departure point for a system of monumental staircases and symbols: at the base of the statue the fountains represent the Tyrrenic and Adriatic seas, and the bronze sculpted groups symbolize Thought and Action; below them are the high reliefs of the triumphal March of Work and Love for the Patria, which converge on a central representation of Rome. Above that stands the statue in golden bronze of Victor Emmanuel on horseback on a pedestal adorned by images of Italian cities. In the upper storey of the arcade there are statues depicting Italian regions and, on top of the arcade, to the right and left respectively sit the two bronze *quadrigae* symbolizing Unity and Liberty. Along with monuments of the Risorgimento, another architectural fashion of the time was the construction of covered galleries. The Victor Emmanuel gallery in Milan (1863) has a triumphal façade inspired by both antiquity and the Lombard Renaissance that faces the Duomo square; in Naples, the Umberto I gallery (1887–90) expressed both contemporary eclecticism and a return to the Renaissance.

One major event, which mobilized city councils, associations, citizens and representatives of Italian communities abroad, was the 'civil pilgrimage' to Victor Emmanuel's grave in the Pantheon in 1884 on the 25th anniversary of the Risorgimento with the intention of expressing national gratitude to the House of Savoy. The choice of date determined that the Risorgimento had officially begun in 1859, thereby expunging the humiliating first war of independence, as well as the democratic revolutions and republics of 1848. Another way of 'making Italians' was by heightening awareness of their country's natural and artistic beauty. During the previous two centuries, the European upper classes had travelled to Italy as the principal destination of the Grand Tour; with this migration, secular travellers had taken the place of the pre-Renaissance religious pilgrims, and the newcomers discovered Italy's classical and humanist culture. Goethe, who spent two years in Italy from 1786, described in his *Travels in Italy* the archaeology and architecture, the natural landscapes and the urban life of Italy. He was also one of the first to move as far south as Sicily, provoking a new interest in the Italian south among European travellers. The Grand Tour tradition was interrupted by the Napoleonic invasion and by the tortuous events of the Risorgimento, but after unification the new state decided to promote an 'internal' Grand Tour to enable Italians to discover more about their own country. In 1863, the leader of the Right Quintino Sella (1827–84) founded the Italian Alpine Club, reflecting an increased interest in the Italian mountains, inspired by the idea of the Alps as a frontier, one from which foreigners had often come and which now must be defended as a national border: national values were thus at the heart of the club. Mountains both represented an arduous challenge in which individuals exercised physical virtue, and a mental pathway for strengthening attachment to the *patria*. While proletarian Italy was forced to emigrate to avoid starvation, the bourgeoisie responded enthusiastically to the idea of travelling. In 1894, the Italian Cyclist Touring Club added to foreign visitors those who were born and lived in the peninsula. Members of the Touring Club were very different from traditional travellers, a distinction evident even from their dress. In an etiquette manual published at the beginning of the twentieth century, the writer Matilde Serao stated that the 'good bourgeois' going on holiday had to pack separate costumes for horse riding, running, playing tennis, playing polo, hunting, rowing, alpine sports, swimming and fencing. New rules for leisure time on holiday were strict on dress codes, to the extent that early century beach life looked like a summer annexe of the bourgeois salon. To this Italy of full summer dress and parasols (to avoid tanning, which at the time was considered plebeian), the Touring Club counterposed physical effort and the more casual cycling costume. Italians visited one another's cities: this was an Italy rooted in its urban culture, which intended to unite the hundreds of cities and thousands of villages not only through travel itineraries and new maps, but also with common ideals and feelings that were to be at the basis of every Italian's education.

The idea of combining travelling and sport in order to 'forge Italians' gained popularity at the same time as the introduction of German methods of physical exercise into schools to eradicate physical defects and combat rickets. A new model of Italian youth is found in Miss Pedani, the female protagonist of the short novel *Amore e ginnastica* ('Love and gymnastics') by De Amicis (1892), an athletic gymnastics teacher whose bookshelves contained atlases, pamphlets on hygiene, swimming and cycling, and the publications of the Italian Alpine Club. In response to a neighbour, she replies to the common view that gymnastics is unimportant:

How can we joke about gymnastics while we have, out of 300,000 conscripts, 80,000 rejects for physical debilitation! Schools are full of pale youngsters, whose chests and arms are like those of a small child, and out of ten girls of the best society you cannot find even two without any constitutional defects . . . Oh! It is a sad joke.

(De Amicis, 2001, p. 30)

De Amicis and the Touring Club were imagining the same Italy, one in which Italians from every part of the country became curious about all its regions, where Italians of different social classes learned geography, gymnastics and good citizenship together at school. The most famous of De Amicis' works was *Cuore* (*Cuore: The Heart of a Boy*), which became, together with Collodi's *Pinocchio*, essential reading for generations of young Italians.

Carlo Collodi (the pseudonym of Carlo Lorenzini, 1826–90) was a former republican converted to the monarchy, who believed in public education as a means of overcoming class differences. His work was intended to reach the masses but also, as Silvio Lanaro has underlined, to transmit the national message from adults to children. In *Viaggio per l'Italia di Giannettino* ('Giannettino's journey across Italy', 1880), Collodi added new elements in the country's landscape to the monuments traditionally listed in atlases of Italy: the factories, new symbols of the Italian worker, served to bring both moral and material improvement to the lower classes, and to create a new industrial and modern architecture. His most famous book, *Le avventure di Pinocchio: Storia di un burattino* (*The adventures of Pinocchio*), follows the vicissitudes of a puppet in an Italy of vagrancy and hunger, disreputable inns and policemen. The educational intent was inserted into a fantasy story in which the wooden puppet Pinocchio, invented by his master Geppetto, becomes a youthful adventurer in a life beyond rules. Dangers are overcome with the help of magical beings such as the fairy with blue hair, a substitute for the mother Pinocchio could not have; a sense of guilt always accompanied his adventures, because Pinocchio acted against Geppetto's will and the rules of society, in particular those of its central institution, the school. Collodi's story imparted to children the value of hard work, honesty, school attendance and obedience to parents. When Pinocchio decides to run away from home in order to avoid going to school, the talking cricket (representing the voice of his conscience) tells him: 'Woe to those children who rebel against their parents, and who run away from their homes. They will never be happy in this world, and sooner or later they will repent it bitterly.' Despite these messages, Pinocchio has been interpreted as the anti-*Cuore*: it makes no reference to king or nation, and leaves much space for fantastic adventures.

Cuore by De Amicis is a post-Risorgimento diary of a Piedmontese child, apparently addressed to children but in fact targeting a generation of parents that came through the battles of the Risorgimento. The primary school was seen as the laboratory of the nation; unification took place in classrooms, as the book illustrates when a pupil from Calabria arrives at the Piedmontese school, shy and terrified, and the teacher, holding his hand, tells the class:

> You should be pleased. Today a young Italian is entering the school who was born in Reggio di Calabria, more than five hundred miles from here. Cherish your brother who has come from so far away. He was born in a glorious land which gave Italy illustrious men, and which gives her strong workers and brave soldiers, in one of the most beautiful parts of our country, where there are great forests and great mountains, inhabited by people of ability and courage ... Make him see that an Italian boy, no matter which Italian school he sets foot in, finds brothers there.

> (De Amicis, 1986, p. 17)

In the book, respect for the army was another value to be taught at school: at a military parade, the school director explains to the children that they must love the soldiers, who were both poor and *signori* from all parts of the country dedicated to defending it from foreign invasions; children were taught to salute the flag, because 'he who respects the flag when he is small will know how to defend it when he is grown up'. Children were also taught to love the king because he unified Italy and liberated it from foreign tyrants, and to honour Risorgimento heroes. Drawing on Risorgimento ideals, love for the patria and the family – particularly the mother – were firmly intertwined, depicted in the book in the teacher's reading of a text on Mazzini and his love for his mother, his desperate pain at her death, and her survival in his memory as a moral guide. The literary critic, Elio Gioanola, has defined De Amicis as the most extraordinary tear-jerker that literature had ever known: *la mamma* and *la patria*, this universal mother, became the preferred themes of the creative pedagogy of the Ligurian writer. Another writer full of Risorgimento rhetoric was the classicist poet Giosuè Carducci (1835–1907). He was, like De Amicis, a republican who converted to monarchical, anti-socialist and anti-clerical ideas, including a hatred of foreign influences in literature. Carducci had a great impact on the generation that would later support Italy's entry to the First World War.

As well as the army, schools, the Touring Club and literature, a contribution towards making Italians also came from cookery books: the conditions of extreme poverty in most of Italy did not prevent the continuation of Italian cuisine in the nineteenth century, and in 1891, Pellegrino Artusi from Romagna published a book that became a bible in Italian family homes, *La scienza in cucina e l'arte di mangiar bene* ('Science in the kitchen and the art of eating well'). As Carol Helstolsky has noticed, its impact in providing Italians with a common language regarding the preparation of food and attitudes towards eating was still evident years later, but at the time it was written 'his formula of middle-class sobriety, simplicity of presentation, and attention to regional difference proved to be the right formula for a national cuisine'. One of the elements that unified Italy was indeed diet – mainly bread. The variety, between classes and regions, came principally from the type of flour, which was the common ingredient involved in producing different types of bread, polenta or pasta. The poverty of the Italian diet was emphasized by social scientists and reformers, as in earlier centuries. They explored the living standards of the rural population to argue that poor nutrition brought with it other problems such as illness, short stature and intellectual inferiority. Observers of the southern question affirmed that southerners ate fewer proteins than northerners and were therefore less productive. The real difference, however, was not geographical but social: class disparity was emphasized by the difference in food consumption. Maize spread to dominate the agrarian landscape of the northern regions; eating only maize-based polenta (which lacked vitamins) caused pellagra, an illness that had social, as well as physical consequences. The disease progressed through three phases (the three Ds): dermatitis, diarrhoea and dementia – the origin of expressions like 'to be mad with hunger' or 'the madness of monophagy'. Italian psychiatrists at the time did not know how to cure what they believed to be a mental disease for which there seemed to be no obvious cause.

In the nineteenth century, flour was the basis of another dish invented in Naples that would become as important as pasta in the identity of Italians: pizza. An oven for pizzas already existed in the district of Capodimonte at the time of the Bourbon King Ferdinand II. Under the new state, a pizza that became very popular was made with tomatoes (red), mozzarella (white) and basil (green) to represent the colours of the Italian flag. As Franco La Cecla has explained, there are two different stories about this pizza – it could have been made for the occasion of the visit of Queen Margherita of Savoy (1851–1926, married to Umberto I), and therefore named in her honour, or the pizza already existed and, in honour of the queen's visit, it 'suddenly found a name, a sense, and a historical function'. Italian national identity crystallized around national food – pasta and pizza – which became the gastronomic symbols in which regional differences were dissolved. Italian emigration, together with the dissemination of Artusi's book, extended the same process around the world, as the millions of Italians who crossed the Alps and the Atlantic reproduced the dishes they were familiar with in Italy, which in turn stimulated exports from Italian food companies trading in pasta, tinned tomatoes and olive oil. Even emigrants who had the opportunity to try new types of food continued to eat as they had done in Italy.

CONTESTING THE NATION: THE CATHOLIC CHURCH

In the centre of the Campo de' Fiori in Rome, among the market stalls and wandering Romans and tourists, stands a monument to Giordano Bruno. The philosopher is wrapped in a Dominican habit, carries an open book in his hands; his face, with his head covered by a hood, appears thoughtful, severe and absorbed. The inscription simply says: 'For Bruno, from the century by him foreseen, here where the stake burned'. The statue was unveiled in June 1889 on Pentecost Sunday. It was a spectacular ceremony attended by thousands of people. The square was crowded with stalls and banners carrying quotations from Bruno, like the one he addressed to the judges who condemned him: 'You shake more by pronouncing this condemnation than I do by hearing it.' The procession, starting from Piazza Esedra consisted of former *garibaldini*, rectors and professors of Rome University, representatives of city councils and associations from Nola (the town where Bruno was born), representatives of foreign universities and Italian regions, freemasons, representatives of mutual aid societies, and members of parliament. People gathered at windows and on balconies along the route. The erection of a monument to Bruno in the square (very close to the Vatican) where he had been burned at the stake three centuries before, had an unequivocal political meaning. The Pope, who had threatened to leave Rome if the monument was unveiled, spent the day abstaining from food, prostrate at the feet of St Peter's statue while, as the newspaper *Civiltà Cattolica* put it, 'the revolutionary Hydra occupied the streets of his Rome'. From the 1880s onwards, a thick network of cultural associations named 'Giordano Bruno' spread all over Italy.

Relations between Church and state had been deteriorating since the 1850s, when the Piedmontese parliament approved laws to limit Catholic influence, causing the Church to adopt a yet more intransigent approach to political change in Italy. Fissures continued to exist within the Church. For example, some of Garibaldi's supporters in Sicily were local priests, and in the north many priests who had taken part in the 1848 revolutions wanted an end to Papal temporal power. The divergence between the Church and the elites constituted major changes in a society in which, until the eighteenth century, there was virtual symbiosis between the dominant classes and the Catholic hierarchy, with ecclesiastical control over charities and education, and Church ownership of a large proportion of the land. Civil registries that certified baptisms, marriages and funerals were kept in Church archives, exemplifying very well the condition of a society in which there was no distinction between citizen and Christian. During the Enlightenment, when Clement XIV (Pope between 1769 and 1774) suppressed the Jesuits, a movement of Catholics emerged who were open to reform and to dialogue with Enlightenment thinkers. However, the subsequent Pope, Pius VI (1775–99) condemned the Enlightenment, describing it in apocalyptic tones as the work of the Devil, against which the legacy of the Counter-Reformation had to be regrouped for a deadly confrontation between Christianity and the forces of the modern world. The Papacy calculated that eventually political power would side with the Church to defend the existing order. For the Papacy, the French Revolution and the arrival of the French army in Italy were the final consequences of the dissolution of authority initiated by Martin Luther (and instigated by Satan). The Church's totally negative judgement on the modern age emerged, which implied the necessity of a return to medieval Christianity and, indeed, during the Restoration, with the exception of a few Catholic liberals (such as Manzoni, Gioberti, Rosmini and Tommaseo), the medieval model became the ideal alternative to the modern world.

With the first unification of 1861, the Papal States were restricted to the region surrounding Rome. In 1864, the Pope promulgated one of the most famous encyclicals against modernity: *Quanta cura*, which included a 'Syllabus of Errors', a list condemning uncongenial propositions from earlier centuries, which served as an instrument to attack anti-clericalism and liberalism. The Syllabus was divided into ten sections, which condemned as false various statements concerning, for example, pantheism, naturalism and absolute rationalism; moderate rationalism; socialism, communism, secret societies and liberal clerical societies; and modern liberalism. Some of the condemned ideas (followed by a declaration that the opposite was true) were the following: 'philosophy is to be treated without taking any account of supernatural revelation'; 'human reason ... is the sole arbiter of truth and falsehood, and of good and evil'; 'Protestantism is nothing more than another form of the same true Christian religion, in which form it is given to please God as equally as in the Catholic Church'; 'the Church ought to be separated from the state, and the state from the Church'; 'the Roman Pontiff can, and ought to, reconcile himself to, and come to terms with, progress, liberalism and modern civilization'. The Syllabus provoked negative reaction from the Protestant world and, more surprisingly, met with similar response among Catholics, apart from conservatives. Among the Church's enemies, the Syllabus increased anti-clerical activity, having made it clear that the Church and modernity were incompatible.

In 1870, before the events at Porta Pia, a Vatican council was held in Rome with the object of restoring Papal authority; 774 bishops from around the world, along with deposed secular rulers (for example, the Tuscan grand-duke and the former King of Naples, Francis II) voted in favour of papal infallibility – the dogma stating that the Pope spoke from divine revelation on doctrinal matters and therefore could never be wrong when speaking *ex cathedra* on faith and morals. Unfortunately for the council, two months later, Italian troops entered Rome, putting an end to what remained of the Papacy's temporal power. After Porta Pia, the new state's rulers and the king found themselves in a difficult position; the defeat of the Church had been necessary for the establishment of the new state, but continual confrontation could jeopardize their consolidation of power. Most of the population was illiterate and rural, and connected with the Church through parish networks that had been reinforced from the time of the Counter-Reformation onwards. Moreover, most of these rulers were not radical anti-clericals, but conservatives from privileged backgrounds who were accustomed to having connections with the Church. Opposition to the government was not good for the Church either, as its hierarchy had flourished for centuries thanks to its links with the civil authorities.

The Pope's behaviour was not unjustified at the time, since it was not yet clear that he had lost power permanently; Popes had gone into exile or faced serious crisis in the past, and survived, so it seemed natural that he would seek to return to power by refusing to grant legitimacy to the new state, by instructing Catholics not to vote, and by appealing to Catholic states in Europe to assist the Church – through military means if necessary – to help restore its temporal power. While government policy followed Cavour's ideal of a free Church in a free state, the Pope's *Non Expedit* of 1868 proclaimed the policy of 'neither elected nor electors'. The new state's ambiguous position was also evident in the constitution, especially in Article 1 of the *Statuto*, which established Catholicism as the religion of state. Schooling was another contested issue: De Amicis' school, the 'gym' for the education of Italians, made no reference to religion. The Vatican risked losing the clerical monopoly over the education of the young because of national schools: under the Casati law (named after the minister of education, Gabrio Casati) enacted in Piedmont and Lombardy in 1859 and the rest of Italy in 1861, every community had to have a public primary school with teachers hired by the civil authorities, although religious education was included in the curriculum. The Coppino law of 1877, named after minister Michele Coppino, listed all material to be taught in school without mentioning religion, though it did include the secular liberal 'duties of man and citizen'. While religion continued to be taught, this law caused further controversy.

Following Porta Pia, the government, needing to address international concern, declared the Law of Guarantees, which recognized the Pope's status as an independent sovereign, established his freedom to communicate with Catholics internationally and to conduct diplomatic relations with other countries, and assigned the Vatican a large annual income. While the Pope's attitude did not change for some time, this law did eventually help to smooth the relationship between Papacy and state. Moreover, towards the end of the century, the rise of a social Catholic movement brought signs of change. In the 1870s, local Catholic associations emerged, particularly in the north. A national conference of these groups, the *Opera dei Congressi*, founded in 1874, organized further conferences and pilgrimages, sent petitions to parliament calling for the protection of the Church's interests and called public meetings in protest at the government's anti-Catholic policies. Pius IX died in 1878 and was replaced by Leo XIII, who was Pope until 1903. Leo was as intransigent as Pius, but understood the importance of adapting Church policies to modern times; the encyclical *Rerum Novarum* in 1891 outlined the position of the Church on social policy for the first time, rejecting socialism but maintaining that it was their Catholic duty to engage in public works to ameliorate modern social ills. At a local level this led to the formation of youth groups and credit organizations for peasants and workers. Catholic peasant and worker associations appeared during the last twenty years of the century as a response to the socialist threat.

CONTESTING THE NATION: SOCIALIST ITALY

Cavour's financial policies generated a deficit that deepened each year as a result of preparations for war with Austria. Showing little gratitude for Piedmont's sacrifices for the nation, Italians from other regions complained that, after 1861, all Italy had to pay Piedmont's debts. Loans for Piedmont's debts were taken out repeatedly on the international capital market, on disadvantageous terms. In 1865, Quintino Sella was the first finance minister to explain the reality of the situation; his solution – effective but unpopular – was to increase taxation, especially on flour, the tax most hated by the poor.

In March 1876, the 'historical left' replaced the 'historical right' in government. The term 'left' is misleading, as it was a current within the liberal, monarchic system. The new prime minister, Agostino Depretis (1813–87), was a former Mazzinian now loyal to the monarchy. He was one of the 'new' men in the Italian state: neither from Piedmont nor a noble and, like the other Lombard Benedetto Cairoli and the Sicilian Francesco Crispi, had played an active part in the Risorgimento. The five Cairoli brothers from Pavia all fought as volunteers and two of them were killed, becoming by their sacrifice an example for the 'religion of the *patria*' along with their mother (one of the maternal 'symbols' of the Risorgimento discussed in Chapter 6). These new men all came from the middle classes and from the left, but had all converted to the monarchy during the unification process. While there was no great difference between the right and the left, the latter was nominally committed to greater democracy and a wider franchise, and tended to support progressive taxation and secular education. There was, however, agreement on both sides that Italians must become politically educated in loyalty to the state first – they were not yet ready for liberty and democracy. This belief was reflected in the suffrage, which remained very limited: in 1881, a new electoral law extended voting rights (to 6.9 per cent of the population) according to taxation, so that a greater proportion of the middle classes qualified to vote, but the franchise was still linked to education and literacy and therefore continued to exclude the peasant masses, and particularly southerners. The new leaders of the state feared that reactionary landowners and priests would manipulate these unenfranchised masses. At the same time, the left sought to educate: the Coppino law made primary education free, compulsory and secular up to the age of nine. Another law abolished the tax on flour.

In the 1882 elections, the far left, known as the *Estrema* (radicals, republicans and later also socialists) doubled their number of seats. Economic crisis and anarchist attempts to assassinate political leaders throughout Europe added to the concerns of the ruling class in Italy; hoping to prevent a radicalization of politics, Depretis began an alliance between the left and the right, called *trasformismo*. Differences between the two sides faded further, because, with *trasformismo*, politics were no longer governed by principles, but by expediency. Ministers began to appear in corruption cases, as they could be 'bought' by either side whenever policies were debated.

A radical move towards more authoritarian government came with the arrival of Francesco Crispi as prime minister in 1887. The Sicilian, and former *garibaldino*, held a patriotic view of the soldier as the good citizen, and linked the concept of war with that of nationhood; these ideas were revolutionary during the battles of the Risorgimento, but became reactionary in the new context. Crispi reinforced the monarchy's role as a national symbol ('the monarchy unites us, the republic would divide us'), and was prime minister at the time of the pilgrimage to the Pantheon and one of the creators of the 'religion of the *patria*'. Consistent with his (previously Mazzinian) view of Italy's world mission, he became an advocate of a strong foreign policy, signing the Triple Alliance with Austria and Germany in 1882 and provoking Italy's first foray into colonial imperialism with an invasion of Ethiopia. The massacre of Italian soldiers at Massawa in 1885 and their defeat in 1896 at Adowa confirmed the poor reputation of the Italian army and undermined confidence in the new state. Crispi's domestic policies, notably the ferocious repression directed at the socialist movement, were as disastrous as his foreign policy, and created another enemy for the new state in socialism.

Socialism, first organized by ex-garibaldian and ex-republican elements, emerged in the countryside of the Po Valley, in Sicily, and in the early factories in the north. A new and growing class of factory workers toiled for long hours in unhealthy conditions; wages for women and children were respectively 27 per cent and 17 per cent of those for the male work force; and there was no system of social security, so periods of illness and unemployment took families close to starvation. The first associations for the defence of workers were republican (motivated by a Jacobin and *carbonara* legacy) and anticipated socialist associations, particularly in the Romagna, taking inspiration from Mazzini's opposition to the new state. Mazzini, disappointed with the outcome of unification, had remained in exile. He was distressed by the fact that the idea of the nation did not overcome social conflict, and that nationality was instead an illiberal force that had failed to emancipate the people. Anti-clericalism also became a major element of the new workers' associations – Republican associations created mutual aid societies that competed with the traditional bourgeois philanthropy, which in rural areas were influenced by Catholicism. Even under Depretis, the constitutional freedom of association was accepted only formally, as the Italian government was constantly anxious about the possible existence of a 'state within the state'.

Mutual organizations and co-operatives were established to help workers, often receiving money from employers, who hoped by these means to contain conflict. However, the severe economic crisis during the last two decades of the nineteenth century turned the associations into militant leagues that declared war on employers and demanded better pay and working conditions. Socialist leagues quickly came into conflict with Catholic leagues in rural areas. The major difference between them was that Catholic culture promoted class collaboration and mediated between peasants and landowners, while socialist struggles tended to be highly confrontational. Protests became more effective with the foundation of the Chambers of Labour in 1890, the socialist representatives of which began to take part in local politics. Socialist and Catholic leagues developed divergent local political cultures by providing recreational activities, meeting places and even separate marriage and funeral services. A strong Christian culture was common to both: socialists, despite their anti-clericalism, propagated the idea of Jesus as the 'first socialist', and developed a Christian message (a kind of 'evangelical socialism') that was compatible with the class and egalitarian ideology of Marxism. The first socialist leaders, such as Camillo Prampolini (1859–1930) and Leonida Bissolati (1857–1920) would appear outside village churches, describing socialism to the peasants as a promised land, a 'world upside-down', where the teaching of the Gospels could be put into practice not by obeying the Church authorities but, on the contrary, by fighting against the privileges the Church had shared with the landowners since time immemorial.

The extent of state repression was a consequence of the liberal ruling class's sense of vulnerability. Emergency regulations enshrined in the 1865 Public Security Law were applied on a regular basis. The police had wide-ranging powers to restrict individual freedom. In the 1890s in particular, a state of military rule was frequently declared to deal with mass anti-government protests. Towards the end of the century, the two most important moments of unrest were the Sicilian *fasci* risings and the bread riots in Milan, both bloodily repressed.

A socialist movement developed in Sicily around the shipyards and in the cities of the east coast, from Messina to Catania and Syracuse. The groups that emerged, called *fasci*, were the first in southern Italy to exercise the rights permitted in the *Statuto*, particularly the rights of association and to hold meetings in private and public places; the *fasci* organized huge popular demonstrations for better working conditions and higher salaries, and they held meetings in theatres, squares, cities and villages, selecting significant sites of collective memory and identification. Their most momentous achievement was winning the right to strike, which was confirmed in 1890 in the penal code written by Giuseppe Zanardelli (1826–1903, jurist and prime minister between 1901 and 1903). In 1893, protests spread throughout the countryside, where 300,000 peasants occupied huge landed estates that, despite the number of landless peasants, were left abandoned by absentee owners. New secular ceremonies, full of 'civil' rhetoric, replaced or coexisted alongside traditional local religious rituals such as processions and feasts for patron saints. As in the Po Valley, religion and socialism were tightly intertwined, indicated by the presence of crosses, Madonnas and patron saints at the *fasci*'s demonstrations. The liberal elite, which by this point controlled municipal power and public employment, stood alongside the conservative landowners in demanding that the government repress the *fasci*. The intervention of troops in the repression of the movement unleashed a violent backlash in many villages – arson, assassination, and the invasion and sacking of town council buildings – a violence made considerably worse by further state reaction, which restored social peace in Sicily by killing, arresting and outlawing the *fasci*. Crispi was a former *garibaldino*, yet he also held a sacralized idea of the authority of the state, property and public order, which he was ready to defend by any means.

In May 1898 (fifty years after the 'five days' of 1848), widespread social unrest in Milan again culminated in military repression, in which

Box 7.1   Social protest and music in liberal Italy

Music continued to be an important cultural expression of political conflict. Proletarian protest after Italian unification expressed itself in the composition of republican, socialist and anarchist songs. Many of these referred to the examples of the French Revolution and the Risorgimento, so that new hymns used the music of the *Marseillaise*, the *Hymn to Garibaldi*, or Verdi's operas. Pietro Gori, the most prolific of anarchist songwriters, invented the hymn of the First of May (international workers' day, a date that originated with the hanging of four innocent anarchists in Chicago in 1886) to the tune of *Nabucco*:

> Go, May, the peoples are waiting for you/the free hearts salute you/sweet Easter of the workers/go and shine at the glory of the sun!

While Verdi's arias had inspired the ideal of freedom from foreign oppression during the Risorgimento, they now expressed, with the new words of the workers' hymns, hopes for a new freedom from political and social oppression. Songs of the workers' movement had common themes – fields, factories, barricades, the memory of the 'martyrs', social revolution, human progress, the struggle against tyranny and oppression. *The Ferocious Monarchist Bava*, written immediately after the slaughter in Milan in 1898, follows the effects

⟶

over 100 protesters were killed. State violence was followed by the suppression of newspapers, the closure of socialist and Catholic organizations, and the arrest of opposition party leaders. While socialists and anarchists had taken part in the organization of the riots, the actions were fundamentally the expression of intense economic hardship caused by taxation on flour and a corresponding rise in the price of bread. King Umberto I, the son of Victor Emmanuel and King of Italy from 1878, praised the general responsible for the massacre, Bava Beccaris, and awarded him a medal. This was a dramatic end to the nineteenth century, which clearly demonstrated the repressive and undemocratic nature of the new liberal state. 'Proletarian revenge' opened the new century in an equally dramatic fashion: Gaetano Bresci, an anarchist manual worker from Prato in Tuscany, who had emigrated to America, returned to Italy to avenge the Milanese protesters massacred by Bava Beccaris, and shot

---

Box 7.1   (*continued*)

▐▌▌▶

of that repression in a semi-didactic style (along the classic model of Italian songs by *cantastorie*):

> At the agonizing and painful screams/of a crowd asking for bread/the ferocious monarchist Bava/fed the hungry with lead.//One hundred were the innocent dead/under the fire of the armed Cains/and at the fury of the assassin soldiers/'death to the cowards'! shouted the plebs.//Alas, do not laugh, Savoy thug/if the gun has tamed the rebels/if the brothers have killed the brothers/on your head that blood will fall.//. . . Come on, do cry sorrowful mothers/when the dark evening descends/for the sons thrown in prison/for those killed by fatal lead.

Political songs of the twentieth century continued along the lines of their nineteenth-century origins. As Stefano Pivato has observed, another aspect of continuity was the religious character at the root of the workers' movement ideals, as demonstrated by hymns such as the Italian version of *The International* ('a faith was born in our hearts'), the *Hymn to the First of May* ('sweet Easter of the workers'), or the *Song of the Young Italian Socialists* ('we swear to die/rather than to betray our faith'). Politics were a new 'religion'; protest songs were 'prayers'.

---

the king dead in Monza. After the assassination, it became clear that repression alone would not prevent social revolution, particularly since the grievances of the masses were widely recognized as legitimate. A new, more democratic, phase began under a post-Risorgimento liberal, Giovanni Giolitti (1842–1928).

CONTESTING THE NATION: BANDITRY AND THE 'SOUTHERN QUESTION'

The ministers of the new state were mainly northerners, and those who did come from the south had spent years in exile and had distanced themselves from the problems of their provinces. Sicily had twice initiated a national revolution (in 1848 and 1860), but it was much less

---

Box 7.2   The Bronte episode

The Sicilian writer Giovanni Verga published in 1883 a short story based on an actual incident in the revolution of 1860. In the town of Bronte, west of Mount Etna in the province of Catania, the peasants attacked the town hall and aristocrats' homes, killing members of the local gentry. The revolt was violently suppressed by the *garibaldino* general, Nino Bixio:

> They unfurled a red-white-and-green handkerchief from the church-tower, they rang the bells in a frenzy, and they began to shout in the village square, 'Hurray for liberty!' Like the sea in storm, the crowd foamed and swayed in front of the club of the gentry, and outside the Town Hall, and on the steps of the church – a sea of white stocking-caps, axes and sickles glittering. Then they burst into the little street. 'Your turn first, baron! You who have had folks cudgelled by your estate-keepers!' . . . Sickles, hands, rags, stones, everything red with blood! The gentry! The hat-folks! Kill them all! Kill them all! Down with the hat-folks! . . . Liberty meant that everybody should have his share . . . The next day they heard that the General was coming to deal out justice; which news made folks tremble . . . From afar off, in the remotest alleys of the village as you sat behind your closed door, you could hear those gun-shots firing one after the other, like cannon-crackers at holiday time.

> (Verga, 1984)

---

nationally conscious than either Lombardy or Piedmont. In Sicily, landowners who had opposed the revolution at first turned patriot when Cavour's soldiers provided a chance to put down social disorder. Even the *garibaldini* made it clear in 1860 that national unification took precedence over social issues.

Northern rulers were ignorant about southern Italy, and many of them simply believed it to be a potentially rich area that could become prosperous with good administration; they neglected such realities as 90 per cent illiteracy, the persistence of feudalism in the countryside, or the different forms of criminality that were evolving out of traditions of banditry – like the Neapolitan *camorra* and the Sicilian Mafia. Prefects and police inspectors who were sent to administer Sicily after 1860 believed they were confronting a sort of 'primitive Africa', inclined to violence and far removed from the concept of legal equality. Its peasants seemed ignorant and barbarous, ferocious in rebellion, religious, anti-modern, and therefore unpatriotic. What made the southern situation distinct was the persistence of banditry, which had weakened in most of the rest of the country by the time of Italian unification. In most of the south, banditry, organized by the Bourbons, seemed capable of threatening the very existence of the new state in the two years after 1861: many cities and villages in the mainland south were occupied by armed bandits, and subjected to bloody repression and civil war. Some 90,000 Italian troops were employed to fight banditry, a higher number of soldiers than had been employed during the anti-Austrian war of 1859; and civil war in the south caused more casualties than the wars for independence. Much of the brutality was a result of the reaction of desperate soldiers trying to survive in a hostile country against a fierce enemy.

The situation was different in Sicily, where the Bourbons had never been loved, and the memories of Risorgimento battles were too fresh to permit a reaction favourable to the older dynasties. Part of Sicilian banditry's success was its rejection of conscription; many peasants left their villages and went into hiding, rather than serve in the army. In addition, banditry was linked with the idea of the *faida* – the use of vendetta to redress a wrong (generally murder) between families, a symbol of a society that did not recognize the rule of state law. While banditry was defeated by the state in the southern mainland by 1865, in Sicily it remained endemic, supported by the landowners, who accused the civil authorities of being unable to control the criminals and who therefore 'had to' deal with them in order to avoid trouble. In fact, the landowners did not employ bandits simply to defend themselves, but also to give weight to their own personal vendettas, to damage economic rivals and to control the peasantry.

In his *Enquiry on Sicily* of 1876, Leopoldo Franchetti (1847–1917) explained that 'mafioso' behaviour represented a distinctive characteristic of Sicilian society at all levels. The first serious scholars of the southern question were Franchetti, Pasquale Villari (1826–1917) and Sidney Sonnino (1847–1922), who studied the condition of the peasantry in areas where city dwellers had never penetrated. These scholars inaugurated a tradition of inquiry later named *meridionalismo* ('southern-ism'). They believed that peasants were the real Italians, since the peasantry made up over half of the national population, even though almost all were illiterate. Villari, a Neapolitan liberal exiled by the Bourbons in the 1850s, who lived in Florence, wrote a pamphlet in 1866 entitled: 'Who is to blame?' which, at the time of the third war for independence, suggested that the real enemy of the new state was not Austria, but was instead (as cited in Nelson Moe) 'our colossal ignorance', 'the illiterate multitudes, the unthinking bureaucrats, the ignorant teachers, the child-ish politicians, the impossible diplomats, the incompetent generals, the unskilled worker, the patriarchal farmer, and the rhetoric that eats away at our souls'. The 'quadrilateral' to be fought was not on the battlefield between the fortresses at Mantua, Verona, Peschiera and Legnago, but was the 'quadrilateral of seventeen million illiterates and five million rhetoricians'.

The new state exported the Piedmontese education system to the south, but could not suddenly provide teachers and buildings, and the dissolution of monasteries caused a crisis in the charity system that led to even greater levels of poverty. Banditry contained an element of Catholic reaction against the government's treatment of the clergy. Some bandits were just peasants protesting against high prices, and they were easily manipulated by the Church and the landowners, who had increased their power with unification as electors who controlled local government and local employment, and had acquired both ecclesiastic and communal possessions. Garibaldi's army had been disbanded in 1861 and prisoners were widely released in the 1860s, liberating a mass of the displaced poor and escaped convicts, all of whom were difficult for the new administration to control. Initially, the *garibaldini* were considered a greater threat than the pro-Bourbons. The new state there-fore purged more *garibaldini* than Bourbons from the administration, the military and the judiciary, leaving in place those who were in reality the most corrupt and the most hostile to the existing state.

In 1863, the Pica Laws (called after the right-wing deputy, Giuseppe Pica) gave extensive military powers to the civilian authorities, who could use arrest, detention and summary executions in the provinces affected by banditry, and these powers were used widely. The war against banditry was not only hugely expensive (in terms of both money and men), but it also created public disillusion with the new Italy, and a distorted view of the south as a backward and crime-ridden area, imper-vious to change, and a source of political subversion: the war contributed to the construction of a 'southern question' and a sense of southern 'difference', which was to dominate the understanding of the south. The main reason why a more serious political crisis did not occur was the weakness of the various opponents; despite disrupting and undermining government authority, Bourbon reaction never justified the alarm it caused, and the Church had effectively withdrawn from politics. Republicans and revolutionaries did not constitute a real threat, and the parliamentary left was ineffective in the 1860s.

Apart from a few serious scholars, the southern question was in the main analysed by writers, particularly within the current of *verismo*, a current influenced by Zola's and Flaubert's naturalism in France. *Verismo* was contemporary to the emergence of positivist culture, which arrived in Italy largely thanks to Villari – who applied experimental scientific methods to history and literature in his research on banditry; to the philosopher Roberto Ardigò (1828–1920); and to the anthropologist Cesare Lombroso (1835–1909). The major representatives of Italian realism were three Sicilian writers: De Roberto (author of *The Viceroys*, a masterpiece on the Sicilian aristocracy at the time of unification), Giovanni Verga (1840–1922) and Luigi Capuana (1839–1915). Verga, born in Catania to a family of landowners and brought up in an atmosphere of liberalism and patriotism, retains a place in Italian literature as the guide to the world of humble people. His short stories and novels showed a historical piety, which was not sentimental and did not imply identification, but simply expressed the commitment of a writer who recognized the moral validity of the Sicilian lower classes. In this lay the main difference between his masterpiece, *I Malavoglia*, and Manzoni's: while Manzoni had also described historical reality, he was a romantic idealist who believed that events were ultimately governed by Providence, while Verga's realism examined social reality in its material and casual simplicity (one just needs to think about the ironic name 'Providence' given, in Verga's novel, to a boat that sinks and causes ruin to the Malavoglia family). In his use of language, he sought to adhere fully to the way his characters spoke (though dialect was present in the syntax rather than the vocabulary); he collected proverbs and sayings in the villages. Capuana did the same, though he was more important as a theorist of *verismo* and as a literary critic than as a writer. In *I Malavoglia*, Verga used proverbs as symbols of an ideological fixity that gave an aura of sacred authority to decisions apparently taken for practical and immediate needs, but nevertheless consistent with a metaphysical wisdom. To both Verga and Capuana, proverbs were also the expression of a traditional way of life, closer to nature, in contrast with the turbulent passions of the big city, a contrast they experienced as they both moved to Milan (a characteristic of Italy's best realists was that they were Sicilians who wrote about their region from Milan, as detachment was fundamental in their understanding of the island). But they also represented a society that was bound to disappear, as shown by *I Malavoglia*, where proverbs were associated with the generation of the grandfather, Padron 'Ntoni, and not with that of his grandson 'Ntoni, who rejected them. Verga's realism was evident in his desire to avoid depicting Sicilian villages as picturesque and idyllic, and the novel eventually demonstrated how the law of economic self-interest prevailed over the traditional family values of the Malavoglia clan.

Another great writer of the end of the century was Italo Svevo (pseudonym of Ettore Schmitz), born in Trieste (still under the Habsburgs) in 1861; like Verga, he rejected the Risorgimento rhetoric, but, influenced by the arrival of psychoanalysis in Italy, turned his attention to the self, producing beautiful novels such as *Confessions of Zeno*, *A Life* and *As a Man Grows Older*, which were both anti-romantic (describing inept and defeated ordinary people in ordinary life) and anti-naturalistic (focusing on autobiographical subjects).

ITALIANS ABROAD

Prior to unification, the mass migration of poor workers and peasants occurred alongside the process of Risorgimento. In some of their aspects, the Risorgimento and emigration were rebellions against poverty in the countryside, clerical and aristocratic privilege in the cities, and foreign interference and occupation. This raised the question of whether nationalists could succeed in turning the peasantry into Italians abroad more easily than at home. Could it be easier to make Italians once they had left Italy? One problem with such a project was that political and economic emigration did not always follow the same routes: urban nationalists and exiles chose mainly European destinations, while most of the poor and rural migrants moved to north and south America and Australia.

A wave of emigration followed the unification of Italy, mainly from Sicily, Venetia, Tuscany and Calabria; emigrants saw themselves as workers of the world rather than supporters of their own new state, something that held true for southerners in particular, who felt despised by their own rulers, who treated them as racially inferior and rebellious criminals. In fifty years, 16.6 million Italians left the country – although many later returned. The principal reasons for the mass exodus were deep seated agricultural crisis: the fall in the price of wheat, the erosion of customary and paternalist bonds of rural society caused by industrialization (which created precarious new conditions of life for the peasantry), the conditions of poverty because of the lack of adequate land reform, and, in some cases, the awareness of the peasants' miserable conditions resulting from socialist proselytizing in the countryside. The large demand for labour in the plantations, mines and factories of northern Europe and America presented a solution. Most emigrants from southern Italy moved to north America, leaving from the port of Naples, and most of those from northern Italy moved to south America, leaving from the port of Genoa. Two-thirds of emigrants were men, half of them peasants; 90 per cent were manual labourers. Initially, it was mainly men who left, a development that was made possible by the women who remained on the land taking on all the productive and family work.

How did emigrants know where to go? Usually, they already had contact with experienced emigrants through family, friends or neighbours; within a network of men sharing the same trade, some became labour recruiters for employers abroad; such recruiters were active in an entirely male world of cafés, *osterie* (pubs), trade fairs and markets. Most of the temporary or seasonal emigration was between Italy and northern Europe, while emigration to America tended to be more definitive. An impressive number of emigrants returned to Italy as soon as they had accumulated enough money: between 1905 and 1920, 80 to 90 per cent of emigrants from Venetia and Friuli returned from across the Alps, while 40 per cent returned from the Americas. No other country's emigration has comparable figures. The creation of 'Italian villages' abroad and the high numbers of those who returned to Italy provide good counter-arguments to the notion of an absence of national identity after unification that is often repeated in textbooks. In addition, the emigrants' perception of the wider world remained confused, so that it was difficult to substitute loyalty to the new host country for loyalty to an Italian identity; for example, any non-European country was indistinctly defined as *'la Merica'*. The result of emigration was the emergence of another Italy replicated around the world with a huge variety of official and non-official associations, cultures of origin that persisted but were at the same time modified by their new environments; mass emigration too created 'a history of Italy'. The Italian press in foreign countries is an example of how many histories of Italy existed, and of how varied the concept of Italianness could be; Italy was perceived in different ways by Risorgimento exiles, liberal patriotic societies, and Catholic, and later Fascist and anti-Fascist, newspapers. As research by Emilio Franzina has shown, the experience of emigration expressed itself largely through music, as emigrants carried mandolins and other instruments in their baggage and wrote songs about their experience. One of the most famous songs, *Mamma mia dammi cento lire* ('Mother, give me 100 lire'), was adapted from a well-known ballad, *La maledizione della madre* ('The mother's curse'), in which a daughter wanted to marry the king of France and disobeyed her mother, who was against the marriage; running away from her mother, the girl drowned in a river. In the new version, the daughter asks her mother for 100 lire to emigrate to America, rebels against her mother's objection though she is supported by her brothers, and dies in the middle of the ocean when the ship is wrecked. The song was just one of many on the theme of tragedies at sea, which were all too common, and a constant fear for emigrants.

The state promulgated the first emigration law in 1888, which dealt with the organization of sea transportation for emigrants, with the stipulation of contracts with shipping companies and regulation of conditions during the journeys. The latter were shameful by any standard – there was a minimum requirement of only one square metre per person on the boats – and there was no interest in emigrants once they arrived at their destination. One rule decreed that married women could not emigrate without their husbands' consent, while men's choices were restricted by conscription as they could be called up for service even while abroad, while their sons could also be conscripted if they kept their Italian nationality.

TOWARDS INDUSTRIALIZATION: WOMEN'S WORK BETWEEN FIELDS AND FACTORIES

Between 1880 and 1910, Italy experienced a huge increase in the urban population, particularly in the north, where industries (mainly textiles) began to appear. In Milan, which during that period began its transformation into the economic capital of Italy, the population almost doubled, from 322,000 to 579,000. The diffusion of industry increased exchanges between city and countryside, particularly in northern regions, where the urban propertied class invested capital in rural improvements such as hydraulic works and land reclamation. The first industries were also largely dependent on rural production and on the rural population. One example of this is the spread of silkworm cultivation from the seventeenth century: spinning was a family industry that was entirely reliant on rural activity; it augmented meagre rural earnings and depended on the cultivation of mulberry trees and silkworm farming as well as on the spinning mill. During the nineteenth century, many landowners who lived in cities established small factories with spinning mills where women workers produced cloth. From the mid-century, this development gave rise to a mushrooming textile industry in the valleys of the Olona, Lambro and Adda rivers in Lombardy, and in the Piedmontese and Venetian valleys (around Biella and Schio, respectively). Women did most of their work from home, were dispersed in different areas of the countryside, were low paid and politically unorganized, and performed the work in addition to their other tasks in the fields. Skilled jobs in factories were given to men, with the justification that women must marry and bear children, and the continuity of their work could not therefore be guaranteed. The diversification of industrial occupations meant that women's industrial work was limited to one phase in their lives, before they married; this in turn led many women to postpone marriage and childbirth, as well as to the tragic abandonment of illegitimate children to foundling hospitals – at the time of Italian unification, the Milan foundling hospital had over 5,000 admissions a year. Women continued to work in factories and fields until the moment they gave birth, a reality starkly at odds with the advice of medical literature of the period, which was full of suggestions regarding the attention pregnant women must pay to their condition. Women who worked until they gave birth in the industries of the Milanese valleys suffered from a deformation of their pelvis which caused puerperal osteomalacia, a bone disease related to childbirth.

Middle-class urban women began organizing to improve the conditions of these poorer women by devoting themselves to philanthropic work, giving rise to the first women's associations, which combined charity work (the tutelage of young female workers, assistance to prevent the abandoning of children and so on), with educational and political activities. Women were also supported by the Church, which sought to rescue them from socialist propaganda. Priests were very influential in many women's lives; for example, during the confession women could complain about their husbands – not to much avail, as priests generally taught women the virtue of patience. For this reason, many democrats and socialists of the time opposed the extension of the suffrage to women, in the belief that women's social condition inevitably led them to religious dependence and political conservatism. The idea was that, influenced by priests and landlords, women were likely to use their votes in the wrong way. An exception was the Mazzinian and radical feminist

Anna Maria Mozzoni (1837–1920), who wrote an appeal in favour of the vote for women and against marital tutelage as early as 1877, following the hopes raised by the political victory of the left.

Women also wrote about themselves. In the second half of the nineteenth century, with the expansion of the publishing industries, the novel became a consumer product, spawning numerous writers expert in rambling love stories, tear-jerkers and spirited romances, often published as appendices to newspapers and magazines. This development favoured the appearance of a female literature by women and for women, which often promoted the bourgeois values of the family and motherhood, but sometimes considered the question of female emancipation. In both cases, these works were highly rhetorical with little literary value. Perhaps the first female writer of significance was Sibilla Aleramo (pseudonym of Rina Faccio, 1876–1960), author of the feminist autobiography *Una donna* ('A woman', 1906), followed in the twentieth century by many more. Anna Radius Zuccari (1846–1913), known as Neera, was one early author of numerous novels centred on family life, with female protagonists who struggled with their condition but eventually accepted it; however, the most famous female writer of that period was Matilde Serao (1846–1927), a journalist and wife of a famous journalist of the time, Edoardo Scarfoglio. Serao was influenced by *verismo* but fell into patronizing and sentimental formulas when writing about the social problems of her native city of Naples.

'LA BELLE EPOQUE': THE GIOLITTI AGE

The nineteenth century ended with colonial disaster, bloody state repression, and banking and corruption scandals in which the government was directly implicated. Yet, the period between the beginning of the new century and the outbreak of the First World War was an age of optimism: in 1900, a more progressive and democratic government came to power; with the exception of a (European-wide) economic crisis in 1907, the economy expanded rapidly – the national income rose by 38 per cent up to 1907, and a further 20 per cent subsequently; some of the most famous names in the Italian economy appeared during this period: Fiat, Pirelli, Olivetti, Lancia and Alfa Romeo represented Italy's industrial take-off. But after the first fifteen years of the century, Italy lived through two world wars and Fascism, and did not experience a further economic boom until the 1950s and 1960s. What was true for the economy was also true for culture. The early years of the twentieth century were also a culturally prestigious time: between 1901 and 1914, Italy received four Nobel prizes (awarded to Carducci for poetry, Golgi for pathology, Moneta for peace, and Marconi for physics). Also, between the 1860s and 1900, the daily press developed considerably, with the birth of newspapers that still exist today.

However, it is necessary to remember that this rapid industrial and cultural development was patchy, and considerable difficulties remained: poverty was still a major problem, particularly in the south and among the landless peasants in the north (*braccianti*). Politically, the period was defined as the era of Giovanni Giolitti, a liberal Piedmontese statesman who was prime minister through most of the pre-war period, governing with various coalition governments. Giolitti understood that Italy could continue to progress only if it managed to control and absorb internal protest. His major innovations lay in incorporating those forces representing the greatest danger to the Italian state. Giolitti therefore responded to moderate socialist demands, seeking in particular to involve the reformist current of the Socialist Party as, for example, in 1913, with the granting of universal male suffrage. He also opened a dialogue with organized Catholicism in order to gain crucial votes against the growth of socialism, which led to the Gentiloni agreement in 1913 (after Count Vincenzo Gentiloni). However, his policies angered an increasingly hostile extreme right, which turned nationalism into an aggressive and imperialistic idea distinct from its democratic origins in the Risorgimento. This nationalist right became more explicitly anti-parliamentary and anti-democratic (particularly as Giolitti provided openings to the moderate left), and in 1910 the Italian Nationalist Association was founded as its organized expression.

In a 1909 novel entitled *I vecchi e i giovani* ('The old and the young'), the writer Luigi Pirandello (1867–1936, and winner of the Nobel prize for literature in 1934) illustrated the distance that had grown between two generations: those who had experienced the Risorgimento – and had in many cases later betrayed its original ideals – and a new generation born between 1880 and 1890 that felt detached from the Risorgimento vision and was tired of living on memories, focusing instead on the future. Among this latter generation were the futurist avant-garde and the writers for newspapers such as *Il Regno*, *Leonardo*, *La Voce* and *Lacerba*, all of which were published in Florence and attacked the condition of the country they called 'Italietta' (small Italy); one of the motivators of this circle was the founder of the Nationalist Association,

---

Box 7.3   The Futurist manifesto (1909)

1. We want to sing of the love of danger, the habit of energy and rashness.
2. The essential elements of our poetry will be courage, audacity and revolt.

. . .

4. We declare that the splendour of the world has been enriched by a new beauty: the beauty of speed . . . A roaring motor car which seems to run on machine-gun fire is more beautiful than the Victory of Samothrace.

. . .

7. We want to glorify war – the only cure for the world – militarism, patriotism . . .
8. We want to demolish museums and libraries, fight morality, feminism and all opportunist and utilitarian cowardice.

. . .

It is in Italy that we are issuing this manifesto of ruinous and incendiary violence, by which we today are founding Futurism, because we want to deliver Italy from its gangrene of professors, archaeologists, tourist guides and antiquaries. Italy has been too long the great second-hand market. We want to get rid of the innumerable museums which cover it with innumerable cemeteries.

Enrico Corradini (1865–1931). These newspapers were read by a discontented bourgeois public of predominantly young men. In 1911, in an attempt to appease the right, Giolitti embarked on renewed colonial war, this time in Libya – the first war in which Italy used aircraft in combat. The modernity of the new flying machines was exalted by the intellectuals of futurism, a movement founded by Filippo Tommaso Marinetti (1876–1944). The nationalists desperately wanted Italy to be involved in a glorious war, and the praise of war appeared in all their writings. As Arno Mayer has argued, futurism, for all its admiration of modernity, remained linked to a nineteenth-century bourgeois myth of progress and technology, explicit in its collusion with capitalist industry and accompanied by a reactionary, anti-socialist and anti-feminist ideology. The periodicals influenced by futurism carried a nationalist, imperialist line, full of expressions such as 'Italy's absolute leader', 'colonial expansionism', 'cult of progress and speed, of sport and physical strength' (as

Gioanola has commented, 'Mussolini had nothing to invent himself').
Centred in Milan and Florence, futurism also flourished in Sicily;
Marinetti exalted metropolises, industry and the modernity of the northern spirit, but also, as Claudia Salaris has argued, the instinctive improv-
isation and the 'enthusiasm for the primordial force of landscape
belonging to the dream of a southern dimension'. Marinetti himself felt
'a bit Sicilian': born in Alexandria in Egypt, the first Italian land he
touched was Sicily; futurism in Sicily was one of the movement's first
and most enduring incarnations.

The fervour for war also stimulated more moderate voices; the elderly
poet, Giovanni Pascoli (1855–1912), a Romagnol pupil of Carducci who
had been an internationalist in his youth, represented perhaps better than
anyone else the transition from the Risorgimento to twentieth-century
nationalism, when he gave a famous speech in favour of war, claiming
that Italian peasants needed land – in the shape of colonies – and that
Italy, 'the great proletarian', had finally 'moved'. His 'national socialism' met with approval from landowners and industrialists, since it did
not threaten the class system: the nation was 'proletarian' compared with
other European nations. Corradini's writings were very similar, especially his political novels; he addressed these to Italian emigrants, whom
he considered lost to the Fatherland unless they could be brought back to
fight in a national war. On the eve of the Libyan war, which was opposed
by the socialists, a climate of nationalist enthusiasm engulfed the bourgeois cafés in Italy and a new popular song was played by civic groups
in the streets and in theatres, stirring novel emotions:

> Where does the most prosperous soil hide?/Where does the sun smile most
> magnificently?/On the sea that links us to golden Africa,/the Italian star
> shows us a treasure.//Tripoli, beautiful soil of love,/May this song come
> fast to you./May the tricolour flag fly/on your towers with the sound of the
> cannon!//Do navigate, o battleship:/The wind is favourable and the season
> is pleasurable./Tripoli, delightful land,/will be Italian with the sound of the
> cannon.

The Libyan war ended in victory in 1912, though it was only a relative
one: Italian rule was limited to the coast, and it took the Fascist regime
years of violent repression in the 1920s to extend Italian control over the
entire country, and the population continued to rebel against their colonial rulers. The nationalists wanted the war from the start, but were
unhappy with the way it was prosecuted: they argued for a more inten-

sive campaign and hoped for a more definite outcome. Despite the war being in part conducted for them, these criticisms aggravated the nationalists' relationship with Giolitti's government. The nationalist right, together with the Futurists, constituted the largest element of the interventionist movement of 1914–15 which culminated, as we shall see, in the 'radiant days' of May 1915.

The radical position of the nationalists was pushed further right by the 'red week' of June 1914, characterized by strikes and violent clashes with the police all over Italy at a time when many cities and towns were run by socialist councils. The spark for this widespread workers' protest was a police massacre at Ancona; three workers were killed during an anti-militarist demonstration calling for the release of the anarchist Augusto Masetti, who had shot and wounded a colonel and shouted 'up with anarchy, down with the army!' while departing for Libya in October 1911. The link between social protest and pacifism was evident during the red week, and would continue in various ways throughout the duration of the Great War. During the red week, the trade unions proclaimed a general strike, supported by the socialist newspaper *Avanti!* (edited from 1912 by Benito Mussolini, from Romagna). The symbolism of the French Revolution and of 1848 were resurrected in Italy by the protests; pews taken from churches were piled up in the streets, serving as both barricades and an anti-clerical demonstration; protesters talked of revolution and a republic. The fear of revolution among industrialists and the middle classes turned into anger at Giolitti's government, which was accused of not repressing the protest – though the predicted revolution failed to take place because the reformist leaders of the socialist trade unions called off the strikes.

When the First World War broke out in August 1914, Italy was still part of the Triple Alliance negotiated by Crispi in 1882, but decided at first to remain neutral. However, by May 1915, Italy had changed its position to support France and Britain. Neither the Entente powers (France, Britain and Russia) nor the central powers (Germany and Austria) wanted Italy to join with their enemies, not because they thought the Italian army was an ally worth having, but because Italian involvement would divert resources to a new front in the Alps. For this reason, Britain and France promised Italy convenient territorial gains, in case of war. The secret Treaty of London of 1915 committed Italy to join the Entente and declare war on Germany and Austria-Hungary; in return, Italy would receive the Trentino, South Tirol, Trieste and Gorizia, Istria (but not Fiume) and northern Dalmatia if the Entente won. To many 'democratic' interventionists (including republicans, reformist socialists and Italians living in the Trentino and Trieste areas that were still part of the Habsburg Empire) this treaty raised the prospect of liberating lands that were still 'unredeemed' and waging a final war for Italian independence against Austria: thereby finishing the task of the national Risorgimento. For the nationalists and Futurists the war was an opportunity to turn Italy into a great power, no longer the 'proletarian' among European nations, no longer Giolitti's 'Italietta'. A final vote in favour of war was taken in parliament on 20 May 1915 under a conservative prime minister, Antonio Salandra (1853–1931), with the Socialist Party as the only opposition.

As Chapter 8 will show, intervention was supported by Italian intellectuals influenced by nationalism and Futurism, whose writing demonstrated a fundamental shift from nineteenth-century democratic nationalism to an aggressive imperialism. As the Socialist Party continued to oppose the war (with the exception of the reformists, who had been expelled from the party in 1912 after their support for Giolitti's Libyan war, and had founded the small Italian Socialist Reformist Party), Mussolini, until 1914 an anti-militarist revolutionary and editor of the party newspaper, turned interventionist. This move, which has often been explained simply by reference to his opportunism, was not peculiar to Mussolini, and was partly a result of a conviction that socialism need not necessarily be separate from the idea of the nation. Mussolini's meetings with socialists from the 'unredeemed lands' of the Trentino (particularly Cesare Battisti) in 1909 persuaded him eventually that socialism must be reconciled to the idea of the *patria* – this mixture of socialism and nationalism became evident in November 1914, when Mussolini wrote his first interventionist article in *Avanti!*, and was consequently expelled from the party:

> The national question is a reality for the socialists too.
> The example of the Trentino is one that forces even the most radical of the neutralists to think. If these 'Italian' people revolted against Austria, how could we, as socialists ... oppose an Italian intervention? Now, the Trentino has morally rebelled. As a minority party with long-term aims we cannot take any military responsibility, but if the Italian bourgeoisie, which has a duty to confront national issues, moved against Austria-Hungary, we – by opposing a war – would only sacrifice the Trentino and favour Austria-Hungary, which is – socialists must remember – the very pillar of European reaction.
>
> ('Nations and Internationalism', *Avanti!*, 18 October 1914)

With financial assistance from Italian and French industrialists, Mussolini founded an interventionist newspaper, *Il Popolo d'Italia*. His declaration of interventionism, a few short weeks after his article in *Avanti!*, added elements to the discussion of socialism and nation similar to the ideas of the Futurists and many anti-socialist interventionists. As Chapter 8 shows, the distinctions within the interventionist movement were to fade as the war progressed:

> I am embarking on an audacious project and I do not hide its difficulties from myself.
> The cry is one word which I would have never pronounced in normal times, but which I instead raise, aloud and with no compromises, with certain faith, today: a fearful and fascinating word: *war*!
>
> ('Audacity!', *Il Popolo d'Italia*, 15 November 1914)

What allowed Mussolini and many democratic interventionists to overcome the questions posed by their socialist and pacifist origins was the decision to accept that class struggle must be suspended for the greater good of the nation in times of war:

> The socialists cannot ignore the existence of national issues. One cannot ignore existing facts, and national problems do exist, they are complex and profound. At times, they overwhelm class issues and they interrupt the evolution of class struggle.
>
> ('The terms of the problem', *Il Popolo d'Italia*, 19 November 1914)

While democratic interventionists such as Bissolati drew on the memory of the Risorgimento to maintain the war's democratic aims of liberating the Trentino and Trieste from the Austrians (as well as defending Serbia and Belgium from Germany), Mussolini also recalled the lost battles of Italian unification, battles that – in his view – demanded revenge, since only through victory in war could the unification process be completed. War, not education or literature, was now necessary to 'make Italians':

> War must reveal Italians to themselves. First of all, it must dissolve the ignoble legend according to which Italians do not fight, it has to delete the shame of Lissa and Custoza, it has to demonstrate to the world that Italy is able to fight a war, a great war. We must repeat it: *a great war*. Only a great war can give the Italians the notion and the pride of their Italianness, only war can 'make the Italians', as D'Azeglio said.
>
> ('The first of Italy's wars', *Il Popolo d'Italia*, 14 February 1915)

SUGGESTED FURTHER READING

A. Lyttelton, *Liberal and Fascist Italy, 1900-1945* (Oxford: Oxford University Press, 2002) provides an excellent introduction to the period. M. Carlson, *The Italian Stage: From Goldoni to D'Annunzio* (London: McFarland, 1981) and S. Stewart-Steinberg, *The Pinocchio Effect: On Making Italians (1860–1920)* (Chicago: Chicago University Press, 2007) are useful starting points for a study of Italian literature during the nation-making process. The development of Italy as a nation can also be explored through a study of mass emigration, as in D. Gabaccia, *Italy's Many Diasporas* (Seattle, Wash.: University of Washington Press, 2000), and of Italian food, as in C. Helstolsky, *Garlic and Oil: Food and Politics in Italy* (Oxford: Berg, 2004). A very interesting and readable account of the position of southern Italy in this period is N. Moe, *The View from Vesuvius: Italian Culture and the Southern Question* (Berkeley, Calif.: University of California Press, 2002).

8

From Hunger to Hedonism: Italy in the Twentieth Century

CHRONOLOGY

Mussolini; Marshal Badoglio becomes prime minister; armistice with the Allies in September; foundation of the Italian Social Republic; foundation of the Committee of National Liberation

1944   Liberation of Rome in June

1945   Partisan insurrection and liberation of northern Italy in April; Mussolini shot

1946   Referendum votes for republic to replace monarchy

1948   New Constitution; Christian Democracy wins elections

1978   Former prime minister Aldo Moro kidnapped and murdered by the Red Brigades

1991   Communists rename themselves Democratic Party of the Left

1992   Revelations of high-level corruption spark arrests and investigations; collapse of Christian Democracy and the birth of the 'Second Republic'

THE ITALIAN PEOPLE BETWEEN PEACE AND WAR

'Sacred selfishness': with these words, prime minister Antonio Salandra justified the shift in alliance that took Italy into the First World War on the side of the Entente in 1915. This cynical image confirmed the ideas that many contemporary Europeans held about Italy, especially among its former allies. Austro-Hungarian propaganda depicted Italian soldiers as sinister dwarfs with a regimental feather in their hats and a knife behind their backs, and represented Italy as a country of cunning people dating back to Machiavelli's time (a country of *machiavellici*); after unification, Italy had inherited from Piedmont the art of 'managing': of changing alliances when it suited them. The Austrian chancellor referred ironically to Italian 'waltz turns' as both Germany and Austria tried to persuade Italy not to turn its back on them.

However, this view of diplomatic opportunism does not do justice to the reasoning and feelings of what has been called the 'interventionist piazza'. Confrontation between interventionists and neutralists in Italian cities saw the former prevail between autumn 1914 and spring 1915, not because they were the majority of the population but because they were the most visible and noisy. This was due in part to the support they received from much of the press and from industrialists, but it was also because the futurists and nationalists were consistently able to mobilize bourgeois and student urban groups in their support. It is indeed impossible to ignore the links between the Italian intellectual world of the *belle époque* (the Giolitti age) and the entry of Italy into the First World War.

239

In 1904, the futurist newspaper *Il Regno* had welcomed the outbreak of the Russian–Japanese war: 'War, finally, has broken out'. This fervent welcome for war continued in the Italian futurist and nationalist press in 1911–12, and again in 1914–15, with hymns to violence, greetings to the 'new world', to 'war as the only hygiene for the world and its sole moral educator'. Such writing continued for a full decade, and characterized a period in which war was awaited, described, and prepared for psychologically. These intellectuals also regarded war as a way out of Giolitti's weak democratic *Italietta*, and attacks on the parliamentary system began to appear in the writings of, for example, Giovanni Papini and Giuseppe Prezzolini, and continued to grow in strength as the government dithered over intervention in 1914 and 1915. A number of their declarations and appeals were expressed as a populist 'revenge of the piazza' against the alleged 'betrayal' of diplomats and politicians.

Forces of the moderate left also sided with the war – republicans, radicals, socialist reformists such as Leonida Bissolati and Cesare Battisti (who lived in Trent under the Austrians), as well as some revolutionary socialists, including Mussolini. In a speech to parliament in December 1914, Bissolati declared:

> It is not in line with socialist spirit to tell the proletariat: Serbia, this Piedmont of young *Slavia*, is about to succumb to Austrian lead; Belgium, the Belgium of Wanderwelde and Anseele is gasping for breath under German bullying . . . France . . . struggles to defend her life, renewing the heroic resistance of the Commune . . . but all this, Italian proletariat, does not concern you.

In the province of Cremona, one of Bissolati's followers wrote in the local interventionist newspaper: 'In order to secure more fighting for civilization and for the proletariat, in order to affirm the principle of democracy, in order to maintain a sense of the word "international", we say: War!'. The writer of these words was Roberto Farinacci, later organizer of some of the most violent episodes of Fascist *squadrismo* in Italy.

Educated in the ideals of the Risorgimento, one of Bissolati's spiritual guides was the poet Carducci, Bissolati's professor at the University of Bologna. In Carducci's poetry, Bissolati saw the Italy of the Risorgimento, born out of the ruins of a divided, clerical and medieval Italy. Believing in the ideal of the war as the conclusion of the Risorgimento, the reformist socialists began to abandon Marx in favour of Mazzini, to place nation before class. Thanks to this Risorgimento mystique, the war became invested with a romantic aura; Bissolati himself, a war volunteer, was portrayed by the interventionist press as a romantic hero, as if the war had taken him, at over fifty years of age, directly from parliament to the battlefield. Far from praising the war (as the futurists and nationalists did) as a revolutionary or imperialist act, the reformists lent their support in the name of principles such as reform and the safeguarding of democracy in Europe: an interpretation that proved very difficult to sustain, not only because the 'progressive' Entente included Tsarist Russia, but also because the development of the war soon united the different wings of interventionism against pacifists and socialists. At the end of the conflict, democratic interventionists became implicated in the social consequences of war by taking part in 'patriotic blocs' with the nationalist right in the 1919 elections, against the socialists, not grasping that the real danger to Italian democracy did not come from those who had been neutralists, but from the patriots with whom they had been allied throughout the duration of the conflict.

Another public soldier–interventionist figure was Mussolini, whose role as editor of *Il Popolo d'Italia* was concerned with cementing the link between soldiers and the Fatherland. However, while Mussolini's war diary, published in instalments in *Il Popolo d'Italia*, was the self-depiction of a leader in the making, and portrayed in his war adventures his leadership of ordinary soldiers the first 'star' of interventionism and post-war nationalism was the poet Gabriele D'Annunzio (1863–1938). Born in Pescara, D'Annunzio was educated in Prato and later moved to Rome, where the success of his poetry won him access to the most prestigious bourgeois salons and cultural circles; his poetry focused obsessively on the self, embodying a decadent aestheticism in an exaggerated style. His poems became very fashionable and allowed him to live an extravagant life characterized by numerous scandals that served both to publicize his literary work and to create his image as a celebrity who secured much space in the media of the time. The First World War provided D'Annunzio with an opportunity for national acclaim in piazzas all over Italy; he was hailed as an extraordinary orator and interventionist propagandist, a 'first-hour' volunteer and 'political educator of the nation'. As Mario Isnenghi has remarked, his speeches were cha--racterized by the will to renovate all the cultural and political traditions of the country's past in an attempt to 'remake' Italians: the myth of Rome and the maritime republics, the Savoy monarchy and Garibaldi; an entire repertory of classicism used to propagate the idea of a just and sacred war in which the role of the individual Italian citizen was to be devoted and submissive.

Interventionism was mainly an urban, bourgeois phenomenon. However, the common image of an immobile peasant mass waiting passively to be directed by others does not reflect the reality of the war years; in fact, sections of both the peasantry and the industrial working class demonstrated actively against the war. During the 'red week', social and anti-war protest continued to be linked. The slogan launched by the socialist Angelo Tasca (1892–1960) in August 1914 – 'between France and Germany, we choose the International' – was welcomed by socialists and anarchists, including Errico Malatesta (1853–1932) who, in December 1914, explained in a letter to *Avanti!* that the hope for a German defeat did not justify participation in the conflict: instead of 'a massacre between brothers', the masses had to 'invoke peace among mankind and war against oppressors'.

Studies of the 'radiant May' of 1915 (when interventionists demon-strated in piazzas around Italy) have often tended to leave out the neutralist activity that took place at the same time. In Turin, opposition to the war was stronger than anywhere else; almost every worker parti-cipated in the May Day demonstration and strikes continued throughout the month, only ending with the capitulation of the Socialist Party which, at that point, had to face the inevitability of war. Acts such as desertion assumed symbolic value among the masses. Police reports showed the collective and organized character of desertion throughout the war years, particularly in the centre–north. After October 1917, censored letters from families to soldiers suggested that they 'acted as at Caporetto'. Desertion and open forms of rebellion were not, however, limited to the north; between 1917 and the end of the conflict in southern Italy and in Sicily, demonstrations against the war arose from the necessity of having men to work in the fields – during these protests, women and children carried white flags and demanded peace, bread and revolution.

As Isnenghi has demonstrated, while intellectuals and officers conti-nued to advocate the reassuring ideology of peasants as the patient instru-ments of the nation's will, during 1917 a contradictory process began to unfold around two major events that transformed the face of the war, and imposed reality over ideological mystification: the August revolt in Turin, and the Caporetto defeat in October. When crowds began demon-strating for peace and bread in a large industrial workers' city such as Turin, echoing the slogans of the Russian Revolution (the first phase of which had taken place in February 1917), the liberal state realized the great risk it faced. The high number of arrests that followed the riots re-launched the anti-militarist campaign. Armaments workers were urged to bring their guns to the piazza: 'Let us put an end,' one anarchist leaflet appealed, 'to this systematic destruction of the human race.' A few months later, the Austrians defeated the Italian army at Caporetto (in present-day Slovenia) taking 300,000 prisoners, while another 300,000 soldiers disbanded and fled. The 'liberated' lands of Friuli and half of Venetia were abandoned in a general retreat along the line of the River Piave. To the liberal ruling class, this was not only a military defeat. Caporetto heightened a long-held fear that Italian soldiers (mainly pea-sants and southerners with no interest in 'liberating' Trent and Trieste) would not continue to fight. In 1915, the interventionists had overcome the neutralists, but the majority of the population had not supported the war; the ruling class understood well enough that some of the liberals were also unhappy about the war, and that the socialists and many Catholics opposed it. Universal male suffrage had been granted under Giolitti in 1913, just prior to the conflict, after half a century of unifica-tion during which the dominant classes continued to believe that the Italian people were not mature enough to be given voting rights. Would those who gave their vote in 1913 also be ready to give their blood? Would the Italian peasant simply continue to obey in silence?

These questions and fears were behind the interpretation of Caporetto as a military strike, as thousands of soldiers threw away their guns and fled, refusing to fight. Did this mutiny herald the start of a revolutionary process, as in Russia? Was the retreat influenced by defeatist propaganda carried out by socialists and Catholics? Though Catholics were divided regarding the war, many of the leaders of Catholic peasant organizations were more intransigent than the socialists in their pacifism. Shortly before Caporetto, two powerful slogans circulated in the army: the demand from the leader of the Socialist Party, Claudio Treves, for 'not another winter in the trenches', and the definition of the war as a 'useless slaughter' by Pope Benedict XV (Pope between 1914 and 1922). The Fascist historian Gioacchino Volpe later explained the phenomenon of Catholic pacifism by the fact that many Catholic leaders worked among the peasantry, and that no party who wanted the peasants on its side could support the war: 'because, if the Libyan war, with a vague perspec-tive of land to be conquered and some religious colouring had found them not too ill-disposed, the present war left them indifferent'.

Subsequent historical research, particularly by Giorgio Rochat, has proved that the major responsibility for the defeat lay with the army generals (so that the behaviour of the rank-and-file soldiers was an effect rather than a cause of Caporetto); however, contemporary accusations turned from blaming soldiers to pointing at the alleged 'political instigators'. After Caporetto, while the new head of the army Armando Diaz (who replaced Luigi Cadorna) inaugurated a new phase of 'persuasion' and material improvements for soldiers, anti-pacifist repression on the home front became fierce, including local trials of pacifists and interventionist-led persecution of anyone suspected of defeatism. Episodes of verbal and physical assault carried out by interventionists – who were protected by the judiciary and the police under the justification that they were defending the Fatherland – represented an early premonition of Fascist squad violence after the war.

The final victory at Vittorio Veneto and on the River Piave was won a year after Caporetto. A 'greater' Italy came into being, expanding to include Trent and Trieste within its borders, but at the cost of 600,000 dead. The gap between nationalist rhetoric and the reality of war persisted in the aftermath of the conflict, in the erection of memorials to 'unknown soldiers' and sites of patriotic pilgrimage at a time when returning peasants found themselves in conditions of poverty that were worse than before the war. This gulf between the experience of ordinary soldiers and the triumphal rhetoric of the nation is evident in the texts of war songs, particularly the wartime song *Gorizia* and the post-war *The Legend of the Piave*. *Gorizia*, written in 1916 after a battle that cost the life of 50,000 Italian and 40,000 Austrian soldiers, expresses the tragedy of the massacre and the soldiers' hatred for nationalism ('O Gorizia, may you be cursed/for every heart which feels conscience/it was painful to depart/and for many there was no return') and for the upper classes who wanted the war, to whom it promises vengeance ('You call a field of honour/this land on the other side of the border/Here we die crying assassins/one day you will be cursed'). *The Legend of the Piave*, a 1918 anthem to the victory, is a poetic narration of the war which has the River Piave as its protagonist ('The Piave whispered calm and tranquil at the passage/of the first infantrymen on the 24th of May [1915]'); the main shift is between Caporetto ('The Piave whispered: the foreigner returns!') and a proud and patriotic reaction that brought to the final victory ('No, said the Piave, no, said the soldiers,/never again may the enemy step forward!/We saw the Piave inflate its banks/and the infantrymen fighting the waves./Red with the blood of the arrogant enemy,/the Piave ordered: go back, o foreigner!').

THE DEFEAT OF ITALIAN DEMOCRACY

The number of soldiers killed in the conflict meant that in almost every Italian family there was a veteran, a prisoner, someone maimed in the war, a widow or orphans. Thus the war continued well into the post-war years as the wartime experience and its consequences influenced both behaviour and choices. The parliamentary elections of November 1919 were a referendum on the war, counterposing interventionist and neutralist parties. A few months earlier, in March, groups of interventionists, nationalists and futurists had gathered in Milan at San Sepolcro to found a new political movement, the *fasci di combattimento*. The group was led by Benito Mussolini who produced a programme full of ideological confusion – it was republican, in favour of votes for women, anti-Vatican and nationalist at the same time, encompassing the varied origins of the Fascist movement – but it was also clearly in favour of Italian imperialism and expressed a will to conquer power:

> We can declare with total certainty that the Fatherland today is greater . . . Because we feel greater, because we have experienced this war, in as much as we have wanted it, it was not imposed on us, and we could have avoided it.

By claiming responsibility for the conflict and for the victory, the Fascists implied that it was now them, and not those who had opposed the war, who had the right to decide the destiny of the nation:

> The meeting of 23 March . . . accepts the supreme postulate of the League of Nations which presupposes the integration of each nation, an integration which in the case of Italy must be carried out in the Alps and in the Adriatic with the reclaiming and annexation of Fiume and Dalmatia. We have 40 million inhabitants on an area of 287,000 square kilometres . . . in ten or twenty years our population will be 60 million. But if we look around we see England which, with 47 million inhabitants, has a colonial empire of 55 million square kilometres . . . We want our place in the world.

Despite Fascism's vaguely asserted opposition to imperialism, the *fasci*'s programme in fact clarified the imperialist aims of the movement, with its demand for Dalmatian annexation and its indication that a confrontation with Italy's former allies over the question of colonies was now an open possibility. Italy, therefore, was 'greater', but not as great as it deserved to be. In September 1919, proclaiming Italian rights to Slav territory, D'Annunzio led a military occupation of Fiume (in present-day Croatia), which continued until the end of the following year.

Meanwhile, workers in industrial areas began to occupy factories: red flags flew from chimneys, and revolutionary slogans appeared on factory walls; workers organized 'factory councils' to demonstrate their ability to organize both the workforce and factory production collectively without employers. A similar pattern was followed in the countryside, where peasants in the Po Valley and Apulia occupied land and organized 'farm councils'. Giolitti believed that agreement with the trade unions could be brought about through granting reforms. As revolution seemed imminent, Italian socialism showed itself to be more reformist than revolutionary and called off the strikes; in 1921 at Livorno, Antonio Gramsci, one of the organizers of the council movement in Turin, founded the Italian Communist Party. By then, revolution had been defeated, and the 'black biennial' replaced the 'red biennial'; powerfully portrayed in Bernardo Bertolucci's later film *1900* (1976), Mussolini's *fasci* moved decisively to the right by setting up armed squads and helping landowners in the repression of peasant protest.

The *squadristi* were mainly veterans and accomplished with ease punitive expeditions carried out with hand grenades, staves, knives and guns against socialist co-operatives, trade union headquarters, left-wing newspaper offices and city councils controlled by the left. Several hundred workers, peasants and union leaders died in this 'one-way' civil war, which saw the forces of the left unprepared and less well-armed. The *Arditi del Popolo*, founded in June 1921 by socialists, communists and anarchists, represented the most militant anti-Fascist group; not supported by any left-wing party and outlawed by the government as an armed association (a status not attributed to the Fascist squads), the *Arditi* could only be successful locally. In August 1922, supported by a large part of the population, they defended Parma against a major Fascist offensive led by Farinacci and Italo Balbo. However, they were finally defeated by a Fascist violence that benefited from the complicity of the state. Indeed, the police and the liberal authorities did not stop the violence, believing that Fascism could avert the revolutionary threat. The Liberal government looked quite favourably on the growth of Fascism. Implementing his usual tactic of *trasformismo*, Giolitti included Fascists in his coalition for the 1921 elections, a fact that inevitably encouraged the police to ignore Fascist violence during that period. Patriotic Italians had been angry with the government after the Versailles Treaty – which did not give Italy the colonies it craved – and believed that Giolitti's conciliatory attitude towards strikes was of a piece with his government's weakness in the area of foreign policy. The Fascists, who demanded territory and opposed strikes, grew significantly during 1920 and 1921. But how was it possible to move from *squadrismo* to power?

The use of squads by landowners was called 'agrarian Fascism', and grew quickly and unexpectedly. Even Mussolini was surprised by their success – he had always claimed that Fascism was essentially an urban phenomenon (just as interventionism had been). Agrarian Fascism created the figure of the *ras* – a local *duce*, often not under Mussolini's direct control, such as Farinacci in Cremona, Dino Grandi in Bologna and Balbo in Ferrara. The apparently reactionary nature of agrarian Fascism contradicted Mussolini's revolutionary Fascist rhetoric. The solution to the difficulties this contradiction entailed came with the decision to organize a Fascist 'march on Rome' in October 1922.

During the course of the month, the Fascists began to take over authority in local provinces and regions. These smaller 'marches on the provinces' continued as Fascist columns converged on the capital from different parts of Italy. There were many references and symbols reminiscent of D'Annunzio's earlier march on Fiume, but the Fascists also employed Garibaldi's slogan: 'Rome or death'. About 50,000 people marched towards the capital, while thousands were simultaneously taking power in local centres all over Italy: they took over the offices of city councils and prefects, seized weapons and destroyed the headquarters of the anti-Fascist press. The march was organized by four men known as the *quadrumviri*: Cesare Maria De Vecchi, a landowner, and Emilio De Bono, a general, were monarchists; Michele Bianchi was a former revolutionary syndicalist; and Balbo was a former republican. These four men symbolized the divergent origins of Fascism, which interventionism had first brought together. While the *quadrumviri* were co-ordinating the columns marching towards the capital, Mussolini waited in Milan, uncertain perhaps as to whether the Fascist march would be successful. Emilio Lussu, the veteran democratic interventionist and anti-Fascist writer observed, in his novel *The March on Rome and Thereabouts*, that Mussolini stayed close enough to Switzerland in order to flee there if things went badly wrong further south.

Around fifty people (Fascists, army officers, policemen and anti-Fascists) were killed in the days leading up to the march on the capital; there was illegal activity, violence, destruction and intimidation. It is difficult now to imagine a political movement in a modern democracy taking over the public sites of power across a country in just a few days. The police resisted occasionally, but often they did not; and there was no longer any division within the movement, because by this point Mussolini was its undisputed leader. Fascist propaganda later insisted that the Italian problem was the division between nation and state: Italy was a nation, but it needed a strong state and it was this that the Fascists claimed they had achieved on 28 October, when the king appointed Mussolini to the office of prime minister. Yet the memory of that day remained controversial under the regime, even in Fascist imagery. On the one hand it became a source of legitimacy, by providing a revolutionary myth of the regime's origins: on 28 October every year citizens were summoned together to remember the significance of the date. On the other hand, it was an embarrassing and difficult memory for all those conservatives who supported Fascism and yet retained power within the regime. How was a phase of illegality and bloodshed to be represented once Fascists constituted the government? A popular film under the regime was *A Noi!* ('To us'), partly filmed during that part of the march that had started out from Naples; but it was heavily edited, so that the final version showed no violence at all, portraying a disciplined army of blackshirts, with people welcoming them everywhere, a force which understood that its destiny was to accomplish a revolution and to win a form of mass plebiscite. At the decennial Exhibition of the Fascist Revolution, which opened on 28 October 1932, an effort was made to present a historic continuity from the interventionist marches of 1914 to the Fascist marches of 1922 – both were interpreted as insurrections against an internal enemy (the alien, the defeatist, the neutralist, the Bolshevik) in which a disciplined people triumphed. The reality was very different: the columns that marched towards Rome were far from disciplined. They assaulted trains, walked or arrived on old bicycles, were unorganized, hungry, tired and wet (it rained continuously). Mussolini arrived in Rome only when asked to form a government, and only at that point did the Fascists receive the order to march into the capital. By then, the revolution was effectively over – though in fact it had never started.

Anti-Fascism was not definitely defeated at this point, and it took a number of years for Mussolini to initiate his dictatorship. When the 1924 elections were conducted using means of violence and intimidation around the country, the socialist MP Giacomo Matteotti (1885–1924) decided to denounce this situation in the chamber:

No Italian elector has been free to decide according to his own will ...
[*interruptions and protests from the right*] ... No elector has been free to
say whether he approved or not the politics, or better the regime, of the
Fascist government. No one was free, because every citizen knew *in
advance* that if he dared to oppose the regime, a political group in the hands
of the government would have nullified his vote and his response ... [*interruptions and protests from the right*] ... To reinforce the government's
intentions, there is an armed militia ... [*clapping from the right, and shouts
of 'Viva la milizia!'*] ... I am talking about elections. There is an armed
militia which has the following fundamental and declared purpose: to
support a prime minister who is the leader of Fascism, and not to support,
as the Italian army does, the head of the state ... and particularly in rural
Italy these militias were present at the polling stations in great numbers.

Other democratic politicians had been physically attacked (for example,
Francesco Saverio Nitti and Giovanni Amendola), and Matteotti
expected to be next. In June 1924 he was kidnapped, as recent research
has demonstrated, by members of the Fascist secret police; Liberal opponents asked the king to dismiss Mussolini, but he refused. The opposition abandoned parliament in protest and moved to the Aventine Hill. In
July, Mussolini told the Fascist Grand Council: 'It is not possible to step
back now! Fascism did not achieve power through the normal ways. It
did so with the March on Rome, an insurrectional act. If no one resisted,
it was because it was clear that it was pointless to resist destiny.' The
significance of this speech was to confirm the legend of insurrection, but
it also stated the truth about a ruling class that had not stopped Fascism
in 1922 and would not do so now. In August, Matteotti's corpse was
discovered outside Rome.

Unable to legislate, the Aventine secession had been a mistake;
however, it was important from a moral point of view – those who took
the decision to leave parliament erected a moral barrier between the
opposition and Fascism, rejecting any compromise. Despite its defeat,
this represented a strong moral message, which could be passed on to the
next anti-Fascist generation. Matteotti endured in popular memory as a
defender of civil freedom and democracy, his last speech representing
the ultimate challenge to the illegality of Fascism and bringing him
martyrdom. In the thousands of messages received by his family he was
called a 'martyr', an 'apostle', the 'new Christ', 'hero' and 'teacher';
these were expressions typical of both a Risorgimento civil religious
rhetoric, and a Christian religion understood by the rural masses of Italy.
As most anti-Fascists who had not been assassinated or imprisoned had

---

Box 8.1 Bourgeois anti-Fascism: Non Mollare ('Do not give up')

One evening in January 1925, a history professor, Gaetano Salvemini, met with a group of friends and former students in Florence and decided to launch a clandestine newspaper, as the freedom of the press no longer existed. Moving rapidly between offices to avoid Fascist surveillance, the group published 2,000–3,000 copies of each edition. The newspaper could not publish more than two issues at any one printshop, as the premises were discovered and burned out by the Fascists. Reference to democratic legality, civil liberties and the honour of a people reminded the paper's readership of the ideals of the Risorgimento, of the struggle for Italian unification against the Austrians, and of the victory in the Great War. Italy would not have peace, they argued in February 1925, until 'the shame of this regime is erased, a regime which uses, as instruments of government ... destruction, intimidation, assault, homicide and arson'. The Fascists were not solely responsible for such criminal acts; the Italian people deserved some of the blame for enduring Fascism passively, showing 'little moral vigour' in a 'serious symptom of the low level of our public morality': 'We do not believe that the murder of a Member of Parliament [Matteotti], ordered by the prime minister, can be regarded, in Italy, as a second-ary event' (June 1925). The last issue of the paper (which could no longer be published because of the destruction of printing offices, protracted physical violence and the arrests of contributors) drew pessimistic conclusions regarding the fundamentally unequal conditions of the struggle:

> Fascism has been compared to an occupation army: it is precisely true ... Many people in Europe are blaming the Italians because they do not revolt against such oppression. But a revolt is, for the moment, technically impossible. Was it possible to blame the Belgian people for not revolting against the German invaders? It is exactly the same thing. Fascism has at its disposal 200,000 blackshirts, all the military forces of the state, 100,000 policemen, and the possibility of providing immunity to all the criminals who are now willing to act against the anti-Fascists.
>
> (October 1925)

---

fled into exile by 1926, Matteotti became a symbol for anti-Fascism abroad, and many committees were named after him. The legacy of the *Arditi del Popolo* continued too, as many militants joined the International Brigades during the Spanish Civil War in 1936–9 and the Resistance during the Second World War.

MUSSOLINI'S ITALY

The destruction of democratic institutions occurred in a short period between 1925 and 1927: laws against the freedom of the press and for the censorship of critical newspapers, the dissolution of political associations and any political party other than the PNF (National Fascist Party), a new Penal Code that transformed Italy legally into a totalitarian state, the reinstatement of the death penalty, the abolition of mayors and local city councils and their replacement by *podestà* (nominated by the government), the neutralization of parliamentary powers so that only the Grand Council of Fascism (the supreme body of the Fascist party created in December 1922) remained, the institution of the Special Tribunal for State Security to deal with political opponents, and the establishment of the *confino* to keep opponents for years, without trial, in remote villages in the south or on islands, were all put in place during these two years. These measures indicated a desire to return to a pre-Enlightenment age, with values and priorities that challenged the Enlightenment heritage: authority came to be preferred to liberty, and the rights of men and citizens were deemed to be outweighed by those of the *patria*, which was in turn identified with the Fascist state. As a result, many non-Fascists had to pretend to be Fascists, or risk being ostracized by the *patria* and losing their rights. In the late 1920s, and particularly in the 1930s, it became impossible to work in the public sector without a party membership card (which for this reason began to be called the 'bread card'). Fascism did not organize elections, but instead imparted directives from above; increasingly, as the dictatorship progressed, Mussolini became the central figure as the founder of the party, the head of the government, and *Duce* (Leader) of the Italian people – a Latin term (*Dux*) that did not mean anything in juridical terms but was supposed to indicate the existence of a mystical relationship of trust and communion between leader and led.

Indeed, as Emilio Gentile's research has demonstrated, Fascism organized a political-religious mobilization based on faith and, when referring to Mussolini, employed a vocabulary more suited to religion than to politics. The attribution of qualities such as omnipotence, youth and immortality were encouraged by Vatican support for the new cult: Pope Pius XI (Pope between 1922 and 1939) claimed that Mussolini had escaped death (after several attempts on his life), which proved that God had saved him for the well-being of the nation. Mussolini was also omnipresent, taking advantage of the invention of the radio – thousands of loudspeakers appeared in Italian piazzas – and by travelling around the peninsula as no prime minister had done before, giving speeches everywhere. Italians saw him in the flesh, and participated in what became a collective political 'theatre', answering rhetorical questions posed by the *Duce* with pre-arranged slogans. The foremost stage was Piazza Venezia in Rome, where Mussolini established his office and gave speeches from a balcony overlooking the Vittoriano monument of Italian unification now renamed the 'Altar of the *Patria*' in honour of victory in the Great War, with the addition of the symbolism of the 'Unknown Soldier' to that of the Risorgimento. In this way, Fascism anointed itself heir to the Risorgimento, the process of national 'becoming' that the war and post-war period had completed. Gatherings in Piazza Venezia appeared in endless LUCE films shown in Italian cinemas, together with images updating viewers on the achievements of the regime, its public works and architecture, and on the activities of *Il Duce*. Mussolini did not 'do politics' in the old way: he got up very early in the morning, rode horses, fenced, flew as his own pilot from city to city, spoke other languages, wrote, swam, threshed wheat, signed international treaties, received the world's powerful, and made proclamations to the masses. *Carri di tespi*, small mobile theatres, took plays and opera around Italy, and LUCE films could be seen even in small villages, in mobile cinemas. A key slogan of the time was 'going towards the people'.

Tradition and modernity, conservatism and revolutionary slogans coexisted in the culture and politics of Fascism, which promoted both a new 'futuristic' Italy of modern cities with white concrete buildings, a militaristic country of battleships and aeroplanes but simultaneously a country in which the peasantry was the pillar of the nation. The moral and physical health of the peasantry was held up as an example for eugenic purposes, while ruralization was linked to the desire for an increase in population, which in turn furthered the aim of imperialist expansion. LUCE films pictured Italians travelling on holiday by train and by car, and joyful songs such as *Mille lire al mese* ('1,000 lire a month') created the imagery of the petit-bourgeois dream, though in reality, both the first mass-produced Fiat cars (called *Balilla*) and tickets for rail travel were very expensive, and most people travelled to work on foot or by bicycle; economic depression and protectionism led to a general decrease in consumption that was at odds with Fascist propaganda.

Women were the principal object of a demographic campaign linked by the regime to its need for greater military power. Welfare and maternity incentives encouraged Italians to marry and have a large number of offspring; new laws opposing 'crimes against the health and purity of the race' made contraception illegal and turned abortion into a crime against the state, carrying a penalty of 2–5 years imprisonment. From 1933, the institution of Mother and Child Day (24 December) brought women with large numbers of children from all over Italy to Rome to be awarded prizes. The laws and ideology surrounding women's fertility were supported by the Catholic Church, which came to an agreement with the Fascist state in 1929 (known as the Lateran Pacts) that ended more than fifty years of Papal hostility towards the Italian state. Fascism was again propelling Italy backwards by establishing conservative policies at the same time as broadcasting a message of novelty and revolution. This position is exemplified in the case of the regime's attitude to women: Fascism did not encourage women simply to stay at home and breed, as the Catholic Church had always preferred, but also to play a revolutionary role in the regime by producing and educating new generations of Fascist warriors. The female reaction to these policies was just one example of the way the population refused to comply with those aspects of the system that called for personal sacrifice: women continued to use birth control as much as they were able, despite its illegality. If the population did grow under Fascism it was as part of a generalized European trend of falling infant mortality and rising life expectancy.

Linked with the demographic campaign was the reclamation of marshes, though it remained limited to central Italy and was not attempted in the poorer areas of the south, which remained prey to malaria. After the Great War, the Sicilian Mafia had expanded its control over land on the island, as many landowners called for protection against the threat of land redistribution and the demands of the peasantry. Like Fascist squads in other parts of Italy, the Mafiosi were ready to shoot socialists and trade unionists. Fascism became rooted in the south, particularly after the March on Rome, when many liberals and landowners joined the winning side. Between 1925 and 1931, the state conducted a fierce campaign against the Sicilian Mafia, reminiscent of the post-unification campaign against banditry unleashed by the liberal state. The campaign brought about the destruction of many criminal associations and families, but by the 1930s the Mafia had begun to reorganize, by which point state propaganda had ceased to mention Sicilian criminality.

In terms of art and architecture, the Fascist regime had incorporated and developed aspects of the Futurist movement. In 1914, a few years after Marinetti had published the Futurist Manifesto, the architect Antonio Sant'Elia published the Manifesto of Futurist Architecture. Italian architecture, ran the Manifesto, like its literature, painting and music, should destroy Italy's past and traditions, should embrace modernity to the extent that every age ought to rebuild its cities, and should be both functional and rational. This movement was supported partly by the Fascist regime and was realized in many 1930s public buildings in Italian cities, including the railway stations in Florence, Milan and Rome, and new cities such as Sabaudia on the reclaimed Pontine marshes. The architect Marcello Piacentini rationalized this style further, proposing a 'Fascist style' that hinted at the Roman past but added what he called a 'virile nakedness' in buildings with sharp-cornered pillars and giant columns to provide a sense of monumentalism.

Fascism was both a return to the past in terms of law and politics and an entirely new form of 'mass' dictatorship. It took advantage of the existing rhetoric of a 'religion of the *patria*', a powerful ideological component that had first been raised during the Risorgimento, then strengthened by victory in the Great War, and which could now be conveniently disseminated by the new technology of radio and cinema, which developed at just the right time for the regime. The myth of ancient Rome was revived once more, with Mussolini cast as a new Augustus, his regime seen as a new imperial age, symbolized by the introduction of a new calendar, the foundation of new towns such as Littoria, youth associations named 'Youth of the Lictors' and 'Sons of the She-Wolf' and the adoption of the Roman salute. Perhaps the best single example of all the elements of the Fascist discourse is the Fascist anthem *Giovinezza* ('Youth'), which was played at most public events, and sung by children in schools:

> Salute, o heroic people/Salute, o immortal Fatherland!/Your children have been reborn/With faith in the Ideal//The value of your warriors/The virtue of your pioneers,/The vision of Alighieri/Shines today in every heart//*Youth, youth/Spring of beauty/Your song rings and goes/Through the*

sorrows of life//Within Italy's borders/The Italians have been remade/Mussolini has remade them/For tomorrow's war//For the joy of work/For peace and for the laurel/For the shame of those/ Who have disowned the Fatherland//*Youth, youth* . . . /The poets and the craftsmen,/The lords and the peasants/with the pride of the Italians swear faith to Mussolini//There is no poor town/which does not join the ranks,/which does not unfurl the flags/of Fascism the redeemer//*Youth, youth* . . .

Consistent with the rhetoric of an empire that would be rebuilt through the acquisition of colonies, and with the foundation of five new towns on the reclaimed Pontine marshes in central Italy in the 1930s, Mussolini also set restrictions on emigration. Fascist propaganda insisted that Italians no longer needed to leave their country, and that one day, once Italy had its empire, emigrants could return to work in the Fatherland and its colonies, no longer exploited by others, but as employers themselves. In the meantime, Italians abroad were supposed to maintain their Italianness, while at the same time they were to 'be remade' just as, in the words of *Giovinezza*, they were being remade in the Fatherland. Institutions like the *Fasci* abroad intended to transform Little Italies around the world into little Fascist Italies, microcosms of the Mussolini experiment in Italy. Much of the *Fasci* propaganda was mere rhetoric – Isnenghi has defined Fascism as a 'regime of words': however, these were words that many wanted to believe were facts, as the exiled Professor Salvemini had to acknowledge on arrival among the Italian community of New York:

> [These emigrants were] hard workers, linked to their families by heroic bonds of sacrifice. Arrived in America, illiterate, shoeless and with bags on their shoulders, they had to face unheard-of difficulties and suffering, despised by everybody because they were Italians. And now they heard, even from Americans, that Mussolini had made Italy a great country, where no one was unemployed, where everyone had a bath at home, where trains were on time, and that Italy was respected and feared in the world. Whoever challenged this view, not only destroyed their ideal Fatherland, but also hurt their personal dignity. Italy and the Italian government and Mussolini were in their imagination an indivisible whole; to criticise Mussolini meant to fight Italy and to offend them as individuals.
>
> (Salvemini, 1973, p. 625)

Any discussion of the question of the extent of popular consensus achieved by the regime has to take all these aspects into consideration:

the Italian population took part in political demonstrations as mass rituals, and millions of Italians privately, at school, or at summer camps, wrote letters to Mussolini demonstrating belief in his cult – around which the organizational energies of the regime were permanently mobilized. However, the image of all Italians as convinced Fascists who were ideologically and politically involved is as misleading as that of all Italians as non-Fascists forced to take part in the regime's initiatives. It would be simplistic to think that most Italians accepted Fascism out of convenience or because they were forced to. The expression 'honest dissimulation' (first used in Counter-Reformation Italy, as was shown in Chapter 5), has been used to describe the attitude of those who took part in rallies and meetings, who represented the regime in their jobs, who saluted *Il Duce* and wore a black shirt – including artists and intellectuals such as the poet Giuseppe Ungaretti, Luigi Pirandello and all the professors and scientists who swore oaths of loyalty to the regime. As Isnenghi has suggested, it would be more honest to acknowledge that many believed in what they were doing, and that they identified with one of the many variants of Fascism – whether with the San Sepolcro programme, the resurrection of a new Roman empire or, later, the emergence of a new Nazi–Fascist European order. As Isnenghi has argued, Fascism was a 'fruit of Italian history'; it can, therefore, be considered a 'poisonous fruit', but not an extraneous one 'fallen, who knows how, from another tree'.

WORDS THAT DID NOT BECOME REALITY: FASCIST WARS AND DEFEATS

Domestic policies regarding, for example, the education of youth, women or the rural campaign, were strictly linked with the grandiose aims of the regime's foreign policy. The 1920s have been defined as a period of 'pacific' foreign policy because, despite the regime continuing to make clear its discontent with the Versailles Treaty, there was no practical possibility of overturning it. In 1923, when four Italian soldiers were killed in the Greek part of Corfu while on a League of Nations mission, Italian forces bombarded and occupied the island, killing at least fifteen civilians. The League forced Italy to leave Corfu, and for the rest of the 1920s Mussolini focused on the 're-conquest' of Libyan territory, where Italian occupation had, after the 1911 war, remained geographically limited and precarious. The Libyan campaign was a rather traditional colonial war, efficient and ruthless, accompanied by little clamour or propaganda, and later removed from national memory and historiography, until recent studies by Italian historians Angelo Del Boca and Giorgio Rochat. The most difficult area to control was Cyrenaica, where the population resisted occupation. In 1930, the Italian army deported more than 80,000 semi-nomads to concentration camps, where they lived in overcrowded conditions with a lack of food and hygiene, resulting in the deaths of half their number in three years. In a solemn proclamation in 1932, Marshal Pietro Badoglio announced the 'pacification' of Libya. The Libyan deportation and genocide was up to that point the gravest crime that could be laid at the door of Italian colonialism.

The victory of Nazism in Germany boosted Italy's chance of pursuing a revisionist foreign policy. Mussolini's speeches and articles in the Italian press increasingly included attacks on the League of Nations and on disarmament. In 1932, Mussolini wrote an entry for the XIVth volume of the Italian Encyclopedia entitled 'the doctrine of Fascism' in which he stated: 'Peace is foreign to Fascism, as all international institutions for peace are . . . Only war can bring all human energies to the highest pitch and can ennoble peoples who fight.' But how was Italy's power to be felt in the world? How and where was the new empire to be built and through a war against whom?

Mussolini's starting point in the quest for total power was inevitably the Great War, which according to the Fascists had entitled Italy to the Slav-inhabited Adriatic coast, but which Italy had failed to acquire. As research by Rochat and MacGregor Knox has demonstrated, the Allies and the neighbouring Slavs came to be regarded as a major obstacle to Italian ambitions. The other area of Fascist interest was the Mediterranean, which Mussolini claimed must again become a Roman sea. Ethiopia was not Mussolini's first choice as an area for new territory, though he had expressed interest in colonies there since 1925. It was only in 1932, when it became clear to Italian leaders that France would not tolerate Fascist forays into the Balkans, that Mussolini began planning the invasion of Ethiopia, which was an independent state and a member of the League of Nations. However, when Italy invaded Ethiopia in October 1935, conquering it by May 1936, the only intervention from the League was economic sanctions – a measure that rallied Italians behind the dictatorship and marked the highest point of consensus with the regime. The League gave Mussolini an enormous opportunity to dramatize Italy's struggle as a virtuous one against the greedy and plutocratic Western powers, whose ruthless immorality made them a much more dangerous enemy than Ethiopia. The regime began to describe Italy as a besieged nation; in the diplomatic correspondence of Mussolini's ambassador to London, Dino Grandi, the British capital was described as the enemy's most dangerous trench and headquarters – this was a war fought, he believed, not on the Ethiopian Tigrai, but on the British Thames. Militarily, the two enemies were not well matched; Haile Selassie, Emperor of Ethiopia, had a much smaller army, little artillery and a very limited air force, while Italy employed modern weaponry against the civilian population. More than 2,000 bombs containing poison gas, which was forbidden by international conventions, were dropped, to destroy Ethiopian resistance.

Subsequently, Mussolini's policy was characterized by open hostility to the Western powers in the Mediterranean, intervention in Spain, the introduction of racial laws, the annexation of Albania, and entry into the Second World War. These steps became feasible because of the growth of a domestic consensus around the African victory and the license for aggression that German dominance conferred. After the Ethiopian war, more 'glorious' enterprises became necessary in order to maintain support at home. Foreign policy became the main feature of the regime in the late 1930s, which also served to keep Italians 'mobilized' at home. The most important domestic policy change during those years were the racial laws of 1938, which decreed that Jews who had been born abroad, many of whom came from Nazi Germany, must be deported, that marriages between Aryans and Jews were forbidden, that Jews could no longer hold public office, could not join the National Fascist Party, and could not own more than fifty hectares of land or run any business with over 100 employees. As a result, 6,000 Italian Jews left the country in the following three years, Jewish-run firms closed down, Jewish children were expelled from state schools, one in twelve university teachers lost their jobs, and others left in protest. The laws outraged not only the business and academic elite but also the Church, which regarded them as a breach of the 1929 Concordat because they prohibited mixed marriages between Catholics and baptized Jews. For many Jews the laws posed a serious problem of financial survival: with the exception of very wealthy families, many found themselves suddenly without employment and had to live in precarious conditions. In the autobiographical novel, *The Garden of the Finzi-Continis*, Giorgio Bassani recalled the experience of his own family, an average wealthy Jewish household from Venetia:

My father had volunteered in the war and joined the fascist party in 1919; I myself had belonged to the GUF [Fascist University Groups] until just now. In fact, we'd always been the most normal people you could think of, so normal we were downright banal, in fact, and for this reason it seemed to me really ridiculous that now he should suddenly expect us to behave in an exceptional way, just like that, out of the blue.

(Bassani, 1974, p. 135)

The decision to attack the Jews was an extension of Mussolini's long-held anti-Africanism; laws were issued in Ethiopia from August 1936 outlining a system of racial separation. However, while many Jews anticipated a racist campaign from the time of the Ethiopian war, others expressed incredulity. As Primo Levi recalled, in *The Drowned and the Saved,* instead of confessing to being a political opponent when he was caught by the Fascist police in 1943, he declared himself a Jew, for which he was sent to Auschwitz. There were two separate phases of the persecution which, despite being different in nature and purpose, are utterly interconnected: between 1938 and 1943 there was an attack on the rights of Jewish people, followed by physical persecution between 1943 and 1945. During the first phase, Jews lost significant civil rights; and during the second, deportations to German extermination camps resulted in the deaths of almost 10,000 people.

Anti-Fascist exiles benefited from the backlash against the racial laws and from the changed climate of opinion. Also having a major impact on anti-Fascism, Italian and German intervention in the Spanish Civil War in 1936 witnessed Garibaldi battalions of the International Brigades fighting Italian troops as well as Franco and anticipating, within Spain, the Italian civil war of 1943–5. In March 1937, at Guadalajara, anti-Fascist brigades proved themselves capable of defeating the Italian militia sent to help the Spanish Nationalist rebels. Anti-Fascist exile Carlo Rosselli launched the slogan 'Today in Spain, tomorrow in Italy', suggesting that Spain was the first stage of the Italian resistance. However, neither he nor his brother Nello would experience it: they were assassinated by the Fascists in Paris in 1937.

In May 1939, Italy and Germany signed the 'Pact of Steel' in which, unlike previous international alliances, the allies had to support one another in offensive wars or actions, not only in those of defence. Also, the Pact was based on the concept of a common civilization and ideology. When Italy invaded Albania in April 1939, the Fascist press portrayed it as a peaceful endowment of civilization upon a population that had always wanted to be united with the destiny of Rome. In reality,

---

Box 8.2   The Jews and Italian society before the racial laws

During Napoleonic rule, Jews acquired equal rights with Catholics, and while some rights were withdrawn during the Restoration it was not possible to reverse the tide completely – Jews were sent back to the ghettoes only in the Papal States. The ghetto was definitively abolished following the liberation of Rome on 20 September 1870. Classicist historian and anti-Fascist exile Arnaldo Momigliano emphasized that Catholic indifference allowed the Fascists and the Nazis to employ anti-Semitism:

> Whatever we write on the period that ends up with Fascist and Nazi collaborationists sending millions of Jews to concentration camps (and my mother and my father were among the victims there), one statement needs to be repeated. This huge slaughter would have never occurred without the indifference, which had continued for centuries, towards Jewish fellow-countrymen. Indifference was the final product of the Church's hostility, for which the only solution to the Jewish question was 'conversion'.

With the Lateran pacts of 1929, Catholicism became the state religion. This changed the juridical condition of other religions that had been considered equal to the Catholic Church under the Liberal Zanardelli's *Penal Code* of 1889. After 1929, other religions were considered hierarchically inferior to the Catholic Church. Anti-Semites and pro-Nazis such as Giovanni Preziosi and Telesio Interlandi reinforced their campaign, particularly after 1934, when a cell of the clandestine anti-Fascist group *Giustizia e Libertà* was caught in Turin and it emerged that many anti-Fascists were Jews. The identification of Jews with anti-Fascism became a constant propaganda argument from the regime, and Jews began to be attacked on a scale previously unheard of.

Mussolini decided to develop a 'parallel' war, so that when Germany provoked wider war (which seemed very likely at that point) Italy would not be too dependent on its ally: indeed, when Italy entered the Second World War, it continued its Balkan orientation with an attack on Greece in October 1940. Italy's period of 'non-belligerence' after the German invasion of Poland in September 1939 was not one of 'neutrality', since Mussolini never intended to be neutral, but of holding back in order to be better prepared militarily. In June 1940, Italy entered the war at the last moment, shortly before the French were defeated, in the hope of gaining some of the spoils of victory.

It quickly became clear that war propaganda was composed of hollow words that bore little relation to reality, as the Italian army was defeated in Greece (rescued only by German intervention) and northern Africa. Indeed, many young Fascists who had earnestly believed in the regime's war were disillusioned by defeat and became anti-Fascists, and, in some cases, later partisans. One of them, the writer Nuto Revelli, an extraordinary narrator of the 'war from below', confronted reality during the battle in the Western Alps against France:

> Let us also reflect on the frozen soldiers. 2125: too many in a military campaign that lasted a few days and was fought on our own land. They wore pieces of cloth on their feet: cloth instead of socks, which wrapped the foot in a shoe of poor quality leather. It was like walking with bare feet in the snow . . . the uniforms were made of fake wool, the same that we brought, together with those cardboard shoes, to the Greek–Albanian front and to Russia . . . Not to speak of the weapons . . . the artillery was outdated, a military residue of the First World War.

In 1941, the general of Revelli's military academy informed the soldiers that they were going to Russia, and added:

> 'The war is going badly . . . Remember that the responsibility of the army's incompetence falls back on Fascism, not on the army.'
> Those words hit me like a punch in my stomach.

One of the most moving memories of the Russian campaign, first published in 1953, was written in a German camp in 1944 by the *Alpino* (member of the Alpine troops) Mario Rigoni Stern, and is a testimony of how the *Alpini* first and foremost fought a battle to preserve their life in the face of inhuman conditions. The collapse of the army was accompanied by the collapse of the home front under the weight of the news of military defeats, hunger and Allied bombing.

The Allied landings in Sicily in June 1943 precipitated Mussolini's fall. With the war almost lost, on 25 July 1943, the king – for the first time since the March on Rome – decided to act against Mussolini after the Fascist Grand Council had voted in favour of Mussolini's dismissal. *Il Duce* was arrested, and Marshal Badoglio became the new prime

Box 8.3   Italy under the bombs

The bombing of Italian cities began immediately in June 1940, when Turin and Genoa were hit for the first time, followed by attacks on Milan, Naples and Taranto. Successive attacks in 1942 and 1943 were much heavier than those of 1940–1, and by the first half of 1943 all Italian regions had been bombed. In June 1943, Rome was hit for the first time. After the Allied landing, the bombing of southern Italy began, by both the Allies and the Germans. In 1943, after the heavy raids on Turin, Milan and Genoa – by then in ruins – workers went on strike, demanding peace. Women, who were disproportionately victimized by the bombing, played a major role in organizing shelters and helping refugees as well as organizing demonstrations against the regime over the lack of civilian defence. The writer Natalia Ginzburg, née Levi, who was from a Jewish anti-Fascist family in Turin, described in her famous autobiographical book how the bombing, more than anything else, revealed the reality of war to Italians:

> We supposed that the war would overwhelm us and turn our lives upside-down. On the contrary many people remained unaffected in their houses, living as they had always done. When, however, everyone was thinking that they had got away with it at little cost, and that there would be no upheavals of any sort, no destruction of homes, nor flights nor persecutions, all of a sudden bombs and mines exploded everywhere; houses collapsed, and the streets were full of ruins, soldiers and fugitives. There was not a single person left who could pretend that it was nothing, shut his eyes, or stop his ears, or hide his head under the pillows, there was not one. The war was like that in Italy.
>
> (Ginzburg, 1967, p. 151)

minister. Mussolini's was a silent fall, imposed from above, but it was immediately welcomed from below: as the radio announced the news, the summer evening saw massive crowds in the streets and piazzas, cheering and shouting that the war and Fascism were over. The writer Cesare Pavese, in one of the most famous novels of wartime Italy, described the arrival of the news on a Piedmontese hill, where he lived with his landlady and her mother:

Next day the news arrived . . . The people went down into the town, talking at the top of their voices. Elvira knocked at my room and called to me through the door that the war was over. Then she came in, and without looking at me because I was getting dressed, told me, red in the face, that Mussolini had been thrown out. I came down and found Egle and her mother. We listened to radio – London this time – I could no longer doubt that the news was true. Her mother said: 'But is the war over?' 'No; it's just beginning now', I said cynically.

(Pavese, 1965, p. 40)

Although the radio made clear that the war would continue, the population could not see any reason to go on fighting once the regime had fallen. Moreover, as a famous Piedmontese partisan song (entitled *Badoglieide*) later reminded them, Fascism was still there with Badoglio 'made fat by Fascism', responsible for the war in Ethiopia, for the shameful aggression against France, for the massacre of the *alpini* in Russia and, finally, for having left the Fascists in power and put anti-Fascists in prison: 'the shirt was no longer black/but Fascism remained in power'. There was a mass reaction against the symbols of the dictatorship: images and statues of Mussolini were taken down, images of Roman lictors on public buildings destroyed, and streets renamed; the enraged population needed to reject an entire age, to leave the past and part of themselves behind – most people having been, or behaved as, Fascists under the regime. In the meantime, secret bargaining between the Allies and Badoglio led to an armistice on 8 September and the Germans suddenly became the enemy. Again, the popular reaction was a delighted belief that the war was really over. The army collapsed and everyone escaped who could, starting with the king and Badoglio, who abandoned Rome to German vengeance and sought refuge in Allied-liberated southern Italy. Soldiers left the field without orders in a large-scale repeat of Caporetto, pursuing what seemed the only sensible idea: to go home – the title of a famous film made later in 1961, *Tutti a casa* by Luigi Comencini. The partisan Beppe Fenoglio (author of the well-known novel *Johnny the Partisan*), told in *Primavera di bellezza* ('Spring of beauty') of the shock with which a group of soldiers greeted the news:

The uniform wrapped them like a symbol of shame and death, the guns they were holding no longer felt like honourable national weapons, but like individual tools good for hunting or banditry.
. . .
As the soldier said, this is the complete forty-eight [1848]. Never again will there ever be an army in Italy.

It was difficult to cross Italy and escape from the Germans; some 600,000 Italian soldiers were deported to German internment camps. Women took on a major role of defending, feeding and helping Italian and Allied soldiers, thus demonstrating that, despite the lack of a state to give orders, civil society continued to function, and a country named Italy still existed. Which Italy, however? Fascist Italy had died, and the army and the state had collapsed. Some historians claimed, therefore, that 8 September represented the 'death of the Fatherland'. This was certainly the way that Fascists felt: one of them, the young Carlo Mazzantini, expressed these feelings in his wartime memoir *A cercar la bella morte* ('Looking for the beautiful death'): 'There was no more Italy; there was no more government, no more army . . . Italy had become nothing more than a territory with a population occupied by a foreign army.'

The masses sought ways to survive hunger and the bombing, and waited for the end of the war, welcoming the Allies as liberators as they progressed from southern to northern Italy. Such attitudes expressed weariness and opportunism, but also the attraction of the myth of America – the rich country to which many Italians had emigrated – which was symbolized during those months by soldiers bringing food, cigarettes and chocolate as the first products, for many Italians, of a world of consumption they had admired in the Hollywood movies they had still been permitted to watch under the regime. The death of the old *patria* corresponded to the birth of a new one – no longer that of Mussolini who, rescued by the Germans, had established a Fascist republic controlled by the Nazis between the west of Lake Garda and Venice (the Salò Republic), and no longer that of Badoglio or the House of Savoy, irredeemably compromised by contact with the past regime. The new Italy was born in the mountains where partisan groups began to organize to fight Fascism and Nazism. It was for this reason that the republic founded in 1946 declared itself 'born of the Resistance'. The names that partisans chose for their armed groups were those of the heroes of the Risorgimento (Garibaldi, Mazzini, Mameli), and of the heroes of anti-Fascist martyrdom such as Matteotti, Gramsci and Rosselli. The indication was that the time had come for a genuine second Risorgimento, more democratic than the first, with reference not to Cavour and the monarchy but to the republican and radical components of the unification struggle.

ITALIAN ART OF THE RECONSTRUCTION

The years of reconstruction were also years of economic boom; while Italian cities were still in ruins, the economy and society began to change and to prepare for what was later called the 'economic miracle' (between the mid-1950s and the mid-1960s). New forms of artistic expression, particularly in cinema, architecture and design, began to indicate society's strong desire to break with the war and with the Fascist past. After the war, the finest achievements of Italian art were in cinema. Neo-realist cinema, compared by art historians to the realism of Italian painting at the time of Caravaggio, was characterized by a civil passion, which rejected both traditional and Fascist rhetoric, and was aimed at discovering the real Italy in its backwardness and misery (the Christian Democrat leader, Giulio Andreotti, Italy's prime minister for many years under the republic, said that neo-realism 'badly served the Fatherland'), but also in its faith in the ability to renew itself. Neo-realism was characterized by a philosophy and an aesthetic that distinguished Italian cinema from that of other nations: it combined 'humanitarian sympathy' with 'gentle cynicism' which, as an American film review of *Bicycle Thieves* by Vittorio De Sica (1948) put it in 1949, 'Italians alone carry as their trademark'. Neo-realism was a new Italian Renaissance that shared with fifteenth-century humanism an emphasis on the role of the individual. Poor Italians lived as miserably as the poor in other countries, but their protests tended to take more individual forms, unaided as they were by any institution (the protagonist of *Bicycle Thieves*, for example, could not get any help from either the police or the Communist Party). Neo-realist cinema portrayed pity for humanity without offering any solution to its problems and, like the Commedia dell'Arte in the seventeenth century, could be seen, as described by Herbert Jacobson, an 'old Italian recipe for living'.

The term neo-realism was borrowed from the nineteenth-century literary genre *verismo*, which already enjoyed public popularity. As a reaction to Futurism and decadence, this current re-emerged after the war through writers such as Alberto Moravia who, in *Time of Indifference*, portrayed a bourgeoisie without ideals, captured in the banality of its conversations; or Corrado Alvaro, who revealed in detail the Calabrian rural world. The writer Italo Calvino, who described the non-heroic side of the Resistance movement in his book *The Path to the Spiders' Nest*, explained that neo-realism was the cultural climate for his generation, which they could share, for example, even during a journey on a train:

'crammed with people and bags of flour and oil drums, [where] every passenger would recount to complete strangers the adventures which had befallen him'. The same image can be found in the journey by boat to Sicily described by Elio Vittorini in *Conversation in Sicily*.

Neo-realism also influenced Italian architecture. At the end of the Second World War, over three million houses had been destroyed or badly damaged. During the reconstruction, the Italian architectural and design avant-garde focused for the first time on the needs of the working classes. These were years of democratic idealism and enthusiasm, and architects wanted to reconcile new developments in housing with the new democracy. For an architect such as Ernesto Rogers, the vision of prefabricated buildings in the middle of nowhere represented the physical manifestation of hopes for the future, though neo-realist cinema did not see the boom in such a positive light: in 1960, Federico Fellini's film, *La Dolce Vita*, juxtaposed the 'miracle' with the decadence and shallow voyeurism of the protagonists, interpreting the new buildings in the periphery of Rome like signs of despair and desolation of a dream gone wrong. Plans designed to increase employment and build workers' homes denoted a reaction against the anonymity of 1930s' 'rationalist' architecture. A return to the Baroque age was proposed in the use of different façades and balconies with roofs and external stairs. Newly-created districts were supposed to look as if they were the product of historical sedimentation, hinting at the human and social ups and downs expressed by the architecture of earlier ages.

At the same time, new furnishings and new interior design developed to become a symbol of regeneration from the late 1940s onwards. The 'ideal home' of the boom years that followed was not designed around the needs of everyday life, but emerged instead from the dream kitchens of America as seen in Hollywood films and, later, in television soap operas. Italian companies such as Zanussi began production for the middle classes and for export. As Ginsborg has observed, the economic crisis of the 1970s did not interrupt the growth in prosperity – by 1975, 92 per cent of families had a television, 94 per cent a refrigerator, and 76 per cent owned a washing machine – and the housing situation improved significantly by the end of the 1970s. A process of aestheticization began, focusing on the sculptural form of objects; Ernesto Rogers coined the slogan 'from the spoon to the city' to indicate that everything now had to be 'designed'.

ITALIAN SOCIETY DURING THE REPUBLIC

In 1945, in the first issue of *Il Politecnico*, the writer Elio Vittorini reflected on the consequences of Fascist crimes:

> For some time it will be difficult to say if anyone has lost or won in this war. But it is certain that a lot has been lost. The dead, if we count them, are more children than soldiers: the ruins are of cities that had enjoyed 25 centuries of life.

At the same time, he was reflecting on the responsibility of an entire culture in allowing those crimes to happen and, correspondingly, on the responsibility of that culture to now shape a democratic society. In the post-war years, anti-Fascist authors who had been forced into silence for years under Fascism produced a wealth of literary works; many of these books had been written during the dictatorship but had gone unpublished. In 1945, Carlo Levi published *Christ Stopped at Eboli*, an account based on his experience of the *confino* that brought to public attention the problems of southern Italy. While in exile, Ignazio Silone described a desperate peasant universe in Abruzzo under Fascism in the novel *Fontamara*, first published in Italy in 1945. From 1948, Gramsci's *Prison Notebooks* began to be issued, including his revealing reflections on Italian society since the Risorgimento. It was as if novelists and poets had suddenly returned to life after a long hibernation, as Carlo Levi wrote in 1950, as if everyone could be a politician:

> Everyone still seemed to be living in the exciting atmosphere of the Resistance, and no one thought that there was any difference between politicians and ordinary people; everyone acted naturally, in an independent world where there were no barriers in the factories, at work or in the local government of the Liberation Committee. Just like any miracle, that active and creative freedom lasted very briefly, but at the time it was real, you could touch it with your hand and you could see it written on people's faces. (Levi, 2007, p. 45)

Following a popular referendum in 1946, Italy became a republic. For the first time, the country had real universal suffrage with the introduction of female voting. The Italian Constitution of 1948 combined the aspirations and values of the anti-Fascist parties. Their unity, however, was soon disrupted by the Cold War; because Italy was in the Western sphere of influence, Western leaders wanted to prevent a revived Italian

---

Box 8.4   The Republican Constitution

Based on anti-Fascism and created by the leaders of the parties that had taken part in the Resistance, it was the most democratic constitution in the Western world. It reflected the awkward compromise between the left and the Catholics visible in the many emphases on 'work', 'progress', 'people' and 'equality', as well as the persistence of the agreement between the formerly Fascist state and the Church. Decentralization, the rejection of militarism and the protection of minorities all marked a will to reverse Fascist trends and policies:

Article 1:
   Italy is a democratic republic based on labour.

Article 3:
   (1) All citizens have equal social status and are equal before the law, without regard to their sex, race, language, religion, political opinions, and personal or social condition.
   (2) It is the duty of the republic to remove all economic and social obstacles that, by limiting the freedom and equality of citizens, prevent full individual development and the participation of all workers in the political, economic, and social organization of the country.

                                                                        ⫸

Communism from coming to power. The United States and the Vatican strongly backed the Christian Democrat Party, who consequently won the first national elections, held in 1948.

Norman Lewis, an English officer stationed in Italy, observed as early as 1944 that Christian Democracy was the most likely party to run Italy after the war: not tainted by compromise with Fascism (or by too much compromise with anti-Fascism, as its contribution to the armed resistance had been minimal), backed by the Church, industrialists and landowners, and enjoying an existing network of religious organizations around the country (particularly in rural areas), run by an army of nuns and priests. The time when the Catholic Church had been an enemy of the state had now passed.

The elections of 1948 represented a fight not just between political parties, but between two ideas of civilization. Christian Democrat elec-

---

Box 8.4 (*continued*)
⫸

Article 5:

The republic, one and indivisible, recognizes and promotes local autonomy; it fully applies the administrative decentralization of state services and adopts principles and methods of legislation meeting the requirements of autonomy and decentralization.

Article 6:

The republic protects linguistic minorities by special laws.

Article 7:

(1) State and Catholic Church are, each within their own reign, independent and sovereign.

(2) Their relationship is regulated by the Lateran Pacts. Amendments to these pacts which are accepted by both parties do not require the procedure of constitutional amendments.

Article 11:

Italy repudiates war as an instrument offensive to the liberty of the peoples and as a means for settling international disputes; it agrees to limitations of sovereignty where they are necessary to allow for a legal system of peace and justice between nations, provided the principle of reciprocity is guaranteed; it promotes and encourages international organizations furthering such ends.

---

tion posters showed monsters destroying families with the Kremlin in the background, or the image of a citizen in the polling station with the words: 'God can see you, Stalin can't.' In a famous film from 1952 (*Don Camillo*, from a successful novel by Giovanni Guareschi, *The Little World of Don Camillo*) a priest from a Po Valley village tries to refuse to baptize the baby of the Communist mayor, Peppone, by telling his wife that he could not be sure of the child's legitimacy, since Communists believed in free love. The message was that Communists opposed the family (the most important value in Italian life) but also that even Communists, though in theory irreligious, wanted to baptize their children.

While the Church had been deeply rooted for centuries in the countryside, peasant revolts in the late 1940s and early 1950s demonstrated a Communist militancy that stemmed from experiences under Liberal Italy (like those of the Sicilian *fasci* and the land struggles in the Po Valley during and after the Great War), destroyed by agrarian Fascism but reborn after the Liberation. The peasants of the Po Valley and Apulia, Sicily, Calabria and central Italy became the protagonists in a bitter struggle against landowners to implement promised land reform. As had been the case in the socialist struggles of Liberal Italy, Communism was fused with utopian, religious and mystical elements of peasant culture. In 1950, of the two million hectares the government had promised to co-operatives, only 250,000 had been assigned; between 1945 and 1952, the police killed 84 peasants during demonstrations (mainly in the south, with numerous deaths in Calabria, Apulia and Basilicata); in Sicily, it was often the Mafia that opened fire, as in the 1947 massacre at Portella della Ginestra carried out by the bandit Salvatore Giuliano. The state struggle against Communism also extended to the northern factories, where workers could easily be dismissed for political reasons, and the police shot at workers during trade union demonstrations, particularly between 1947 and 1953, under Christian Democrat interior minister Mario Scelba. At the same time, in the Cold War context and in a country with the largest Communist Party in the Western world, the Italian and American secret services organized an illegal, anti-Communist, clandestine network called 'Stay Behind' codenamed *Gladio*, which was intended to prevent a Communist take-over in Italy, and only came to light in the 1990s. This situation, together with coalitions (of the Christian Democracy, the Liberal Party and, from 1963, the Socialist Party) which helped to maintain a permanent DC (*Democrazia Cristiana*) majority, has been called a 'blocked system' or 'imperfect bi-polarism' because it made it practically impossible for the PCI to enter government. In 1960, an attempt by Christian Democracy to govern in alliance with the reborn Fascist party (the Italian Social Movement – MSI, founded in 1946), as well as the decision to grant permission to the MSI to hold its national congress in Genoa (where the resistance had been particularly strong), revealed that the memory of the civil war was still very much alive. A mass demonstration was organized in Genoa against the MSI and the then Christian Democrat prime minister, Fernando Tambroni, which attracted 100,000 protesters. Despite facing police violence, the movement spread to other cities, from Piedmont to Sicily, forcing the MSI to abandon its meeting and Tambroni to resign. What struck contemporary observers was the presence of many young people protesting alongside partisans, a protest not only against the prospect of a return of Fascism but also against the power and corruption of politicians, the violence of the police and industrialists, and the fact that, in order to find work, recommendations of priests were more relevant than a worker's skill. As Carlo Levi wrote in 1960, it was protest for a freedom to be gained and not just for a freedom to be defended.

The protests of the 1960s reached their climax in 1968–9. In 1967, a democratic priest, Don Lorenzo Milani, wrote *A Letter to a Teacher*, which challenged the class character of Italian schools and became a standard text for a generation of students in schools and universities; Italian students protested against authority, against the dominant culture, and against the individualistic values of the economic boom. In 1969, the revolt moved to the factories, with mass strikes at Fiat and all over Italy during the so-called 'hot autumn'. These protests were also a consequence of the growth in the working class, a proletariat that was mainly rural and southern in origin, semi-skilled and concentrated in large factories. Workers' wages were among the lowest in Europe, and outside the factory their basic needs – adequate transport, medical care, schooling for children and housing – were not being met. The protest thus expanded to embrace the rest of society, generating new forms of collective action that brought families together in a network of solidarity. In the families of political militants, women began to break with their roles as housewives, roles that had intensified in the post-war years of economic boom, with a diminished need for women to work outside the home, children staying at school for longer, and with constant Christian Democrat propaganda and TV advertising which insisted that a woman's duty was to stay at home. Women organized protests outside factories and took part in the occupation of housing. By taking this path, the movement of protest moved first from universities and schools to factories, and then into wider society and the individual family. Democratic currents within the Catholic Church, following a thread that had been present for centuries, proposed again that the Church should be on the side of the poor and not on the side of the powerful. To the left of the Communist Party, which had never been committed to revolution, radical anti-capitalist groups emerged with names such as *Lotta Continua* ('The Struggle Continues'), *Potere operaio* ('Workers' power') and, in the 1970s, *Autonomia Operaia* ('Workers' autonomy'). A famous protest song of the time, alarming to both industrialists and politicians, included the refrain: 'What do we want? We want everything/continuous fight in the factory and outside it/Communism shall triumph'.

A response came, in different phases between 1969 to 1980, through a series of atrocities later known as 'the strategy of tension'. In

---

Box 8.5   Two intellectuals reflect on the strategy of tension

The playwright Dario Fo (winner of the Nobel prize for literature in 1997) sided with the left-wing movement and dedicated a play to Pinelli: *The Accidental Death of an Anarchist*, while the poet, writer and film director Pier Paolo Pasolini wrote a reflection on the responsibility of intellectuals in unmasking the Christian Democracy and neo-Fascist violence in Italy:

> I know. I know the names of those responsible for what is called a 'golpe' [coup] (which is in fact a series of golpes instituted as a system to protect power). I know the names of those responsible for the slaughter in Milan on 12 December 1969. I know the names of those responsible for the slaughter in Brescia in 1974. I know the names of those who, in between going to mass, have ensured political protection for old generals, for young neo-Fascists ... I know these names and I know all the facts (attempted violence against institutions and murders) of which they are guilty. I know. But I have no evidence. I do not even have clues. I know them because I am an intellectual, a writer, one who seeks to follow all current events, to know everything that is published, to imagine all the facts that are not known or that are kept silent.

> (Pasolini, 'What is this golpe?', *Il Corriere della Sera*,
> 14 November 1974)

December 1969, with factories occupied and high levels of social conflict all over Italy, a bomb exploded in Piazza Fontana in Milan, killing sixteen people. Giuseppe Pinelli, an anarchist interrogated about the event in a police station, died by falling from a window in the building. An inquiry carried out by journalists and left-wing militants, and published a few months later, documented the links between the murders, the secret services and the Italian state. The 'long 1968' continued in Italy for a decade, shrouded in a climate of violence. Neo-Fascists committed further atrocities, detonating a bomb in Piazza Loggia in Brescia in 1974 which killed eight people, and another at Bologna railway station in 1980 in which eighty-five people were killed; then, from the mid-1970s, red terrorism (based on the Red Brigades, first created in 1970) began to kidnap and kill targeted politicians.

In the mid-1970s, the Communist Party decided for the first time to support the Christian Democrats in a defence of Italian democracy from terrorism, both black and red, a collaboration known as the 'historic compromise'. In 1978, the Red Brigades kidnapped the Christian Democrat leader responsible for the dialogue with the Communist Party, Aldo Moro. Following the refusal of his party and the Vatican to deal with the terrorists, Moro was assassinated less than two months later. In the same year, the famous Sicilian writer Leonardo Sciascia wrote an enquiry based on a careful study of the letters Moro sent from his 'people's prison'. Sciascia claimed that the Christian Democracy had decided to leave Moro to his destiny on purpose, worried by his strategy of including the Communist Party in the government (his absence from parliament was 'more productive' than his silence). Sciascia commented sarcastically on the Christian Democrat line of the 'strong state':

> It is as if a dying man had risen from his bed . . . The Italian state has revived. The Italian state is alive and strong, safe and sound. For a century, for over a century it has consorted with the Sicilian Mafia, the Neapolitan Camorra, the Sardinian bandits. For three decades it has exploited corruption and incompetence, wasted public funds in streams and rivulets of unpunished embezzlement and fraud . . . But now, confronted with Moro's sequestration by the Red Brigades, the Italian State rises up strong and impressive.
>
> (Sciascia, 2004, p. 49)

In confronting the Moro family's request that a deal should be made for his life, the DC found valuable assistance in the Vatican. Only a few hours before the Red Brigades' ultimatum, Pope Paul VI wrote a public letter to the terrorists defining Moro as a 'dignified and honest man' and pleading in the name of Christ: 'I am begging you, I am kneeling in front of you, please set Aldo Moro free.' He added, however, the words: 'simply and unconditionally'.

Between the late 1970s and the early 1980s, organized crime offensive by the Mafia and Camorra started to increase and expand geographically. In 1977, the cover of the German magazine *Der Spiegel* expressed Italy's image abroad: a dish of spaghetti topped with a P38 gun instead of Parmesan cheese.

This image was overcome in the 1980s as Italy emerged from the economic and social crisis. The new decade was symbolized by victory in the football World Cup in 1982, and by a new consumer age that was considerably more hedonistic than during the 1960s economic miracle. This time, the cover of *Time* magazine showed a new image of Italy: the designer Giorgio Armani in triumphant mood, promoting the idea that 'all Italians are stylish'. Nevertheless, the success of Italian fashion, football and food all over the world could not prevent the development of a new political crisis, which led to the collapse of the Italian political system at the beginning of the new decade – the end of the 'First Republic'. The 1980s were characterized by the re-launch of the Mafia offensive; organized crime had until then taken advantage of links with a section of the political class (principally the Christian Democrats). In 1982, the Communist MP Pio La Torre, author of the first attempt to propose legal measures against the Mafia, was killed and many other assassinations followed – including anti-Mafia prefects such as Carlo Alberto Dalla Chiesa and the magistrates who organized a large-scale trial against the Mafia in 1986–7 in which some important crime bosses were given life sentences. After the results of this trial were confirmed in the early 1990s, the *mafiosi* avenged themselves on ex-allies who had been unable to save them, such as the Christian Democrat Salvo Lima, and on the magistrates who had organized the trial, Giovanni Falcone and Paolo Borsellino, murdered in 1992. Many Christian Democrats, including some of the most powerful politicians in the Italian Republic, such as Antonio Gava and Giulio Andreotti, began to appear in public trials accused of having links with the Mafia.

However, the links between the government and the Mafia only came to light in the 1990s. The optimism of the 1980s had been embodied in the figure of the Socialist Party leader, Bettino Craxi. The party, which had been overtaken on the left by the Communists since the first republican elections, had been allied to the DC for almost two decades and had broken every link with its past. Not only was the party no longer on the side of the workers, but it also became involved in a corrupt system characterized by the mutual and illegal exchange of favours between parties in the government and the centres of industrial and financial power. Among the latter, the entrepreneur Silvio Berlusconi, who had built up a private television empire, won the passage of a law sanctioning his right to broadcast his channels nationally – largely a result of Craxi's efforts on his behalf. After a massive trial in the early 1990s that was dubbed 'Tangentopoli' (Kick-back City), in which a collection of magistrates demonstrated the corruption of the existing governing class, Berlusconi could present himself as the founder of a new political party that was fit to govern a new Italy – *Forza Italia*. From the ashes of the DC and with the fall of the Berlin Wall, new parties appeared: National Alliance – the renamed MSI – declared that it had left its Fascist past

---

Box 8.6   The anti-Mafia reaction in Palermo in the early 1990s

We commit ourselves to educate our children to respect others, with a sense of duty and justice. We commit ourselves not to get used to the current dishonesty, and not to comply with it passively simply because 'everybody does'. We commit ourselves not to ask as a favour what is owed to us as a right. We commit ourselves not to sell our vote at any price ... We commit ourselves to resist, by legal means, the impositions of the Mafia. We commit ourselves not to forget Giovanni Falcone and all those who died fighting the Mafia, and to remember them as if they were relatives who gave their lives for us.

('The Commitment', read at a wake in a church in Palermo
following a 40,000-strong demonstration over Falcone's death,
13 June 1992)

---

behind, while the Left Democrats (part of the former PCI) abandoned their Communist identity, to the regret of many militants, who adhered instead to a reformed left-wing organization, *Rifondazione Comunista*. The reaction against politics initially seemed to favour an entirely new party, the Northern League, which pointed to Rome and to southern Italy as the sources of corruption, and proposed, after more than a century of unification, the re-division of Italy. These political changes together marked the beginning of a 'Second Republic'.

A CONSUMER SOCIETY

The definition of 'consumer society' is applied specifically to the significant change in consumer patterns in society during the post-Second World War period – a definition of a particular variant of capitalism characterized by the primacy of consumerism. In Italy, consumer culture developed with the economic boom, fusing together aspirations that originated in other countries, in particular the United States, with local (national and regional) elements that helped to generate new forms of collective identity. Remo Bodei has observed that once the period of Fascist autarchy had ended and their horizons widened, Italian citizens, who did not easily identify with the state, began to look 'outside' for a higher standard of living – particularly to the American 'liberator'. As Franzina has remarked, America again became *la Merica* of many years earlier, that is to say, the country of a better future'; many Italians began to dream of a land of pleasures and comfort, and for them the United States represented a 'reproducible prosperity'.

However, the period called the 'consumer age' only began to take shape from the end of the 1950s, in part because Italians were still poor, and because spending and consuming were not part of a lifestyle culturally acceptable to the Church and the left. Italian cinema illustrates this slow transition: a kind of 'lexicon of the country's journey along the road to reconstruction', neo-realist cinema did not embrace the emergence of the Hollywood values of social climbing or enrichment condemned by the Church and the communists. This gap was reflected in notions of feminine beauty: compared to the female stars from Hollywood, the actress Anna Magnani (who starred one of the first neo-realist films, Roberto Rossellini's *Rome Open City*, in 1945) represented a woman of the people, a real woman in her thirties – not typically beautiful, but passionate, instinctive and strong. But by the late 1950s there emerged new models of Italian beauty and sexuality, personified by Gina Lollobrigida (whose hairstyle was copied by women all over Italy) and Sophia Loren. The new generation of glamorous female stars were ignored in the Catholic press because they were considered to be too sexually provocative.

In the 1960s, the fall in unemployment and wage rises prompted a division of daily life between work and leisure time – the latter intended to be time for consumption. Under Fascism, leisure time had been organized by the regime; after-work societies were forced on workers, although they also provided the opportunity for socializing in the evenings. After the war, the left and the Catholics set up their own social organizations, resulting in the birth of the ARCI (Italian Cultural Recreational Association), a democratic organization for leisure time (organizing film shows, exhibitions and excursions); the ANPI (National Association of Italian Partisans) organized for former partisans; and the UDI (Italian Women's Union) for women. Communist festivals called *Festa dell'Unità* (from the title of the newspaper *Unità,* founded by Gramsci in 1924) became popular, open-air social occasions held every summer in Italian cities, towns and villages. The ACLI (Christian Association of Italian Workers) represented the Catholic version of the ARCI and was supported by a dense network of parish organizations that had existed in Italy for centuries. ARCI and ACLI still exist, though they entered a period of crisis from the 1970s with the emergence of a new left-wing culture based on direct action that sought to distance itself from political parties, a decline which continued in the 1980s and 1990s, first with the challenge of consumerism that encouraged new forms of socialization, then with the 'fall of ideologies' that followed the end of the Cold War.

One novel transformation in the 1960s was holiday travel. Holidays were no longer a luxury enjoyed by the bourgeoisie as they had been when the Touring Club was first founded in the nineteenth century, but were now within the reach of workers and their families. Italians began to explore their own country in their millions: between 1959 and 1965 the number of Italians who took a holiday doubled, and doubled again in the following decade, reaching 20 million in 1975. Internal migration began to break down regional barriers: many Italians from southern regions and rural areas moved to the northern industrial cities in the 1960s. Between 1958 and 1963, one million people moved from the south to central and northern Italy. Among the principal destinations were the provinces of Milan, Turin and Rome, followed by Genoa, Florence and Bologna. In the area surrounding Milan, whole new towns were developed, whose inhabitants commuted to Milan every day, while the city centre was redesigned with elegant skyscrapers, such as the Pirelli and the Velasca towers. The journalist Giorgio Bocca described this development in a 1963 article in *Il Giorno* as the 'factory of the new Italians':

> The Milanese industrial belt, which is made up of many names: Cinisello – Rho – Cologno – Sesto, etc., is not a city but a malignant growth of a city; dwellings which multiply like cells gone mad, underpasses, rail tracks, block of flats, closed streets, a little bit of countryside which is neither green nor yellow, more flats, smoke, smell. How is it possible that people who only a few days ago left the blue sea of Sicily or the delightful smell of Calabrian mountains live here? . . . The village-cities of the belt (Sesto has more than 80,000 inhabitants) are as hostile an environment to immigrants . . . as America was to the men who conquered it . . . But those who think that a new Italian can be born here, hopeful and proud of his adventure like the American, are probably wrong.

> (Bocca, 'The factory of the new Italians', *Il Giorno*, 3–8 September 1963)

Emigration and tourism both had an impact on Italian architecture. As more social housing developed around industrial areas, motorways and hotels appeared all over Italy because of tourism; a new architecture transformed coastal areas, while fishing villages were transformed into tourist resorts, with the addition of reproduced city entertainment in the shape of cinemas, theatres and cafés. In the mountains, tourists joined forces with traditional alpinists, and skiing villages began to appear; the growing popularity of winter holidays also had an impact on the landscape as ski slopes came to replace woods. Mass seaside holidays were typical of a consumer culture composed by mundane pastimes, having fun, exposing increasingly more of the body, and the importance of appearing 'fashionable'. Unlike the liberal age, the purpose of holidays was not merely cultural, but also to have good time. Men and women began to spend time together and gender role distinctions began to fade.

Holidays were linked to the increase in individual mobility. The *Autostrada del Sole* (the 'motorway of the sun' connecting northern and southern Italy) was opened in 1960. Fiat produced the Seicento car in 1954, and the cheaper and internationally famous smaller Cinquecento in 1957. Significant sections of the lower classes gained access to private motor transport: between 1950 and 1964, the number of private vehicles on the roads increased from 342,000 to 4,670,000. Weekend trips by Vespa scooter or Cinquecento diminished regionalism, as these 'miracle vehicles' took Italians all round the peninsula. The scooter company Piaggio created the Vespa in 1946 (it appeared on the roads by 1948); it was not too expensive, had a modern aerodynamic design and low maintenance costs. Young people who left the cities on Sundays on Vespas were free from the influence of their parents, and this development also changed the relationships between the sexes at a time when parental control over young people's sexual relations was very strict, and when, at the Catholic *oratorio* (parish club), girls and boys were kept as separate as possible during recreational activities. A number of films contributed to creating the Vespa myth, such as *Roman Holiday* (1953), in which Gregory Peck takes Audrey Hepburn around Rome on a Vespa; and *Pane amore e fantasia* (1953) and *Poveri ma belli* (1956), portraying an image of Italians who were 'poor, but handsome'. The birth of Vespa clubs around the world marked the product's success in the Western world; in Italy, such clubs organized collective trips to the countryside, showing that tradition continued to coexist with modernity; in this sense, the policy of the Vespa clubs was in harmony with that of the Touring Club – supporting internal tourism yet seeking to discipline the behaviour of those who experienced it.

Television arrived in Italy in 1954, building on the success of radio that had been used in the 1930s by Mussolini to underpin the totalitarian system. After 1946, radio did not simply have a duty to inform and became mainly a provider of light music, songs and variety shows. Public taste was for easy-listening songs – which remained in the memory like 'summer torments' – with titles such as *Abbronzatissima* ('Very tanned') or *Una rotonda sul mar* ('A pavilion by the sea'). The TV advertising programme *Carosello* showcased stylish kitchens and introduced modish furniture, as well as new products, to the country. Advertisements were not breaks in the middle of programmes, but were grouped together into short, discrete programmes in the evenings, entertaining the audience with little stories and comic sketches to make the brand names and images of their products memorable. In November 1954, Mike Buongiorno began *Lascia o raddoppia* ('Double or quit?'), the first television quiz show, which filled bars and emptied cinemas. Buongiorno's showgirls became as famous as actresses. Quiz shows were successful because they incorporated elements of theatre, soap, film and music, and the protagonists were ordinary people, making it easy for others to identify with them. Mike Buongiorno was an Italian-American who appeared so ordinary and conformist that he gave weight to the notion that anyone could reach such heights. Historians have regarded the introduction of television as being as important as Dante's *Divine Comedy* or the expedition of the Thousand, because it united Italy linguistically and unified dialects more effectively than decades of education had done.

The impact of consumption, with the migration of workers from rural areas to the north, disrupted traditional habits that had lasted for centuries. For example, as Luisa Passerini has explained, the fashion for female underwear undermined the concepts of the trousseau and the dowry, and the arrival of electrical appliances in Italian kitchens also contributed to female emancipation, freeing women from laborious housework. In the 1960s an ideology of female emancipation became associated with consumption; though it also created new forms of power, based on processes of emulation and identification; gradually, forms of opposition began to emerge to what came to be defined, negatively, as 'consumerism'. This criticism came predominantly from the left, though also from part of Catholic culture, and gave life to forms of radical protest in the 1960s–1970s. An anxious Pier Paolo Pasolini wrote in 1973 that not even Fascism had been able to do what the civilization of consumerism had been able to achieve: hedonistic ideology had nullified the differences between right and left; the television culture was standardizing behaviour and expectations, and Italians' quality of life had become the entire expression of their identity.

The transition in Italy from the attraction of consumerism to its criticism was represented in music as well as in cinema. After the Liberation, new songs encouraged Italians to forget the past, erasing civil war memories in order to make Italians dream of a happier life – in part for political reasons. The desire to forget was encapsulated in the annual Sanremo festival of Italian song that was shown every year on television. This was not (and has never been, up to the present day) 'good music'; yet despite its limited artistic value, the festival still rates highly in the sentimental history of Italian society. In 1958, Domenico Modugno triumphed at the festival with the song *Volare*, coinciding with the arrival of '45s' – 45 rpm records – and the juke box, which some historians have taken as the symbolic start of the economic miracle:

> I think that a dream like that will never return/I painted my hands and my face with blue/Then suddenly, I was taken by the wind/And I began to fly in the endless sky.//Flying oh, oh/Singing oh, oh/In the blue sky, painted in blue/so glad to be up there//And I was flying and flying, happily higher than the sun/and more/While the world was slowly disappearing so far away/A sweet music was singing only for me//Flying oh, oh . . .

Other television programmes, such as *Canzonissima*, focused entirely on one particular form of music, the *canzonette* (light songs) and showcased the most acclaimed singers.

However, from the mid-1960s, some Italian songs became overtly political, more closely connected with the concerns that neo-realist cinema had expressed. In 1960, both *La Dolce Vita* and Luchino Visconti's *Rocco and His Brothers* were released, the first set in Rome, the second in Milan, both reflecting critically on the morality of economic prosperity, illustrating the excitement and freedom provided by the boom, but also the idea that something more valuable had been lost. *Cantautori* (singer-songwriters) such as Fabrizio De André wrote poetic songs that sided with the outcasts of society and against the values of the dominant class. De André was influenced by his study of centuries of Italian poetry, and by Genoese and Sardinian dialect and traditional music, and he identified with 1968 leftism; De André's songs revived the first examples of poetry in the Italian language, like the thirteenth-century Tuscan poet, Cecco Angiolieri, who raged against Popes and emperors in the beautiful sonnet *S'i fosse foco* ('If I were fire'). De André sympathized with the protest against bourgeois values in, for example, the *Canzone del Maggio* ('Song of May', 1973), with its menacing opening lines:

> Even if the month of May/hardly affected you at all,/Even if the fear of confronting reality,/made you turn away,/Even if your car/Was not torched,/Even if you absolved yourselves,/It concerns all of you.

The rejection of a civilization based on work and consumption was expressed in a youth culture. In music (Bob Dylan) and contemporary art (Pop Art) this protest was influenced by the United States – by the same country that had exported the model that was now under attack. As Robert Lumley has observed, American involvement in Vietnam provoked instances of anti-Americanism, creating bonds between Europeans and Americans who opposed both war and consumerism. Reactions among Italians were in fact more complex than simple acceptance or rejection of the American model. For example, the earliest kinds of advertising showed how traditional elements were used to modify the appeal of American products and to reinterpret their message in ways which applied to an enduring local culture. In the 1950s, even while magazines and newspapers were full of gossip about Hollywood celebrities, advertising continued to reflect reality and the traditions of the Italian family, promoting more sober forms of consumption and attempting to reconcile consumerism with Catholicism, and with habits and values that remained very different from those on the other side of the Atlantic.

The protests of 1968 left their mark on many areas of Italian society – in attitudes towards authority, in relationships between the sexes, and in governmental reforms granted under pressure from the movement. The legacy of the feminist movement led to the passage of the laws on divorce (1970, confirmed with a referendum in 1974) and on abortion (1978, confirmed with a referendum in 1981) – the latter putting an end to the dangerous recourse of vulnerable women to illegal abortions. However, while it took almost ten years for the Italian state to defeat the radical movements, the protesters did not overturn the core values of capitalism and consumerism. With the defeat of the movements, there was a return to nuclear family consumer values in the 1980s.

Italians experienced a 'second economic miracle', even more indulgent than the first, after the economic crisis in the 1980s. A new generation emerged in America: the *yuppies*, devoted to consumption as a lifestyle. These people bought and flaunted branded objects and fashionable clothes, creating a mass culture that also travelled to Italy – where rich yuppies were christened the *paninari* ('burger eaters'). The *paninari* met in new, American-style 'fast-food' bars, adopted right-wing values, and boasted in their branded clothes about being rich adolescents with a right to consume.

The history of Italian food followed the path of Italian consumption more generally, a compromise between the imposition of an American model and the resistance of a centuries-long tradition. After 1945, the Italian food industry, which had until then been limited by autarchy and war, began to invent new products and to become competitive on the world market – Motta and Algida ice creams, and Pavesi and Motta crackers in the 1950s; and Perugina and Ferrero sweets and chocolate in first half of the 1960s. By the end of the 1960s, the Italian food industry was able to compete with the rest of Europe. One example is the invention of espresso machines, which were exported and imitated abroad from the 1950s; their modern design being one of the symbols of Italy's economic miracle, alongside Vespas and Fiat cars.

Food modernization and mass consumption have progressively 'Westernized' Italy, but this process is not by any means complete. Research in this field has demonstrated that Italian food has not been significantly transformed over the last two centuries, and that Italians, by resisting standardization and Americanization more than other European countries, still use the ingredients of the past in their cuisine – they simply eat more than before. The TV advertising programme *Carosello* (broadcast every evening between 1957 and 1976) represented a compromise between Catholic values and the values of consumerism, and this synthesis persisted during the 1970s with resistance to the Americanization of food and consumer habits. One example is the publicity and success of *Mulino Bianco* ('white mill') biscuits. In those years of engaged, radical and, at times, violent politics, Italian society was deeply divided between the dominant anti-consumerist forces of Communists and Catholics. *Mulino Bianco* had to take into account the anti-industrial prejudice of the Italian public, and its publicity and packaging focused on a return to nature and the traditional values of the countryside, reflecting the suspicion that Italian housewives had of mass-produced food. This mistrust persisted into the hedonistic 1980s, when prejudice against industrial consumerism seemed to wane: the continuation of such advertisements played on the hope that people wanted breaks from city life (at least at the weekends) and confirmed a belief in the value of natural ingredients. While shopping centres and big supermarkets have proliferated everywhere in Italy, their number is still the lowest of any country in Europe. McDonalds has been more contested in Italy than anywhere else, and the American coffee chain Starbucks, which has opened almost everywhere in the world and in every major European country, has no branches in Italy. The worldwide organization *Slow Food* which, like the Touring Club, promotes the knowledge of local culture and traditional products, has its headquarters in Piedmont. For these reasons, the Italian path to the modern consumer age has been described as an alternative one to the world of conventional mass consumption.

Perhaps the most revealing example of the dichotomy between Italian modernity and tradition is that of espresso coffee, created for the first time with the invention of a 'cream coffee' machine by the Milanese firm Gaggia in 1948. Since then, Italian firms and coffee roasters have insisted on the modern design of the machines, and on the 'cult' aspect of drinking espresso, a symbol of urban life. Yet in the 1980s, the Turin-based firm Lavazza, which is, in terms of both distribution and marketing, the most popular of coffee roasters among Italians, still focused its advertising on tracing a link between the new, modern, espresso culture and the old history of Italy's famous cafeterias, where the intellectual and political elite met from the eighteenth century onwards. Goldoni's *La bottega del caffè* (see Chapter 5) and traditional Venetian culture were used to describe Lavazza's view of Italian cafés:

> Casanova, *doges* and ladies, soft armchairs and extravagant masks of an eternal carnival. It is the Venice of the eighteenth century that meets at Florian café. And after that, Habsburg magnificence and Risorgimento yearnings, Dannunzian frenzy and the progeny of poets, painters and scholars. From three centuries the history of Venice and of Italy meet at Florian; the first premises in Italy to serve a precious cup of steaming coffee. Lavazza, today, intends to defend this tradition.
>
> ('Florian: da 300 anni Venezia si specchia in un caffè', *Bargiornale*, no. 3, March 1987)

The sense of an enduring culture, continuous across the centuries, is evident in manifestations of social life as well. In the summer of 2007, posters for the *Festa dell'Unità* in northern Italian cities organized by the political centre-left showed a medieval painting of a Commune, and bore the slogan: 'the good government of the cities'.

SUGGESTED FURTHER READING

Two very useful syntheses are P. McCarthy (ed.), *Italy since 1945* (Oxford: Oxford University Press, 2000) and J. Foot, *Modern Italy* (Basingstoke: Palgrave, 2003). Among the many works on Fascist Italy, J. Pollard, *The Fascist Experience in Italy* (London: Routledge, 1998) is a collection of translated and contextualized primary sources. First published in 1973, A. Lyttelton, *The Seizure of Power: Fascism in Italy, 1919–1929* (London: Routledge, 2004) is still the most authoritative account in English on the origins of Fascism. R. Ben-Ghiat, *Fascist Modernities: Italy, 1922–1945* (Berkeley, Calif.: University of California Press, 2001) is an innovative work on the cultural history of Italy in the inter-war period. Excellent introductions to the post-war period are the two volumes by P. Ginsborg, *A History of Contemporary Italy: Society and Politics, 1943–88* (London: Penguin, 1990) and *Italy and Its Discontents: Family, Civil Society, State, 1980–2001* (London: Allen Lane, 2001). D. Forgacs and R. Lumley (eds), *Italian Cultural Studies* (Oxford: Oxford University Prees, 1996) is a lively introduction to modern Italian culture. R. Gordon, *An Introduction to Twentieth-Century Italian Literature: A Difficult Modernity* (London: Duckworth, 2005) provides an overview of the complex responses of Italian literature to the challenges of the century.

9

. . . .

Conclusion

In a recent address to the students of the Johns Hopkins University in Bologna, Cardinal Biffi argued that it was necessary to return to the values that have unified Italy: 'and they are only two: religion and pasta'. As this book has sought to demonstrate, there are also other elements of continuity that have shaped Italian identity throughout the centuries – art and architecture, a unitary literate culture, and particularism in relationships between cities and countryside, between religion and politics, between family and civil society.

While the urban population and economy have been, until recent times, small in comparison with the rural population and agriculture, Carlo Cattaneo attempted to find a unitary thread in Italian history through the history of its cities. His analysis was prompted by the fact that, from the Middle Ages, Italy experienced a much higher degree of urban development than did any other European country. The landed aristocracy, together with the professional bourgeoisie, controlled power in the cities and took part in commerce; peasants were never far from the cities, and movement of population between the two was constant. Feudal links also united communes and countryside, as representatives of feudal families took part in the government of the communes; the submission of the countryside to the city was often a result of agreements between city governments and feudal lords. The history of Italy is thus a history of the relationship between the rural and urban worlds, between feudal and mercantile power.

Mountains and sea are also the protagonists of Italian history. The Alps have always constituted the most important physical and symbolic frontier for Italians. It was from beyond the Alps that the barbarian invasions first arrived, and, throughout the centuries, it was from beyond the Alps that most of the emperors came who dominated Italy for centuries; with the formation of Italian nationalism, the Alps became a contested frontier between Italy and Austria, symbolizing the enmity between the two countries: the Austrians went back to their side of the Alps in 1848, only to return after having crushed the revolutions and defeated the Italian army; in the fight to obtain Trentino in the First World War, the population of Venetia saw the return of the Austrians after the defeat at Caporetto. In 1848, an anti-Austrian cry resounded all over the peninsula: 'down with the barbarians'; when the Allies bombed Italian cities in the Second World War, in order to persuade Italians to turn against the Fascist regime and to sabotage the Germans, they threw leaflets to civilians which carried the message: 'Italian people! Mussolini has called back the barbarians from the north.' After unification, as part of its programme of 'making Italians', the liberal ruling class focused on the Alps as a symbol of Italianness, and alpine excursions up to the Fascist period were used as a way of strengthening patriotism.

Like the Alps, the Mediterranean constituted a frontier, and one that involved most of the peninsula and its islands. There was never a historical distinction between cities on the sea and those inland; for centuries, inland cities had been linked to the sea by rivers and canals, both natural and artificial. For example, Mantua, a city of the north Italian plain, had ships of its own; Venice sent its ships all the way inland to Lake Garda; Florence was connected to Livorno via the River Arno and the Navicelli Canal; using the River Adige, wood was transported from the Alps to Verona and Venice. Coastal cities lived in symbiosis with inland villages, as did Genoa with the mountain areas of Liguria. Cities confined within their walls did not exist. Invaders also came from the Mediterranean, an area where Italy had major interests throughout the period. The maritime cities – Venice, Genoa, Pisa and Amalfi – controlled a large part of the commercial traffic of the Mediterranean, while Venice dominated most of the Adriatic. Both liberal and Fascist foreign policy later looked back at this maritime tradition to justify Italy's new imperial interest in expanding into North Africa and the Balkans.

While cities continued to be at the centre of economic and cultural growth, the major loser in Italian history was the peasantry. It was certainly not the case that the peasant masses were always the passive object of decisions taken in the cities, nor did their illiteracy mean that they had no culture. The history of the peasantry has been one of ruthless exploitation on the part of landowners, of extreme poverty and of the violent repression of any attempt at revolution; it has also been a history of resistance to conscription, taxation and war. The peasantry's last defeats came in the twentieth century, in the aftermath of the First World

War and the rise of Fascism; and at the end of the 1940s, when Christian Democracy and the Mafia made land reform impossible. The most dramatic social conflict throughout the history of Italy has indeed been between the ruling elite and peasants. Because of this, it sometimes proved possible during moments of political crisis or war for an outside enemy to mobilize the peasantry of a particular Italian state on their behalf against the local ruling class: at the time of the 'Viva Maria' revolts in Tuscany at the end of the eighteenth century, or of the anti-Jacobin massacres in Naples at the time of Napoleon's invasion, or in Austrian-occupied Lombardy, when the Austrian General Radetsky threatened to arm the peasantry against the Milanese liberals.

Another constant element of Italian life across the centuries, involving in particular art, politics and cuisine, has been loyalty to the local city: even cities in the same region (for example, Siena, Pisa and Florence) were political and artistic rivals, and even the formation of region-states (such as Lombardy, the Venetian Republic, Tuscany, the Papal States, and the Kingdom of Naples) in the fifteenth century could not break down the barriers of local loyalty. Nevertheless, a unitary art did result from the constant exchange between cities and the fact that artists travelled regularly across the country. All over Italy, open-air collective life meant paying particular attention to ornamental architecture in squares and on external façades, to urban spaces as monumental units. Art reflected the country's peculiar relationship between city and countryside, with the fashion for villas in rural areas and the taste for ornamental gardens, which were designed to fuse together art and nature: the 'Italian garden' can be found from Piedmont to Sicily. Another specific aspect of Italian art has been the continuous influence exerted between the sacred and profane, and the unanimous rejection of the Protestant hostility to the cult of images.

The period of Baroque art was followed by a revival of classicism (neo-classicism), sustained by the myth of ancient Rome and a renewed interest in archaeology, but which was also present in the rhetorical and triumphal nationalist architecture of liberal Italy and of the Fascist period. After the Second World War, in an attempt to leave the Fascist past behind, architecture and art turned again to the examples of the Renaissance and the Baroque age, creating new 'models' with neo-realist cinema, new forms of design and new buildings that were intended to bear witness to the persistence of a centuries-long tradition.

The development of an Italian language and literature also mediated between the existence of local elements and the evolution of a unitary experience. While the spoken vernacular was, until unification, very varied, an Italian written literary and commercial language emerged as early as the Middle Ages. Following the influences of the Sicilian and the Tuscan schools of the thirteenth century, poetical language was brought closer to the language of the people, first of all by Dante; commercial language was also developed during the communal age, despite the existence of regional variants and dialects. Boccaccio wrote the *Decameron* in a Tuscan Italian full of influences from Bologna, Venice, Milan, Naples and Sicily. Throughout the long period preceding the Risorgimento, from the thirteenth to the eighteenth centuries, the sense of belonging to a literary community continued and was rooted everywhere in Italy in the civilization of city courts. In the nineteenth century, this Italy of the aristocracies was challenged by a new Italy of the bourgeoisie, which in turn claimed the right to lead the people and interpret their interests. Like the first, this was also a literary Italy. The Risorgimento intellectuals never hesitated to root their patriotic ambitions in literary imagery. Foscolo's project was to entrust literature with the duty of re-founding Italy by revisiting Italy's great ancestors (even when they were not, strictly speaking, men of letters): Michelangelo, Machiavelli and Galileo. In the histories of Italian literature from that period, great importance was indeed attributed to philosophers, artists, and scientists and not just to writers. For example, Giordano Bruno and Giovan Battista Vico were ascribed a more central role than poets such as Ariosto or Marino.

Writers in the nineteenth century believed that an old community had ended and a new one was being born. The old community was founded on the conventions of the court, on love poems, on the language of Petrarch. The new one was to give precedence to action over contemplation, ethics over aesthetics, to bring together the world of writing and the world of popular military endeavour: literature and music had to create collective passions that could rouse the people to violent political action in order to unify Italy as a nation. It was the age of the historical novel and of the opera; Risorgimento writers entrusted them both with the responsibility of providing a model for the moral and political redemption of Italy. After unification, the project of creating an Italian community was again entrusted to literature; this was the object, for example, of De Sanctis, in his *History of Italian Literature* (1870–1): to rewrite the history of Italy by setting aside the elements of its past considered shameful in order to rescue moments of glory from the country's literary heritage and to announce an equally glorious future. In

1874, the poet Carducci made a speech entitled *Presso la tomba di Francesco Petrarca* ('At Francesco Petrarch's grave'), arguing that Italy was its literature: 'when Metternich said that Italy was a geographical expression, he had not understood that Italy was a literary expression, a poetical tradition'.

During the period of liberal Italy, the triumphant romanticism of the Risorgimento, underlined by the popularity of opera (the origins of which lay in the tradition of singing and reciting literature, from the first examples of Italian poetry onwards), was replaced by another history, born of disillusionment and regret, of indifference and opportunism, of social climbing and political 'transformism'. This history was narrated in a post-unification literature hostile to the national rhetoric: Verga and Capuana, De Roberto and Svevo wrote novels that had no moments of triumph but spoke instead of an Italy overwhelmed by a sense of tragedy. This was the history of losers, of communities whose traditional livelihoods had been swept away by modernity, or of parvenus unable to win acceptance in the new social context; of opportunists who recycled themselves into the new state only to continue their lives in the old way. The continuity in terms of literature between Risorgimento, Fascism and anti-Fascism consists of this ambivalent bond between literature and national identity. Yet once again, after the experience of wartime resistance, literature was expected to build a new Italy.

Like language and art, Italian food also expressed great regional variety; but a continuous process of exchange from region to region has produced a unitary diet. The use of vegetables rather than meat, of products based on a variety of flours (pasta, gnocchi, polenta, focacce), of wine rather than beer, of olive oil rather than butter (typical also of northern Italy, with the oil-producing areas around Lake Garda and in Liguria), have characterized a cuisine very different from that on the other side of the Alps. Local cuisine distinguished Italians from their invaders. In a Commedia dell'Arte written in 1632, *La Lucilla costante* by Fiorillo, the masked Pulcinella addresses the Spanish rulers with the words: 'Ah, Spaniard, enemy of macaroni!' Gastronomic guides of Italy appeared from the thirteenth century onwards. It was food, more than language, that unified Italy in the nineteenth century; as Piero Camporesi remarked, *Scienza in cucina e l'arte di mangiar bene* ('Science in the kitchen and the art of eating well') by Artusi had more of an impact in making Italians than did Manzoni's *The Betrothed*. Behind the triviality of food, it is possible to find one of the most successful aspects of Italianness. Historian Ruggiero Romano calculated that between the first edition of Artusi's book in 1891 and the 1970 edition, 640,000 copies had been sold – a huge number considering that it is a book typically passed down through the generations from mother to daughter. Its influence has been even wider than this, since it became the inspiration behind a number of other equally successful cookery books, the *talismani* and *cucchiai d'argento* (Ada Boni's *Talismano della felicità* – 'Talisman of happiness', and *Cucchiaio d'argento* – 'Silver spoon', have continued to be re-published from the interwar period onwards).

Another central element of the country's identity is religion, and its peculiar relationship with politics. The early-twentieth-century historian Benedetto Croce pointed out in his *A History of Italy*, that it was a mistake to yield to the temptation to write the history of Italy as the history of separate states, because the Catholic Church had diffused to the whole of Italy the same religious message. Because of its presence on Italian soil, the Church never regarded Italy as it regarded other countries: it constantly interfered in Italian politics and saw itself as the 'Roman' or 'Italian' Church at the same time as it proclaimed its universality. From the last centuries of the first millennium, a unification of religious beliefs was established in the whole of Italy around Christianity and the Roman Church. This process took place over several centuries. From the time of Gregory VII onwards, exploiting the mythical image of imperial Rome, the Church was able to place itself at the head of the entire Western Christian world, first through the Crusades, and, from the thirteenth century, through the expansion of the mendicant orders. From the ninth century onwards, a great majority of Popes and their closest collaborators were indeed Italian, a symbiosis that intensified from the thirteenth century, when the Papacy concluded political alliances with a number of Guelph cities (such as Lucca and Florence), and sought systematically to appoint Italians in the various chapter houses in French or English cathedrals. While canonists of the thirteenth century elaborated the precept *ubi Papa, ibi Roma* ('where the Pope is, there is Rome'), in the Avignon period Italian public opinion never accepted the dissociation between the Papal institution and its residence on the River Tiber. Catherine of Siena expressed the most intimate beliefs of her Italian contemporaries when she passionately argued that the Papacy could not remain absent from the Roman site of the tombs of the apostles St Peter and St Paul, the source of its legitimacy, without grave peril.

In the final period of the Middle Ages, the Church gained substantial benefit from encouraging a cult of the saints, which allowed local communities or special groups to choose their particular saint – who would then, it was believed, intercede on their behalf when they had particular aspirations to fulfil. One of the factors that helped to give the Italian people a sense of unity was the visibility of the sacred, manifested in the honour bestowed on the graves and relics of the saints and martyrs, and on any traces (the footprints, fingerprints of saints, and so on) that confirmed the reality of the spiritual world and the possibility of communication between this world and the afterlife. It is therefore not surprising that the links between Italy and the Byzantine world, still very close in the eighth century, began to fade when the emperors at Constantinople decided to ban the use of icons and relics. From north to south, the whole peninsula unanimously rejected a decision that challenged the popular and sentimental belief in the mediating role of religious images.

Catholic identity penetrated Italy's civil and family ethics profoundly. It succeeded most in the peasant world, and in general among the poor, who found in the evangelical message a promise of redemption and consolation. That elementary need for protection and comfort was at the root of the immense diffusion of Marian devotion, which, as the historian André Vauchez has written, belonged to the people even more than it did to institutions. The Virgin represented the most physical aspect of religion, the one that most closely involved the sphere of emotions and feelings in contrast to the desiccated sphere of theological detail and abstract dogma. However, it would be wrong to think that devotion to the Virgin developed entirely separately from the religious institutions of the time; indeed, it was encouraged by the Church and by political institutions from the Middle Ages onwards. The two social levels, the 'people' and the ruling class, converged in the cult: the image of the Madonna in art was both a genuine artistic choice and a theme regularly commissioned by patrons of the arts. The local feasts to the Virgin brought together both civil religion (the Virgin of a certain town) and the wider Marian cult. This is still evident today, when statues of local Madonnas are carried around some Italian villages, and processions led by the representatives of the Church and of local authorities.

From the 1990s, when churches began to empty across Europe, Pope John Paul II created more saints than his predecessors had done over the previous five centuries; and Pope Benedict XVI appears to be continuing this trend. Since the Fascist period, the crucifix has been present in Italian schools and public buildings, and images of the Madonna (joined by other saints) adorn the walls of private homes and hospitals. Recurrent episodes of crying Madonnas (always checked by the Church authorities to verify their veracity) have been easy to find in Italian newspapers right up to the present day. Popular religiosity also has its seamy side, however. The *bestemmia* – the use of a rich variety of swear words against God, the holy family and saints – is typical of the whole country, though with some local variants, dictated by the existence of different local patron saints.

In the 1960s, the writer Umberto Eco analysed a popular type of literature, which he described as 'thaumaturgic underground'. With titles such as *La voce della Madonna* ('The voice of the Madonna') or *Araldo di Sant'Antonio* ('St Antonio's herald'), these pamphlets circulated all over Italy, asking readers for donations to charitable activities; in exchange, people expected to receive future grace or recompense. Eco calculated that, in Milan, one family in three received a copy by post, and that around one million copies were distributed within Lombardy alone; in southern regions, even more prone to thaumaturgic advertising, the numbers were higher. The historian Sergio Luzzatto has recently demonstrated how the most famous Italian saint of the twentieth century, Padre Pio, became popular after the First World War when stigmata allegedly appeared on his body. From his village in Apulia, in the difficult and violent post-war years, Padre Pio was able to meet the need for miracles and divine signs of the Italian people; the cult expanded all over Italy and is still alive today, symbolizing a country 'suspended between archaism and modernity': 2,714 official prayer groups devoted to Padre Pio existed in Italy in 2005, and in the following year about six million pilgrims visited his village in Apulia, San Giovanni Rotondo (in the same year, a similar number of pilgrims went to Jerusalem). The popularity of Padre Pio grew particularly during Fascism, representing an example of the clerico-Fascist alliance, and reached its climax under Pope John Paul II, who made him a saint in 2002.

Links between religion and politics have always characterized Italian history. As Jeremy Boissevain has remarked, Catholic religion represented a strong ideological basis for a political system based on clientelism. Research by Piero Brunello on nineteenth-century letters of recommendation to Fedele Lampertico (1833–1903), a moderate Catholic politician in Vicenza, demonstrates a use of language that placed powerful politicians on the same level as the saints. The use of nepotism and clientelism in Italian society has long-term roots from at least the time of the *signorie* onwards. Though Italy is considered a 'modern' Western democracy, the use of the recommendation and the exploitation of a corrupt nepotistic system still govern a large part of the job market. When interrogated on the provision of favours (such as jobs and tax exemptions) in exchange for votes, a former Christian Democrat answered, in 1995: 'Please let me explain: this is not clientelism, this is Christian charity.' There is a belief, reiterated by many other politicians, that the system of recommendation has helped many poor people, and has thus addressed the issue of social inequality. As Brunello has explained, this culture originates from the deep-rooted belief in the role of mediator ascribed to saints: it is more effective, rather than to address God directly, to act through patron saints, who are closer to God than the supplicant and therefore more likely to persuade Him; religious patronage and political clientelism continue to sustain each other.

The use of clientelism to achieve personal objectives also suggests a lack of faith in the state typical of all Italian regions. Gramsci described in his *Prison Notebooks* the negative effects of the Risorgimento as a 'passive revolution', in which the ruling elite failed to integrate the popular masses into the new state. As Ginsborg has remarked, the lack of identification between people and state had the effect of accentuating the antagonism of the lower classes and their propensity for self-organization, making them open to class ideologies, both Marxist and anarchist. Revolutionary minorities were at times able to win a wide base of support, as they did at the time of the Sicilian *fasci* (1891–3), or during the red week (1914) or the red biennial (1919–20), and again after the Second World War, during the peasant strikes of 1949–50, or the case of radical politics between 1968 and the late 1970s.

After unification, the repressive nature of the state encouraged Italians to concentrate on the one structure in civil society over which they could exercise any control – the family. Long-term explanations for the lack of faith in the state focus on the experience of centuries of foreign domination and on Catholic teachings about the family. During the Renaissance, the importance of the family was also emphasized by humanists such as Leon Battista Alberti. The journalist Tullio Altan argued in 1985 that 'in the largest part of Italian society, in both the north and south, there prevailed, and there still prevails, the moral viewpoint of the individualistic Albertian family'. According to the historian Giovanni Levi, the roots of the central role of the family are to be found in the long-term history of the country and are intimately linked with the Catholic model of family life. The co-existence of two centres of power in Italy, the state and the Church, meant that the country developed a weak institutional identity, which in turn led to the strengthened role of the family; this model also had a positive effect, as it offered an alternative to the extreme capitalist mentality of the Protestant countries and prevented the emergence of intense class polarization that has characterized, for example, Britain and, even more, the United States.

As Ginsborg's research has demonstrated, attachment to the family coexisted at times with the experience of collective action and radical politics. In 1949–50 the great mobilizations of the peasantry in the south and the state repression that followed sparked further protest and expressions of solidarity centred on the village rather than the family. During that period, a Communist mass culture spread in the countryside with the establishment of *Case del Popolo* (meeting halls) and the festival organized by the newspaper *Unità*. Another attempt to engage in civil society and to challenge the individualism of the family came with the protest of 1968, when Italian students attacked the dominant culture of family values and the individualistic ethic encouraged by the economic 'miracle'. At the same time, the protests of the industrial workforce went beyond the demand for higher wages to address issues outside factory life, such as adequate transport for commuters, medical care, improved schooling and higher standards of housing. All these social issues encouraged forms of collective action that involved the whole family. Women took part in the illegal occupation of dwellings and rejected the Christian Democratic model of woman as solely a mother and wife. More than in the 1940s, the nuclear family itself came under attack.

However, the economic crisis of the 1970s did not interrupt the growth of family prosperity, and while the protest left important legacies it was not able to overcome the core values of capitalism and consumerism; with the defeat of the movement of the left, nuclear family consumer values were reasserted in the 1980s. Stephen Gundle has observed that the optimism of the 1980s, with its focus on the present (on affluence, comfort and consumption), was more appealing than the pressure to build a different future that characterized the ideology of the left. The attractions of Hollywood defeated the myth of Moscow; and the optimism of Craxi, and later of Berlusconi, defeated the values of the left. The fascination with the image of the 'star', which arrived in Italy in the 1920s with Hollywood cinema, became widely diffused in the 1950s when TV advertising and light music, very different from the realist message of Italian home-grown cinema, propagated an ideal of happiness. Berlusconi won the election in 1994 not only because of the support of the Mafia and the Vatican, but also through a successful advertising campaign characterized by images of blue skies, happy and wealthy families, and the slogan 'for a new Italian miracle'.

To say that Italian families feel no attachment to the state does not mean that there has never been a sense of nationalism in Italy. This book has emphasized how different ideas of nationalism existed during the process of unification, and has followed them through to the Fascist period. It is important to examine these differences, in order to understand recent public debate on Italy as a nation. The conservative and monarchic idea of the nation that was passed on by the Liberal elite to Crispi and, through the Great War, to Mussolini, was only one possible option. Intellectuals, political militants and writers proposed different views of the Italian future, often from exile. For example, Giuseppe Mazzini's civil ideal of nationhood was centred on the concepts of unity, independence from foreigners, and republicanism; when the Piedmontese king began the first war of independence against Austria in 1848, Carlo Cattaneo wrote that the Savoy monarchy would be even worse than previous tyrants, and proposed a democratic, republican and federalist model (as Ruggiero Romano has remarked, despite recent manipulation of his thought by the Northern League, he proposed a federalism that unified, not one that divided Italy); some Risorgimento patriots, such as Pisacane, believed that the revolution had to involve the peasant masses, a view that constituted one of the origins of Italian socialism.

Fascism claimed that it was restoring the glories of ancient Rome and renewing the Italian people; it represented an extreme nationalism and militarism. Yet the years of Fascism showed both continuities and ruptures with earlier versions of the nation, and despite the triumph of the Fascist ideal in the first half of the 1920s, rival versions continued to develop abroad thanks to the network of anti-Fascist exiles who returned to Italy during the period of the Resistance. Between the end of the nineteenth century and the mid-twentieth century, Italy was also a nation abroad thanks to mass emigration, and those migrants took with them different aspects of Italian history and identity that reflected the differences at home.

There were thus many different 'Italies' opposed to each other during the process of nation-building, some surviving, some disappearing. Paolo Macry has suggested that historians should focus on the moments of crisis, on the collapse of the states, on the losers as well as on the winners, and on all those who changed sides in the process. In this way it is possible to find the many 'Italies' that lost out in the political and ideological struggle and not only the one that finally triumphed. Franco Benigno has reminded us how, in seventeenth-century Naples at the time of Masaniello (see Chapter 5), women occupied the city centre, and wandered about armed with all kinds of weapons; women also had central roles in the revolutions of the nineteenth century, behind the barricades, or organizing collections for the *garibaldini*, or during the plebiscites for Italian unification (even if they could not vote); and during the First World War they provoked pacifist protests all over Italy. However, Italian feminists in the second half of the nineteenth century had to confront a widespread belief, among the left, that the majority of women were too heavily influenced by the Catholic Church and would be unable or unwilling to vote for progressive causes; women continued to count for very little in Italian politics, and obtained the right to vote only in 1946. In Naples in 1860, at the dawn of unification, many intellectuals, soldiers and politicians who had until then worked for the Bourbons sought to recycle themselves into the new liberal class, negotiating (among themselves too) their move to the side of the 'Piedmontese'. Others took up arms and joined the bandits in a ferocious war against the new state. At that point, the outcome of the conflict was still open, and, if it now seems inevitable that Italy would eventually be unified, it was not inevitable that it would be unified in any particular way; the ideas of the nation that failed to win out did not disappear entirely but continued to exert an influence on cultural and political life or even re-emerged at a later date.

The nation built after unification was characterized by the politics of *transformism*, a phenomenon so deep-rooted in the history of Italy that it cannot be restricted to a particular period. According to the political scientist Giorgio Galli, the bourgeoisie's failure to build a powerful liberal party in the middle years of the nineteenth century nullified any role the parliamentary opposition might play, from Cavour's *connubio* (the alliance between right and left in parliament over particular issues) to the transformism of the 1870s; from Giolitti's alliances in the first decade of the twentieth century to Mussolini's one-party state; and finally to the Christian Democratic 'blocked' system (which created a system of alliances in order to prevent the Communist Party from ever entering government). Transformism meant to transform political parties, eliminating distinctions between right and left by creating alliances on specific programmes or laws; the result was the reduction of political life to a set of politicians who created clienteles, who above all had the satisfaction of their own interests at heart. The pejorative meaning of transformism thus derived from a system that placed private above public interest, creating a gap between public rhetoric and the reality of private motive, and between public argument and private agreement. Giulio Bollati noticed that this finally led to a divorce between politics and culture, a union that had been fundamental to the process of the Risorgimento.

The primacy of politics during the Resistance was a reaction to both liberal transformism and Fascist de-politicization, and the partisans saw the Resistance as a second Risorgimento. In 1943, the partisan Altiero Spinelli wrote: 'we live at a time when politics have so much penetrated human relations to have become a question of life or death for an infinite mass of people'; civilization, for those who contributed to the liberation of Italy and to the drafting of the Constitution of 1948, implied the existence of people who 'intended to maintain a firm scale of values'. The compromise that had been reached at the time of the Risorgimento between the monarchy and Italian democratic forces was finally broken after the armistice of 8 September 1943, when the Italian army collapsed after the shift in alliance that brought Italy over to the side of the Allies, Nazi Germany occupied the country, and the monarchy fled from Rome in order to save itself. The new Risorgimento was going to be republican, to be based on the values and ideas of Italy that had been suppressed at the time of Italian unification.

In its young history, Italy as a nation has taken part in a high number of military conflicts. It also suffered a number of defeats, caused chiefly by a lack of military preparation and the ineptitude of Italian military leaders. One of the consequences of this has been the creation of a stereotype of the Italian who 'cannot fight'. According to Girolamo Arnaldi, the origins of this can be found as early as the Middle Ages; at the time of the wars between Italian region-states and the German emperors (when Italian states claimed they were fighting a war 'for Italy'), Italians began to acquire the reputation for being poor soldiers. Arnaldi finds one of the reasons for this in the lack of a militaristic culture in Italian society because of the limited success of poetic accounts of aristocratic knights (which were very popular in other European countries), for whom the most honourable feelings were courage in war and loyalty. Instead of this feudal chivalric conception of life, Italy's literature produced the novella, whose heroes were merchants and artisans, not warriors and knights; the best example was Boccaccio's *Decameron*. According to Machiavelli, the use of mercenaries, who had no loyalty to a particular state, was a major cause of Italy's military weakness. Historians have explained how united Italy took part, often for reasons of nationalistic prestige, in unnecessary conflicts, badly prepared and ineptly led. The result has often been to blame a largely peasant army for alleged cowardice, or to deplore the widespread presence of pacifism in Italian society. The presence of the Catholic Church, disloyal to the state but rooted among the peasant masses, was one of the reasons for Italian pacifism; another was the spread of socialism from the end of the nineteenth century, which also encouraged the tendency among the peasantry not to want to be involved in war. The levels of desertion in the First World War were higher than in any other European country. During the Second World War, not only the soldiers but also the home front withdrew their support after the first military defeats and the bombing of cities. An Italian anti-Fascist exile in London, Marie Louise Berneri (daughter of Camillo Berneri, a well-known anarchist militant killed during the Spanish Civil War), wrote in praise of Italian cowardice:

> Italian soldiers had to be sneered and laughed at. If the government did not teach the British people to despise them, who knows, the British tommy might have begun to think that there must be a reason why the Italian did not fight – that he had nothing to fight for, and he might even have begun to wonder if he had anything to fight for himself.
>
> ('Liberating Italy with Bombs', *War Commentary*, June 1943)

Linked with the view that Italians do not want to fight is the myth of the 'good-hearted Italian', which has won particular support since the Second World War. Historians Angelo Del Boca and Gianni Oliva have conducted detailed research on the brutal behaviour of Italian soldiers from unification onwards, and have shown that Italians acted in specific situations just as violently as the soldiers of other armies, particularly from the early Fascist period to the end of the Second World War, and that the image of the Italian soldier as 'good-hearted' is a myth that Italians have used to absolve themselves during the Republican years of any accusation of wartime atrocity. Del Boca has also demonstrated how the totalitarian attempt by the Fascist state to transform Italians meant the transformation of an otherwise docile rural population into an army of brutal warriors; to replace a non-existent national military tradition with slogans such as 'believe, obey, fight' resulted in mass atrocities committed during the wars in Ethiopia and the Balkans. Atrocities such as the establishment of concentration camps in Libya in the 1920s, or the use of poison gas to exterminate the Ethiopian resistance in 1936, have until recently been obscured in the public memory. Another episode, still largely ignored, is the case of Italian atrocities in the Balkans, particularly in Albania, Slovenia and Croatia, during the Second World War. In order to 'pacify' Slovenia, Mussolini supported a plan of mass deportation to concentration camps as part of an operation of ethnic cleansing in which Italians sought to destroy Slovenian and Croat cultural identity. During the war of resistance against the Italian occupiers, Yugoslav partisans killed some 4,000 Italian soldiers, throwing them into natural crevasses called *foibe*. This terrible episode has been at the centre of political debate in Italy up to the present time, while the death, deportation and torture of up to 50,000 Slovenians has been ignored, despite the objective results of a joint research project established in 1993 and conducted by a mixed commission of Italian and Slovenian historians.

The debate on these issues has been particularly lively in Italy since the end of the Cold War, which reopened conflicts over the history of the recent past, allowing the heirs of communism and Fascism to enter the sphere of government; in 1994, the former Fascist party, the National Alliance, joined a government coalition of the Northern League (the secessionist party founded in the 1980s) and *Forza Italia*, a party founded by the owner of a publishing and television empire, Silvio Berlusconi. When the government fell and a centre-left government was established in 1996, the new president of the chamber, Luciano Violante, made a speech in favour of 'national reconciliation':

> The Resistance and the war of liberation involved only a part of the country and a part of the political forces. I ask myself what that part of Italy which believes in those values . . . must do in order that the struggle for freedom from Nazi–fascism might become a national value and how we might leave behind, in a positive manner, the lacerations of the past. I ask myself whether the Italy of today should not start reflecting on the defeated of yesterday. Not because they were right, or for some kind of unacceptable argument that the two sides were equivalent. We must try to understand . . . the reasons why thousands of young men, and above all, young women, chose to fight for Mussolini and the Republic of Salò, and not for the side that represented rights and freedom.

The renewed sentiment of national reconciliation saw an attempt to reconstruct the memory of the recent past in order to forget, or to bridge over, formerly traumatic divisions, symbolized by the key dates of 8 September 1943 (which some historians have called the 'death of the Fatherland') and 25 April 1945, when Italians entered a bitterly contested democracy. Resistance, anti-Fascism, and the Constitution began to be attacked as rhetorical 'past things' no longer able to unify

Italians, who were now one people under the tricolour flag. The sentiment of sharing the nation's grief together was meant to reconcile the conflicting memories of a people who were now to be united, as Remo Bodei has remarked, through the pathos of 'belonging to a one and only destiny'. According to Giovanni Levi, this was an expression of a long-term tendency in Italian political life, characterized by the continuous search for mediation – an ideal with a religious origin, linked to the Catholic sense of sin. Against this tendency, Italian intellectuals such as Isnenghi or Bodei have suggested that the existence of a number of separate and not necessarily reconcilable memories is an advantage for a democracy; the experiment attempted by Fascism, to create a monolithic 'us', should not be revived.

The last section of the book analysed Italian society and culture during the Republican period after 1945: how the economic miracle changed the life of Italians; the links between political power and Catholicism under Christian Democracy; the communist challenge and the creation of a communist mass culture within Italian society; the relationship between new values of American consumerism and European integration on the one hand, and on the other the persistence of a culture and traditions that have endured for centuries. When the Allies landed in Sicily in 1943, America was once again perceived as the land of plenty to which many Italians had emigrated from the nineteenth century onwards. As the writer Leonardo Sciascia explained in his collection of short stories *Sicilian Uncles*, so many Sicilians had relatives in America that they did not perceive American soldiers to be foreigners. People in the villages could be found wearing American clothes, and some Sicilians were supported economically by their American relatives. The child protagonist of one of the stories, 'The Aunt from America', describes the wartime graffiti 'viva America, viva the forty-ninth star' and how he believed with fanatical commitment that the forty-ninth star on the American flag would represent a Sicily separated from the rest of Italy. Reconstruction made its way between the myth of American liberation and the will to create a renewed national myth. The invention of new products was perceived as the way to create an exportable Italian life style: these products (such as espresso machines and Vespa scooters), as well as new consumer habits, were presented as symbols both of economic modernity (the transformation of Italy into an industrial country) and of cultural modernity (the 'made in Italy' image). In the 1960s, the foreign press labelled the Italian economic miracle a 'second Renaissance', founded on revolutions in design and culture. Two decades of economic growth and cultural creativity transformed the way of life of many Italians, evident in the birth of a mass urban society (the consequence of large-scale internal migration), in the tension between Catholicism and consumerism, in new roles for women, but also expressed more negatively through the rivalry between Christian Democracy and the Communist Party in an age of terrorism and state corruption. From the 1980s to the present, the increased popularity of Italian style abroad, generated by fashion, food, home furnishing, fast cars, luxury items and tourism, has created what historians and sociologists have called the 'icon of Italy'. Even in the 1970s, the 'lead years' of terrorism, there was a renewed interest in Italy's committed ('organic') intellectuals, particularly among the European left; and in the 1980s, an Italian path to hedonism developed, partly in opposition to American models imposed all over the world: Italy responded to fast food with slow food, to standardized chains with independent bars, and with the survival of small shops alongside the arrival of huge supermarkets and shopping centres.

Italians have reacted more enthusiastically than any other country (perhaps together with Belgium and Germany) to European unification; one reason for this was the defeat in the Second World War, but there are longer-term reasons, such as the persistence of a Catholic universal tradition; the cosmopolitanism of many intellectuals who had to spend large parts of their lives in exile; of artists who were summoned to other European courts for a large part of the medieval and early modern period; or the emigration of peasant masses who had to leave the country because of poverty.

In the 1970s and 1980s, terrorism, the strategy of tension and the discovery that part of the political class had colluded with illegal secret services and the P2 Masonry lodge, all revealed how weakly-rooted democracy was, both at the highest levels of the Italian state and at the political fringes of society. Other aspects of the Italian model in the post-war years have included the continued survival of the Mafia and the Camorra, and a political system that has produced continual government crises (though this did not necessarily imply that the system was inherently weak, since Christian Democracy was able to retain power for forty years). Salvatore Lupo has argued that the Mafia originated in the episodes of banditry in the nineteenth century, and was transformed into a powerful economic system that expanded beyond Sicily and, thanks to the pattern of Italian emigration, outside Italy as well. The French writer Stendhal had already recognized in the nineteenth century that the presence of bandits in Italy was not an irremediable evil, but what he called an 'inconvenience necessarily inherent to the various localities'. Indeed, at certain times in the past, determined leaders had been able to suppress the phenomenon. Cola of Rienzo, who in 1347 led a republic in Rome, 'cleaned up the region from the bandits who were already infesting it' (Stendhal). At the heart of the centuries-long problem lies what journalist Paolo Sylos Labini has defined as the 'habit' of acceptance or 'tolerance' towards illegality, again a product of a Catholic morality that privileged forgiveness over justice. The Mafia and its links with the state – demonstrated by impartial judicial investigation, particularly in the case of Christian Democracy and of Berlusconi's new party – remains another archaic element that has survived into the Italy of the third millennium.

Bibliography

CHAPTER 1

Amory, Patrick, *People and Identity in Ostrogothic Italy, 489–554* (Cambridge: Cambridge University Press, 1997).

Arnaldi, Girolamo, *Italy and its Invaders* (Cambridge, Mass.: Harvard University Press, 2005).

Auerbach, Erich, *Introduction to Romance Languages & Literature: Latin-French-Provencal-Italian-Spanish* (New York: Capricorn Books, 1961).

Auerbach, Erich, *Literary Language and its Public in Late Latin Antiquity and in the Middle Ages* (London: Routledge & Kegan Paul, 1965).

Azzara, Claudio, *L'Italia dei barbari* (Bologna: Il Mulino, 2002).

Bakhtin, Mikhail, *Rabelais and his World* (Bloomington, Ind.: Indiana University Press, 1984).

Cammarosano, Paolo, *Italia medievale. Struttura e geografia delle fonti scritte* (Rome: Nuova Italia Scientifica, 1992).

Centro italiano di studi sull'Alto Medioevo, *Il secolo di ferro: mito e realtà del secolo X* (Spoleto: Il Centro, 1990).

Christie, Neil, *The Lombards* (Oxford: Basil Blackwell, 1995).

Giardina, Andrea and Vauchez, André, *Il mito di Roma: da Carlo Magno a Mussolini* (Rome/Bari: Laterza, 2008).

Giorcelli Bersani, Silvia (ed.), *Romani e barbari: incontro e scontro di culture* (Turin: CELID, 2003).

Horden, Peregrine and Purcell, Nicholas, *The Corrupting Sea. A Study of Mediterranean History* (Oxford: Blackwell, 1999).

Kreutz, Barbara, *Before the Normans: Southern Italy in the Ninth and Tenth Centuries* (Philadelphia, Pa.: University of Pennsylvania Press, 1991).

La Rocca, Maria Cristina, *Italy in the Early Middle Ages, 476–1000* (Oxford: Oxford University Press, 2002).

Luperini, Romano, Cataldi, Pietro, Marchiani, Lidia and Tinacci, Valentina, *La scrittura e l'interpretazione*, Vols 1–3 (Palermo: Palumbo, 2004).

Markus, R. A., *Gregory the Great and his World* (Cambridge: Cambridge University Press, 1997).

Pirenne, Henri, *Medieval Cities: Their Origins and the Revival of Trade* (Princeton, NJ: Princeton University Press, 1969).

Pohl, Walter, *Kingdoms of the Empire: The Integration of Barbarians in Late Antiquity* (Leiden: Brill, 1997).

Salvatorelli, Luigi, *San Benedetto e l'Italia del suo tempo* (Rome/Bari: Laterza, 2007).

Tabacco, Giovanni, *The Struggle for Power in Medieval Italy: Structures of Political Rule* (Cambridge: Cambridge University Press, 1989).

Vian, Giovanni Maria, *La donazione di Costantino* (Bologna: Il Mulino, 2004).

Vauchez, André (ed.), *Roma medievale* (Rome/Bari: Laterza, 2006).

Ward-Perkins, Bryan, *The Fall of Rome and the End of Civilization* (Oxford: Oxford University Press, 2005).

Wickham, Chris, *Early Medieval Italy: Central Power and Local Society* (London: Macmillan, 1981).

Wickham, Chris, *Land and Power: Studies in Italian and European Social History, 400–1200* (London: British School at Rome, 1994).

Wickham, Chris, *Framing the Middle Ages: Europe and the Mediterranean, 400–800* (Oxford: Oxford University Press, 2005).

Wolfram, Herwig, *History of the Goths* (Berkeley, Calif.: University of California Press, 1988).

Primary sources

Constantine I, *A Treatise of the Donation Given unto Sylvester Pope of Rome by Constantine* (Amsterdam: Theatrum Orbis Terrarum, 1979).

Gregory I, the Great, *Dialogues* (Washington, DC: Catholic University of America Press, 1977).

Procopius of Caesarea, *History of the Wars* (Cambridge, Mass: Harvard University Press, 1960–8).

CHAPTER 2

Abulafia, David, *The Two Italies: Economic Relations between the Norman Kingdom of Sicily and the Northern Communes* (Cambridge: Cambridge University Press, 1977).

Abulafia, David, *Italy, Sicily and the Mediterranean, 1100–1400* (London: Variorum Reprints, 1987).

Abulafia, David (ed.), *Italy in the Central Middle Ages, 1000–1300* (Oxford: Oxford University Press, 2004).

Albertoni, Giuseppe and Provero, Luigi, *Il feudalesimo in Italia* (Rome: Carocci, 2003).

Ascheri, Mario, *Le città stato* (Bologna: Il Mulino, 2006).

Barbero, Alessandro, 'Il castello, il comune, il campanile. Attitudini militari e mestiere delle armi in un paese diviso', in *Storia d'Italia*, Annali 18, *Guerra e pace*, ed. Walter Barberis (Turin: Einaudi, 2002).

Barbero, Alessandro, *Terre d'acqua. I vercellesi all'epoca delle crociate* (Rome/Bari: Laterza, 2007).

Brown, Peter, *The Cult of the Saints: Its Rise and Function in Latin Christianity* (Chicago: University of Chicago Press, 1981).

Browsky, William, *A Medieval Commune: Siena under the Nine, 1287–1355* (Berkeley, Calif.: University of California Press, 1981).

Camporesi, Piero, 'Cultura popolare e cultura d'elite fra Medioevo ed età moderna', in *Storia d'Italia*, Annali 4, *Intellettuali e potere*, ed. Corrado Vivanti (Turin: Einaudi, 1981).

Cattaneo, Carlo, *Le città considerate come principio ideale delle istorie italiane*, in *Scritti storici e geografici*, ed. Gaetano Salvemini and Ernesto Sestan, Vol. 2 (Florence: Le Monnier, 1957).

Cattaneo, Carlo, *Geografia e storia della Sardegna* (Rome: Donzelli, 1996).

Dean, Trevor, *Crime and Justice in Late Medieval Italy* (Cambridge: Cambridge University Press, 2007).

De Rosa, Gabriele, Gregory, Tullio and Vauchez, André (eds.), *Storia dell'Italia religiosa*, Vol. 1, *L'antichità e il Medio Evo* (Rome/Bari: Laterza, 1993).

Dessì, Rosa Maria, 'Pratiche della parola di pace nella storia dell'Italia urbana', in Centro Italiano di Studi del Basso Medioevo, *Pace e guerra nel Basso Medioevo* (Spoleto: Fondazione Centro Italiano di Studi sull'Alto Medioevo, 2004).

Dionisotti, Carlo, *Geografia e storia della letteratura italiana* (Turin: Einaudi, 1967).

Duby, Georges, *L'An Mil* (Paris: Juillard, 1967).

Epstein, Steven, *Genoa and the Genoese, 958–1528* (Chapel Hill, NC: University of North Carolina Press, 1996).

Flori, Jean, *Le crociate* (Bologna: Il Mulino, 2003).

Golinelli, Paolo, *Città e culto dei santi nel Medioevo italiano* (Bologna: CLUEB, 1996).

Housley, Norman, *Crusading and Warfare in Medieval and Renaissance Europe* (Aldershot: Ashgate, 2001).

Jones, Philip, *The Italian City-State: From Commune to Signoria* (Oxford: Clarendon Press, 1997).

Loud, G. A., *The Age of Robert Guiscard: Southern Italy and the Norman Conquest* (Harlow: Longman, 2000).

Matthew, Donald, *The Norman Kingdom of Sicily* (Cambridge: Cambridge University Press, 1992).

Montanari, Massimo, *Alimentazione e cultura nel Medioevo* (Rome/Bari: Laterza, 1988).

Muzzarelli, Maria Giuseppina and Campanini, Antonella (eds), *Disciplinare il lusso. La legislazione suntuaria in Italia e in Europa tra Medioevo ed Età Moderna* (Rome: Carocci, 2003).

Nicol, Donald M., *Byzantium and Venice: A Study in Diplomatic and Cultural Relations* (Cambridge: Cambridge University Press, 1988).

Petrucci, Armando, *Writers and Readers in Medieval Italy* (New Haven, Conn.: Yale University Press, 1995).

Placanica, Augusto, *Storia della Calabria dall'antichità ai giorni nostri* (Rome: Donzelli, 1999).

Pryor, John, *Commerce, Shipping, and Naval Warfare in the Medieval Mediterranean* (London: Variourum Reprints, 1987).

Ravegnani, Giorgio, *I bizantini in Italia* (Bologna: Il Mulino, 2004).

Ravegnani, Giorgio, *Bisanzio e Venezia* (Bologna: Il Mulino, 2006).

Renouard, Yves, *Gli uomini d'affari italiani del Medioevo* (Milan: Rizzoli, 1995).

Waley, Daniel, *The Italian City-Republics* (London: Weidenfeld and Nicolson, 1969).

Waley, Daniel, *Siena and the Sienese in the Thirteenth Century* (Cambridge: Cambridge University Press, 1991).

Webb, Diana, *Patrons and Defenders: The Saints in the Italian City-States* (London: Tauris, 1996).

Primary sources

Francis of Assisi, *Canticle of the Sun* (Boston: Shambhala, 2002).

Giacomo da Lentini, *The Poetry of Giacomo da Lentino, Sicilian Poet of the Thirteenth Century*, ed. Ernest Langley (Cambridge, Mass.: Harvard University Press, 1915).

Jacopone da Todi, 'On the Heart's Jubilation', in *The Lauds*, trans. Serge and Elizabeth Hughes (London: SPCK, 1982).

Thomas Aquinas, *Political Writings*, ed. R. W. Dyson (Cambridge: Cambridge University Press, 2002).

CHAPTER 3

Auerbach, Erich, *Mimesis. The Representation of Reality in Western Literature* (Princeton, NJ: Princeton University Press, 2003).

Baratto, Mario, *Realtà e stile nel Decameron* (Rome: Editori Riuniti, 1996).

Bloch, Marc, *The Royal Touch* (London: Routledge & Kegan Paul, 1973).

Boccardi, Giancarlo (ed.), *Caterina da Siena. Una santa degli europei. Dalle lettere di Caterina: un fervido messaggio per l'Europa dello spirito, alla ricerca delle proprie radici cristiane*, 2nd edn (Siena: Cantagalli, 2003).

Cardini, Franco and Montesano, Marina, *La lunga storia dell'Inquisizione. Luci e ombre della leggenda nera* (Rome: Città Nuova, 2007).

Chastel, André, *Storia dell'arte italiana*, Vol. 1 (Rome/Bari: Laterza, 2002).

D'Avray, David, *Medieval Marriage: Symbolism and Society* (Oxford: Oxford University Press, 2005).

Dean, Trevor (ed.), *The Towns of Italy in the Later Middle Ages* (Manchester: Manchester University Press, 2000).

De Seta, Cesare, *Roma. Cinque secoli di vedute* (Naples: Electa, 2006).

De Stefano, Antonino, *La cultura alla corte di Federico II* (Bologna: Zanichelli, 1950).

Evangelisti, Silvia, *Nuns: A History of Convent Life, 1450–1700* (Oxford: Oxford University Press, 2007).

Frosini, Giovanna, *Il cibo e i signori. La mensa dei priori di Firenze nel quinto decennio del secolo XIV* (Florence: Accademia della Crusca, 1993).

Frugoni, Chiara, *Le origini del nostro futuro*, Vol. 2 (Bologna: Zanichelli, 2003).

Fumagalli, Vito, *Matilde di Canossa* (Bologna: Il Mulino, 1996).

Furlan, Francesco, *La donna, la famiglia, l'amore: tra Medioevo e Rinascimento* (Florence: Olschki, 2004).

Kessler, Herbert and Zacharias, Johanna, *Rome 1300: On the Path of the Pilgrim* (New Haven, Conn.: Yale University Press, 2000).

Kirschner, Julius and Wemple, Suzanne (eds), *Women of the Medieval World* (Oxford: Basil Blackwell, 1985).

Larner, John, *Italy in the Age of Dante and Petrarch, 1216–1380* (London: Longman, 1980).

Le Goff, Jacques, 'L'immaginario urbano nell'Italia medievale (secoli V–XV)', in *Storia d'Italia*, Annali 5, *Il paesaggio*, ed. Cesare De Seta (Turin: Einaudi, 1982).

Martellotti, Anna, *I ricettari di Federico II. Dal Meridionale al Liber de Coquina* (Florence: Olschki, 2005).

Martines, Lauro (ed.), *Violence and Civil Disorder in Italian Cities, 1200–1500* (Berkeley, Calif.: University of California Press, 1972).

Martines, Lauro, *Power and Imagination: City-States in Renaissance Italy* (London: Pimlico, 2002).

Montanari, Massimo, *Uomini, terre, boschi nell'occidente medievale* (Catania: CUEM, 1992).

Nada Patrone, Anna Maria, *Il cibo del ricco e il cibo del povero: contributo alla storia qualitativa dell'alimentazione: l'area pedemontana negli ultimi secoli del Medio Evo* (Turin: Centro Studi Piemontesi, 1981).

Omicciolo Valentini, Rosella, *Mangiare medievale. Alimentazione e cucina medievale tra storia, ricette e curiosità* (Latina: Penne e Papiri, 2005).

Opiz, Claudia, 'La vita quotidiana delle donne nel Tardo Medio Evo', in *Storia delle donne in Occidente*, dir. G. Duby and M. Perrot, *Il Medio Evo*, ed. Christiane Klapisch-Zuber (Rome/Bari: Laterza 1995).

Power, Eileen, *Medieval Women* (Cambridge: Cambridge University Press, 1995).

Quondam, Amedeo, *Petrarca, l'italiano dimenticato* (Milan: Rizzoli, 2004).

Rubinstein, Nicolai and Ciappelli, Giovanni (eds), *Studies in Italian History in the Middle Ages and the Renaissance*, Vol. 1, 'Political Thought and the Language of Politics. Art and Politics' (Rome: Edizioni di storia e letteratura, 2004).

Schmitt, Jean-Claude, *Medioevo 'superstizioso'* (Rome/Bari: Laterza, 2007).

Skinner, Patricia, *Women in Medieval Italian Society, 500–1200* (Harlow: Longman, 2001).

Tabacco, Giovanni, *The Struggle for Power in Medieval Italy: Structures of Political Rule* (Cambridge: Cambridge University Press, 1989).

Tenenti, Alberto, *L'Italia del Quattrocento. Economia e società* (Rome/Bari: Laterza, 2004).

Primary sources

Alberti, Leon Battista, *The Family in Renaissance Florence (Della famiglia)*, trans. Renée Neu Watkins (Columbia, SC: University of South Carolina Press, 1969).

Alighieri, Dante, *The Divine Comedy*, trans. Charles S. Singleton (Princeton, NJ: Princeton University Press, 1970–5).

Alighieri, Dante, *Literature in the Vernacular (De Vulgari Eloquentia)*, trans. Sally Purcell (Manchester: Carcanet, 1981).

Alighieri, Dante, *Dante's Il Convivio (The Banquet)*, trans. Richard Lansing (New York: Garland, 1990).

Alighieri, Dante, *Monarchy*, trans. Prue Shaw (Cambridge: Cambridge University Press, 1996).

Anonymous Tuscan author, *Libro della cucina del secolo 14* (Bologna: Forni, 1970).

Anonymous Venetian author, *Libro per cuoco*, in *Arte della cucina in Italia*, ed. E. Faccioli (Turin: Einaudi, 1992).

Boccaccio, Giovanni, *Esposizioni sopra la Comedia di Dante*, ed. Giorgio Padoan (Milan: Mondadori, 1994).

Boccaccio, Giovanni, *The Decameron*, trans. G. H. McWilliam (London: Penguin, 1995).

Folgore da San Gimignano, *Sonetti dei mesi*, in *Poeti del duecento*, ed. G. Contini (Milan, Ricciardi, 1960).

Ventura, Guglielmo, *Memoriale Guilelmi Venturae civis Astiensis*, in *Rerum Italicarum Scriptores*, XI (Milan 1727); Italian translation in A. Paravicini Bagliani, *La vita quotidiana alla corte dei papi nel Duecento* (Rome/Bari: Laterza, 1996).

CHAPTER 4

Barberis, Walter, 'Uomini di corte nel Cinquecento', in *Storia d'Italia*, Annali 4, *Intellettuali e potere*, ed. Corrado Vivanti (Turin: Einaudi, 1981).

Baron, Hans, *The Crisis of the Early Italian Renaissance: Civic Humanism and Republican Liberty in an Age of Classicism and Tyranny* (Princeton, NJ: Princeton University Press, 1966).

Battisti, Eugenio, *L'Antirinascimento* (Milan: Garzanti, 1989).

Black, Christopher, *Early Modern Italy: A Social History* (London: Routledge, 2001).

Brucker, Gene, *Living on the Edge in Leonardo's Florence* (Berkeley, Calif.: University of California Press, 2005).

Brucker, Gene, *Giovanni and Lusanna: Love and Marriage in Renaissance Florence* (Berkeley, Calif.: University of California Press, 2005).

Burke, Peter, *The Fortunes of the Courtier: The European Reception of Castiglione's Cortegiano* (London: Polity, 1995).

Burke, Peter, *The Italian Renaissance: Culture and Society in Italy* (London: Polity Press, 1999).

Calabria, Antonio and Marino, John (eds), *Good Government in Spanish Naples* (New York: Peter Lang, 1990).

Celenza, Christopher, *The Lost Italian Renaissance: Humanists, Historians, and Latin Legacy* (Baltimore, Md.: Johns Hopkins University Press, 2004).

Chabod, Federico, *Scritti su Machiavelli* (Turin: Einaudi, 1982).

Connell, William J. and Zorzi, Andrea (eds), *Florentine Tuscany: Structures and Practices of Power* (Cambridge: Cambridge University Press, 2000).

Cozzo, Paolo, *La geografia celeste dei duchi di Savoia. Religione, devozioni e sacralità in uno Stato di età moderna* (Bologna: Il Mulino, 2006).

Dionisotti, Carlo, 'Discorso sull'umanesimo italiano', in C. Dionisotti, *Geografia e storia della letteratura italiana* (Turin: Einaudi, 1967).

Fazio, Ida, 'La famiglia', in *Storia della Sicilia. Dalle origini al Seicento*, ed. Francesco Benigno and Giuseppe Giarrizzo (Rome/Bari: Laterza, 2003).

Ferraro, Joanne M., *Family and Public Life in Brescia, 1580–1650* (Cambridge: Cambridge University Press, 1993).

Finucci, Valeria (ed.), *Renaissance Transactions: Ariosto and Tasso* (Durham, NC: Duke University Press, 1999).

Fiume, Giovanna, *Madri: storia di un ruolo sociale* (Venice: Marsilio, 1995).

Furlan, Francesco, *La donna, la famiglia, l'amore: tra Medioevo e Rinascimento* (Florence: Olschki, 2004).

Garin, Eugenio, *L'uomo del Rinascimento* (Rome/Bari: Laterza, 2007).

Godman, Peter, *From Poliziano to Machiavelli: Florentine Humanism in the High Renaissance* (Princeton, NJ: Princeton University Press, 1998).

Hankins, James, *Renaissance Civic Humanism: Reappraisals and Reflections* (Cambridge: Cambridge University Press, 2000).

Hay, Denys and Law, John, *Italy in the Age of the Renaissance, 1380–1530* (London: Longman, 1989).

Haydn, Hiram, *The Counter-Renaissance* (New York: Grove Press, 1960).

Ianziti, Gary, *Humanistic Historiography under the Sforzas: Politics and Propaganda in Fifteenth-Century Milan* (Oxford: Clarendon Press, 1988).

Klapisch-Zuber, Christiane, *Women, Family and Ritual in Renaissance Italy* (Chicago: University of Chicago Press, 1985).

Mackenney, Richard, *The City-State, 1500–1700. Republican Liberty in an Age of Princely Power* (London: Macmillan, 1989).

Martin, John and Romano, Dennis (eds), *Venice Reconsidered: The History and Civilisation of an Italian City-State, 1297–1797* (Baltimore, Md.: Johns Hopkins University Press, 2000).

Martines, Lauro, *The Social World of the Florentine Humanists, 1390–1460* (London: Routledge, 1963).

Matthews Grieco, Sara F., 'Corpo, aspetto e sessualità', in *Storia delle donne. Dal Rinascimento all'età moderna*, ed. Natalie Zemon Davies and Arlette Farge (Rome/Bari: Laterza, 1991).

Mazzacurati, Giancarlo, *Il Rinascimento dei moderni. La crisi culturale del XVI secolo e la negazione delle origini* (Bologna: Il Mulino, 1985).

Muir, Edward, *The Culture Wars of the Late Renaissance: Skeptics, Libertines, and Opera* (Cambridge, Mass.: Harvard University Press, 2007).

Niccoli, Ottavia, *Prophecy and People in Renaissance Italy* (Princeton, NJ: Princeton University Press: 1990).

Niola, Marino, *I santi patroni* (Bologna: Il Mulino, 2007).

Panizza, Letizia (ed.), *Women in Italian Renaissance Culture and Society* (Oxford: European Humanities Research Centre, 2000).

Panofsky, Erwin, *Studies in Iconology: Humanistic Themes in the Art of the Renaissance* (New York: Harper & Row, 1972).

Pozzi, Mario (ed.), *Discussioni linguistiche del Cinquecento* (Turin: UTET, 1996).

Reinhardt, Volker, *Il Rinascimento in Italia* (Bologna: Il Mulino, 2004).

Russell, Camilla, *Giulia Gonzaga and the Religious Controversies of Sixteenth-Century Italy* (Turnhout: Brepols, 2006).

Sapegno, Maria Serena, 'Italia, Italiani', in *Letteratura italiana*, dir. Asor Rosa, Vol. 5, *Le questioni* (Turin: Einaudi, 1986).

Zapperi, Roberto, *Tiziano, Paolo III e i suoi nipoti: nepotismo e ritratto di Stato* (Turin: Bollati Boringhieri, 1990).

Zapperi, Roberto and Walter, Ingeborg, *Il ritratto dell'amata. Storie d'amore da Petrarca a Tiziano* (Rome: Donzelli, 2006).

Wilson, Bronwen, *The World in Venice: Print, the City, and Early Modern Identity* (Toronto: University of Toronto Press, 2005).

Wolf, Hubert, *Storia dell'Indice. Il Vaticano e i libri proibiti* (Rome: Donzelli, 2006).

Primary sources

Ariosto, Ludovico, *Orlando Furioso*, trans. Guido Waldman (Oxford: Oxford University Press, 1983).

Castiglione, Baldassarre, *The Book of the Courtier*, trans. Charles S. Singleton (New York/London: W. W. Norton, 2002).

Cellini, Benvenuto, *My Life*, trans. Julia Conaway Bondanella and Peter Bondanella (Oxford: Oxford University Press, 2002).

Della Casa, Giovanni, *Galateo of Manners and Behaviours (1576)*, trans. Robert Peterson (Bari: Adriatica Editrice, 1997).

Gioia, Melchiorre, *Nuovo Galateo* (Milan: Guigoni, 1886).

Guicciardini, Francesco, *Carteggi* (Rome: Istituto storico italiano per l'età moderna e contemporanea, 1938–1972).

Guicciardini, Francesco, *The History of Italy*, trans. Sidney Alexander (New York: Macmillan, 1969).

Guicciardini, Francesco, *Guicciardini's Ricordi*, trans. Ninian Hill Thomson (Leicester: Allandale Online, 2000).

Machiavelli, Niccolò, *Florentine Histories*, trans. L. F. Banfield and H. C. Mansfield (Princeton, NJ: Princeton University Press, 1988).

Machiavelli, Niccolò, *Discourses on Livy*, trans. H. C. Mansfield and N. Tarcov (Chicago: University of Chicago Press, 1996).

Machiavelli, Niccolò, *The Prince*, trans. William J. Connell (Boston, Mass.: Bedford/St Martin's, 2005).

Vasari, Giorgio, *Lives of the Painters, Sculptors and Architects*, trans. Gaston de Vere (London: David Campbell, 1996).

CHAPTER 5

Ago, Renata, *Il gusto delle cose. Una storia degli oggetti nella Roma del Seicento* (Rome: Donzelli, 2006).

Astarita, Tommaso, *The Continuity of Feudal Power: The Caracciolo di Bienza in Spanish Naples* (Cambridge: Cambridge University Press, 1992).

Astarita, Tommaso, *Between Salt Water and Holy Water. A History of Southern Italy* (New York: W. W. Norton, 2005).

Benigno, Francesco, 'La Sicilia in rivolta', in *Storia della Sicilia. Dalle origini al Seicento*, eds Francesco Benigno and Giuseppe Giarrizzo (Rome/Bari: Laterza, 2003).

Bianconi, Lorenzo, *Music in the Seventeenth Century* (Cambridge: Cambridge University Press, 1987).

Burke, Peter, *The Historical Anthropology of Early Modern Italy* (Cambridge: Cambridge University Press, 1987).

Carlson, Marvin, *The Italian Stage: From Goldoni to D'Annunzio* (Jefferson, NC: McFarland, 1981).

Castagno, Paul, *The Early 'Commedia dell'arte' (1550–1621): The Mannerist Context* (New York: Peter Lang, 1994).

Cochrane, Eric W., *Florence in the Forgotten Centuries, 1527–1800* (Chicago: University of Chicago Press, 1974).

Cochrane, Eric W., *Italy 1530–1630* (London: Longman, 1988).

Croce, Benedetto, *Storia dell'età barocca in Italia. Pensiero – Poesia e letteratura – Vita morale* (Bari: Laterza, 1957).

Dandelet, Thomas and Marino, John (eds), *Spain in Italy: Politics, Society and Religion, 1500–1700* (Leiden: Brill, 2007).

De Martino, Ernesto, *Sud e magia* (Milan: Feltrinelli, 2006).

DeMolen, Richard, *Religious Orders of the Catholic Reformation* (New York: Fordham University Press, 1994).

De Rosa, Gabriele, Gregory, Tullio and Vauchez, André (eds), *Storia dell'Italia religiosa*, Vol. 2, *L'età moderna* (Rome/Bari: Laterza, 1994).

Elliott, John, *Richelieu and Olivares* (Cambridge: Cambridge University Press, 1984).

Enggass, Robert and Brown, Jonathan, *Italy and Spain, 1600–1750: Sources and Documents* (Englewood Cliffs, NJ: Prentice-Hall, 1970).

Fano, Nicola, *Le maschere italiane* (Bologna: Il Mulino, 2001).

Ferraro, Joanne, *Marriage Wars in Late Renaissance Venice* (Oxford: Oxford University Press, 2001).

Ferrone, Vincenzo, *The Intellectual Roots of the Italian Enlightenment* (New York: Humanity Books, 1995).

Findlen, Paula, *Possessing Nature: Museums, Collecting, and Scientific Culture in Early Modern Italy* (Berkeley, Calif.: University of California Press, 1994).

Firpo, Massimo, *Riforma protestante ed eresie nell'Italia del cinquecento* (Rome/Bari: Laterza, 1993).

Foa, Anna, *Giordano Bruno* (Bologna: Il Mulino, 2002).

Fosi, Irene, *La giustizia del papa. Sudditi e tribunali nello Stato Pontificio in età moderna* (Rome/Bari: Laterza, 2007).

Gallico, Claudio, *Monteverdi: Poesia musicale, teatro e musica sacra* (Turin: Einaudi, 1979).

Gallo, Francesca, 'La nascita della nazione siciliana', in *Storia della Sicilia*, ed. Francesco Benigno and Giuseppe Giarrizzo, Vol. 2, *Dal seicento a oggi* (Rome/Bari: Laterza, 2003).

Gentilcore, David, *From Bishop to Witch: The System of the Sacred in Early Modern Terra d'Otranto* (Manchester: Manchester University Press, 1992).

Ginzburg, Carlo, *Cheese and the Worms: The Cosmos of a Sixteenth-century Miller* (London: Penguin, 1992).

Ghirelli, Antonio, *Storia di Napoli* (Turin: Einaudi, 1992).

Hanlon, Gregory, *Early Modern Italy* (Basingstoke: Palgrave, 2000).

Marino, John (ed.), *Early Modern Italy, 1550–1796* (Oxford: Oxford University Press, 2002).

Niola, Marino, *I santi patroni* (Bologna: Il Mulino, 2007).

O'Malley, John (ed.), *The Jesuits: Culture, Sciences, and the Arts, 1540–1773* (Toronto: University of Toronto Press, 1999).

O'Malley, John, *Trent and All That: Renaming Catholicism in the Early Modern Era* (Cambridge, Mass.: Harvard University Press, 2000).

Parronchi, Alessandro, *Caravaggio* (Milan: Medusa, 2002).

Pollak, Martha, *Turin, 1564–1680: Urban Design, Military Culture, and the Creation of the Absolutist Capital* (Chicago: University of Chicago Press, 1991).

Prodi, Paolo, *Il sovrano pontefice: un corpo e due anime, la monarchia papale nella prima età moderna* (Bologna: Il Mulino, 1982).

Repishti, Francesco and Schofield, Richard, *Architettura e controriforma. I dibattiti per la facciata del Duomo di Milano, 1582–1682* (Milan: Electa, 2003).

Robin, Diana, *Publishing Women* (Chicago: University of Chicago Press, 2007).

Rosa, Mario, 'La chiesa meridionale nell'età della controriforma', in *Storia d'Italia*, Annali 9, *La Chiesa e il potere politico dal Medioevo all'età contemporanea*, ed. Giorgio Chittolini and Giovanni Miccoli (Turin: Einaudi, 1986).

Ruggiero, Guido, *The Boundaries of Eros: Sex, Crime and Sexuality in Renaissance Venice* (Oxford: Oxford University Press, 1985).

Scaraffia, Lucetta, *Loreto* (Bologna: Il Mulino, 1998).

Sella, Domenico, *Italy in the Seventeenth Century* (London: Longman, 1997).

Snyder, Jon, *Writing the Scene of Speaking: Theories of Dialogue in the Late Italian Renaissance* (Stanford, Calif.: Stanford University Press, 1989).

Sodano, Giulio, '"Sangue vivo, rubicondo e senza malo odore". I prodigi del sangue nei processi di canonizzazione a Napoli nell'età moderna', *Campania Sacra*, 26, 1995.

Tedeschi, John, *The Prosecution of Heresy: Collected Studies on the Inquisition in Early Modern Italy* (Binghamton, NY: MRTS, 1991).

Villari, Rosario, *The Revolt of Naples* (Cambridge, Mass.: Polity Press, 1993).

Villari, Rosario (ed.), *Baroque Personae* (Chicago: University of Chicago Press, 1995).

Zarri, Gabriella, 'Monasteri femminili e città (secoli XV–XVIII)', in *Storia d'Italia*, Annali 9, *La Chiesa e il potere politico dal Medioevo all'età contemporanea*, ed. Giorgio Chittolini and Giovanni Miccoli (Turin: Einaudi, 1986).

Primary sources

Alfieri, Vittorio, *The Prince and Letters* (Toronto: University of Toronto Press, 1972).

Campanella, Tommaso, *The City of the Sun*, trans. A. M. Elliott and R. Millner (Milan: Feltrinelli, 1991).

Commynes, Philippe de, *The Memoirs of Philippe de Commynes*, trans. Isabelle Cazeaux (Columbia, SC: University of South Carolina Press, 1969–1973).

Locke, John, *Two Treatises of Government and a Letter Concerning Toleration*, ed. Ian Shapiro (New Haven, Conn.: Yale University Press, 2003).

Manzoni, Alessandro, *The Betrothed*, ed. David Forgacs and Matthew Reynolds (London: J. M. Dent, 1997).

Parini, Giuseppe, *The Day: Morning, Midday, Evening, Night*, trans. H. M. Bower (London: Routledge, 1927).

Stendhal (Marie Henri Beyle), *I briganti in Italia* (Genoa: Il Nuovo Melangolo, 2004).

CHAPTER 6

Aliberti, Giovanni, *La resa di Cavour. Il carattere nazionale italiano tra mito e cronaca (1820–1976)* (Florence: Le Monnier, 2000).

Ascoli, Albert Russell and von Hermeberg, Krystyna, *Making and Remaking Italy: The Cultivation of National Identity around the Risorgimento* (Oxford: Berg, 2001).

Banti, Alberto Mario, *La nazione del Risorgimento. Parentela, santità e onore alle origini dell'Italia unita* (Turin: Einaudi, 1999).

Banti, Alberto and Ginsborg, Paul, 'Per una nuova storia del Risorgimento', in *Storia d'Italia*, Annali 22, *Il Risorgimento*, eds Alberto Banti and Paul Ginsborg (Turin: Einaudi, 2007).

Bartolini, Francesco, *Rivali d'Italia. Roma e Milano dal Settecento a oggi* (Rome/Bari: Laterza, 2006).

Beales, Derek and Biagini, Eugenio, *The Risorgimento and the Unification of Italy* (London: Longman, 2002).

Berengo, Marino, *Intellettuali e librai nella Milano della Restaurazione* (Turin: Einaudi, 1980).

Berengo, Marino, *Cultura e istituzioni nell'Ottocento italiano* (Bologna: Il Mulino, 2004).

Biscuso, Massimiliano and Gallo, Franco, *Leopardi antitaliano* (Rome: Manifestolibri, 1999).

Black, Jeremy, *Italy and the Grand Tour* (New Haven, Conn.: Yale University Press, 2003).

Brunello, Piero, *Voci per un dizionario del Quarantotto: Venezia e Mestre, marzo 1848– augosto 1849* (Venice: Comune di Venezia, 1999).

Caffiero, Marina, *La repubblica nella città del Papa. Roma 1798* (Rome: Donzelli, 2005).

Carnazzi, Giulio, 'Introduction' to Pietro Verri, *Osservazioni sulla tortura* (Milan: Rizzoli, 1988).

Carpanetto, Dino and Ricuperati, Giuseppe, *Italy in the Age of Reason, 1685–1789* (London: Longman, 1987).

Coppa, Frank, *The Origins of the Italian Wars of Independence* (London: Longman, 1992).

D'Amelia, Marina, *La mamma* (Bologna: Il Mulino, 2005).

Davis, John, *Conflict and Control: Law and Order in Nineteenth-Century Italy* (London: Macmillan, 1988).

Davis, John (ed.), *Italy in the Nineteenth Century, 1796–1900* (Oxford: Oxford University Press, 2000).

Duggan, Christopher, *The Force of Destiny: A History of Italy since 1796* (London: Penguin, 2007).

Eisenstein, Elizabeth L., *The First Professional Revolutionist: Filippo Michele Buonarroti (1761–1837)* (Cambridge, Mass.: Harvard University Press, 1959).

Ferrone, Vincenzo, *I profeti dell'illuminismo* (Rome/Bari: Laterza, 1989).

François, Etienne, 'Il caffè', in Heinz-Gerhard Haupt, *Luoghi quotidiani nella storia d'Europa* (Rome/Bari: Laterza, 1993).

Fruci, Gian Luca, 'Il sacramento dell'unità nazionale. Linguaggi, iconografia e pratiche dei plebisciti risorgimentali, 1848–70', in *Storia d'Italia*, Annali 22, *Il Risorgimento*, ed. Alberto Banti and Paul Ginsborg (Turin: Einaudi, 2007).

Ginsborg, Paul, *Daniele Manin and the Venetian Revolution of 1848–49* (Cambridge: Cambridge University Press, 1979).

Ginsborg, Paul, 'Romanticismo e risorgimento: l'io, l'amore e la nazione', in *Storia d'Italia*, Annali 22, *Il Risorgimento*, ed. Alberto Banti and Paul Ginsborg (Turin: Einaudi, 2007).

Greco, Gaetano and Rosa, Mario (eds), *Storia degli antichi stati italiani* (Rome/Bari: Laterza, 2006).

Gregory, Desmond, *Napoleon's Italy* (London: Associated University Presses, 2001).

Isnenghi, Mario (ed.), *I luoghi della memoria. Strutture ed eventi dell'Italia unita*, 3 vols. (Rome/Bari: Laterza, 1997).

Kimbell, David, *Verdi in the Age of Italian Romanticism* (Cambridge: Cambridge University Press, 1981).

Laven, David and Riall, Lucy (eds), *Napoleon's Legacy: Problems of Government in Restoration Europe* (Oxford: Berg, 2000).

Lovett, Clara, *The Democratic Movement in Italy, 1830–1876* (Cambridge, Mass.: Harvard University Press, 1982).

Macry, Paolo, *Ottocento. Famiglia, élites e patrimoni a Napoli* (Turin: Einaudi, 1988).

Macry, Paolo, *Giocare la vita. Storia del lotto a Napoli tra Sette e Ottocento* (Rome: Donzelli, 1997).

Mack Smith, Denis, *Cavour and Garibaldi: A Study in Political Conflict* (Cambridge: Cambridge University Press, 1985).

Malatesta, Maria, 'Il caffè e l'osteria', in *I luoghi della memoria. Strutture ed eventi dell'Italia unita*, ed. M. Isnenghi (Rome/Bari, Laterza, 1997).

Menozzi, Daniele, 'Tra riforma e restaurazione', in *Storia d'Italia*, Annali 9, *La Chiesa e il potere politico dal Medioevo all'età contemporanea*, ed. Giorgio Chittolini and Giovanni Miccoli (Turin: Einaudi, 1986).

Meriggi, Marco, *Gli stati italiani prima dell'unità. Una storia istituzionale* (Bologna: Il Mulino, 2002).

Pensa, Maria Grazia and Pizzamiglio, Gilberto, 'L'idea di nazione nella storiografia letteraria italiana del settecento', in *Cultura e nazione in Italia e Polonia dal Rinascimento all'Illuminismo*, ed. Vittore Branca and Sante Graciotti (Florence: Olschki, 1986).

Pillepich, Alain, *Napoleone e gli italiani* (Bologna: Il Mulino, 2005).

Quondam, Amedeo and Rizzo, Gino (eds), *L'identità nazionale. Miti e paradigmi storiografici ottocenteschi* (Rome: Bulzoni, 2005).

Riall, Lucy, *The Italian Risorgimento: State, Society and National Unification* (London: Routledge, 1994).

Riall, Lucy, *Garibaldi: Invention of a Hero* (New Haven, Conn.: Yale University Press, 2007).

Sarti, Roland, *Mazzini: A Life for the Religion of Politics* (London: Praeger, 1997).

Soldani, Simonetta, 'Il Risorgimento delle donne', in *Storia d'Italia*, Annali 22, *Il Risorgimento*, ed. Alberto Banti and Paul Ginsborg (Turin: Einaudi, 2007).

Spagnoletti, Angelantonio, *Storia del Regno delle Due Sicilie* (Bologna: Il Mulino, 1997).

Venturi, Franco, *Italy and the Enlightenment: Studies in a Cosmopolitan Century* (London: Longman, 1970).

Primary sources

Abba, Cesare, *The Diary of One of Garibaldi's Thousand*, trans. E. R. Vincent (Oxford: Oxford University Press, 1962).

Alfieri, Vittorio, *The Prince and Letters* (Toronto: University of Toronto Press, 1972).

Balbo, Cesare, *Speranze d'Italia* (Turin: UTET, 1948).

Cuoco, Vincenzo, *Saggio storico sulla rivoluzione napoletana del 1799* (Manduria: Lacaita, 1998).

D'Azeglio, Massimo, *Things I Remember* (London: Oxford University Press, 1966).

De Amicis, Edmondo, *Impressioni di Roma* (Florence: Faverio, 1870).

De Roberto, Federico, *The Viceroys*, trans. Archibald Colquhoun (London: Harvill, 1989).

De Sanctis, Francesco, *History of Italian Literature (1870–1871)*, trans. J. Redfern (Oxford: Oxford University Press, 1930).

Foscolo, Ugo, *Sepolcri, Odi, Sonetti* (Milan: Mondadori, 2001).

Foscolo, Ugo, *Last Letters of Jacopo Ortis*, trans. J. G. Nichols (London: Hesperus, 2002).

Gimma, Giacinto, *Idea della storia dell'Italia letterata* (Naples: Mosca, 1723).

Gioberti, Vincenzo, *Del Primato morale e civile degli italiani* (Turin: UTET, 1946).

Goldoni, Carlo, *La bottega del caffè* (Milan: Rizzoli, 2004).

Gramsci, Antonio, *Sul Risorgimento* (Rome: Editori Riuniti, 1967).

Gramsci, Antonio, *Prison Notebooks*, trans. Joseph A. Buttigieg and Antonio Callari (New York: Columbia University Press, 1991).

Leopardi, Giacomo, *Leopardi's Canti*, trans. Joseph Tusiani (Fasano: Schena, 1998).

Leopardi, Giacomo, *Discorso sopra lo stato presente dei costumi degl'italiani* (Milan: Rizzoli, 2001).

Leopardi, Giacomo, *Zibaldone di pensieri* (Milan: Mondadori, 2007).

Manzoni, Alessandro, *The Count of Carmagnola and Adelchis*, ed. Federica Brunori Deigan (Baltimore, Md.: Johns Hopkins University Press, 2004).

Manzoni, Alessandro, *Storia della colonna infame* (Milan: Rizzoli, 2007).

Mazzini, Giuseppe, *The Duties of Man and Other Essays*, trans. Thomas Jones (London: J. M. Dent, 1955).

Nievo, Ippolito, *The Castle of Fratta*, trans. Lovett F. Edwards (Oxford: Oxford University Press, 1957).

Puoti, Basilio, *Regole elementari della lingua italiana* (Parma: Fiaccadori, 1843).

Ruffini, Giovanni, *Lorenzo Benoni, or Passages in the Life of an Italian* (Edinburgh: 1853).

Ruffini, Giovanni, *Doctor Antonio* (Leipzig: Tauchnitz, 1861).

Stendhal, *Rome, Naples and Florence*, trans. Richard N. Coe (London: Calder, 1959).

Tomasi di Lampedusa, Giuseppe, *The Leopard* (London: Vintage Classics, 2007).

Verri, Pietro, *Osservazioni sulla tortura* (Milan: Rizzoli, 1988).

CHAPTER 7

Agulhon, Maurice, *Marianne into Battle: Republican imagery and symbolism in France, 1789–1880* (Cambridge: Cambridge University Press, 1981).

Bevilacqua, Piero, *Breve storia dell'Italia meridionale dall'Ottocento a oggi* (Rome: Donzelli, 1993).

Bevilacqua, Piero, De Clementi, Andreina and Franzina, Emilio (eds), *Storia dell'emigrazione italiana*, 2 vols (Rome: Donzelli, 2001).

Cardoza, Anthony, *Patrizi in un mondo plebeo. La nobiltà piemontese nell'Italia liberale* (Rome: Donzelli, 2005).

Carlson, Marvin, *The Italian Stage: From Goldoni to D'Annunzio* (London: McFarland, 1981).

Cirese, A. M., *Intellettuali, folklore, istinto di classe: note su Verga, Deledda, Scotellaro, Gramsci* (Turin: Einaudi, 1976).

Collodi, Carlo, *Viaggio per l'Italia di Giannettino* ('Giannettino's journey across Italy', 1880).

Collodi De Bernardi, Roberto, 'Il granoturco e i maccheroni', in *Ambiente e società alle origini dell'Italia contemporanea, 1700–1850*, ed. Lucio Gambi (Milan: Electa, 1990).

De Marco, Laura, *Il soldato che disse no alla guerra. Storia dell'anarchico Augusto Masetti (1888–1966)* (Caserta: Spartaco, 2003).

Dickie, John, *Darkest Italy: The Nation and Stereotypes of the Mezzogiorno, 1860–1900* (New York: St Martin's Press, 1999).

Di Gesù, Matteo, *Dispatrie lettere. Di Blasi, Leopardi, Collodi: letterature e identità nazionali* (Rome: Aracne, 2005).

Duggan, Christopher, *Francesco Crispi: From Nation to Nationalism* (Oxford: Oxford University Press, 2002).

Ferrante, Lucia, Palazzi, Maura and Pomata, Gianna, *Ragnatele di rapporti. Patronage e reti di relazione nella storia delle donne* (Turin: Rosenberg and Sellier, 1988).

Foa, Anna, *Giordano Bruno* (Bologna: Il Mulino, 1998).

Gabaccia, Donna, *Italy's Many Diasporas* (Seattle: University of Washington Press, 2000).

Gabaccia, Donna and Iacovetta, Franca (eds), *Women, Gender and Transnational Lives: Italian Workers of the World* (Toronto: University of Toronto Press, 2002).

Gioberti, Vincenzo, *On the Civil and Moral Primacy of the Italians* (Turin: UTET, 1946).

Gioanola, Elio, *La letteratura italiana*, Vol. 2, *Ottocento e novecento* (Milan: Librex, 1985).

Goethe, Johann Wolfgang von, *Travels in Italy* (Whitefish, Mont.: Kessinger, 2007).

Helstolsky, Carol, *Garlic and Oil: Food and Politics in Italy* (Oxford: Berg, 2004).

Hobsbawm, Eric and Ranger, Terence (eds), *The Invention of Tradition* (Cambridge: Cambridge University Press, 1992).

La Cecla, Franco, *La pasta e la pizza* (Bologna: Il Mulino, 1998).

Lanaro, Silvio, 'Il Plutarco italiano: l'istruzione del "popolo" dopo l'unità', *Storia d'Italia*, Annali 4, *Intellettuali e potere*, ed. Corrado Vivanti (Turin: Einaudi, 1981).

Lanaro, Silvio, *Nazione e lavoro. Saggio sulla cultura borghese in Italia, 1870–1925* (Venice: Marsilio, 1988).

Lanaro, Silvio, *L'Italia nuova. Identità e sviluppo, 1861–1988* (Turin: Einaudi, 1988).

Lumley, Robert and Morris, Jonathan (eds), *The New History of the Italian South: The Mezzogiorno Reconsidered* (Exeter: Exeter University Press, 1997).

Malato, Enrico (ed.), *Storia della letteratura italiana* (Rome: Salerno, 1995).

Mayer, Arno, *The Persistence of the Old Regime: Europe to the Great War* (London: Croom Helm, 1981).

Moe, Nelson, *The View from Vesuvius: Italian Culture and the Southern Question* (Berkeley, Calif.: University of California Press, 2002).

Pivato, Stefano, *Bella ciao. Canto e politica nella storia d'Italia* (Rome/Bari: Laterza, 2005).

Pivato, Stefano, *Il Touring Club Italiano* (Bologna: Il Mulino, 2006).

Powell, Cecilia, *Italy in the Age of Turner: 'The Garden of the World'* (London: Merrell Holberton, 1998).

Ramella, Franco, *Terra e telai. Sistemi di parentela e manifattura nel biellese dell'Ottocento* (Turin: Einaudi, 1983).

Ridolfi, Maurizio, *Il circolo virtuoso. Sociabilità democratica, associazionismo e rappresentanza politica nell'Ottocento* (Florence: Centro Editoriale Toscano, 1990).

Ridolfi, Maurizio, *Il Partito della Repubblica: i repubblicani in Romagna e le origini del PRI nell'Italia liberale (1872–1895)* (Milan: Angeli, 1990).

Russo, Luigi, *Giovanni Verga* (Rome/Bari: Laterza, 1995).

Salaris, Claudia, *Sicilia futurista* (Palermo: Sellerio, 1986).

Schneider, Jane (ed.), *Italy's 'Southern Question': Orientalism in One Country* (Oxford: Berg, 1998).

Soldani, Simonetta and Turi, Gabriele, *Fare gli italiani. Scuola e cultura nell'Italia contemporanea*, 2 vols (Bologna: Il Mulino, 1996).

Stewart-Steinberg, Suzanne, *The Pinocchio Effect: On Making Italians (1860–1920)* (Chicago: Chicago University Press, 2007).

Tobia, Bruno, *Una patria per gli italiani* (Rome/Bari: Laterza, 1998).

Weber, Eugen, *Peasants into Frenchmen: The Modernization of Rural France, 1870–1914* (Stanford, Calif.: Stanford University Press, 1976).

Primary sources

Aleramo, Sibilla, *Una Donna* (Milan: Feltrinelli, 2007).

Artusi, Pellegrino, *La scienza in cucina e l'arte di mangiar bene* (Florence: Giunti, 1998).

Carducci, Giosuè, *Presso la tomba di Francesco Petrarca*; *Del rinnovamento letterario in Italia*, in Carducci, *Opere*, VII, *Discorsi letterari e storici* (Bologna: Zanichelli, 1935).

Collodi, Carlo, *The Adventures of Pinocchio* (London: Armada, 1977).

De Amicis, Edmondo, *Cuore: The Heart of a Boy* (London: Peter Owen, 1986).

De Amicis, Edmondo, *Amore e ginnastica* (Milan: Mondadori, 2001).

Serao, Matilde, *Il ventre di Napoli* (Naples: Del Delfino, 1973).

Verga, Giovanni, *I Malavoglia*, ed. M. D. Woolf (Manchester: Manchester University Press, 1972).

Verga, Giovanni, 'Liberty', in *Short Sicilian Novels*, trans. D. H. Lawrence (London: Dedalus, 1984).

CHAPTER 8

Agarossi, Elena, *A Nation Collapses: The Italian Surrender of September 1943* (Cambridge: Cambridge University Press, 1999).

Albanese, Giulia, *La marcia su Roma* (Rome/Bari: Laterza, 2006).

Alberoni, Alberto, *Consumi e società* (Bologna: Il Mulino, 1964).

Arvidsson, Adam, *Brands: Meaning and Value in Media Culture* (London/New York: Routledge, 2006).

Baldoli, Claudia, *Bissolati immaginario. Le origini del fascismo cremonese dal socialismo riformista allo squadrismo* (Cremona: Cremonabooks, 2002).

Baldoli, Claudia, *Exporting Fascism: Italian Fascists and Britain's Italians in the 1930s* (Oxford: Berg, 2003).

Ben-Ghiat, Ruth, *Fascist Modernities: Italy, 1922–1945* (Berkeley, Calif.: University of California Press, 2001).

Berezin, Mabel, *Making the Fascist Self: The Political Culture of Interwar Italy* (Ithaca, NY: Cornell University Press, 1997).

Berghaus, Günter, *Futurism and Politics: Between Anarchist Rebellion and Fascist Reaction, 1909–1944* (Oxford: Berghan, 1996).

Bianchi, Bruna, *La follia e la fuga. Nevrosi di guerra, diserzione e disobbedienza nell'esercito italiano (1915–1918)* (Rome: Bulzoni, 2001).

Bocca, Giorgio, 'The Factory of the New Italians', *Il Giorno*, 3–8 September 1963.

Bodei, Remo, *Il noi diviso. Ethos e idee dell'Italia repubblicana* (Turin: Einaudi, 1998).

Brunello, Piero, *Storia e canzoni in Italia. Il Novecento* (Venice: Comune di Venezia, 2000).

Brunetta, Gian Piero, *Storia del cinema italiano*, 4 vols (Rome: Editori Riuniti, 1993).

Capuzzo, Paolo (ed.), *Genere, generazioni e consumi: l'Italia degli anni sessanta* (Rome: Carocci, 2003).

Ceschin, Daniele, *Gli esuli di Caporetto: i profughi in Italia durante la Grande Guerra* (Rome/Bari: Laterza, 2006).

Cheles, Luciano and Sponza, Lucio (eds), *The Art of Persuasion: Political Communication in Italy from 1945 to the 1990s* (Manchester: Manchester University Press, 2001).

Crainz, Guido, *Storia del miracolo italiano. Culture, identità, trasformazioni fra anni cinquanta e sessanta* (Rome: Donzelli, 1996).

Crainz, Guido, *Il paese mancato: dal miracolo economico agli anni Ottanta* (Rome: Donzelli, 2003).

De Grazia, Victoria, *How Fascism Ruled Women: Italy, 1922–1945* (Berkeley, Calif.: University of California Press, 1991).

Dickie, John, *Cosa Nostra: A History of the Sicilian Mafia* (London: Coronet, 2004).

Dickie, John, *Delizia! The Epic History of the Italians and their Food* (London: Sceptre, 2007).

Dorfles, Piero, *Carosello* (Bologna: Il Mulino, 1998).

Fincardi, Marco, *C'era una volta il mondo nuovo. La metafora sovietica nello sviluppo emiliano* (Rome: Carocci, 2007).

Follini, Marco, *La DC* (Bologna: Il Mulino, 2000).

Foot, John, *Milan Since the Miracle: City, Culture and Identity* (Oxford: Berg, 2001).

Foot, John, *Modern Italy* (Basingstoke: Palgrave, 2003).

Forgacs, David, *Italian Culture in the Industrial Era, 1880–1980* (Manchester: Manchester University Press, 1990).

Gentile, Emilio, *The Sacralization of Politics in Fascist Italy* (Cambridge, Mass.: Harvard University Press, 1996).

Gibelli, Antonio, *La grande guerra degli italiani, 1915–1918* (Milan: Sansoni, 1998).

Gillette, Aaron, *Racial Theories in Fascist Italy* (London: Routledge, 2002).

Ginsborg, Paul, *A History of Contemporary Italy: Society and Politics, 1943–88* (London: Penguin, 1990).

Ginsborg, Paul, *Italy and its Discontents: Family, Civil Society, State, 1980–2001* (London: Allen Lane, 2001).

Gordon, Robert, *A Difficult Modernity: An Introduction to Twentieth-Century Italian Literature* (London: Duckworth, 2005).

Gundle, Stephen, *Between Hollywood and Moscow: The Italian Communists and the Challenge of Mass Culture, 1943–1991* (Durham, NC: Duke University Press, 2000).

Isnenghi, Mario, *Breve storia dell'Italia unita a uso dei perplessi* (Milan: Rizzoli, 1998).

Isnenghi, Mario, *Le guerre degli italiani. Parole, immagini, ricordi, 1848–1945* (Bologna: Il Mulino, 2005).

Isnenghi, Mario, *Il mito della grande guerra* (Bologna: Il Mulino, 2007).

Jacobson, Herbert L., 'De Sica's "Bicycle Thieves" and Italian Humanism', *Hollywood Quarterly*, vol. 4, no. 1, Autumn, 1949, pp. 28–33.

Joseph, B. W., Reichlin, B. and Shugaar, A., 'Figures of Neorealism in Italian Architecture', *Grey Room*, no. 5, Autumn, 2001, pp. 78–101.

Knox, MacGregor, *To the Threshold of Power, 1922–1933: Origins and Dynamics of the Fascist and National Socialist Dictatorships* (Cambridge: Cambridge University Press, 2007).

Levy, Carl (ed.), *Italian Regionalism: History, Identity and Politics* (Oxford: Berg, 1996).

Lumley, Robert, 'Between Pop Art and Arte Povera: American Influences in the Visual Arts in Italy in the 1960s', in *Across the Atlantic: Cultural Exchanges between Europe and the United States*, ed. Luisa Passerini (Brussels: Peter Lang, 2000).

Luperini, Romano, *Letteratura e identità nazionale: la parabola novecentesca*, in

Letteratura e identità nazionale nel novecento, ed. Romano Luperini and Daniela Brogi (San Cesario di Lecce: Piero Manni, 2004).

Lupo, Salvatore, *Storia della mafia dalle origini ai giorni nostri* (Rome: Donzelli, 1993).

Lupo, Salvatore, *Il fascismo. La politica in un regime totalitario* (Rome: Donzelli, 2000).

Mangiameli, Rosario, 'La Sicilia dalla prima guerra mondiale alla caduta del Fascismo', in *Storia della Sicilia*, ed. Francesco Benigno and Giuseppe Giarrizzo, Vol. 2, *Dal seicento a oggi* (Rome/Bari: Laterza, 2003).

McCarthy, Patrick, *Italy since 1945* (Oxford: Oxford University Press, 2000).

Morris, Penelope (ed.), *Women in Italy 1945–60* (Basingstoke: Palgrave, 2007).

Oliva, Gianni, *Foibe. Le stragi negate degli italiani della Venezia Giulia e dell'Istria* (Milan: Mondolibri, 2006).

Passerini, Luisa, *Fascism in Popular Memory: The Cultural Experience of the Turin Working Class* (Cambridge: Cambridge University Press, 1987).

Passerini, Luisa, 'Donne, consumo e cultura di massa', in *Storia delle donne. Il Novecento*, dir. Georges Duby and Michelle Perrot, ed. Françoise Thébaud (Rome/Bari: Laterza, 1997).

Pollard, John, *The Vatican and Italian Fascism, 1929–1932: A Study in Conflict* (Cambridge: Cambridge University Press, 1985).

Pugliese, Stanislao (ed.), *Fascism, Anti-Fascism, and the Italian Resistance. 1919 to the Present* (New York: Rowman & Littlefield, 2004).

Ridolfi, Maurizio, *Le feste nazionali* (Bologna: Il Mulino, 2003).

Rochat, Giorgio, *Le guerre italiane, 1935–1943: dall'impero d'Etiopia alla disfatta* (Turin: Einaudi, 2005).

Salvati, Mariuccia, *Il Novecento: interpretazioni e bilanci* (Rome/Bari: Laterza, 2004).

Snowden, Frank, *Violence and Great Estates in the South of Italy: Apulia, 1900–1922* (Cambridge: Cambridge University Press, 1986).

Stille, Alexander, *Benevolence and Betrayal. Five Italian Jewish Families under Fascism* (London: Vintage, 1993).

Ventrone, Angelo, *Il nemico interno. Immagini, parole e simboli della lotta politica nell'Italia del Novecento* (Rome: Donzelli, 2005).

Vercelloni, Luca, 'La modernità alimentare', in *Storia d'Italia*, Annali 13, *L'alimentazione*, ed. Alberto Capatti, Alberto De Bernardi and Angelo Varni (Turin: Einaudi, 1998).

Wilson, Perry, *Gender, Family and Sexuality: The Private Sphere in Italy, 1860–1945* (Basingstoke: Palgrave, 2004).

Primary sources

Bassani, Giorgio, *The Garden of the Finzi-Continis* (London: Quartet Books, 1974).

Bissolati, Leonida, *La politica estera dell'Italia dal 1879 al 1920* (Milan: Treves, 1923).

Calvino, Italo, *Due interviste su scienza e letteratura*, in Italo Calvino, *Una pietra sopra, Discorsi di letteratura e società* (Turin: Einaudi, 1980).

Calvino, Italo, *The Path to the Spider's Nest*, trans. Archibald Colquhoun (New York: Ecco Press, 2000).

Croce, Benedetto, *A History of Italy, 1871–1915*, trans. Cecilia M. Ady (Oxford: Clarendon, 1929).

Fenoglio, Beppe, *Primavera di bellezza* (Turin: Einaudi, 2006).

Fo, Dario, *The Accidental Death of an Anarchist* (1970), trans. Simon Nye (London: Methuen, 2003).

Ginzburg, Natalia, *Family Sayings*, trans. D. M. Low (London: Hogarth Press, 1967).

Guareschi, Giovanni, *The Little World of Don Camillo*, trans. Una Vincenzo Troubridge (London: Gollancz, 1951).

Levi, Carlo, *Christ Stopped at Eboli*, trans. Frances Frenaye (London: Penguin, 1982).

Levi, Carlo, *L'Orologio* (Turin: Utet, 2007).

Levi, Primo, *The Drowned and the Saved*, trans. Raymond Rosenthal (London: Summit, 1988).

Lewis, Norman, *Naples '44. An Intelligence Officer in the Italian Labyrinth* (London: Eland, 2002).

Mazzantini, Carlo, *A cercar la bella morte* (Venice: Marsilio, 1995).

Milani, Lorenzo, *A Letter to a Teacher*, trans. Nora Rossi and Tom Cole (Harmondsworth: Penguin, 1970).

Pasolini, Pier Paolo, *Lutheran Letters*, trans. Stuart Hood (Manchester: Carcanet, 1983).

Pavese, Cesare, *The House on the Hill*, trans. W. J. Strachan (London: Peter Owen, 1965).

Revelli, Nuto, *Le due guerre. Guerra fascista e guerra partigiana* (Turin: Einaudi, 2005).

Rigoni Stern, Mario, *Il sergente nella neve. Ricordi della ritirata di Russia* (Turin: Einaudi, 2007).

Salvemini, Gaetano, *Memorie di un fuoruscito* (Milan: Feltrinelli, 1973).

Sciascia, Leonardo, *The Moro Affair*, trans. Sacha Rabinovitch (London: Granta Books, 2004).

Vittorini, Elio, *Conversazione in Sicilia* (Milan: Rizzoli, 2006).

Volpe, Gioacchino, *Il popolo italiano tra la pace e la guerra, 1914–1915* (Rome: Bonacci, 1992).

CONCLUSION

Abulafia, David, *Italy, Sicily and the Mediterranean, 1100–1400* (London: Variorum Reprints, 1987).

Albertoni, Giuseppe and Provero, Luigi, *Il feudalesimo in Italia* (Rome: Carocci, 2003).

Arnaldi, Girolamo, *Italy and its Invaders* (Cambridge, Mass.: Harvard University Press, 2005).

Asor Rosa, Alberto, *Scrittori e popolo. Il populismo nella letteratura italiana contemporanea* (Turin: Einaudi, 1964).

Asor Rosa, Alberto, 'La cultura', in *Storia d'Italia*, Annali 4, Vol. 2, *Dall'Unità ad oggi: La cultura* (Turin: Einaudi, 1975).

Asor Rosa, Alberto, *Genus Italicum. Saggi sulla identità letteraria italiana nel corso del tempo* (Turin: Einaudi, 1997).

Bartoli Langeli, Attilio, *La scrittura dell'italiano* (Bologna: Il Mulino, 2000).

Benigno, Francesco, *Specchi della rivoluzione. Conflitto e identità politica nell'Europa moderna* (Rome: Donzelli, 1990).

Benigno, Francesco and Torrisi, Claudio, (eds), *Elites e potere in Sicilia dal medioevo ad oggi* (Rome: Donzelli, 1995).

Bevilacqua, Piero, *Tra natura e storia. Ambiente, economie, risorse in Italia* (Rome: Donzelli, 1996).

Bodei, Remo, *Il noi diviso. Ethos e idee dell'Italia repubblicana* (Turin: Einaudi, 1998).

Boissevain, Jeremy, *Friends of Friends. Networks, Manipulators and Coalitions* (Oxford: Basil Blackwell, 1974).

Bollati, Giulio, *L'italiano. Il carattere nazionale come storia e come invenzione* (Turin: Einaudi, 1996).

Brilli, Attilio, *Il viaggio in Italia. Storia di una grande tradizione culturale* (Bologna: Il Mulino, 2006).

Brunello, Piero, 'Avere santi in Paradiso. Modelli linguistici e culturali nelle lettere di raccomandazione in Italia', *Altrochemestre. Documentazione e storia del tempo presente*, vol. 5, 1997.

Brunello, Piero and Pes, Luca, 'Madonne che piangono', *Altrochemestre. Documentazione e storia del tempo presente*, vol. 3, 1995.

Capatti, Alberto and Montanari, Massimo, *Italian Cuisine. A Cultural History* (New York: Columbia University Press, 2003).

Cattaneo, Carlo, *Le città considerate come principio ideale delle istorie italiane*, in *Scritti storici e geografici*, ed. Gaetano Salvemini and Ernesto Sestan, Vol. 2 (Florence: Le Monnier, 1957).

Cuaz, Marco, *Le Alpi* (Bologna: Il Mulino, 2005).

Del Boca, Angelo, *Italiani, brava gente? Un mito duro a morire* (Vicenza: Neri Pozza, 2005).

De Mauro, Tullio, *La cultura degli italiani*, ed. Francesco Erbani (Rome/Bari: Laterza, 2005).

Eco, Umberto, *Apocalypse Postponed*, ed. Robert Lumley (London: British Film Institute, 1994).

Galli, Giorgio, *I partiti politici in Italia: 1861–1943* (Turin: UTET, 1995).

Ginsborg, Paul, 'Family, culture and politics', in *Culture and Conflict in Postwar Italy: Essays on Mass and Popular Culture*, ed. Zygmunt Baranski and Robert Lumley (London: Macmillan, 1990).

Jossa, Stefano, *L'Italia letteraria* (Bologna: Il Mulino, 2006).

Gramsci, Antonio, *Sul Risorgimento* (Rome: Editori Riuniti, 1967).

Gundle, Stephen, 'Il sorriso di Berlusconi', *Altrochemestre. Documentazione e storia del tempo presente*, vol. 3, 1995.

Isnenghi, Mario, *La tragedia necessaria. Da Caporetto all'otto settembre* (Bologna: Il Mulino, 1999).

La Cecla, Franco, *La pasta e la pizza* (Bologna: Il Mulino, 1998).

Levi, Giovanni, 'Responsabilità limitata', *Altrochemestre. Documentazione e storia del tempo presente*, vol. 5, 1997.

Lupo, Salvatore, 'La Mafia', in *Storia della Sicilia*, ed. Francesco Benigno and Giuseppe Giarrizzo, Vol. 2, *Dal seicento a oggi* (Rome/Bari: Laterza, 2003).

Macry, Paolo (ed.), *Quando crolla lo stato. Studi sull'Italia preunitaria* (Naples: Liguori, 2003).

Monti, Aldino, *I braccianti* (Bologna: Il Mulino, 1998).

Musella, Luigi, *Il trasformismo* (Bologna: Il Mulino, 2003).

Niola, Marino, *I santi patroni* (Bologna: Il Mulino, 2007).

Procacci, Giuliano, *Storia degli italiani* (Rome/Bari: Laterza, 1998).

Raimondi, Ezio, *Letteratura e identità nazionale* (Milan: Bruno Mondadori, 1998).

Romano, Ruggiero, *Paese Italia. Venti secoli di identità* (Rome: Donzelli, 1997).

Sciascia, Leonardo, *Sicilian Uncles*, trans. N. S. Thompson (Manchester: Carcanet, 1986).

Spinelli, Altiero, *Machiavelli nel secolo XX. Scritti del confino e della clandestinità, 1941–1944*, ed. Piero Graglia (Bologna: Il Mulino, 1993).

Sylos Labini, Paolo, 'Introduzione', in Saverio Lodato and Marco Travaglio, *Intoccabili* (Milan: Rizzoli, 2006).

Various authors, *Le vie del Mezzogiorno: Storie e scenari* (Rome: Donzelli, 2002).

White, Jonathan, *Italy: The Enduring Culture* (London: Leicester University Press, 2000).

White, Jonathan, *Italian Cultural Lineages* (Toronto: University of Toronto Press, 2007).

Wilson, Peter H., *The Holy Roman Empire, 1495–1806* (London: Macmillan, 1999).

Zinn, Dorothy Louise, *La raccomandazione. Clientelismo vecchio e nuovo* (Rome: Donzelli, 2001).

Index